D1045397

ALSO BY LESTER C. THUROW

Poverty and Discrimination
Investment in Human Capital
The Impact of Taxes on the American Economy
The Economic Problem (with Robert L. Heilbroner)
Generating Inequality: The Distributional Mechanisms of the Economy
*The Zero-Sum Society: Distribution and the Possibilities for Economic
    Change*
Five Economic Challenges (with Robert L. Heilbroner)
Economics Explained (with Robert L. Heilbroner)
Dangerous Currents: The State of Economics
The Management Challenge: Japanese Views

THE ZERO-SUM

Lester C. Thurow

SOLUTION

Building a World-Class American Economy

SIMON AND SCHUSTER   NEW YORK

Copyright © 1985 by Lester C. Thurow
All rights reserved
including the right of reproduction
in whole or in part in any form
Published by Simon and Schuster
A Division of Simon & Schuster, Inc.
Simon & Schuster Building
Rockefeller Center
1230 Avenue of the Americas
New York, New York 10020
SIMON AND SCHUSTER and colophon are registered trademarks of
Simon & Schuster, Inc.
Designed by Eve Kirch
Manufactured in the United States of America

10 9 8 7 6 5 4 3 2 1

Library of Congress Cataloging in Publication Data
Thurow, Lester C.
  The zero-sum solution.
  Includes bibliographical references and index.
  1. United States—Economic conditions—1981–
2. United States—Economic policy—1981–
I. Title.
HC106.8.T5 1985   338.973   85-14480
ISBN: 0-671-55232-5

ACKNOWLEDGMENTS

This book benefited from many conversations with my colleagues at MIT. Various arguments were shaped on the basis of presentations to a wide variety of groups. But perhaps most of all I should thank my secretary, Mary Lane, for putting up with me during the process of writing it.

OTTO ECKSTEIN
A Great Teacher, A Good Friend, A Super Human Being

PREFACE

In 1979 I wrote a book that was entitled *The Zero-Sum Society* when it was published in 1980. At the center was the thesis that America faced a set of structural problems, such as slow productivity growth, whose solutions required that significant economic losses be distributed to politically powerful interest groups. I argued that Americans would be better off in the long run if solutions were found, but that significant groups of Americans would be worse off in the short run. If more investment in plant and equipment was part of the solution to the productivity problem, Americans would have to consume less to permit more investment. Those who would be forced to consume less would have a lower standard of living and might fight attempts to impose losses upon them.

The losses imposed upon Americans by efforts to solve their problems would be at least as large as the benefits gained for some significant period of time—hence the title *The Zero-Sum Society*. America must pass through a zero-sum society to restore economic prosperity.

That book provoked two reactions. My unfriendly critics argued that the thesis was wrong. The American problem was too much government. Get government out of the economy and off the backs of the people and the economy would painlessly right itself.

My friendly critics agreed with the thesis but thought that I had

11

left them hanging. I had accurately described the problem but had not provided a solution.

Not surprisingly, the political process decided to test the thesis of my unfriendly critics. After all, if a painless prescription exists, why would any sensible person choose the painful prescription? A painless solution may not exist, but it is certainly worth a try. Such an experiment was conducted during the first four years of the Reagan Administration. The whys and wherefores will be examined in detail later in this book, but we now know the results. The painless prescription did not work.

Instead of stopping inflation painlessly by simply printing less money, inflation had to be stopped with a maxi-recession in 1981 and 1982 that drove unemployment up to levels not seen since the Great Depression. Instead of a supply-side recovery based on more investment and less consumption, America had a classical Keynesian demand-side recovery in 1983 and 1984. National savings rates were at all-time lows. By early 1985 no one was predicting further falls in unemployment; yet it was still at rates that formerly were seen only in the worst of recessionary times.

There was a weak cyclical recovery in productivity in 1983 and early 1984, but at the end of the first quarter of 1985 productivity was where it had been at the end of the second quarter of 1984: nine months with no productivity growth in America—a dismal record. In 1980 other industrial countries were just catching up with American productivity levels. By 1985 significant numbers of those countries had passed American productivity levels. In 1980 America was competitive on world markets: it had a $2 billion surplus on current account. By 1984 America was massively noncompetitive on world markets: it had a current account deficit of $102 billion.

To finance a noncompetitive economy and maintain a facade of prosperity, America had to begin massive foreign borrowings. In 1982 America had net foreign assets of $152 billion. By the spring of 1985 it had spent all those assets, and sometime in early 1986 it would pass Brazil to become the world's largest net debtor, with international debts of over $100 billion.

At home the policies that were supposed to produce a balanced Federal budget by 1984 had in fact produced America's largest-ever deficit. By 1985 the boom generated by Keynesian aggregate-demand policies was over, and rising international trade deficits were threatening to convert slow growth into no growth. For a limited period of time this threat can be held off by using the Federal Reserve Board to lower interest rates, but lower interest rates cannot by themselves hold off a rising trade deficit forever.

Given that the painless prescription has not worked, it is time to return to reality. Given the reality of the zero-sum dilemma, what should be done? This is the question that my friendly critics asked concerning *The Zero-Sum Society*, and it is the question that *The Zero-Sum Solution* attempts to answer.

The answer is that we must engage in a massive mobilization to build a world-class American economy. If America's international military power were as weak as its international economic power, Americans would instantly put aside their immediate economic self-interests and rally around a common effort to re-create a world-class military power. And while doing so they would give consideration to equity and ensure that all were carrying their fair share of the load.

I believe that if Americans understand their position vis-à-vis their economic competitors, and understand the long-run significance of failing as a world-class economy, and further understand what must be done to create a world-class American economy, they will rally around an effort to build one.

This book attempts to build that very understanding. Where are we now in the world economy? Where are we likely to be ten years from now if we do nothing? What will happen if we fall behind the rest of the industrial world and are defeated on world markets? What must be done to make the American economy competitive in world markets? These are the questions that I attempt to answer.

America is now in a competitive fight for its economic life. Not since World War II has it been so significantly economically challenged. If one believes that competition is healthy, responding to the current international challenges can make the American economy better than it has ever been. I believe that Americans in all walks of life can and will respond to that challenge.

The Zero-Sum Solution is *Building a World-Class American Economy.*

CONTENTS

INTRODUCTION

Of the last five presidential elections the Democratic party has lost four—three by record or close to record amounts. It has lost with a candidate from its left wing, George McGovern, and a candidate from its right wing, James Carter. It has lost with a political outsider, James Carter, and it has lost, first narrowly and then finally by an enormous margin, with two old-pro New Deal insiders, Hubert Humphrey and Walter Mondale. In its only victory, a very narrow victory, the Democratic party needed the help of the Watergate scandal to force an incumbent President out of office and southern pride in the first presidential candidate to come from that region since the the Civil War to win. Both were temporary one-time factors that do not provide a basis for future success.

The problem is not bad luck, not a bad selection procedure, and not bad candidates. The problem is more fundamental. The New Deal, the platform upon which Democrats have been running for fifty years, has run out of political steam and has come to a natural resting point. Democrats desperately need a new vision, a new central organizing principle, to replace it. The programs that made Democrats the majority party for most of the past half century will, if not modified, make the Democrats the minority party for the next half century.

17

The vision imparted by Franklin Roosevelt in the New Deal contained three central elements. First, Keynesian aggregate demand management—expenditure increases or tax cuts—would be used to prevent depressions or deep recessions. Second, a social safety net—Social Security, unemployment insurance, health insurance—would be established to help the poor, but even more important politically, those same programs would reduce economic uncertainties for the middle class. The middle class would not have to worry about falling into poverty when old age, unemployment, or illness struck. Third, a commitment to equal access, education, and training would open up economic opportunities for everyone, but especially those discriminated against—blacks, Hispanics, women.

Given the onset of the Great Depression, it is not surprising that such policies broke three-quarters of a century of Republican dominance and made the Democratic party into the majority party. Except for the very rich, most of the nation stood to gain if Democratic policies were adopted. Over time the New Deal policies were adopted and most of the nation did gain. Speaker Thomas P. O'Neill is right when he says that the Democratic party created America's middle class.

Lyndon Johnson's Great Society programs can be seen as the logical culmination of the New Deal. With the Great Society programs in place "more of the same" no longer made sense. It was not that the New Deal–Great Society policies failed—precisely the opposite. It was that they succeeded and came to natural stopping points.

Social Security is a good example. It was started by Franklin Roosevelt, but in the mid-1960s the elderly still had per capita incomes well below those of the non-elderly and an incidence of poverty that was twice that of the non-elderly. Helping the elderly made sense. No one wants to fall into poverty when they retire. In the late 1960s and 1970s Social Security benefits rose rapidly. As a consequence by the mid-1980s the elderly had higher per capita incomes and a lower incidence of poverty than the non-elderly.[1] Few Americans wish to make the elderly rich and the non-elderly poor, yet this is precisely where a simple business-as-usual expansion of Social Security is leading. Achieving intergenerational parity is a reasonable goal; superiority for the old is not. As a central focus of political attention Social Security had come to a natural stopping point. Democrats could continue to defend Social Security against actual and imagined attacks from Republicans, but they could not advocate further expansions of the old programs that had always been their political meat and potatoes.

In education, training, and equal opportunity, the same natural stopping points have been reached. The percentage of the population with a high school degree has more than doubled since the 1930s and is now approaching 90 percent. In half a century college education has gone from an almost exclusive preserve of the rich to something which half of all high school graduates begin and almost one-quarter finish. American education needs to be improved, but that is a very different, much messier, problem than simply expanding it.

One can demonstrate statistically that an equal-opportunity society has not yet been created. After correcting for education and experience, the average black, Hispanic, or female is still paid less than the comparable white male. But the gross visible abuses have vanished. Blacks, Hispanics, and women show up in jobs where they were in the past never seen. No one is explicitly denied the right to vote.

While affirmative action programs are necessary to achieve equal access in areas where it is virtually impossible to prove individual discrimination, affirmative action is a crude device that does reduce the opportunities for members of the majority groups that have not themselves discriminated against anyone. Non-discriminating members of the majority group are not eligible to compete for some of the good jobs that are being reserved for members of economic minorities. This is especially true in no-growth periods such as that from 1979 through 1982.

As a result affirmative action programs do not command the moral ascendancy and political salability of equal opportunity—even to those such as women who would potentially benefit. President Reagan gutted the Equal Employment Opportunity Commission, but he won the female vote. The answer is not to abandon the goal of real equality of access but to embed the programs for reaching it in an economy where the negative side effects on innocent bystanders are minimized. Affirmative action in a no-growth economy is very different from affirmative action in a rapidly growing economy.

Because most of its programmatic goals had been achieved when the Democratic party was asked, "What have you done for the average citizen *lately* and what are you planning to do for the average citizen in the *future*?" it did not have an answer. If one had an above-average income, one voted for the Democrats not out of self-interest but out of altruism or history.

Governor Mario Cuomo's inspiring keynote speech at the 1984 Democratic presidential nominating convention illustrates the point. It was full of references to Democratic traditions of helping the poor, but there was nothing in his speech as to how the Democrats were going to help today's average citizen who was not poor. Democrats may have made that average citizen into an average citizen with $25,000 in family income, but that was in the past. As long as the Republicans did not threaten to rip up the social safety net or the existing educational ladders, the average citizen had no reason to vote Democratic. The average voter was also smart enough to know that further expansions of the New Deal programs would require higher taxes from him—not someone else. The Cuomo appeal to altruism is not wrong, it is right, but it does not win elections by itself.

This was confirmed in the 1984 election results. If only those with family incomes below $20,000—approximately the bottom 40 percent of the population—could have voted, Mondale would have won.[2] The bottom 40 percent of the population had something to gain by a further expansion of the New Deal programs, but the other 60 percent did not. Voters accurately perceived and voted their self-interest.

Helping those less fortunate than oneself is a Democratic principle that should be cherished and extended, but it cannot by itself be a platform for political success. Most Americans have some altruism, but that altruism must be mixed with a substantial amount of self-interest.

While many of the Democratic social programs had come to natural stopping points, the country's macroeconomic problems had changed. In the 1930s, 1940s, 1950s, and 1960s, growth was assured if recessions were avoided or limited. All of the problems of economic growth could be solved with Keynesian aggregate demand management. But as America's underlying rate of productivity growth (output per hour of work) slowed down from a healthy 3 percent per year in the 1950s and first half of the 1960s to an unhealthy less than one-half of one percent per year in the late 1970s and early 1980s, what had been true was no longer true. Full employment was not enough. There was in fact a supply problem in the American economy. If rapid productivity growth could not be regenerated, Americans were not going to enjoy a rapidly rising standard of living in the future.

The problems of slow productivity growth were magnified by the emergence of a world economy. It was correct to say that the American economy had died and was replaced by a world economy. More importantly as far as Americans were concerned, this world economy was no longer populated by industrial countries that were inferior to America technologically but by countries that were generally America's technological peers and in some areas its superiors. America no longer had the huge economic and technological edge, the effortless superiority, that it enjoyed after World War II. Instead of the perpetual trade surpluses enjoyed earlier, America had large trade deficits in the 1980s. America was not a competitive supplier on world markets.

Viewed as a real solution, President Reagan's supply-side economics (the notion that tax cuts and expenditure cuts can cure all of America's economic problems) was and is silly. Viewed as a diagnosis of a problem, however, it was and is correct. Low productivity growth and the resulting lack of international competitiveness require a supply-side solution. By default Democrats have the opportunity to suggest real supply side solutions—solutions that increase rather than reduce equity.

When the New Deal emerged, America had only one economic problem—unemployment. There were no inflationary problems in the Great Depression. Prices were falling. Keynesian economics provides answers for depressions, recessions, and high unemployment, but it does not provide answers for inflation. Keynesian fine tuning (carefully making small adjustments in aggregate demand) was once thought to be the answer, but it wasn't. Modern industrial economies are inflation prone; and adjustments of aggregate demand, no matter how careful, cannot keep the economy operating at full employment without inflation, given the inevitable occasional inflationary shocks flowing from sectors such as food and oil.

Given this inflationary reality, Keynesian prescriptions became not instruments for running economies at full employment but instruments for deliberately creating recessions to hold inflation in check. Unemployment came to be not something to be avoided but something to be deliberately created to control inflation. This change, however, undercut Democratic claims that they were better able than Republicans to deliver prosperity. Given the reality of inflation, they weren't.

Both parties would use unemployment to control inflation. In 1982 President Reagan pushed unemployment up toward 11 percent; President Carter had never dared to go above 8 percent. Using unemployment to stop inflation, however, hurts Democrats much more than Republicans politically, since most of those deliberately thrown into unemployment to cure inflation come from traditionally Democratic voting groups, such as blue-collar workers and low-income white-collar workers. If Democrats were going to use unemployment to stop inflation, they weren't much better than Republicans and had little to offer the groups that had learned to vote Democratic in the Great Depression to avoid unemployment.

As a result Keynesian-Democratic demand management policies also came to a natural stopping point. They could be used to stop depressions or maxi-recessions, but to use them in this circumstance no longer made Democrats unique. Republicans were willing to do the same, and in 1983 and 1984 President Reagan became a super-Keynesian stimulating the economy with large budget deficits in the aftermath of the 1981-82 maxi-recession. But if traditional demand management policies could not be used to generate an economy which persistently ran at full employment without inflation, Democrats were no better than Republicans at delivering prosperity.

This lesson was driven home to the electorate in the Carter Administration. Democrats were given a chance to restore a full-employment non-inflationary economy, but they failed on both counts. Based on the record, the Democrats did not deserve to win the 1980 election and the electorate was wise enough to know it. The time had come to try something different.

Living in the past without a vision of the future makes it difficult to get elected, but more importantly it makes it difficult to govern. President Carter knew that the future was different, but he and his party were still tied to the past. They knew that a simple expansion of New Deal and Great Society programs was not called for, but they did not know what *was* called for. Not having a central vision of where America should be going, the Carter Administration responded to short-run political pressures, but without a central organizing principle they did not know which pressures to heed—and which to ignore. Since the political pressures run in all directions, simply responding to them quite naturally led to the adoption of inconsistent policies. In the end it was fair to say that the only consistent thing about the Carter Administration was its inconsistencies.

If "getting the government out of the economy and off of the backs of the people" were to produce rapid growth without inflation over a long period of time, Democrats would be left with only one issue—fairness. For metaphorically, such a laissez-faire policy is equivalent to throwing the bottom 40 percent of the population overboard to speed up the economic ship for the remaining 60 percent. Statistically, the bottom 40 percent of the population has fallen behind and has not participated in the 1983–1984 economic recovery. Perhaps the growing economic gap between the majority and the minority would eventually reach the point where the majority was willing to do something about it, but history has few examples of the majority altruistically being willing to make major sacrifices in their own standard of living to help those less fortunate than themselves without the advent of a crisis where they also feel threatened (the Great Depression) or the advent of an actual revolution. To argue that things must get worse before they can get better is also the height of nihilism. It is not the basis upon which a future Democratic platform should be constructed.

Fairness is an issue, but it is not the only issue left to Democrats. As the next chapter will demonstrate, America's fundamental problems remain unsolved. The long-run trend rate of growth of productivity is still low. America is every day becoming less competitive on world markets. Current policies are not capable of running the U.S. economy at full employment without inflation for any lengthy period of time. In 1984 America was enjoying a temporary economic boom, a cyclical recovery from a maxi-recession, that masked the underlying problems, but those problems are still there awaiting a solution. It is the task of the Democratic party to develop a set of solutions to these problems. Honest realistic solutions can be designed and sold.

In 1984 it was doubtful that anyone would have been willing to listen to an alternative set of solutions even if they had been developed. Americans wanted to believe that their economic problems could be solved painlessly with tax cuts. If it had been true, it would have been so nice for most of us.

Eventually an intellectual window will open. The American economy is in a very literal sense running on borrowed money. The policies of President Reagan produced a recovery in 1983 and 1984 but they also produced trade deficits of $69 and $123 billion. It is a simple mathematical fact of life that no country can forever run such huge balance of trade deficits. The foreign lending necessary to finance them will end as foreigners come to feel that they have enough of their liquid assets invested in an ever more deeply indebted United States of America. When the lending stops, the dollar falls. Since 12 percent of the GNP is imported, a falling dollar generates a substantial amount of inflation. A 30 to 40 percent fall in the value of the dollar (the amount that would be necessary to restore balance in the balance of trade) would generate about 4 percentage points of inflation. This would be an inflationary shock as large or larger than the OPEC oil shocks. To stop inflation and to prevent the dollar from falling too far, the Federal Reserve Board is apt to do what central banks always do in such circumstances and apply its economic brakes, raising interest rates, and pushing the American economy into its next deliberately created recession.

Events, not arguments, will make it obvious that the Reagan-Republican policies are not long-run solutions to America's problems. When these events occur, however, ideas and arguments become important. Americans will be willing to listen, but will the Democrats have anything to say?

They will if they remember two things. First, the central task of the next quarter century is to regain American competitiveness. Unless that is done, America's standard of living can only slip relative to that of the rest of the industrial world. Second, America is more than a simply statistical aggregation of individuals. It is a community, a society, where socially organizing to help each other leads to a more attractive society, a more equitable society, and a more efficient society than one where each individual is left to make it on his or her own. In a good society social organization is central.

To hold on to American markets and to compete in world markets will require changes in America's standard operating procedures. Change is a political process. Historically the Democratic party has been the party of change. In the future it will be the task of the Democratic party to lead toward those changes that will be necessary to insure America's position in the new world economy that is emerging.

PART ONE

Where Are We?

1 / 1985: Where Are We?

Midway through the 1960s it looked as if the American economy was about to achieve a sustained orbit of non-inflationary growth and prosperity unmatched in American history. Inflation was minimal, just 1.6 percent per year from 1960 to 1965; unemployment was falling, reaching 4 percent in December 1965. Productivity had been rising at a healthy 3.7 percent rate, leading to the expectation that real standards of living would double by 1984.[1]

LOOKING BACKWARD

It was not to be. Instead of entering a period of sustained prosperity, the United States was about to embark on a cyclical roller coaster with an ever wilder ride ahead. Under the pressures of the Viet Nam war inflation would slowly accelerate through the last half of the 1960s. To control inflation the American government would engineer its first deliberate recession in 1969.

Then the 1970s struck. Food and energy shocks came in rapid succession. Governments responded by repeatedly slamming on their fiscal and monetary brakes. The roller coaster entered a sickening era of ups and downs. Moreover at the end of each of those swings the economy was in worse shape than it had been at the beginning—inflation and unemployment were higher; productivity growth was lower.

By 1982 the economy seemed about ready to achieve a sustained orbit of inflationary decline. In the five years from 1977 to 1982 inflation averaged 8.1 percent. Unemployment rose, reaching 10.6 percent in December of 1982. Productivity growth (0.2 percent per year) essentially stopped, leading to the expectation that real standards of living would not double until the year 2329—essentially never.

From 1982 to 1984 everything seemed once again to turn around. The economy boomed. Unemployment fell, reaching 7.4 percent in December 1984. Inflation averaged less than 4 percent, and productivity rose at a 3 percent rate. What happened? Was it permanent, or was it just another upswing preceding yet another downswing?

What Happened?

When President Reagan came into office in January 1981, Reaganomics meant two things—monetarism (a slow, steady rate of growth of the money supply) and supply-side economics (cutting taxes to increase savings and work effort).[2] Neither part worked as planned. Instead of the boom promised when the Reagan Administration entered office, tight monetary policies and high interest rates stopped the economy dead in its tracks—producing a maxi-recession in 1981 and 1982.

Unknowingly and to some extent unnoticed, Reaganomics was, however, about to undergo a major transfiguration. As the 1981-1982 maxi-recession lengthened, it became increasingly clear that monetarism wasn't working as planned, but other events intervened to kill monetarism before it might otherwise have died a natural death. On Friday, August 13, 1982, the Reagan Administration learned that Mexico on the following Monday would not be able to make required repayments on its international loans. Over the following weekend the Reagan Administration had a choice. It could refuse to lend Mexico the necessary funds and take a chance that some of America's largest banks would collapse in the aftermath of a Mexican default. Or it could lend Mexico what was needed to repay its bankers. But if it did the latter, the money would be turned over to the American banks and would constitute a large increase in the American money supply.

Quite wisely the Reagan Administration decided not to take a chance on financial panic. Mexico was lent the billions it needed. In the twelve months following the August 1982 Mexican crisis, the American money supply grew almost twice as fast as it did in the twelve months prior to the crisis; and the rate at which the best corporations borrow money (prime) fell from 15.5 percent to 10.5 percent. What had been a policy of slow monetary growth was reborn as a policy of rapid monetary growth.

To make sure that the metamorphosis wasn't missed by the public, the change was overtly proclaimed by the Chairman of the Federal Reserve Board, Paul Volcker, in a speech shortly after the Mexican crisis. Since government agencies, however, never like to admit that an unforeseen crisis has forced them to reverse their policies, they look for "technical" excuses to do what they know needs to be done. In this case the Federal Reserve Board claimed that the development of new money market bank accounts had made it temporarily impossible to accurately measure the money supply and that therefore the Fed could not be expected to control the rapid rate of growth of the money supply that would occur in the months ahead.

This was the most transparent of fig leaves. The money supply could have been measured and controlled if that was what the Fed had wanted to do.[3] And if the announced excuse for temporarily abandoning monetarism were true, it permanently, not temporarily, vitiated the possibility of controlling the money supply. New financial instruments can always be invented, and if their invention makes money supply targets impossible to hit, then money supply targets are always impossible to hit.

The death of supply-side economics cannot be so precisely dated, for it died a slow death from exposure. It simply did not work as planned. In the four years of the Carter Administration, Americans' personal savings averaged 6 percent of disposable income. Since a 6 percent savings rate is less than one-half that found in the rest of the industrial world, such a rate is clearly too low. To raise America's savings rate, the Reagan Administration enacted a series of tax cuts in 1981 designed to substantially cut the taxes of high-income Americans on the grounds that they were precisely the Americans who were most likely to save income not taken in taxes. During the hearings on these tax cuts Reagan supporters testified that as much as 70 percent of the tax cuts would be saved.

It did not happen. When the tax cuts were fully effective, America's personal savings rate first dropped to 5 percent in 1983 and then rose to 6.1 percent in 1984. But there was no significant increase in personal savings. When it came to the bottom line, Americans of all income classes were spenders, not savers. The 1981 tax cuts empirically demonstrated that high-income Americans did not in fact have a high marginal propensity to save out of extra take-home income generated from tax cuts. Nor did they go to work in record numbers. Labor force participation rates rose almost four times as fast under President Carter as they did under President Reagan.

America's consumption behavior, however, converted what was supposed to be supply-side economics into demand-side economics. Instead of more saving and the resultant investment pulling the economy up, higher consumption expenditures would push it up.

The shift toward consumption in private budgets was matched by a similar shift in public budgets. Led by a doubling of the defense budget, Federal government spending rose 39 percent, from $661 billion to $917 billion, between the first quarter of 1981 and the fourth quarter of 1984. Combined with large tax cuts, the Federal deficit rose from $43 billion to $176 billion with a peak deficit of $211 billion reached in the fourth quarter of 1982.[4]

Although it was never publicly admitted, the Reagan Administration had become "born again Keynesians," converted to easy money, large tax cuts, big increases in government spending, and huge deficits. Midway through his first term of office President Reagan had adopted precisely the policies which he had spent a lifetime denouncing.

In 1982 such policies were appropriate. Keynesian demand-side economics was developed to rescue the world from the economic avalanche of the Great Depression. In late 1982 America needed to be rescued from the quicksands of the worst recession since the Great Depression. Large budget deficits and easy money were the correct prescription to get the economic engines restarted in 1982.

IS IT PERMANENT?

In 1983 and 1984 the United States was in the midst of a cyclical recovery that was being politically sold as if it were permanent prosperity. While the selling job was successful, the stable expansion began to look more and more like a mirage. Almost as President

Reagan's election tide rolled in, a tide of bad economic news began to roll out.

As the election polls closed, Budget Director David Stockman opened his books and revealed that the budget deficits were going to be much larger than previously supposed—above $200 billion and trending upward rather than below $150 billion and trending downward. Little further improvement was to be expected in unemployment. While a 7 to 7.5 percent unemployment is better than the almost 11 percent of 1982, it is a dismal rate if one remembers that such rates used to be seen only at the depths of a recession. What used to be America's worst unemployment rate was now its best unemployment rate. If America had been running a balance in its balance of trade instead of $123 billion deficit, 3 million Americans who were not working in 1984 would have been working. Those 3 million extra jobs would have gotten America a long way back toward a more reasonable level of unemployment.

While an inflation rate which seems to have stabilized around 4 percent looks good relative to the recent past, it also is dismal if it is the best that can be achieved in the aftermath of double-digit unemployment. Such inflation rates in the late 1960s and early 1970s brought demands for wage and price controls to end what was then viewed as an intolerable rate of inflation. Such rates are now the best that the economy can achieve right after it has been put through the wringer of almost 11 percent unemployment and four years of no growth from the first of 1979 through the fourth quarter of 1982. Historically, a 4 percent inflation rate is also a very high jumping off point from which to commence the next inflation surge.

As far as inflation and unemployment are concerned, the cyclical roller coaster continues to exist. Americans were enjoying the thrill of a cyclical recovery in 1984, but ahead lie more sickening bouts with inflation and unemployment, for the nature of the system has not been altered.

During the 1984 election the Reagan Administration pointed to 1983's productivity rebound (a 2.7 percent rate of growth) as evidence of a new long-run trend. In fact the 1983 results were nothing but the standard cyclical swing (in a recovery overhead labor is spread across more units of output and productivity temporarily grows), and right after the election the Labor Department announced that American productivity was actually falling in the third quarter of 1984. At the end of the first quarter of 1985 productivity was no higher than it had been in the second quarter of 1984. Nine months had passed with no productivity growth.

Nothing is more important than restoring American productivity growth, yet nothing is being done to do so. Nothing could help in the task of restoring productivity growth more than the elimination of frequent and persistent recessions, but nothing is being done to change the structural characteristics of the economy to get America off its up-and-down roller coaster.

Part of the answer as to whether the recovery is permanent is to be found in historical experience. While Keynesian economics works if the problem is to end the Great Depression or a maxi-recession such as that of 1981–82, Keynesian economics does not work if the problem is to persistently run a modern industrial economy at full employment without inflation. This failure has repeatedly been confirmed here and abroad. Sooner or later too much aggregate demand or the inevitable external shock rekindles the inflationary fires. Keynesian economics must then be turned on its head to produce recessions and unemployment. Higher unemployment is the only known cure for inflation in Keynesian economics. There is no other solution. Both old practitioners and new converts to Keynesianism confront this reality. When the economy reaches full employment or faces another inflationary shock, the Reagan Administration, just as the Carter Administration in its time, will have only deliberately induced recessions to fall back upon.

The costs and benefits of such recessions can be seen in an analysis of the reasons for the improvement in inflationary performance between 1979–80 and 1982–83. As the data in Table 1 indicate, 37 percent (2.9 percentage points out of 7.8 percentage points) of the measured decline in inflation from 1979–80 to 1982–83 occurred because of good luck. The prices of energy, farm products, and imports were falling rather than rising. None of these declines were caused by American economic policies. When these prices quit falling (and they inevitably will, since no price can fall forever), inflation will automatically accelerate, since falling commodity prices will no longer be offsetting some portion of the inflation in other industrial prices. Good luck is better than bad luck, but good luck is not a long-run solution to the inflationary problem.

While there is no doubt that high unemployment can control inflation, the costs are high. If unemployment is given credit for reducing the inflation flowing from previous excess demand and for

TABLE 1[5]
CONTRIBUTIONS TO DISINFLATION

	Inflation		
	1979–1980	*1982–1983*	*Improvement*
Shock Inflation	2.3%	−0.6%	−2.9%
Energy Prices	1.7	−0.1	−1.8
Farm Prices	0.4	−0.1	−0.5
Foreign Exchange Rate	0.1	−0.4	−0.5
Core Inflation	9.0	6.9	−2.1
Labor Costs	5.0	4.5	−0.5
Capital Costs	4.0	2.4	−1.6
Demand Inflation	0.2	−1.9	−2.1
Unexplained Residual	1.0	0.3	−0.7
Total Inflation (CPI)	12.4	4.6	−7.8

driving labor and capital costs down, over 6 million man-years of extra unemployment were required to reduce the inflation rate by 4.2 percentage points from 1979–80 to 1982–83. What happened—almost 11 percent unemployment, 35 percent of the nation's capital capacity idle, no economic growth from the beginning of 1979 through the end of 1982, tens of thousands of firms and individuals filing for bankruptcy, a worldwide industrial shutdown, the third world at the edge of default, a banking crisis—could by no stretch of the imagination be described as the immediate boom scenario outlined by the Reagan Administration when it took office in January 1981. At an enormous price modest inflationary gains were achieved.

If statistics and history are not persuasive as to the lack of permanence in the 1983–1984 recovery, consider logic. To solve the inflation problem without deliberately raising unemployment requires the solution of a structural problem that remains unsolved. The essence of the problem can be seen in the second OPEC oil shock in 1979. OPEC doubled the price of oil and America's imported oil bill rose from 2 to 5 percent of the GNP.[6] At the same time America's GNP was not growing. As a result, at the beginning of 1980 there was only 97 percent as much left to be divided among Americans as there had been at the beginning of 1979. Mathematically, the average American standard of living had to fall 3 percent.

The bad news could have been delivered in two ways.

(1) If wages (and other incomes) had fallen 3 percent, a balance

could have been restored between American incomes and the products left to be purchased by Americans. Such a decline in wages would have let unit costs of production fall for domestic products and these price declines would have counterbalanced the initial rise in energy prices, producing a non-inflationary economy.

(2) Alternatively, as actually happened, everyone could have attempted to preserve his standard of living with a wage hike. In 1979 wages rose 9 percent. Without an equivalent gain in productivity, however, such a wage hike merely adds 9 percent to production costs, and prices must now go up 12 percent (3 percent because of oil price hikes and 9 percent because of wage hikes). Real standards of living must still fall 3 percent, but now America also faces a 12 percent inflation rate.

No one wants to accept a fall in his standard of living yet the fall was inevitable given what happened—a sharp rise in the price of imported oil and a deterioration in America's terms of trade (the rate at which America trades exports for imports). Each individual American thinks that if he can raise his wages faster than the rate of inflation that he can then be the exception to the general rule—and he is right. As each of them seeks to become the exception, however, they collectively make the general inflationary problem worse. What is individually rational (possible) is socially irrational (impossible). Yet each American knows that no one can divide nonexistent output and that his real wage rate cannot on average rise faster than his productivity.

If productivity is not growing, the average real American wage rate cannot grow after correcting for inflation, regardless of how fast money wages are growing. If productivity is not growing, the only non-inflationary wage gain is no wage gain. If any worker's wages rise faster than inflation, then some other worker's wages must rise slower than inflation. The problem is not knowing such "facts of life." Every American knows the "facts of life." What Americans do not know is how to deliver the bad news to themselves in such a way that they will accept it without making the problem worse.

In many ways inflation is simply the easiest way to deliver the bad news about slower productivity growth or a deterioration in the terms of trade. Everyone can blame inflation on someone else, usually the government, and not have to confront the fact that his wages are stagnant because his productivity is stagnant. Instead of employers having to tell their employees that they will get no wage increase this year because employers and employees have not learned how to work together more efficiently, the employer distributes a 5 percent wage gain, everyone mentally congratulates himself on his intelligence and hard work, and then bitterly complains when that 5 percent wage gain is taken away from him in the form of a 5 percent rate of inflation.

The cure for inflation is not found in remedying stupidities in the government at the Federal Reserve Board or in accepting permanently higher unemployment. If Americans want a full-employment society without inflation, they will have to discover a better way to cope with unfavorable changes in the terms of trade and techniques for reaccelerating the rate of productivity growth.

Logically, inflation and unemployment remain unsolved problems. Democrats can lead the way in discovering and adopting real long-run solutions that will make it possible to persistently run the American economy at full employment without inflation. The last thirty years have witnessed ten recessions, the last five deliberately induced to stop inflation. There hasn't been an accidental recession in the American economy since that of 1960–61. There is no need to have ten recessions in the next thirty years. There is no need to deliberately induce recessions to fight inflation.

LOOKING FORWARD

Looking forward, two problems loom on the horizon. One springs from the deficit in America's balance of trade; the other springs from the deficit in the Federal budget. Much of America's prosperity in 1983 and 1984 was literally due to borrowed money—money borrowed to finance foreign deficits; money borrowed to finance government deficits. Permanent prosperity cannot be based upon borrowed money, for no one, country or person, can forever borrow faster than his income is growing. Eventually lenders quit lending, and when this happens painful changes in lifestyle are forced upon the borrower. This happened to Mexico in 1982 and it will happen to the United States at some point in the future.

The United States' balance of trade deficit was $123 billion in 1984. Some of this deficit could be financed from the interest and dividends received on past American investments in foreign countries, but America had to borrow heavily to finance its 1984 purchases. The United States shifted from being a net creditor nation (owed more than it owes) to being a net debtor nation (owing more than it is owed) in early 1985 and is projected to have a net debt of $94 billion by the end of 1985.[7]

The United States hasn't been a net debtor nation since World War I. Between then and 1982 America accumulated $152 billion worth of net foreign assets. The magnitude of the current borrowing can be seen in the fact that America will liquidate almost seventy years of asset accumulation in a little more than two years. To preserve today's standard of living Americans are literally mortgaging tomorrow's standard of living.

The origins of the problem are simply put. The monetary policies practiced by the American government to control inflation in the late 1970s and early 1980s produced very high interest rates relative to those in other industrial countries. Those high American interest rates looked attractive to foreign investors. As they moved their funds into the United States to take advantage of high interest rates, the value of the dollar had to rise. German and Japanese investors sold marks and yen to buy the dollars they wanted. With foreign investors demanding dollars and selling their own local currencies, the value of the dollar rose substantially above the level where American exports and imports balanced.

With fiscal pump priming, imports into a rapidly expanding American economy rose faster than American exports into a still stagnant world economy. Normally this would have led to a quick fall in the value of the dollar, but the normal inclination was offset by high interest rates. With high interest rates much of the rest of the world wanted to keep its cash balances in the United States. As a result the outward flow of dollars from the trade deficit was matched with an inward flow of dollars on the capital account.

When foreigners put their money into the United States they finance our trade deficit, but much of the money goes into government bonds and also helps finance the government deficit. If this flow of foreign funds did not exist, the interest rate that would be needed to attract enough American funds to finance the Federal deficit would be much higher than it is. American interest rates are high, but they would be even higher without foreign lending.

A dollar which rises above the level that can be justified by American productivity, however, generates a number of adverse consequences. In the short run, American firms find that they cannot compete on world markets and that they lose market share at home and abroad. Once lost, American firms find in the long run that it is hard to rebuild their market shares, since their foreign competitors have established service networks and developed customer loyalty they did not previously have. In addition, with rapidly expanding markets taken from American producers, foreign firms find they can afford to make investments in new technologies that American firms with contracting markets cannot afford to make. American firms cannot earn the profits necessary to develop new products and processes, and they know that even if they were able to borrow the necessary funds, foreign producers would quickly undercut their best possible prices because of the high-valued dollar. As a result they don't invest in new American production facilities. Offshore production becomes the preferred mode of competition.

With an enormous persistent deficit in the American balance of payments, economic fundamentals (what economists call purchasing power parity) indicated that the dollar should have been falling in 1984, but it wasn't. How can this be?

There are two approaches to sorting out such a conundrum. Those who believe in the all-wise, never-wrong virtues of financial markets search for rational factors which would justify a high-valued dollar. They point to rises in American interest rates in the first half of 1984. With a bigger differential between American and foreign interest rates, more foreigners want to hold their money in the United States. To do this they have to buy dollars and sell their local currency.

But foreign currencies also went up in the last half of the year when American interest rates were falling. To explain this they point to the fact that the American recovery is much faster than that in the rest of the world. Foreigners want to get in on the American boom. To do this they have to buy dollars and sell their local currency. But most of the foreign currencies flowed into bonds rather than the equities that one would expect if foreigners wanted a "piece of the action." To explain this they point to political uncertainties in Latin America and much of the rest of the third world. Such uncertainties lead to capital inflows into safe political havens such as the United States. But money was also flowing out of countries such as Japan where no one worries about political stability.

While there is probably a bit of truth in each of these suggestions, they just don't explain the magnitude and persistence of what went on in 1984. To do this it is necessary to return to history and think of the great financial bubbles—and ensuing panics. Leave the world of the rational and enter the world of the irrational.

Meet the tulip craze. In 1633 the price of tulip bulbs started to rise. More and more speculators were sucked into the market. Three years later in 1636 individual bulbs were selling for hundreds of dollars. The Dutch were not stupid. They knew that bulbs were not "worth" hundreds of dollars and that prices would eventually fall. In the long run the value of tulip bulbs could not be greater than the costs of growing them—the agricultural equivalent of today's purchasing power parity. But they were willing to pay hundreds of dollars because they thought that bulbs would go even higher. Each speculator thought that he would be the smart one who would make a killing and get out before the inevitable crash came. Most were wrong. The crash actually came early in 1637. Most were caught, their fortunes were swept away, they were left in financial ruin. But note that it took four years for the rational facts about tulips to overwhelm irrational beliefs about tulips.

Meet the South Sea Bubble. In 1720 the South Sea Bubble burst in Great Britain. The value of the shares of the South Sea Company, a company engaged in fishing and slaving in the South Sea, had been rising over the previous seven years but exploded by a factor of 10 in six months. Yet the British knew that there were very few fish to be caught or people to be made into slaves in the South Sea. A few months before the peak, what may have been the world's smartest man, Sir Isaac Newton, sold his shares for a 7,000 pound profit, with the statement that he could "calculate the motions of heavenly bodies, but not the madness of people."[8] Even the world's smartest man, however, could not resist the temptation of rapidly rising prices. He later reentered the market for shares and eventually lost 20,000 pounds when the stock eventually crashed, wiping everyone out. In the words of the times the stock market was "a roaring Hell-porch of insane and dishonest speculators."

The Great Depression followed in the aftermath of just such an "irrational" speculative surge. By the fall of 1929 a farm depression had already been under way for several years and the nation's GNP had already ceased to grow, but the stock market continued to bound upward in greater and greater leaps until those fatal days in October.[9] In that case it took ten years to clean up the resulting mess.

The upsurge in the value of the dollar ought to be called "The Great Dollar Bubble." Currency speculators understand that the dollar is already too high and must inevitably fall, but they think that in the short run it might go even higher. They are the smart ones who will buy dollars today, sell their dollars tomorrow when the dollar's value is even higher than it is today, take their profits, and get out before the dollar falls and wipes them out. History teaches us that most of them will be wiped out just as such bubble speculators have been wiped out in the past.

There is nothing like greed and the belief that they are smarter than everyone else, however, to fog the minds of otherwise rational men. Today's dollar speculators are just as greedy and no smarter than those in 1637, 1720, and 1929. They will come to the same end and be wiped out. No one knows when, but the panic will inevitably set in and speculators will flee from the dollar as they once fled from tulips. The lucky will get out of the dollar before it peaks and keep what profits they have already made, but few will be lucky. Being human, most will stay in the market looking for that last dollar of gain. Once smitten with the tulip craze or the dollar craze, one needs to be financially smitten to get over it.

Everyone understands that no country can forever run a deficit in its balance of payments. But as the dollar stays high longer than anyone believed possible, analysts start to talk as if the impossible is possible. *Business Week*, for example, in October 1984 stated that the dollar would stay high for another ten years.[10] For this to be true, the United States must be able to run large trade deficits for the next ten years. It just isn't possible, and the impossibility can be seen in some simple arithmetic. The United States' trade deficit essentially doubled from 1983 to 1984 and will grow very rapidly with the dollar at the values of early 1985, but be conservative and assume that the trade deficit only grows by $30 billion per year.

In 1984 the United States borrows $110 billion to finance its trade deficit. In 1985 America must borrow $140 to finance its trade deficit, but in addition it must borrow $11 billion (assuming a 10 percent interest rate) to pay interest on 1984's borrowings. In 1986 the United States must borrow $170 billion to finance its trade deficit, $14 billion to pay interest on 1985's deficit, $11 billion to pay interest on 1984's deficit, and $1.1 billion to pay interest on the interest payments that were borrowed in 1985. Altogether it must borrow $457.1 billion dollars in just three years. The rest of the world is not about to lend the United States that sum of money.

The dollar will come down, generating an inflationary shock as it does so. According to the statistical evidence, it would take a 30 to 40 percent fall in the value of the dollar from the levels of early 1985 to eliminate America's trade deficit. If the dollar were to fall 30 percent, a falling dollar would directly generate 3.6 percentage points of inflation since 12 percent of the GNP is imported. But American firms such as General Motors would also raise their prices if foreign competitors such as Toyota were forced to raise the price of imported cars because of a falling dollar. This indirect inflationary effect is in fact apt to be bigger than the direct effect. Put these direct and indirect price effects together with a base inflation rate between 4 and 5 percent and the American economy is quickly back to double-digit inflation.

The normal response to a falling currency and inflation is tight money. But if it took a 19 percent prime rate to force inflation out of the system while the government was pumping a $62 billion Federal deficit into the system in 1981, what kind of a prime interest rate would it take if the government has a $200 billion-plus deficit? Clearly interest rates would have to be much higher than they were at the previous peak.

The size of America's trade deficit is a function of the overvalued dollar but the downward trend in its trading position is a function of low productivity growth. U.S. productivity has simply been growing much more slowly than that of the competition since World War II. In the six years from 1977 through 1983 productivity in American manufacturing grew one-half as fast as that in Germany, one-third as fast as that in France, and less than one-third as fast as that in Japan.[11] Outside of manufacturing American performance was even worse.

In 1983 the United States was enjoying a cyclical rebound in productivity while its industrial competition was still mired down in a slow recovery from the 1981–82 recession. Manufacturing productivity grew at 4.2 percent. Yet in the same year manufacturing productivity grew at 4.6 percent in Germany, 6.1 percent in France and 6.2 percent in Japan.[12] In a good year American productivity growth was below that of the competition in a bad year. Given this reality, problems of international competitiveness will be with Americans even after the dollar falls.

When it comes to the value of the dollar, one thing is unknown and one thing is known. What is unknown is the issue of timing. No one knows, or can know, when the dollar will fall, for that is a matter of psychology. It could be tomorrow, six months from now, a year from now, or it might already have happened by the time this book reaches the bookstores. What is known is that the dollar will fall. The dollar will fall just as tulips and every other overvalued asset have fallen. No one can repeal the financial laws of gravity.

Each day nervous treasurers of multinational companies are comparing the gains they make from higher American interest rates with the foreign exchange losses that they will incur if the dollar falls. Each German treasurer knows that if he moves 300 million marks into the United States when the exchange rate is 3 marks to the dollar his $100 million in American investments will only return 200 million marks when the exchange rate has fallen to 2 marks to the dollar. Such losses easily wipe out all of the gains from higher interest rates. Such losses often get corporate treasurers fired. Each treasurer wants to be in dollars earning those higher interest rates but also wants to be the first person out of the dollar when the fall begins.

It is not necessary to have a decline in American interest rates for the dollar to fall. Even if interest rates should stay high forever, America's trade deficit and the borrowing necessary to finance it are growing rapidly. At some point the rest of the world inevitably decides that they have lent enough of their assets to the United States and that they do not want to increase the proportion of their assets held in dollar loans—whatever the rate of return. At this point the lending quits and the dollar falls.

Whatever the triggering event, the fall of the dollar is apt to be very rapid when it begins. Historically this is what has happened each time currencies started to move since the world went onto the flexible exchange rate system in August 1971, but more importantly it is what should happen if investors are not financial masochists. Everyone wants to rush out of the dollar at the same time to prevent the foreign exchange losses that he would otherwise suffer, for the last person to bail out of the dollar loses the most. He has exchanged his money at the least favorable rates.

Moreover, if the dollar is overvalued by 30 percent, then it is apt to overshoot and fall by more—for this is the history of flexible exchange rates in the last decade. A 50 percent fall for a 30 percent overvalued currency would not be at all surprising.

A falling dollar generates inflation but it also causes what economists call a deterioration in the terms of trade. Since the price of imports has gone up and the price of exports has gone down, it now takes a larger volume of exports to buy the same volume of imports.

This means that after Americans pay for the imports that they need there are fewer goods and services left over to be divided among Americans. The result is a noticeable reduction in the American standard of living. A 50 percent fall in the value of the dollar would reduce American standards of living by about 6 percent.

At some point foreigners will also demand repayment of the loans made in the early 1980s. At this point Americans will have to produce more than they are consuming to give foreigners what they are owed. Today's Americans are in a very real sense borrowing from abroad to enjoy a standard of living that cannot be sustained. When the loans are repaid American standards of living will have to fall.

While foreign borrowing will eventually show up in a balance of payments crisis, domestic borrowing to finance the Federal deficit will show up in a very different but no less serious manner. In 1983 the Federal government borrowed $183 billion or 5.5 percent of the GNP to finance its deficit. At the same time individual Americans were saving 3.3 percent of the GNP. Since government borrowing represents funds withdrawn from the pool of savings available for investment to pay for public consumption, the Federal deficit essentially represents a flow of negative savings. If the personal flow of savings is added together with the Federal government's flow of negative savings the net result is a negative savings rate of 2.2 percent. This can only be accomplished by borrowing savings from the business sector, from state and local governments, or from abroad.

The problem with government deficits is not that they cause recessions, not that they cause inflation, not that they cause high interest rates—although they may lead to all three of these—but that they lower the aggregate savings rate in a society that already has a very low savings rate. With less savings fewer funds are available for investment, and the country's long-term rate of growth falls below what it otherwise would be. From the point of view of long-term economic growth and international competitiveness the Federal government ought to be running a surplus and be contributing to savings rather than running a deficit and subtracting from savings.

The short-term effects of the deficits depend upon how our policymakers react to them. Deficits represent an infusion of Keynesian aggregate demand into the economy. With a $200 billion deficit, the current recovery is not going to abort into a recession. The mechanisms whereby a government deficit leads to a recession run through the Federal Reserve Board. As the economy recovers and approaches full employment the Federal Reserve Board begins to worry about potential or actual overheating (inflation) of the economy because of the large influx of Keynesian stimulation. The Fed tightens monetary policy to offset fiscal policy; interest rates rise, bringing interest-rate-sensitive industries (autos and housing) tumbling down; and the American economy slips into another recession.

Alternatively, the deficits in the balance of payments grow to the point where they are larger than the deficits in the Federal budget. At this point the aggregate demand pumped into the economy from the Federal deficit is eclipsed by the aggregate demand siphoned out of the economy from the balance of payments deficit. The net effect is to brake the growth of American demand and to push the economy into a recession.

Which happens first depends upon the relative rates of growth of inflation, the balance of payments deficit, and the Federal deficit; but there is an automatic abortion built into the current recovery.

In America's previous attempts to drive its economy with one foot on the fiscal accelerator and the other on the monetary brakes, the monetary brakes have had an ugly habit of seeming to have no effect until they were applied so hard that they suddenly grabbed and brought the economy to a screeching halt. Based on recent history, there is not much reason to believe that fiscal brakes and monetary accelerators can be simultaneously and smoothly applied.

The cures for the Federal deficit problem are as economically clear as they are politically murky. Economically the United States will have to raise taxes significantly, since it is not possible to eliminate the deficit with budget cuts. This can be seen in some simple budgetary arithmetic.[13] The government deficit is essentially two-thirds as large as the defense budget. The Defense Department is not going to be cut by two-thirds. The deficit is three-fourths as large as the expenditures on pensions and health care for the elderly. The elderly are not going to have their pensions cut by three quarters. And if defense (the President loves it), aid to the elderly (the President promised not to cut it), and interest on the national debt (it is a legal obligation) are excused from budget cutting, then all of the rest of the Federal government spends an amount of money just about equal to that of the Federal deficit. To cure the Federal deficit by cutting social programs other than Social Security and Medicare would force the elimination of all other Federal civilian activities—no roads, no weather bureau, no FBI, etc. Clearly this is not going to happen and the need for a major tax increase is back on the table.

The tax arithmetic is equally unattractive. The entire Federal personal income tax only raises $300 billion. To eliminate a $200 billion budget deficit with a surtax would require not a 5 percent surtax, not a 10 percent surtax, but a 67 percent surtax. Such a surtax is not apt to be legislated.

When there are no good options and not even any "least bad" options, it does not take a genius to predict that nothing will be done without the impetus of a crisis. But budget deficits do not lead to quick crises. The inflation which flows from too much budget stimulus occurs only slowly. During the Viet Nam war it took five years to raise America's inflation rate from the 2 percent of 1965 to the 5 percent of 1970. Similar inflation will only slowly accelerate over the next five years if the budget deficit is not eliminated. The slower growth which results from large deficits and the negative savings which they represent also shows up only slowly. Looking backward over the decades, Americans will see that their standards of living have grown more slowly than those of the rest of the industrial world, but nothing dramatic will be occurring at any moment in time.

Americans are now enjoying the calm in the eye of the hurricane. They have not entered a new era of permanent prosperity. A maxi-recession is behind them, they are now enjoying current prosperity, but ahead of them lie some difficult times. Neither the balance of payments nor the Federal budget can forever remain in deficit. Inflation will not remain as somnolent as it now is. Unemployment hovers at unacceptable levels. The secrets of productivity growth remain elusive.

These are things that need to be done. This book is devoted to outlining what must be done.

PART TWO

The Problem

2 / Falling Behind

America faces a problem that is simply put.[1] The huge technological edge enjoyed by Americans in the 1950s and 1960s has disappeared. Whereas America once had effortless economic superiority, it is now faced with competitors who have matched its economic achievements and may be in the process of moving ahead of it. If present trends continue, America's standard of living will fall relative to those of the world's new industrial leaders, and it will become simply another country—Egypt, Greece, Rome, Portugal, Spain, England—that once led the world economically but no longer does. What is worse, at precisely the moment when America's effortless superiority has vanished, the American economy has been absorbed into a world economy. For most goods there is now a world market, not just an American market. Competition is worldwide, not just American. As a result America faces the difficult task of learning how to compete in a new world economy just at the point when America's relative economic strength is weaker than it has been at any time since World War II.

STAGNANT PRODUCTIVITY

Productivity—output per hour of work—is the best general measure of a country's ability to generate a high and rising standard of living for each of its citizens. No country's citizens can for long enjoy a higher standard of living than they themselves produce, for no one can divide nonexistent output. To consume more, Americans have to produce more. Productivity measures America's ability to produce more of the goods and services, including leisure, that each of us wants.

Productivity is also a measure of America's ability to compete as a high-wage country on world markets. To fall behind on productivity is to fall behind on introducing the new products and the new production technologies that give American products an edge in world markets. If American productivity is not equal to that of the best, America can compete only on the basis of wages that are lower than those of the world's productivity leaders. While it is certainly possible to compete on world markets based on low relative wage rates (most of the world does so), I know of no American who wants to do so. Americans want to compete from a position of equality or superiority —not from one of inferiority.

Manufacturing is probably the best place to look at America's productivity performance vis-à-vis the rest of the world. All manufactured goods are potentially tradeable (they account for 70 percent of America's exports) and essentially homogeneous from country to country. The problems that make precise productivity measurements difficult in government or service activities do not exist in manufacturing. In manufacturing it is possible to make cross-country comparisons without the difficulties that are inherent in attempts to measure comparative standards of living. One does not have to place a value upon differences in the amount of space per person, differences in health care and life expectancy, or differences in the provision of free public services.

The data in Table 2 show the level of manufacturing productivity for seven leading industrial countries in 1983. As the data show, the United States has already been surpassed by Germany and France. Since we know that most of the small northern European countries (Switzerland, Sweden, Norway, Holland, Austria) have productivity rates similar to those of Germany and France, all of northern Europe with the exception of Ireland and the United Kingdom may now have moved slightly ahead of the United States in manufacturing productivity.

TABLE 2
MANUFACTURING PRODUCTIVITY 1983[2,3]

Country	Output Per Hour of Work (1983 prices)	Rate of Growth 1977–82	1983
United States	$18.21	0.6%	4.2%
Germany	20.22	2.1	4.6
France	19.80	3.0	6.1
Italy	17.72	3.6	0.6
Japan	17.61	3.4	6.2
Canada	17.03	−0.3	6.9
United Kingdom	11.34	2.7	6.1

To some it will come as a surprise that Japanese productivity is still slightly behind that of the United States. This is due to the fact that the Japanese manufacturing economy is a peculiar mixture of the superefficient and the real dogs. In America we see only the exporting superefficient industries whose productivity is second to none. Japan's inefficient industries do not export and as a result are simply invisible to American eyes. While average Japanese productivity may be slightly inferior to that of America, it is well to remember that it is possible to drown in a river which is "on average" two feet deep. Where it counts—in exporting industries such as steel, autos, and consumer electronics—the Japanese are second to none.

In Table (2) national measures of productivity are converted into dollars using a purchasing power parity index rather than current exchange rates. Such an index takes into account the prices of goods not traded internationally, since it attempts to measure the purchasing power of a worker's wages. If actual exchange rates had been used, the relative position of the United States would have been much worse. Japanese productivity would, for example, exceed that in the United States. As a result, if the data in Table 1 are in error, they are in error in the direction of making American productivity levels more competitive than they really are.

While America's previous position of economic superiority has clearly ended, its current position is probably not one of inferiority. Germany, the most advanced country, has a 10 percent edge according to the data. But given the vagaries inherent in any such measurements, a 10 percent edge is not an unambiguous lead. The rest of the world has caught up but is not ahead. America's competitive position is one of "an equal among equals."

There is a real danger, however, that America is falling from parity to inferiority if one examines comparative rates of growth of productivity. American productivity growth rates have been below those of Europe and Japan every since World War II, but more importantly they are still below those of Europe and Japan even though these countries have now essentially caught up. In the five years from 1977 to 1982 productivity grew at the rate of 0.6 percent per year in American manufacturing, one-third Germany's growth rate (2.1 percent), one-fifth France's rate (3.0 percent), and essentially one-sixth the Italian (3.6 percent) and Japanese (3.4 percent) rates. In 1983 a cyclical recovery generated a better productivity performance, but the United States was still near the bottom of international productivity rankings. Whatever one believes about the exact location of America's current productivity position (there are those who argue that the U.S. is still slightly ahead), if such differences in growth rates continue to exist for very long, substantial inferiority cannot be far away.

Nor can one argue that manufacturing is somehow misleading relative to other areas of the American economy. Manufacturing is in fact a relatively bright spot in the American productivity picture, growing three times as fast as productivity in all of private industry from 1977 to 1982. Since World War II in the entire private economy productivity growth has fallen from 3.3 percent (1947–65) to 2.4 percent (1965–72), to 1.6 percent (1972–77), and to 0.2 percent (1977–82).[4]

In 1983 and 1984 a cyclical upturn in productivity paralleled the upturn in output, but that upturn in no way reflected a change in fundamental trends.[5] Productivity always rises rapidly at the beginning of a recovery as the costs of overhead workers in sales, finance, and administration are spread across more units of output. The 1983 and 1984 productivity gains were in fact much weaker than what would have been expected from historical experience. If America were back on its old 1947–65 productivity trends, the 1983–84 cyclical upswing in productivity growth would have been at least twice as large as it was. America's poor productivity performance has lasted through four cyclical recoveries and is persisting through the fifth, growth having essentially halted by the second quarter of 1984. Low productivity growth is not a problem on the way to being cured.

Broader comparisons of standards of living, while more controversial, reinforce the problems revealed in manufacturing productivity. A recent English study attempted to compare standards of living for some representative countries using a wide variety of economic, social, cultural, health, climatic, and political indicators.[6] Among the countries ranked, the United States was eighth after France, West Germany, Australia, Japan, Italy, Switzerland, and Sweden. Since many of the small countries of northern Europe such as the Netherlands were not ranked, the American position would have been even lower if these countries had been evaluated. Americans still like to think of themselves as having the world's highest standard of living. It is interesting that the rest of the world no longer sees us in the same light.

The success of American science often leads Americans to exaggerate their competitive position. After all, more Nobel prizes are won by Americans than any other nationality. True, but success in pure science does not correlate well with economic success. If it did, America would not have reached economic parity with Britain at the turn of the century. After 1900 America's economic pre-eminence gradually grew, but America did not become the world's leader in science until after World War II—almost half a century later. Scientific breakthroughs still came from Europe. American mass education economically beat Europe's elite education but lost the race for scientific stardom. Since America achieved its economic success without simultaneously dominating pure science, it should come as no surprise that others, such as the Japanese, can do the same. To most Americans, however, it comes as a shock. The economic competition is somehow being unfair.

There are encouraging signs that American industry is now worried about its productivity performance and starting to take remedial measures, but as yet there is no statistical evidence that the problem is lessening, much less being whipped.

THE DISAPPEARING AMERICAN MARKET

Few industries are now safe from international competition. Indeed it sometimes seems as if all of our consumer durables are made abroad.

In the 1950s and 1960s American firms ventured abroad to establish American-owned multinational firms. In the 1970s and 1980s foreign firms reciprocated. Increasingly what used to be American firms are becoming subsidiaries of foreign firms, or foreign firms are building American subsidiaries. The American auto market has dissolved in a flood of imports and foreign-owned American production facilities. France's Renault bought American Motors; Volkswagen, Honda, and Nissan have all opened auto assembly plants; General Motors has essentially given up on the subcompact car market and is producing them in a joint venture with Toyota. There remains only a world auto market.

Statistically, exports more than doubled from 6 percent of the GNP in 1970 to 12.5 percent of the GNP in 1981.[7] With the high-valued dollar American exports fell from that high point, but in late 1984 imports were running at about 12.5 percent of the GNP. While 12.5 percent might not seem like a very high percentage, it needs to be placed in context. In 1981 Japan exported only 16.5 percent of its GNP.[8] America has become almost as dependent upon international trade as Japan. If intra-European trade is excluded as equivalent to trade between states in the United States, then Europe's exporting percentages are also not far above America's. America is no longer very different when it comes to dependence upon exports. The difference is that the rest of the world knows that it depends upon exports, but this reality has not yet sunk in for Americans.

America is now in a world where transportation costs are unimportant and everything that can be traded is traded or soon will be traded, including many things normally considered untradeable, such as buildings, which with a little ingenuity (prefabricated buildings ready to be assembled) can be traded. Firms that do not fight to capture foreign markets will find that they have to spend all their time defending their home markets. And those with a secure home base will have an advantage in competitive foreign markets.

The reality of a world market is here, a reality which most Americans won't like, for no one likes to go from a position of secure isolated economic superiority to one of insecure competitive equality. Like it or not, however, Americans must cope with the situation that prevails.

EXCUSES FOR DOING NOTHING

The usual human reaction to difficult problems is to deny that they exist. Economic problems are no exception. Excuses for doing nothing abound.

When They Catch Up, They'll Slow Down

In the 1950s and 1960s higher foreign productivity growth rates were dismissed on the grounds that America was the world's technological and productivity leader. It was simply harder to be the leader inventing new technologies than it was to be the follower adopting what the leader had already invented and put into practice. When the rest of the industrial world caught up with absolute levels of American productivity, their productivity growth rates would automatically slow down. America did not need to worry about the productivity growth gap.

Unfortunately the hypothesis was not true. America did need to worry. The rest of the world has caught up with absolute levels of American productivity, but the productivity growth gap has not disappeared.

If being an economic follower is automatically easier than being a leader it is now "we," and not "they," who have the "easy" task; yet "we" are failing. America's productivity growth rates have not reached parity, even though there are now many areas where Americans could copy superior foreign practices rather than having to invent new things for themselves.

It's Just the Product Cycle

If American industry were just being beaten on the tail end of the economy, there would be little to worry about. It is normal that what was once a new high-technology product (steel) should over time become an old low-technology product and production should move offshore to countries that must compete based on low wage rates. What is called "the product cycle" would be at work with its inevitable shifts in comparative advantage. Productive countries abandon old products and move on to new higher-value-added products. But if America is being beaten on the front end of the economy in new products and new production technologies, then something is occurring other than the normal product cycle.

Unfortunately American performance at the front end of the economy is little better than its failure at the back end of the economy. Consider the product gracing the cover of *Time* magazine at the end of 1984—the video recorder.[9] *Time* entitled its cover story "Santa's Hottest Gift: the Magic Box That Is Creating a Video Revolution." The VCR is a brand-new product involving brand-new production technologies.

In just one month, October 1984, Japan made more than 2.6 million video recorders.[10] Video recorders were a multibillion-dollar industry employing hundreds of thousands of people. How many video recorders were being made in the U.S. at the same time? Not one. Some are marketed under American brand names, but not one has ever been made in America—100 percent imported. Half of the video recorders made in Japan were actually being built for the American market.

What is worse, the original patents were held by a small American firm. The pattern continues. In late 1983 a big American firm, Kodak, announced that it had invented a new small lightweight video camera, but that it would be built abroad without even the attempt to manufacture in the United States.[11]

Semiconductor chips were once an American monopoly. But the Japanese captured 54 percent of the market for 64K RAM chips in 1984 and 92 percent of the market for the new 256K RAM chips.[12] In 1984 NEC passed Motorola as the world's second-largest maker of semiconductor chips and took aim at taking world leadership away from Texas Instruments.[13] Not surprisingly, given their gains in chip manufacturing, the Japanese also have taken the lead in larger, faster, easier-to-use supercomputers.[14]

In 1977 American machine tool exports equaled machine tool imports. Since then the American machine tool industry essentially lost its entire export market, and imports had risen to capture 36 percent of the domestic market in 1983.[15] Nor is the problem limited to what are technically classified as machine tools. In the third quarter of 1984 imports accounted for 28 percent of all of the equipment (excluding motor vehicles) purchased by U.S. companies.[16] Given what is estimated to be a 40 percent productivity advantage over their American competitors, it is not surprising that Japanese machine tool builders are doing well.[17]

In May of 1983 General Motors opened bids for twenty-one sophisticated new presses worth well over $100 million. Japanese producers were the low bidders for all twenty-one.[18] IBM announced an agreement where it will sell robots made by the Sankyo Seiki Company under the IBM name as part of its CAD/CAM (computer-aided design/computer-aided manufacturing) and FMS (flexible manufacturing systems).[19] Both major American companies, perhaps the premier American companies—both unable to compete alone.

A non-competitive machine tool industry has competitive ramifications for all the rest of American industry. At the end of 1982 there were thirty robots for every 10,000 employees in Sweden, thirteen in Japan, five in West Germany, but only four in the United States.[20] In 1983 every American robot maker but one lost money (for the industry as a whole, losses amounted to 49 percent of sales). Foreign firms were so far down the learning curve that American firms could only sell their products if they sold them below cost. American production of robots rose 10 percent in 1983, but foreign imports rose 92 percent.[21] Yet can anyone imagine a first-class economy without a first-class ability to make and deploy the new machines upon which a first-class economy depends?

When it comes to fiber optics and telecommunications, a foreign firm was by far the low bidder for installing a glass fiber-optic cable between New York and Washington. The low foreign bid was rejected for an inferior American bid on the grounds that the cable had significant "national defense" implications. With the dismemberment of AT&T and the opening up of a competitive market for telecommunications equipment, foreign imports soared and the U.S. had a deficit in its trade in telecommunications equipment for the first time in 1983, importing 48 percent more equipment than it exported.[22]

Personal computers are one of the many products which seem American, carry American labels, but are much less American than they seem. In the IBM personal computer the cathode-ray tube assembly is made in Taiwan and Korea. The circuit boards are being assembled outside of the United States, and recently IBM announced that it would begin subcontracting the disk drives in Hong Kong. Matsushita is producing the complete IBM PC for the Japanese market, the Middle East, and parts of Europe.[23] The printer for the Apple Macintosh comes with a "made in Japan" label.

The average American nuclear reactor has 5.5 emergency shutdowns per year while the average Japanese reactor has only 0.3 shutdowns.[24] The result is a 70 percent operating rate in Japan and a 56 percent operating rate in the United States—the difference between profit and loss, success and failure. The reason for the difference: carbon separates from stainless steel crystals when subjected to heat higher than 500 degrees centigrade and cracking occurs. The cause of the cracking was found to be too much heat during welding in construction. So the Japanese steel manufacturers went back to develop stainless steel that contained greatly reduced amounts of carbon, and the equipment manufacturers improved their welding technology. Those changes weren't made in America. The result: a successful nuclear power industry in Japan and a dying one in the United States.

In 1982 and 1983 the European Airbus captured over one-half of the world's sales for wide-bodied aircraft. Civilian aircraft have been an American monopoly since the introduction of the Boeing 707.

In 1983 for the third year in a row Japan led the world with the largest number of new drugs brought to market. The number of new American drugs has fallen 50 percent from the levels of the mid-1960s.[25]

The list could be extended, but enough is enough. None of these cases can be dismissed as the inevitable churnings of the product cycle. These products are not old products rightfully drifting off to low-wage countries. They are new products where the competition comes from the high-wage countries that are now jousting with America for world economic leadership. Products such as those just mentioned are America's economic future; and if Americans cannot be competitive in producing them, then Americans will have no high-wage industries in which they can be competitive.[26] Without such industries the American future is one as a low-wage "hewer of wood and hauler of water."

It's Just the Second Industrial Revolution

The current plight of American industry is sometimes dismissed as a sign of the second industrial revolution. The first industrial revolution saw a shift from agriculture to industry; the second industrial revolution represents a shift from industry to services. According to this scenario, services intrinsically generate lower productivity growth rates, and the United States is simply having its second industrial revolution ahead of everyone else.

Industrial revolutions are always painful, but they also make way for new opportunities, for even higher standards of living. "Let them make the computers, we'll do the programming; there's more money in the programming anyway." Such sentiments are often heard, but they do not constitute a viable vision of a successful American future.

Services and hardware usually go together. Consider the example of computer software. Those who design the machines have an advantage in doing the programming if they choose to exercise it. Technical design specifications have to be released before outside programmers can efficiently go to work. There is nothing that says that once foreign computer manufacturers have achieved dominance they have to continue to release such information to American software houses—even if it is to their advantage to do so while American firms are still competing actively on the hardware. In the long run, the people who build the hardware are going to dominate the software —and in any case America needs those hardware jobs to achieve full employment.

Consider an example of perhaps lesser importance. The Japanese have conquered the musical instrument business, but one of my sons and millions of other Americans now take Suzuki music lessons. Goods and services in this case are both subject to foreign competition. Dominance in manufacturing leads first to penetration and perhaps eventually to domination in the complementary services.

While it is true that over 60 percent of the hours of work added to the private American economy between 1977 and 1982 went into services, an examination of where those workers went quickly dispels the belief that services are going to be America's salvation.[27] Thirty-seven percent of all those new service workers went into health care.[28] Whatever you believe about the desirability of more health care, Americans are not going to generate a high standard of living giving each other heart transplants. Rising health-care employment simply reflects rising health-care expenditures. Spending on health care has risen from 5 to over 11 percent of the GNP from 1960 to 1983, but such trends cannot continue. Americans are not forever going to spend larger and larger fractions of their income on health care. Efforts are in fact now under way to cap health-care spending in both the private and public sectors. When those efforts are successful, as they must be, health care expenditures will quit growing faster than the GNP and the rapid growth in health care employment will come to a halt.

Another 33 percent of all of those new service workers went into business or legal services.[29] The number of legal workers in the United States rose 43 percent from 1977 to 1982.[30] Suing each other is good clean fun and generates a lot of jobs, but it is not productive. While lawyers could potentially be an export industry if others had our legal system, the rest of the world has much simpler legal systems and is too smart to adopt ours.

Business services are also dependent upon healthy American industries to which those services can be sold. Otherwise there is no need for business consultants. American consultants have no comparative advantages when it comes to the German market. Some of those business services are also in areas such as accounting, where office automation should severely reduce employment in the near future.

There is little reason to believe that business and legal services offer a bright future for the entire American work force. Whatever the structural weaknesses in American manufacturing (sloppy quality control, short time horizons, adversarial labor-management relations), those same structural weaknesses are also apt to plague the rest of American industry. Our service industries are not without actual and potential foreign competition. The world's largest advertising agency is not American. Foreign banks are very good. If international competition in services isn't yet here it soon will be.

One has only to look at Great Britain to see what happens to service industries when manufacturing collapses. The decline of the City of London as a financial hub is directly traceable to the decline of British industry. As American industry declines, the financial institutions that serve it will also decline. American banks, for example, will get some business from foreign manufacturing firms, but most of the foreign business will go to foreign banks. If anyone thinks otherwise, just remember the large equity positions that Japanese, German, French, and other banks hold in their national industrial firms. Controlling large equity positions, foreign banks can and do tell industrial managers what to do. As a result, foreign banks are in a position to insure that American banks get only the financial crumbs from foreign companies—regardless of whether these companies are operating inside or outside the United States. American banks will rise and fall with American industry just as British banks rose and fell with British industry.

While the pattern of industrial activity is indeed changing, as it

must, America is not now experiencing a benevolent second industrial revolution but a long-run economic decline that affects its future
standard of living.[31]

The Free Market Will Take Care of It

Americans like to think that the free market will automatically take
care of any and all economic problems, but that is because Americans
implicitly believe that they will always be the market winners. It isn't
necessarily so. The efficient may drive the inefficient out of business
in the market, but the inefficient may be Americans while the efficient are foreigners. To play a competitive game is not to be winner
—every competitive game has its losers—it is only to be given a
chance to win.

If anyone believes that a free market economy is an automatic
mechanism for reversing national economic decline, one need only
look at history. In the nineteenth century the British economy led the
world and provided the world's highest standard of living. But around
the turn of the century the British economy was surpassed by the
American economy. The British did nothing, relying upon the market
to reverse the situation. The reversal did not occur. The decline continued—by 1982 reaching the point where British manufacturing productivity was just half of Germany.

Britain's decline cannot be blamed on government interference
with the workings of the free market. The British welfare state, whatever its interventions, was not invented until after World War II,
almost a half century after the British economy had slipped from its
position of pre-eminence. The welfare state neither accelerated nor
reversed Britain's long downward slide.

Free market battles can be lost as well as won, and the United
States is losing them on world markets. Trade deficits of $123 billion
are not marks of economic success.

America's lack of performance cannot be blamed on any of the
simple suggestions which are the common currency of American politics. America has much lower productivity growth and a huge deficit
in its balance of payments with Europe. Yet Europeans spend more
on government social services (in the case of Germany 50 percent
more) than Americans dream of spending. America has much lower
productivity growth and a huge deficit in its balance of payments with
Japan. Yet Japan has government interference in areas where Ameri-

cans don't even dream of government interference. "Administrative guidance" is a way of life in Japan—a nightmare in America. Capitalism is good, socialism is bad. Yet socialistic France has productivity growing three times as fast as capitalistic America. In the most capitalistic of European countries, the German government owns all of the telecommunications industry, three-quarters of the electricity industry, one-half the coal industry, the railroads, three-quarters of the airlines, and one-quarter of the auto industry.[32] Interventions abound, yet among large countries the German economy has the world's highest productivity.

Economic battles are won by combining free markets and individual initiative with social organization. Societies with a well-educated labor force beat those without it. Societies who limit consumer credit to raise personal savings rates beat those who don't. Societies who are willing to raise spending on research and development beat those who cut research and development spending. Individuality is needed, but so is social organization.

THE CONSEQUENCES OF BENIGN NEGLECT

To do nothing about America's lack of productivity growth is to accept a standard of living that gradually falls relative to the world's industrial leaders. Normally it takes more than a single lifetime for countries like Portugal and Great Britain to go from being world leaders to being what might be called semi-underdeveloped countries. The process may be slow but it is not enjoyable. No one likes to experience a decline in his or her relative standard of living. Envy is a wide-spread human emotion.

To do nothing is to lose not only economic leadership but political and military leadership too, for no nation can build or maintain world leadership with a rotting economy. History is full of countries that have tried and failed. As economies decline, the economic resources that must be devoted to maintaining old political or military positions hasten the economic decline, as Portugal learned in Angola and the British in India. Simply raising the portion of the GNP devoted to the defense budget is equally unviable in a democracy.

Political problems arise at home. The United States has always thought of itself as a middle-class country having a form of government that required a strong middle class. Yet under the pressure of economic decline, the American middle class is becoming an endangered species.

If a middle-class household is defined as one with an income between 75 percent and 125 percent of the median household (a range that extended from \$15,663 to \$26,106) in 1983, the American middle class has declined from 27.1 percent of all households in 1968 to 23.2 percent of all households in 1983 (see Table 3). While a rapid economic recovery was under way in 1983, it did not reverse the downward trend—middle-class households fell by another 0.5 percentage points.

TABLE 3
THE MIDDLE CLASS[33]

Year	Bottom (0 to 75%) (of Median) (Household Income)	Middle (75 to 125%) (of Median) (Household Income)	Top (125% and up) (of Median) (Household Income)
1968	36.1%	27.1%	36.8%
1983	37.5%	23.2%	39.3%

Slightly widening the definition of a middle-class household (it cannot be widened very much without starting to count households that are below the official poverty line of \$10,178 for a family of four as middle class) changes the exact percentages who are middle class, but not the downward trend. Of those who have left the middle class, about one-third have fallen out of the middle class and about two-thirds percent have risen above the middle class.

Many fall out of the middle class with enough momentum to land in poverty. The percentage of the population living below the poverty line reached a low of 11.1 percent in 1973, hovered between 11 and 12 percent until 1979, and then began a steep ascent—rising to 15.2 percent in 1983.[34] More than 35 million Americans are now living in poverty. One has to go back to 1965 to find a year with a higher incidence of poverty. While it may be true that "the poor are always with us," it is equally true that they are always with us because we refuse to do anything about it. It would only take \$46 billion, approximately 5 percent of what the Federal government now spends, to completely eliminate poverty in America.[35]

The shrinking middle class and rising incidence of poverty are both closely connected with the expanding number of female-headed households. Thirty-six percent of all female householders with no husband present live in poverty—an incidence of poverty that is almost three times that of male householders with no wife present. American poverty is increasingly concentrated among women and children. In 1983 they accounted for 80 percent of those in poverty.[36] The day is not far off when there will be essentially no non-elderly adult males living in poverty.

To concentrate on those at the bottom of the income distribution, however, is to miss more than half of the action. The proportion of upper-income families is also growing—up from 36.8 percent of the population in 1968 to 39.3 percent of the population in 1983. At the top of the distribution almost 2.5 million (2.8 percent of all households) have an annual income in excess of $75,000 per year. Female householders without a husband present, however, represent only 4 percent of this latter group. High-income female workers are often featured in magazine articles, but they are in fact few and far between.

The decline of the middle class is not completely traceable to women and their job problems, however. Males may not fall into poverty, but they face an economy that is not generating new middle-income male jobs. From 1976 to 1983 the number of middle-income male jobs (jobs paying from 75 percent, $12,054, to 125 percent, $20,090, of median male worker earnings—$16,072 in 1983) declined from 23.4 to 20.4 percent of the male work force. The decline was even larger (from 38.0 to 33.4 percent of the work force) for males who work full-time full year.[37] From 1976 through 1983 male employment has grown by 4.7 million, but 0.9 million middle-income male jobs have disappeared.

The trend continues in the current recovery. From 1982 to 1983 the economy generated 0.5 million new male jobs, but despite this gain in overall employment the economy lost 0.5 million middle income male jobs (a decline from 13.6 million middle-income male jobs in 1982 to 13.3 million in 1983). Of the new jobs actually generated, about one-third were low-income jobs and about two-thirds were high-income jobs.

Those who profess to be unworried about the decline of the middle class rest their optimism on some automatic rebound that will restore the position of the middle class. The usual story revolves around the baby-boom generation. When the baby-boom generation becomes middle-aged they will have middle-class incomes, or so the story goes. But there is simply no economic reason why this should be true. Supply does not create its own demand. A larger supply of middle-aged workers simply means that middle-aged workers have to take jobs with lower earnings than middle-aged workers would have had to take if there had been fewer of them. It is a simple axiom of economics that a larger supply of any commodity leads to a lower price of that commodity. Middle-aged baby-boom workers are not exceptions to this axiom.

The "time will take care of it" argument also fails to fit the data. It is possible to take the 1967 age distribution of households and apply it to the 1982 distribution of income for each age group to see what the 1982 distribution of income would have been if the age distribution of the population had remained constant at 1967 levels. When this calculation is made, the fraction of the households that fall between 75 and 125 percent of the median income actually falls slightly farther (to 23.6 rather than 23.7 percent of the total population). The decline in the middle class is not traceable to fewer middle-aged households but to fewer middle-income households within each and every age group.

The real causes of the decline of the middle class lie elsewhere. Part of the decline in middle-income households in the late 1970s can be traced to recession. Most middle-income households become low-income households when the prime earner is unemployed, as happened to large numbers in the 1970s and early 1980s.

Part of the decline in middle class households can be traced to a rising portion of female-headed households. A household headed by the average full-time full-year female worker ($13,915) doesn't make it into the middle class. Conversely, if a household with an average male worker with full-time full-year earnings of $21,881 in 1983 adds an average female worker, that family leaves the middle class and becomes a high-income family.[38]

In recent years, however, the decline in middle-income households cannot be traced to female heads of household. The decline has been concentrated among male-headed households. From 1977 to 1983 middle-income households dropped from 24.0 to 23.2 percent of the population, but female-headed middle-income households basically held their own, actually rising from 4.8 to 5.1 percent of the population while male-headed middle-income households were falling from 19.2 to 18.1 percent of the population.[39] Male-headed households have just as much at stake in the decline of the middle class as female-headed households.

The real answers are not to be found in demography but in the nature and competitive strength of the American economy. America's new growth industries such as micro-electronics tend to have large groups of low-wage assemblers, large groups of high-wage engineers and designers, but not many middle-income jobs. The highly paid skilled blue collar workers typical of many old industries such as machine tools just don't exist in the same large numbers in these new industries. It is not that these new industries have a bipolar income distribution with more high- or low-income jobs than middle-income jobs but that relative to the industries which they are replacing they have fewer middle-income jobs. When General Motors contracts and McDonald's expands, the economy ends up with fewer middle-income jobs.

To some extent this lack of middle-income jobs is a product of technology (fewer middle-skilled jobs) and to some extent it is a product of a non-union environment. In many industries, such as autos, steel, or machine tools, unions converted jobs that probably didn't merit middle-income wages based on the skills required into middle-income jobs. Earnings were redistributed within the industry toward those with the least skills. Whatever their other failings, unions played an important role in the creation of the middle class.

The major cause of the decline of the middle class, however, is found in the hammering being administered to American industry in international trade. America's middle class earns its living in precisely the places that are most subject to superior foreign competition. The industries that have suffered the most such as autos, steel, and machine tools, have traditionally provided millions of middle-class jobs. When these industries cannot compete, America's middle class cannot compete.

From the point of view of technical economics, a shrinking middle class is of no concern. *Fortune* magazine notes correctly that the growth of high-income households will be a great opportunity to firms producing high income leisure products. Economies can easily be retuned to turn out more necessities for low-income groups, more luxuries for high income groups, and fewer middle income consumer durables.

Social democracies are harder to retune. The real problems are not economic but political. According to American conventional wisdom a healthy middle class is essential to a healthy political democracy. A society of rich and poor with no middle group to mediate between them politically or economically is almost by definition unstable. Yet it is precisely this result that our declining economy is now generating.

The inevitable revolution foreseen by Marx flowed from an economy divided between rich and poor. In this bipolar situation the poor would rise up, destroy the rich, and establish communism. But Marx did not foresee the rise of the middle class, and thus his anticipated revolution occurred only in countries such as Russia or China where the economy failed to produce a middle class. The middle class was devoted to preserving capitalism, chose to alleviate the worst excesses of capitalism with social welfare programs, and gave the poor visible hope that they too could escape from poverty. If American conventional wisdom is right and the middle class really is the social glue that holds society together, then America is in the process of becoming unglued.

Long run social self-interest should lead those whose income places them in the upper part of the income distribution to be concerned about the decline of the middle class, but they also have a more immediate economic self-interest. Today the American middle class is being hammered. The upper-income classes are growing. Tomorrow, however, it is highly likely that the hammering will move on to those upper-income groups.

Today production jobs are moving offshore; tomorrow engineering, design, and managerial jobs are apt to be moving offshore. Consider the General Motors–Toyota joint production facility in California. Auto workers have regained their jobs (the cars will be built in America), but all of the engineering and design work for the car is being done in Japan. If this arrangement foreshadows the future, America regains some middle-income jobs but loses upper-income jobs. Similarly the 13 million video recorders being purchased by Americans but built by the Japanese represent the loss of a lot of engineering, design, and management jobs. What is today a threat to the middle class will tomorrow become a threat to the upper classes.

Eventually the threat will even catch up with the wealthy. Americans have no inherent comparative advantage in owning or running offshore production facilities. As foreign countries become richer and less dependent upon U.S. technology, American owners will be squeezed out. If one thinks otherwise, remember American history vis-à-vis British investors. The British bankrolled much of American industry during the initial start-up phase but were quickly pushed out when British technology was no longer needed. A non-competitive economy such as Great Britain ends up with more poor, but it also ends up with fewer rich.

Among Americans the baby-boom generation stands most at risk. Americans born after 1947 (the start of the baby boom) will have to cope with the economic failure of low productivity growth over their entire working lifetimes and at the end will find a noticeably lower American standard of living than that found abroad. Moreover the baby-boom generation needs a supersuccessful American economy to generate the millions of good jobs that it will take to make room for their expanding numbers. Those born near the end of the baby-boom generation (1963) are not going to find many good jobs opening up through retirements. Similarly, since competition for jobs tends to flow downward from the old to the young, those born in the ten to fifteen years after the baby-boom generation are going to find their route to the top blocked by a derailed baby-boom generation. If the American economy does not expand rapidly, instead of being up-wardly mobile both the baby-boom generation and those immediately behind them are going to be downwardly mobile.

Within the baby-boom generation the "yuppies" (young urban professionals) are going to have most at stake. They are the ones competing for the high-earnings management positions that will be at stake in the upcoming international competition. Some will find jobs with successful foreign corporations in their American operations, but even they will find it much harder to get to the top of these foreign corporations than they would have found it in equivalent American corporations. If anyone thinks differently, count the number of Europeans who head American corporations with successful European subsidiaries.

The disappearance of the middle class and the potential threat to the upper classes is not yet a hot political issue, but it should be one of the central issues in the 1988 election campaign.

REBUILDING THE AMERICAN ECONOMY

A cyclical recovery, as welcome as that may be, is not a cure for America's competitive problems. America is falling behind. That is what $123 billion trade deficits are all about.

Americans do not want to stop economic progress in the rest of the world. It is after all better to live in a rich world rather than a poor one, even if Americans sometimes envy their neighbors. Not only are rich neighbors apt to be much more agreeable than poor ones, they are certain to provide better markets for the goods and services Americans want to sell. To catch up with America other countries had to have an extended period of time when they grew faster than the United States. But there inevitably comes a time, and it is now, when the United States has to accelerate its economic performance to keep from falling behind the rest of the industrial world. America cannot return to the era of effortless superiority, but it can and must rebuild its industrial structure to remain an equal among peers. Americans do not have to accept the current trends toward industrial inferiority.

In many ways what is needed is the moral equivalent of defeat. No society undertakes the painful efforts necessary for reconstruction unless it understands that it has been defeated—that it cannot continue as it has been going, and must rebuild on new ways or lose its traditional economic position. New institutions have to be created, new processes have to be tried, and new habits have to be formed. The basic motive for change is the four-letter word "fear"—the fear of losing what Americans have—but it is important not to let that fear turn into paralysis.

It was this sense of defeat that was the advantage enjoyed by Japan and Germany after World War II.[40] It was not that their factories were blown up and had to be replaced with new factories. If anyone thinks that is an advantage let them blow up their factories and see what happens. The British after all saw much of their industry blown up and simply went on declining.

The real advantage flowing from defeat was a social advantage—a willingness to change old ways for new ways, a willingness to give up old pretensions. Having been defeated, one cannot maintain that the old ways were good ways. The old ways have just failed. They must be replaced. The current cooperative labor-management relationships in Japan, for example, are not an inheritance from ancient Samurai traditions but something that was deliberately forged in the 1950s—and even today does not exist everywhere in Japan—witness the virulent labor-management problems on the Japanese national railways.[41]

Today America is where Britain was around the turn of the century. After a long period of effortless economic superiority, America faces a world full of technologically equal, if not superior, competitors. The question facing America is simple: Does America alter its

institutions and practices to compete successfully over the next century, or does America, as Britain before it, fail to do what is necessary
and gradually slip to a position of clear inferiority?

With manufacturing productivity just half that of West Germany,
Great Britain can without much exaggeration be called a "semi-
underdeveloped country." Is this also to be America's fate half a century from now, or will future historians record that America was still
one of the world's economic leaders?

In some ways it will be painful for America to get back into competitive economic shape. What needs to be emphasized, however, is
not the transitory pain but the ultimate gain. America can restore
vigorous productivity growth, and if it does so, everyone can once
again enjoy a rising standard of living that is the envy of the rest of
the world. Democrats can lead in this restoration.

3 | Slow Productivity Growth

Anemic productivity growth stands as America's central economic problem. If productivity cannot be reaccelerated, Americans can only look forward to a very slow rise in their standard of living regardless of how successful they are in inflation-proofing the economy, lowering unemployment, restoring a more reasonably valued dollar, eliminating budget deficits, or in dealing with any of their other economic problems. Rapid productivity growth is essential to America's future.

When disaster strikes, it is human nature to look for someone to blame—the villain. Such a reaction is easy to understand. If only we could find the villain reponsible for our troubles, all we would need to do is to punish him and the disaster would disappear—or so we all sometimes like to think. Unfortunately in the case of slow productivity growth there is no villain. Or perhaps more accurately, if productivity were viewed as a melodrama all of the actors would wear black hats, none would wear white hats. Each American is part of the problem and each American will have to be part of the solution if there is to be a solution.

Similarly there is no magic button to be pushed—that one single thing which if it were to be done would cure the problem.[1] An autopsy of American productivity growth would record "death by a thousand cuts" when it came to the line "cause of death." No one single thing killed American productivity growth; no one single thing can revive it. Death by a thousand cuts means resurrection with a thousand bandages, and unfortunately a thousand bandages are much harder to apply than one big operation. Each of us is in favor of bandaging the 999 caused by others and leaving the one caused by himself. Each of us envisions a patient that could survive our one cut. Each of us is right. The patient could survive any one cut, but if no cut is bandaged because each of us defends his own cut, the patient bleeds to death. And in this case the patient is our collective economic future.

THE DECLINE IN AMERICAN PRODUCTIVITY GROWTH

American productivity is best analyzed on a three-layer grid. The first grid consists of an industry-by-industry examination of productivity growth. The aim is to find those particular industry specific problems that have led to lower productivity growth. While statistically all of the national decline can be traced to some particular industry, to say that productivity has fallen in some particular industry is not to say that the cause is to be found in that industry. If the real cause of a poor productivity performance was too little capital or an unskilled, poorly motivated work force, these factors would show up as lower productivity in some particular industry, but the real problems would lie elsewhere. The job of the productivity analyst is to separate real industry-specific problems from those that only look as if they are industry-specific problems.

The second grid consists of the capital and labor inputs into the economy. What part of the decline in productivity can be attributed to reductions in either the quantity or quality of capital and labor going into the economy? Since higher real (inflation-corrected) earnings can only be generated by higher productivity, slowdowns in productivity growth must show up as slowdowns in income growth for some factor of production. As a result such slowdowns in income growth can be used to attribute productivity declines to capital and labor. If real hourly earnings or returns to capital are down or growing more slowly, the earnings of these factors are down because they have become less efficient. (Technically the economist is assuming that each factor of production is paid its marginal product and that less labor efficiency does not show up as less income for capital or vice versa.)

As is the case with an industry-by-industry analysis all of the slow-down in productivity growth can be attributed to deteriorations in either capital or labor since declining productivity must be matched by declining incomes for some factor of production. As before, however, attribution is not necessarily causation. If the real productivity problem was an industry-specific problem, such as having to drill deeper (use more resources) to find fewer barrels of oil, then this industry-specific problem would show up as lower average earnings for capital and labor in the oil drilling industry. To diagnose the problem as a capital-labor problem would be to misdiagnose it. Real capital-labor problems must be separated from phony ones.

The third grid is composed of adverse external shocks such as sudden large jumps in energy prices, the imposition of new environmental or safety rules, or droughts that lower farm output per unit of input. Some adverse shocks such as environmental regulations are controllable; others such as droughts are not. At this point, however, the goal is simply to determine what part of the observed decline is caused by factors external to the economy itself.

As a result the productivity analyst must move across this three-layered grid searching for the ultimate causal factors. As is always true in economics, judgment is required to assign causation to different statistical results. Numbers are often true but misleading or meaningless.

SPECIFIC INDUSTRY PROBLEMS

Statistically, the national decline in productivity can be disaggregated into slower productivity growth rates within individual industries and to shifts in output from high productivity industries to low productivity industries. If within industry productivity growth rates are examined, there is unrelieved gloom (see Table 4).

In the 1977–83 period, the latest period for which detailed industry data are now available, every single industry recorded a lower growth rate than it had from 1948 to 1965. While there were no industries with falling productivity in the first period, there were five such industries in the latter period. At the end of each year these industries were slightly less efficient than they had been at the beginning of that year. Other industries had to have substantial positive gains in productivity just to keep the nation from slipping below zero.

TABLE 4
INDUSTRIAL PRODUCTIVITY[2]

Industry	Rate of Growth 1948–65	Rate of Growth 1977–83	Output per Hour of Work 1983	Percent of National Average 1983
Agriculture, Forestry, Fisheries	5.0%	1.4%	$11.34	61%
Mining	4.3	−1.1	22.65	121
Construction	3.4	−2.2	11.36	61
Nondurable Manufacturing	3.3	2.0	21.21	113
Durable Manufacturing	2.8	1.8	21.43	114
Transportation	3.1	−1.6	17.73	95
Communications	5.4	3.5	50.07	267
Electricity, Gas, Sanitary Services	6.3	−0.9	46.24	247
Wholesale Trade	3.2	1.2	23.23	124
Retail Trade	2.6	0.8	11.70	63
Finance, Insurance, Real Estate	2.0	−0.4	49.70	265
Service	1.2	0.3	11.38	61
Private Business Economy	3.3	0.8*	$18.72	100

* U.S. Department of Labor productivity data differ slightly from U.S. Department of Commerce data. Labor Department productivity growth from 1977 to 1983 was 0.6 percent per year.

In addition if low-productivity industries such as agriculture are contracting in size relative to high productivity industries, national productivity expands. Agriculture used to be doing so; it no longer is. Conversely if low-productivity industries such as services are expanding relative to high-productivity industries, national productivity contracts. Unfortunately, in the period from 1977 to 1983 such shifts were working against national productivity growth.

In 1983 productivity was almost five times as high in communications as it was in agriculture, forestry, and fisheries. Such differences are not surprising and do not necessarily indicate that one industry is more efficient than another. Technology dictates, for example, that some industries use much more capital per worker than others. This leads those industries to produce more per hour of work but does not necessarily lead to higher total efficiency (output per unit of all inputs —capital, labor, land, and natural resources combined). If one were trying to rank American industries based on their efficiency, one would want to look at total factor productivity and not labor productivity, but total factor productivity isn't available on a detailed industry-by-industry basis. In any case the current goal is not a ranking of industries based on their overall efficiency but an understanding of why labor productivity is growing more slowly. Shifts from industries with high labor productivity to industries with low labor productivity are not necessarily bad, but they do have negative consequences for measures of national labor productivity.

When such shifts and slowdowns are examined, there seem to be five industry-specific problems:

(1) The Shift Out of Agriculture

From 1948 to 1965 the movement out of agriculture was strongly enhancing national productivity growth. Although agriculture has had an above-average rate of growth of productivity since World War II, it had, and still has, a level of productivity well below that of other industries. In 1948 agriculture's productivity was just 40 percent of the national average. As a result every worker released from agriculture and employed by other industries represented, on average, a 60 percentage point jump in productivity.

From 1948 to 1965, 9.1 billion man-hours of work (or 8 percent of the total number of hours worked in the entire private economy) left agriculture to enter industrial employment. By the early 1970s, however, this process was nearing an end, and from 1977 to 1983 less than 0.2 billion man-hours of work were released from agriculture.[3]

As agriculture declined from 17 to 5 percent of all hours worked, national productivity growth was being enhanced. A very low productivity industry was shrinking and its workers were taking jobs with much higher productivity. But this source of national productivity growth had to end—no industry can forever shrink—as it did after 1972.

If agricultural employment had not been shrinking from 1948 to 1965, American productivity would only have grown at a rate per year of 3 percent rather than 3.3 percent. Thus the shrinkage of agricultural employment explains 12 percent (0.3 percentage points) of the observed drop (2.5 percentage points) in the national productivity growth rate between the 1948–65 and 1977–82 periods.

Identifying a cause does not, however, automatically lead to a solution. America cannot go back to the era when workers were leaving agriculture in massive numbers and contributing to national productivity growth. Agriculture no longer employs a large fraction of the labor force. America is simply faced with a new stage in its development. To get the old rate of productivity growth new sources of productivity growth will have to be found.

(2) A Mystery in Construction

Where construction's productivity was once well above the national average, it is now 39 percent below the national average and 25 percent below its own 1968 peak.[4] While construction productivity grew in 1983 (3.9 percent), it has been falling for most of the past fifteen years.

Because the construction industry builds the plants and installs the equipment used by other industries, a fall in construction productivity is much more important than its own size (6.2 percent of total hours of work) would indicate. If a country's construction industry becomes inefficient, the costs of installing plant and equipment rise for other industries; less plant and equipment can be purchased per dollar spent. These other industries consequently buy less plant and equipment and, having invested less, suffer from slower rates of productivity growth. With inferior construction productivity, U.S. Steel and Nippon Steel, for example, could buy identical steel mills and U.S. Steel would still not be able to compete, since it would cost U.S. Steel more to set up the mill in the United States than it would cost Nippon Steel to set up the same mill in Japan. As a consequence, construction productivity has major ripple effects on the rest of the economy.

If construction productivity had continued to grow at its 1948–65 pace instead of falling at its 1977–83 pace, 13 percent of the decline in national productivity would have disappeared. The decline in construction productivity is a major mystery, however. No one knows what caused it; no one knows how to reverse it.

Various explanations for the decline in construction productivity have been advanced, but none of them is entirely convincing. Inefficient union work rules are one possibility, but this suggestion has to confront the fact that unionized construction is rapidly becoming a smaller and smaller fraction of total construction. If union work rules were the problem, one would expect to see productivity grow as unions become less important in the construction business. In fact the decline in unionization and the decline in productivity have gone hand in hand.

To generate falling productivity from restrictive work rules it is also necessary to argue not just that inefficient work rules exist but that these inefficient work rules have been growing at a very rapid rate. Although such restrictive union practices certainly exist, there simply isn't any evidence that they have been growing.

Some have suggested the problem is caused by statistical weaknesses in the way in which construction productivity is measured. Productivity is simply inflation adjusted real output divided by hours of work. This means that to measure productivity current dollar expenditures on construction must be deflated by some price index to yield real output. Since construction does not produce a homogeneous output, however, inflation is difficult to measure. If construction inflation was being systematically overestimated, then construction output would be simultaneously systematically underestimated, and construction productivity estimates would be too low.

There is some evidence to support such a conclusion. From 1954 to 1977 construction output was officially estimated to have risen 58 percent, but the use of construction materials (tons of steel, concrete, etc.) rose 133 percent. Few believe that 1977 buildings took more than twice as many materials as 1954 buildings.[5] On the other hand the government price index is basically an index constructed from data taken from some major private builders and buyers of construction. If government construction inflation estimates are wrong, then the analyst must believe that major builders, such as the Turner Construction Company, and major users of construction, such as the American Telephone and Telegraph Company and the Bureau of Public Roads, don't know their own construction costs. Few observers want to make such an assertion.

Alternatively, construction productivity may have gotten bogged down in shifts from simple to complex outputs. Where the construction industry used to build simple interstate highways across the wide-open spaces of Kansas it is now building urban interstates, such as the proposed West Side Highway in New York, where millions of wires and pipes have to be moved before construction can even begin. Where the construction industry used to build coal- or oil-fired electrical generating stations, it is now building complex bogged-down nuclear generating plants. Since construction output in the case of electrical generating plants output is measured in terms of kilowatts of installed capacity, long-drawn-out fights over safety show up as fewer plants completed and less output per hour of work in the construction industry.

Or the decline may be a straightforward case where workers have gotten lazy and are simply doing less work per hour than their fathers before them. Within the construction industry most observers think that the decline is real but perhaps exaggerated in the government numbers.

Construction productivity is a major part of America's productivity problem, but no one knows what really caused the decline or what can be done about it.

(3) A Geological Blow in Mining

The reasons for the decline in mining productivity are as clear as those in construction are mysterious. In 1983 mining productivity was 37 percent below where it was in 1972, but there was a simple explanation. Appoximately 80 percent of the answer was found in oil and gas—the major mineral "mined" in the United States. The American oil industry is progressing up a rapidly rising cost curve because of geological depletion. There is a lot of oil yet to be found, but it is much more expensive to find it. Since output is measured not in feet drilled but in oil lifted out of the ground, productivity falls when production declines in old wells and when new wells yield less oil per foot drilled. Because of geological depletion it simply takes many more hours of work to produce a barrel of oil. In addition, any expansion of drilling, such as that which occurred after the first and second OPEC oil shocks, adds hours of work to the mining industry well before it adds more output—oil or gas lifted. In 1983, with a cutback in marginal drilling activities, mining productivity rose 15.2 percent. This did not completely offset the 22 percent decline that had occurred from 1977 to 1982, but it went a long way.

The remaining 20 percent of the decline in mining productivity is to be found in the other minerals mined in the United States. Here environmental protection and occupational safety (third-grid effects) probably played a role—there is little evidence of rapid geological depletion of ore bodies. If open-pit mines have to be filled and the land restored to its natural contours, more hours of work are required to mine a ton of coal. If better ventilation and more tunnel supports are required to protect underground miners, more hours of work are necessary to mine a ton of copper.[6]

To the extent that the productivity problem is caused by fewer accidents or a cleaner environment the measured productivity problem is less of a problem than it seems. In the past fifteen years deaths in underground mining have been reduced from three to two per million hours of work. The air is better to breathe and there is less environmental damage than there used to be in mining areas. Neither of these is counted in conventional measures of mining output, yet they contribute to the well-being of America's citizens. If the benefits of such factors had been included in mining productivity, it would not have declined as much as it did. Such outputs are not counted, since no one knows how to weigh the value of a life saved versus a ton of copper produced. Those interested in environmentalism and mining safety may be faulted for not finding the most efficient ways to get the desired results, but the heart of the productivity problem in mining is not to be found in environmentalism or safety. The measured effects are small, and even those small effects are to some extent a statistical artifact of defects in the way in which mining output is calculated.

If mining productivity had continued to grow at its 1948–65 rate of 4.3 percent per year, however, 6 percent of the national productivity decline would have disappeared. Most of this 6 percent, however, is an uncontrollable geological blow from mother nature—fewer pools of cheap oil yet to be found in the United States.

(4) The Demand for Electricity

Part of the national productivity decline flows from gas, water, and electrical utilities, where productivity growth has fallen from plus 6.3 percent per year to minus 0.9 percent per year. If productivity had continued to grow at 6.3 percent per year in the 1977–83 period, 13 percent of the national productivity decline would have disappeared. While the causes of the decline in utility productivity are crystal clear, clarity unfortunately does not automatically lead to an equally clear solution.

Utilities employ most of their workers installing and maintaining the distributing systems that deliver electricity, gas, or water to their customers. Relatively few workers are employed actually producing electricity, gas, or water. When the demand for utility output rises rapidly, productivity rises rapidly. Output is up but more workers do not have to be employed, since the extra output can be sold through the existing distribution system. Conversely when demand falls, productivity falls. Less output is being produced but almost the same work force is necessary to maintain the distribution system. As a result utility productivity is a direct function of the rate of growth of output. If output grows rapidly, as it did from 1948 to 1965, productivity grows rapidly. If output grows slowly, as it did from 1972 to 1977, productivity grows slowly. If output falls, as it did from 1977 to 1979, productivity falls.

The decline in utility productivity is in a class with oil depletion or agriculture when it comes to public remedies. There are none. If energy prices rise rapidly, energy consumption will fall and productivity must fall with it. Since energy prices seem to have peaked and do not appear likely to rise in the near future, however, one would expect that utility productivity would rebound and continue to grow at the 3.6 percent rate of 1983 in the next few years. Barring another OPEC oil shock, the worst is behind us on the utility front.

Together mining and utilities represent the direct "energy" blow (a third-grid effect) to productivity. The decline in oil mining productivity is one of the reasons that energy prices are up, and higher energy prices lead to lower utility productivity. When these direct effects are added to the indirect effects (industry has to devote a larger part of its investment funds to saving energy rather than raising labor's productivity), the energy shocks probably explain about 20 percent of the national productivity decline. This 20 percent, however, is not an additional 20 percent. It is simply a different way of viewing the decline in mining and utility productivity.

(5) Expanding Services

Services are the mirror image of agriculture. Agriculture was a rapidly declining low-productivity industry; services are a rapidly growing low-productivity industry. While agriculture's decline enhanced productivity growth, the expansion of services dampens it.

Services have been braking national productivity growth since World War II, but the brakes have been gradually tightening as service productivity falls farther and farther behind that of the rest of the economy.[7] Back in 1948, when service productivity was 96 percent of the national average, moving a worker into services only lowered national productivity 4 percentage points. But by 1983 service productivity had fallen to 61 percent of the national average, and every worker who moved into services represented a 39 percentage point decline in productivity.

Services have been growing very rapidly, and from 1977 to 1983 they absorbed 65 percent of all of the hours of work added to the private economy. Of these 7.4 billion hours of new work 36 percent went into health care, heavily into nursing homes, and 36 percent went into business and legal services (accountants, lawyers, consultants, etc.). In the economic expansion from 1982 to 1983 services accounted for more than 100 percent of the gain in full-time equivalent jobs in the private economy. A gain of 560,000 full-time equivalent jobs in services offset a loss of 144,000 full-time equivalent jobs in the rest of private industry. Within services, health and business or legal services accounted for a full 81 percent of the jobs generated in 1983.

Health care in many ways is like safety and environmentalism. Nursing homes account for a major share of the growth of the health-care industry; yet bathing, feeding, and caring for grandmother is intrinsically a labor-intensive, low-productivity industry. If each of us took care of grandmother at home, as the Japanese do, grandmother would not show up as part of the productivity problem. Taking care of grandmother in a nursing home, however, has some advantages in terms of the well-being of the children who do not have to tie themselves to the care of an elderly sick person. Their well-being is not counted in conventional measures of health-care output.

The same problem exists in the rest of the health-care industry. Infant mortality has been cut in half over the last two decades and life expectancy at age sixty-five rose three years in the decade of the 1970s, whereas it was rising at only a half a year every ten years in the decades of the 1950s and 1960s.[8] Lower infant mortality rates and longer life expectancy are worth having. As productivity is measured, however, hours of work devoted to this end will show up as declining productivity. More hours are worked without producing more output, since health-care output is measured in terms of treatments given rather than less illness or longer life expectancy. And even in cases where treatments fail, people feel better knowing that an effort is being made to save their lives. Such feelings have value even if they are assigned no value in productivity statistics.

At the same time a country can be spending too much on health care and have a health-care industry which is a real as well as a statistical drag on national productivity growth. To determine this, however, it is necessary to examine the health-care sector and not just productivity statistics.

When it comes to the growing army of American business and legal consultants, there simultaneously is and is not a measurement problem. Since consultants give advice, it is difficult to measure their output directly. If the quality of their advice is being underestimated in measures of service productivity, however, the unmeasured benefits will show up in higher productivity in the industries taking their good advice. The benefits cannot disappear. With an across-the-board slower rate of growth of industrial productivity, however, there is no evidence that consultants are having large positive effects which are incorrectly being attributed to industries other than their own. Legal and business services are being accorded a very slow rate of growth of productivity in the statistics, and they deserve it.

Legal services are, for example, mostly a zero-sum game which absorbs hours of work. Suppose you fall down on my unshoveled sidewalk and sue me. If you win you get to take some of my old output (income) away from me, but the process does not generate any new output that can increase the total income flowing to the two of us. But since the legal process requires hours of work, the economy's hours of work are up without any equivalent increase in the output and productivity is consequently down.

As rapidly as the service industries are growing, such data underestimate the real growth of service workers. Many service workers are on the payrolls of manufacturing or other industrial firms and are not counted as service workers in the official statistics. If one looks at occupational statistics rather than industrial statistics, American payrolls are now almost evenly divided between 50 million office workers and 50 million factory, service, sales, and farm workers who do everything else that needs to be done in the economy.[9] If office workers are simply a deadweight loss when it comes to raising productivity, numerically it will be very difficult for America to break out of its productivity slump.

Paradoxically, while there is a genuine revolution under way in information processing and office automation, these changes have yet to show up in gains in office productivity. Quite the contrary. Between 1977 and 1982 real output rose 8 percent, yet at the same time clerical employment rose 15 percent and total white-collar employment 18 percent. In contrast blue-collar employment fell 2 percent. The net result was a sharp decline in white-collar productivity that completely offset substantial gains in blue-collar productivity.

American banks illustrate the problem. They have completely

computerized their accounting systems and in their automated tellers probably have more robots than any other American industry, yet employment rose 21 percent from 1977 to 1982, far outstripping the rise in banking output, and productivity fell 2 percent per year. In 1982 it took more hours of work to produce a unit of output with computers and automated tellers than it used to take in 1977 without them.

The U.S. Department of Labor has changed its occupational classifications dropping the distinction between blue- and white-collar jobs so it is not possible to compare 1983 with earlier years; but it is possible to compare 1983 and 1984. If one examines the rate of growth of employment for different occupational categories and compares it with the growth of real output (up 6.8 percent), precision production, craft, and repair workers and operators, fabricators, and laborers experienced productivity gains of 0.9 and 2.0 percent respectively while executive, administrative, and managerial productivity was falling by 0.5 percent. More and more executives were producing less and less per unit of work. In our most recent data office workers were still a lagging sector when it comes to productivity growth.

To make offices into a leading productivity sector will require changes not in the hardware of computers but in the software of office sociology. Consider the different options for using word processors. One option is to equip secretaries with word processors. There is very little productivity to be gained from such a shift. The secretary does exactly what she has been doing, and if she was a good typist making few mistakes the superior speed with which mistakes can be corrected on a word processor makes little difference to her total productivity.

The other option is to equip executives with word processors and require them to do their own typing. A good typist can type faster then he can dictate. Files can be recalled with a personal computer in less time than it takes to explain what files are needed to a file clerk. By getting rid of personal secretaries and file clerks enormous gains in productivity are possible. The executive does his part of the task faster and other people aren't needed to put his decisions and thoughts onto paper. But this requires that executives have good keyboard skills. Traditionally, executives are too important to type. Standards of what important people do have to change. Power and status are tied up with having a personal secretary. Old symbols of power and status have to be discarded. Executives must learn a new skill well. The needed facility can only be acquired with practice and a transition period where executives seem clumsy. No one wants to appear clumsy or incompetent in front of his or her subordinates. As a result, word processors aren't used as they should be used.

The same thing is true in accounting. Here again there is a paradox in an explosion in the demand for accountants—employment up 41 percent from 1977 to 1984—at exactly the same time that accounting is becoming computerized. Here again there needs to be a rethinking as to what must be done and by whom.

With computerized accounting the line of least resistance is to simply order up all of the old accounts more frequently and to add new systems of accounting that could not previously have been calculated. Executives now order up accounts on a daily basis that they used to see only once a month or once a quarter. Tax accounting, cost accounting, management information systems, inventory control—new forms of accounting appear almost daily.

Given these demands it is not surprising that firms need more accountants along with the computerization of accounting, but there is a real question as to whether all of the new and more frequent accounts lead to better, more efficient management. In all likelihood the answer is no. Accounting becomes a form of defensive management just as testing has become a form of defensive medicine. Doctors order up every test they can think of, since they don't pay for the tests and they might come in handy in case they are sued for malpractice. In a similar fashion managers order up every account they can think of, since the costs don't come out of their salaries and they may come in handy in defending what they have done. The real problem is not to computerize a company's accounting but to sit back and ask what accounts a company really needs and how often. A little cost-benefit analysis applied to accounting itself would not hurt.

In the end, office productivity will only flow out of office automation if American white-collar workers are willing to change what the office does and how it operates. Managers must become as willing to order themselves to learn to run a word processor as they now are at ordering a blue-collar worker to learn to run a robot. As yet few office workers seem willing to make needed changes in office sociology.

To get American productivity growing again white-collar workers and service workers are going to have to be at the forefront of the productivity revolution. Getting them there is going to be a management and sociological challenge of the first magnitude.

If service industries had not grown relative to the rest of the economy, however, 12 percent of the observed decline in national productivity would have disappeared. Alternatively, if service employment had grown but service productivity had held pace with that of the rest of the economy (stayed at 96 percent of the national average), 9 percent of the observed decline in productivity would have disappeared. If one adds in the growth of white-collar workers not on service payrolls, even more of the productivity decline could be attributed to the growth of white collar support services.

Services illustrate the complexities of the productivity problem. Bathing and feeding old people may be intrinsically a low-productivity occupation, but every American wants to be bathed and fed when old. Lawyers may be a drag on productivity, but Americans are using them in prodigious numbers. Productivity statistics do not care whether you or some thief has your new stereo, but you care, and hire an "unproductive" security guard.[10] In 1983, 602,000 private security guards (up 40 percent in the previous six years) were on some private American payroll. That is a lot of workers who in a more honest society could be productively employed making new goods and services rather than "unproductively" employed guarding old ones.

When the industry-specific first-grid effects from agriculture, mining, construction, utilities, and services are added together, they provide an explanation for slightly more than half the total slowdown in productivity growth. Where cures are possible they need to be applied, but to a great extent America needs new offsetting sources of productivity growth that up to now have not yet been found. Much of the decline that has been identified is irreversible and none is easily reversed.

The American problem is not so much correcting old bad habits as developing new good habits. Old veins of productive ore have become depleted; new veins will have to be discovered if America is to achieve the productivity performance it needs to match the international competition.

INFLATION, THE BABY BOOM, AND CAPITAL INVESTMENT

Inadequate investment in plant and equipment is a second-grid effect. Although Americans certainly invest too little, the problem is not quite as simple as it seems. Consider the following puzzle: In the years from 1948 to 1965 when productivity was growing at 3.3 percent per year Americans invested 9.5 percent of the GNP in plant and equipment. In the years from 1977 to 1983 when productivity was growing at 0.8 percent per year Americans invested 11.5 percent of the GNP.[11] Investment went up 21 percent while productivity growth fell 76 percent. Why?

The answer is to be found in the baby boom. The average American works with $58,000 (1982 dollars) worth of plant and equipment. To reach average productivity levels, new workers must be equipped with $58,000 worth of plant and equipment. Implicitly the parents of the baby boom generation were promising not just to bathe, feed, and educate their babies but to save $58,000 to equip each of their babies to enter the labor force twenty years later as the average American worker. And for every wife who entered the labor force the family was implicitly promising to save another $58,000. These implicit promises weren't kept.

Investment was up, but the labor force was growing much faster (up from 0.4 percent per year in the mid-1950s to 3 percent per year in the late 1970s). What was once a rising capital-labor ratio is now a falling capital-labor ratio—not because Americans are investing less but because the labor force is growing much faster. With a falling capital-labor ratio, stagnant productivity should come as no surprise.

The amount of equipment per worker—the capital-labor ratio—is one of the key ingredients in any model of productivity growth. New equipment allows labor to produce more output per hour of work, but it is also a carrier of new technologies. To put new, more productive technologies to work, new equipment has to be built to embody the new technologies. New knowledge without new equipment is often useless. One cannot work with robots unless one has robots.

The observed slowdown in the growth of plant and equipment per worker explains about 22 percent of the national productivity decline.[12]

The adverse effects of the baby boom were compounded by two energy shocks and environmentalism. To the extent that investments are made to control pollution or cut energy usage, there are fewer funds left to raise labor productivity. There are no hard official estimates of how much of our plant and equipment has gone into energy-saving investments since 1972, although it must be substantial, but about 5 percent of America's plant and equipment investment has gone into pollution and safety controls. If this investment is sub-tracted from the totals, the slowdown in the growth of plant and equipment per worker can explain something like 25 percent of the total slowdown—perhaps a little more, if one remembers the role of capital as a carrier of new technologies.

The slowdown in the growth of America's capital-labor ratio, how-ever, was not due to stupidity or irrationality. It was a perfectly ra-tional market response to the economic facts of life. Firms invest to raise the capital-labor ratio when it is profitable to do so. Technical change brings about such investments, but they are also brought about by changes in the relative price of capital and labor. When the cost of capital falls relative to the cost of labor, firms find it cheaper to raise production by investing in capital than by hiring more work-ers. With fewer workers and more capital, output per hour of work rises. Conversely, when capital becomes more expensive relative to labor, firms find it cheaper to raise production by hiring more workers and the capital-labor ratio falls. With less capital and more workers, output per hour of work falls.

In the aftermath of a baby boom simple supply and demand pre-dict that as the supply of labor rises wage rates fall. With wages down, capital becomes relatively more expensive. Firms shift technologies, replacing expensive machines with cheap workers. Labor productivity falls. From the point of supply and demand the economy has been behaving precisely as it is supposed to behave. Economic signals have been calling for a reduction in the capital-labor ratio. Whereas the cost of labor (wages plus fringe benefits) was rising 1 percent per year relative to the cost of capital (a cost which includes the initial pur-chase price, the energy cost of operating the plant and equipment, and the interest cost of financing it) from 1948 to 1965, the relative price of labor was falling at an annual rate of 6 percent from 1972 to 1979.[13] Where American workers were once becoming expensive rel-ative to machines, they are now becoming cheap relative to ma-chines.

Given such a sharp shift in the movement of the relative prices of capital and labor, it is not surprising that there was a decline in the capital-labor ratio. Business firms were doing exactly what economic incentives were calling for. One can imagine other offsetting factors (a sharp increase in the savings rate) which if they had occurred would have offset the impacts of population growth, but these poten-tially offsetting factors did not occur.

In some ways America is over the hump with respect to the baby-boom generation. Most of them are now at work, and the growth of the labor force will slow appreciably in the late 1980s and 1990s as the baby-dearth generations following the baby-boom generation enter the labor force. Female labor force participation rates are also rising to levels where the growth in female participation must slow down. Both energy prices and interest costs also seem to be mitigating. As a result some of the decline caused by a slower rate of growth of the capital-labor ratio should disappear without remedial action.

Looking forward the United States should enjoy a productivity rebound into the 1 to 1.5 percent range without doing anything. While better than what has been occurring, such a rate is not adequate. It does not come close to closing the productivity growth gap between America and its international competitors.

Even if the United States were living in a world by itself, 1 to 1.5 percent productivity growth rates would be inadequate if America is to successfully absorb the baby-boom generation. Regardless of the economic rationality of the causes, slow productivity growth is apt to produce unacceptable social and political results. With slow productivity growth, standards of living rise much slower than they have in the past. While Americans could get used to this new reality, the process of lowering expectations is not apt to be smooth. This is expecially true for the baby-boom generation, which will end up with lifetime standards of living lower than those of both their parents and their children. (When older Americans bemoan the fact that their children will not be able to afford the house that they live in, this is precisely the problem to which they are implicitly referring.) A democracy only uneasily lives with what will see itself as a "deprived" generation.

Wanting a different result is a rational social desire but not one which can be implemented by simply liberating free enterprise. The market is giving America the market solution, but it is a solution that Americans don't want to live with and don't have to live with if they are willing to socially organize themselves to change the parameters within which the market works. If Americans, for example, were to save much more, then capital's relative price would fall and labor would once again find itself working with a rapidly rising capital-labor ratio. Such changes don't happen automatically. Institutions and incentives have to be socially restructured to bring about the desired market result. One cannot fight the market, but one can channel it.

THE NEED FOR HIGH-QUALITY COMPONENTS

Many of the factors that explain the decline in American productivity growth also explain the much smaller declines in the productivity growth rates observed in most of the rest of the industrial world. The same adverse factors are affecting everyone but to a lesser degree. While the flow out of agriculture is slowing in most industrial countries, some foreign countries such as France are still experiencing relatively rapid declines in their agricultural work forces. Countries without significant oil and gas industries such as Japan cannot suffer from declining oil and gas mining productivity. With different legal and health systems (the British spend just half as much on health care as the United States), services haven't grown as rapidly abroad. Construction productivity has been falling in Europe, but at a slower pace than in the United States. Since most of America's industrial competitors already had high energy prices before the two oil shocks, they needed to invest less in energy conservation, and demand fell less rapidly in their utility industries. The rest of the world also ended up having a much smaller and somewhat later baby boom generation.

To see what must be done to catch up with the productivity growth rates of the rest of the industrial world, however, it is necessary to step back from detailed statistical analysis and look at the big picture. Catching up with foreign productivity growth is simultaneously simple and complex.

No one can build a high-quality economy out of low-quality inputs just as no one can build a high-quality product out of low-quality components. Yet whenever the basic inputs—capital, labor, management, labor-management relations—going into the American economy are compared with those of the competition they just don't seem to measure up.

Look first at the areas where hard comparative measurements are possible. In 1983 American gross investment (a measure that includes investment in housing) was 17 percent of the GNP. At the same time the French were investing 20 percent, the West Germans 21 percent, and the Japanese 28 percent.[14] If America were to have kept up with the Japanese in terms of plant and equipment investment per worker (and in the long run it must), it would have had to have essentially doubled its investment to 30 percent of the GNP because of its more rapidly growing labor force. In any one year such gaps make little difference, but compounded over a few decades they spell the difference between success and failure.

In a recent test of sixth graders in eight different countries, science students in Sweden placed first, Americans placed sixth. In geography the Swedes were again first and the Americans fourth. In math Americans were last, knowing only half as much as the Japanese.[15] Given such science and math scores it should come as no surprise that Japan produces twice as many engineers per capita as the United States and that with twice as many engineers on the payroll Japanese products seem to be a little better engineered.[16]

In the late nineteenth and early twentieth centuries when America was catching up with Great Britain, America had the best educated labor force in the world. It no longer does. A second-class poorly educated American labor force is not going to beat first-class well-educated German, French, or Japanese labor forces. America invented high-quality mass public education; America is going to have to reinvent it.

America's personal savings rate, 5 percent in 1983, was the lowest in the industrial world by a factor of almost three.[17] Our neighbors the Canadians saved 13 percent, the Germans 14 percent, the Japanese 21 percent, and the Italians 23 percent.[18] It does not take a genius to know that Americans cannot compete on world markets saving less than one-third as much as their competitors.

America's savings rates have not gone down. They never were high. When America's per capita income was twice that of the rest of the world, a 5 percent American savings rate was equivalent in terms of generating investment resources to a 10 percent savings rate in the rest of the world. But that time is over. What was good enough in the past will not be good enough in the future.

America invests less in civilian research and development than any of its major industrial competitors. American civilian R&D spending runs at about 1.5 percent of GNP while our competitors are spending 2 percent.[19] Americans aren't smarter than the Germans or French. German scientists with money will beat American scientists without money most of the time. In the 1950s and 1960s America spent more, not less, on civilian research and development than its competitors.

While it is not so easy to quantify, American management cannot escape its share of the blame. American firms have undeniable problems with quality control. When asked to rate the quality of their cars,

American buyers listed only two American-built cars among the top ten. Management is responsible for quality control. If American products are shoddily built, then American management is shoddy.

Neither can the American government escape its share of the blame. American industry cannot be expected to beat foreign competition if it must simultaneously cope with repeated recessions, high interest rates, and an overvalued dollar. Government has to do more than get out of the way. American firms face foreign firms with local governments in their corner. American firms need the same help and support.

When it comes to that famous bottom line, each major input into the American economy will have to be as good as those of the competition if America is to be competitive. A world-class economy demands world-class inputs. Converting existing American inputs into world-class American inputs will not be an easy task, but it is also not an impossible one. Other countries have done what was necessary to make themselves competitive with America. America can do what is necessary to make itself competitive with them.

4 | International Competitiveness

With trade deficits doubling from $69 to $123 billion between 1983 and 1984, something is clearly wrong with America's competitiveness on international markets. Americans cannot sell as much to foreigners as they wish to buy from foreigners.

Given human nature, it is not surprising that Americans often see the trade deficit as evidence of "unfair" competition. After all, Americans could not be losing if the competition really was "fair," or so Americans would like to believe. Corporations that cannot meet their foreign competition in the marketplace reinforce this feeling with advertisements calling for a "level playing field" or saying they are unable to compete against countries with "closed" markets.

In this context Japan is often held up as the prime example of a country closing its markets to American competition. There is some truth in this charge, but the emphasis should be placed on the word "some." (A suggestion for how the truth in this assertion should be dealt with is develped in Chapter 11.) It is not the whole truth and certainly not the whole explanation for America's trade deficit. If Japan had disappeared in 1984 and none of its exports had been replaced with exports from other countries, America would still have had an $88 billion trade deficit.[1] If Canada and Taiwan had had populations the size of Japan, they would have had bilateral trade surpluses with the United States of $78 and $84 billion respectively.[2] Because of its size and its strength in visible consumer products, American competitive concerns have focused on Japan, but the huge deficit in America's trade balance is not produced by "unfair" competition. It is produced by uncompetitive American products regardless of whether markets are closed or open.

In the short run American desires to buy foreign goods and services can be met with foreign loans and by depleting foreign assets accumulated by Americans in the past. Eventually, however, any country depletes its previously accumulated foreign assets and accumulates debts so large that foreigners are not willing to make further loans.

Countries, or persons who maintain their standard of living by accumulating debt face a triple reduction in their standard of living when the lending stops. First, without foreign lending Americans would suddenly have to reduce their foreign purchases (imports) to a level consistent with American sales (exports) abroad. Second, funds necessary to make interest payments on previously accumulated debts can only be acquired by purchasing less from foreigners than they wish to purchase from Americans—running an export surplus. Imports must fall by more than the amount that would be required to simply balance imports and exports. Third, to repay principal, funds over and above those necessary to make interest payments must be acquired. This can only be done if American purchases of foreign products are even further reduced so that America's export surplus is even larger than that required to pay interest. Depending upon the amount of debt accumulated, these three factors could lead to a large sudden reduction in American standards of living, just as they recently did in Mexico (a 5 percent per capita reduction) and Brazil (an 11 percent per capita reduction).[3] To borrow large amounts of money abroad is to preserve today's standard of living by mortgaging tomorrow's standard of living.

In this context it is important to make a sharp distinction between the Federal government's debt, often referred to as the "national" debt, and America's international debts. They are not the same, and because America has been a net international creditor for so long public attention tends to focus almost exclusively on the "national" Federal government debt. The two also tend to get confused because some of the international debt (but not all) is held in the form of Federal government bonds that are part of the national debt. International debt can be held in many forms—government bonds, corporate bonds, shares, real estate. All represent American assets owned by foreigners.

Viewed from society's perspective, Americans appear on both the asset and liability side of the national debt. As taxpayers Americans owe the national debt, but as bondholders they own the national debt. Thus, if one looks at Americans in the aggregate, the national debt makes them neither richer nor poorer. They owe it to themselves. The national debt takes money out of one American pocket and puts it into another American pocket. Among individual Americans there can, of course, be large differences between what individual Americans owe and what they are owed. The national debt alters the distribution of income among Americans but it cannot alter America's total income.

The same cannot be said for international debts. International debts are much more serious than national debts. With international debts all of the liabilities are held by Americans and all of the assets are held by foreigners. Foreign debts are by definition owed to foreigners—not other Americans. As a consequence foreign debts represent a direct one-for-one future (but no one knows exactly when) reduction in American standards of living. By the very fact that foreigners have accumulated a net creditor position vis-à-vis the United States, they have accumulated the right at some future point in time to come to Americans and demand repayment. At that point the goods and services that are necessary to make those repayments must be taken away from Americans and given to foreigners. Foreigners have accumulated that right since they are today giving Americans goods and services that Americans have not paid for. There are relatively few ways that today's Americans can place burdens on tomorrow's Americans, but the accumulation of international debts is one of them.

Today's solution to the deficit in the balance of payments—debt accumulation—is not a long-run answer to America's competitive problems. If Americans cannot build products foreigners want to buy, Americans will ultimately be forced to accept a lower standard of living. In this case "forced" means that the value of the dollar will fall and that foreign goods and services will become more and more expensive as far as Americans are concerned. The foreign cars, video recorders, and vacations that Americans could yesterday afford they cannot tomorrow afford. If American cars, video recorders, and vacations were exactly equivalent in terms of both price and quality to foreign-made products, Americans would not suffer a reduction in their standard of living when they were forced (because of costs) to shift to domestic substitutes. But they are not equivalent by the very fact that Americans are choosing to buy foreign cars, foreign video recorders, foreign vacations and not their American counterparts. If American products were comparable in price and quality, there would be no trade deficit in the first place. As a result, if Americans are cut off from foreign products they must suffer a reduction in their standards of living.

The amount of the reduction depends upon how much net debt America incurs before the borrowing stops and how much interest must be paid upon that debt. If the econometricians are right, a 38 percent fall in the value of the dollar would have been necessary to restore balance in the balance of trade in early 1985.[4] Since America imports 12 percent of the GNP, a 38 percent fall in the value of the dollar means a 38 percent increase in the price of 12 percent of those things purchased by Americans and as a consequence a 4.6 percent (.38 × .12) decline in the standard of living of the average American. While an income reduction of 4.6 percent may not sound like much, it is an impact more than twice as large as that of the severest of America's post-World War II recessions. When it occurs it is going to be very noticeable to the average American family.

If significant debts have been incurred so that interest payments are substantial, the reduction in American standards of living will be considerably higher. As of early 1985 America had liquidated the $152 billion of net foreign assets that it had owned in 1982 and was moving over the line from international creditor to international debtor. By the end of 1985 America was expected to be almost $100 billion in debt. Sometime in early 1986 it would pass Brazil as the world's largest international debtor.

More importantly, if American productivity continues to grow more slowly than foreign productivity, the 4.6 percent reduction in standards of living is only an initial effect. As long as American productivity growth remains below that of the rest of the world, foreign goods are gradually becoming cheaper—for the same quality, or better quality for the same price—than American goods. This leads foreigners to buy fewer American products and Americans to buy more foreign products. The balance of trade again gets out of balance forcing a further reduction in the value of the dollar and American standards of living to restore balance.

If American productivity grows at 1 percent per year and the productivity of our industrial competitors grows at 4 percent per year, the American dollar must fall by approximately 3 percent per year to maintain a balance in America's balance of trade. With 12 percent of the GNP imported, a dollar falling at this rate causes American standards of living to fall by 0.4 percent (.12 × .03) per year forever. If American productivity growth remains low long enough, America gradually shifts from being a relatively rich country to being a relatively poor country. If West Germany and the United States start with equal standards of living and a 3 percentage point differential in productivity growth, twenty-five years later West Germany has a standard of living more than double that of America.

New products are almost always first introduced in countries with the highest standards of living, since consumers in these countries have the most discretionary income for experimentation with new luxuries. Being closely in touch with the highest-income markets gives producers in those countries an edge in new-product introductions and the associated technologies. New production processes are often associated with new products, but even when they aren't, the richest countries are apt to be the ones doing the most research and development and hence the ones most apt to introduce new production processes such as robots. Being technological leaders in turn attracts the world's best brains, who are interested both in using the latest technologies and being paid incomes that only the highest income countries can afford. The British "brain drain" after World War II was no accident. As a result those who get ahead tend to reap dynamic advantages that keep them ahead, while those who fall behind reap dynamic disadvantages that tend to keep them behind. It is simply much harder to catch up than it is to keep up.

Despite the seriousness of America's competitive position, or maybe because of the seriousness of the situation, the experts seemingly disagree. Some experts see an America with a competitiveness problem; others see no problem. Everyone agrees that no country can forever run huge trade deficits; but some experts seemingly see a problem that will cure itself, while others see a problem that needs to be cured with active public policies. The division is not one, however, with liberals on one side and conservatives on the other.

A recent Commission on Industrial Competitiveness, appointed by President Reagan, reported that the "United States had lost the race for international competition in manufacturing and risks losing it in high technology as well."[5] No cures were suggested, but in a new book Kevin Phillips, the author of the emerging Republican majority thesis, sees a competitiveness problem that will have to be cured with overt public policies.[6] Conversely, Charles Schultze, Budget Director under President Johnson and Chairman of the Council of Economic Advisers under President Carter, has been at the forefront of those arguing that there is no competitiveness problem.[7] Why the differences? Which is right?

Since this is a book on what Democrats have to do to regain their competitiveness politically, let's look at the dispute about international competitiveness among Democrats. The seeming contradiction and its resolution can be seen in two books published in 1984. Robert Lawrence, a Brookings economist, in *Can America Compete?*, seems to be arguing that the United States does not have a competitiveness problem.[8] "U.S. manufacturers, aided only by changes in the exchange rate, were able to compete successfully in an environment characterized by emerging competition from developing countries and Japan and by growing government intervention and protection in Europe."[9] Since this view reflects the collective thinking of most of the economists at the Brookings Institution and is the technical backup for Charles Schultze's attack upon the view that America does not have a competitiveness problem, let me call it the Brookings line. America doesn't have a competitiveness problem.

In contrast *The DRI Report on U.S. Manufacturing Industries*, a collective effort led by the late Otto Eckstein, member of the Council of Economic Advisers under President Johnson, Harvard economist, and head of Data Resources Inc., argues that the United States does have a competitiveness problem.[10] The "decline of position of manufacturing is a major historical development for this country."[11] "There are so few exceptions to the decline of the international position of U.S. manufacturing industries that one must seek more general causes that act on the entire American economy. Without a strongly advancing manufacturing industry, the U.S. economy is hardly likely to maintain its progress in the decades ahead."[12] Let me call this position the Eckstein line. America does have a competitiveness problem.

If America follows the Eckstein line while the Brookings position is correct, it rushes off to fix something that does not need fixing and may end up damaging what it has. Conversely, if America follows the Brookings line while the Eckstein position is correct, it ends up with a standard of living which continually falls relative to the rest of the world. Clearly the correct answer matters, but which answer is correct?

Before closely analyzing the arguments on both sides, however, it is necessary to clear away the underbrush of agreement. As stated in the DRI *Report*, "no degree of cleverness on the part of management, no new-found cooperation between employers and workers, no industrial policies by the federal government can overcome the handicaps of an overvalued dollar and a domestic economy disrupted by credit crunches and recessions every three or four years." Everyone agrees on this point. The disagreements come in the next sentence. "Better national economic and financial policies will not solve our industrial problems, but without them the more specific solutions cannot prove successful."[13] In contrast the Brookings position is that better macroeconomic policies can by themselves solve America's competitive problem.

As is usually the case when two sophisticated sets of analysts differ on the facts, the problem is not really the "facts" but differences in the precise questions being posed. Although Eckstein and Lawrence seem to be posing identical questions they are actually posing quite different questions.

If the question is simply "Can America compete in world markets?" the answer is of course yes and the Brookings position is correct. Bangladesh and other economic basket cases compete successfully on world markets with a balance in their balance of payments. They do so by competing as low-wage countries with low standards of living. If their productivity growth rates lag behind those of the rest of the world, they simply accept a gradual fall in the value of their currency, their relative wages, and their relative standard of living. And this is what Lawrence is arguing when he says that America has been and can be competitive. The U.S. can be competitive and have a balance in its balance of payments according to the Brookings study if the dollar *forever falls* relative to the currencies of other nations.

Suppose for example that American producers are not competitive with Japanese producers with an exchange rate of 250 yen to the dollar. The United States is running a large bilateral and total trade deficit as it was in 1984. Suppose further that the average Japanese wage rate is 2500 yen per hour. Translated into dollars at 250 yen to the dollar, the Japanese wage rate is equivalent to an American wage rate of $10 per hour. If output per hour of work were equal in the two countries, 250 yen per dollar would be an equilibrium exchange rate if American workers were paid $10 per hour, and there would be no competitiveness problem vis-à-vis Japan.

If Japanese productivity is 10 percent higher at 1.1 units of output per hour of work relative to American productivity of 1 unit of output per hour of work, however, there is a competitiveness problem. Since Japanese productivity is 10 percent higher, Japanese prices can be 10 percent lower with equal wages. As a consequence American products cannot be sold and America has a balance of trade problem.

This balance of trade problem can be corrected with a depreciation in the value of the dollar so that only 225 yen are necessary to buy a dollar. At the new exchange rate Japanese workers are paid the equivalent of $11.11 per hour (2,500/225), and their higher wage rate compensates for their higher productivity, so that American and Japanese products can be equivalently priced on world markets.

For the American worker the new exchange rate shows up as a reduction in both relative and absolute wages. Where he and the Japanese worker were both making the equivalent of $10 per hour of work with an exchange rate of 250 yen per dollar, at the new exchange rate of 225 yen per dollar the American worker is making less than the Japanese worker, $10 versus $11.11. At home his real wages fall, since the Japanese video recorder that he was planning to buy for $1,000 (250,000 yen/250 yen per dollar) now sells for $1,111 (250,000 yen/225 yen per dollar).

With low productivity growth there is no alternative. The dollar must and will fall. To hold exchange rates up is simply to drive American firms out of business. Their prices gradually become less and less competitive and they lose market share at home and abroad. If the dollar falls, the United States is competitive in the narrow sense that it has a balance in its balance of payments, but it becomes less and less competitive in terms of standard of living.

If the relevant question is "Can America compete on world markets with wages and a standard of living second to none?," however, the answer is equally clearly no. There is no disagreement in the Brookings document. For what Lawrence proves is that the U.S. can compete successfully *if it has a continual decline in the value of the dollar, in its relative wages, and in its relative standard of living.* As Lawrence states, "*Aided by several devaluations,* U.S. firms were able to compete from 1973 to 1980" (my italics).[14] To be precise, Lawrence finds that American manufacturing could compete but *only* with the help of a 14 percent decline in the relative price of U.S. exports, a 22 percent rise in the price of U.S. imports, and a 13 percent decline in U.S. terms of trade (the rate at which exports are exchanged for imports).[15]

In the broader time period from 1965 to 1982 studied by DRI the U.S. could not compete. Lawrence agrees. He finds that more than half of the job loss in U.S. manufacturing from 1980 to 1982 could be traced to falling exports and rising imports.[16] Once again in the words of Lawrence, "In short, slowing productivity growth is a serious problem from the point of view of living standards. But it is not a cause of decreased competitiveness in international markets."[17] That is of course true if competitiveness is narrowly defined. Wages and standards of living fall relative to those of the world leaders, but America is still competitive.

But such a decline is precisely what Americans don't want and precisely what they are worried about when they talk about competitiveness. They do not want to gradually become low-wage "haulers of water and hewers of wood." They want to compete as a high-wage society with standards of living approximately equal to those of the world's economic leaders.

Both books give the right answers to the questions they pose, but the DRI book poses the right question.

The Lawrence book is only interesting for the light that it sheds on how fast American wages and standards of living would have to fall to remain competitive. In attempting to show that the U.S. competitive problem is due solely to macro-economic variables such as changes in the GNP, Lawrence estimates econometric equations to explain historical movements in American exports and imports. The aim is to estimate U.S. and foreign income and price elasticity of demand for imports. As incomes and prices change, what could be expected to happen to U.S. demands for foreign products and foreign demands for U.S. products?

Lawrence's equations show that to regain a balance in manufactured goods the U.S. would need a 38 percent decline in the value of the dollar (as of January 1, 1985), and that thereafter the dollar would have to forever fall by 0.4 percent per year to maintain balance.[18] This latter calculation, however, is made on the assumption that the U.S. GNP growth rate continues to remain one-third below those of the rest of the world, as it was from 1964 through 1980. Yet I know of no American who thinks that growing one-third slower than the rest of the world is an acceptable long run goal.

If the U.S. were to grow at the same rate as the rest of the world, the annual fall in the value of the dollar would have to be 1.8 percent per year according to the Lawrence equations. The 38 percent decline in the value of the dollar would have a noticeable negative impact on American standards of living; and while 1.8 percent per year may not seem like much, it is just such small persistent differences that led Great Britain to slip from number one in the world economically at the turn of the century to a position near the bottom of industrial countries when per capita GNP's are evaluated eighty years later.

Lawrence's equations also give us some insight into recent slippages in the U.S. competitive position. For both imports and exports Lawrence estimates two equations—one with data from 1964 to 1980 and one with data from 1964 to mid-1983.[19] By comparing the two equations it is possible to isolate the structural deteriorations that have occurred in the American position in the 1981–83 period. Such a comparison reveals a systematic deterioration in U.S. competitive strength. After correcting for changes in the value of the dollar, foreigners over those three years were buying fewer (1 percent less) U.S. exports when their industrial production rose than they previously had, and they were becoming more sensitive to the price of U.S. exports, cutting their purchases back more (9 percent greater) than they previously did when American prices rose. On the import side a given increase in the American GNP led to a bigger (14 percent more) rise in imports than it previously had, and a fall in foreign prices led to a bigger rise (6 percent more) in American imports than it previously had.[20]

Such shifts are the mark of a country whose exports are becoming less unique, less competitive, and must more and more be sold as simply cheaper rather than better. Conversely, foreign exports into the United States are becoming more unique, more competitive, and less and less have to be sold simply based on price. Relative to their incomes and after correcting for the effects of a high-valued dollar, Americans want more foreign products than in the past, while foreigners want fewer U.S. products relative to their incomes than in the past. Bigger and bigger American price reductions are needed to secure foreign markets, while foreigners can charge higher and higher prices without losing their American markets.

If the addition of three years of extra data to the Lawrence equations moves them consistently toward a more adverse American position, as it does, strong underlying adverse trends are running against the United States and will gradually enlarge the annual decline in the value of the dollar necessary to remain competitive. Extrapolating forward to the end of 1984, the Lawrence equations predicted a rise in the deficit in manufacturing trade, but the actual rise in the deficit was twice as large as that predicted.[21]

There is also every reason to believe that the Lawrence equations underestimate the magnitude of the adverse shift against the United States. The extra three years of data were added in the context of a rapid military buildup. Military spending is a captive market for American manufacturing. Americans don't ask for competitive foreign bids on military equipment. If they did, all of our naval ships would be made in Japan. But this means total manufacturing looks much stronger than civilian manufacturing would look if separated out.

In addition, the period has been one of protection. The percentage of U.S. manufactured goods protected by non-tariff restrictions has risen from 20 percent in 1980 to 35 percent in 1983. If such protection had not occurred, the adverse shift against the United States would have been much larger than that estimated by Lawrence.[22]

While America was running a trade surplus in high-technology products in the 1970s, in the 1980s it has been moving rapidly toward a trade deficit.[23] It already has a large bilateral deficit in high-tech products vis-à-vis Japan and is just barely holding its own vis-à-vis Germany.[24] Since countries lose their home markets last for the things that they do best, an inability to compete against Japan and Germany on high-tech products such as semiconductor chips or machine tools in home American markets has to be taken very seriously.

The heart of America's competitiveness problem is to be found in low productivity growth. As previously noted, America has lagged behind in productivity growth since World War II and continues to do so in the most recent period for which comparative data are available. While productivity levels are contentious (there are those who argue that the U.S. is not yet behind), data on rates of growth are not contentious. Eveyone agrees that the U.S. growth rates are low. This means that even if the rest of the world has not yet passed us in absolute productivity, it is a only question of time until they do so. And given that it will take a substantial amount of time—a minimum of five to eight years—to turn America's productivity growth rate around, the time to start making that turnaround is now, regardless of whether America is or is not yet behind in absolute terms.

Part of the contentiousness of "competitiveness" springs from the issue of industrial policies. Those against industrial policies are almost forced to argue that the U.S. does not have a structural competitiveness problem. For if it did they would have to advocate some form of industrial policies to cure the competitiveness problem. Industrial policies, as we shall see later, are an area where in many senses the word is more controversial than the substance. Much of the controversy is theological (how much respect should be paid to the god of free enterprise) and has focused on the rather narrow issue of whether the United States does or does not need a public investment bank. The Brookings line is to come down against industrial policies and Lawrence dutifully has a chapter attacking the industrial policy straw man of central planning where some government agency attempts to pick winners and losers. As a policy that would of course be a loser, and Lawrence has no problem deflating it. But in the next chapter, entitled "More Appropriate Structural Policies," Lawrence essentially embraces industrial policies without being willing to use the name. What is thrown out by the front door is dragged in by the back door.

Industrial policies, including the recommendations of Lawrence, will be examined in Chapter 9, but it is important to distinguish arguments about whether the U.S. has a competitiveness problem from those about how it should be solved. Whatever is believed about the right solutions, the U.S. has a competitiveness problem in that *all* of the data show that it cannot compete on world markets without a *perpetually falling dollar.* Even President Reagan's competitiveness commission agrees.

To accept a falling dollar as a solution to America's competitiveness problem is to accept an economy that competes on the basis of low wages and not higher productivity. If a nation decides to compete based on low wages, its industrial structure gradually shifts toward those low-productivity labor-intensive products where low wages are important and away from high-technology products where innovation and efficiency are important. The economy is technically competitive and has achieved a balance in its balance of payments, but when Americans say that they want to be competitive they are saying something quite different. They are saying that they want to compete based on efficiency and innovation and a standard of living second to none.

None of the things that Americans will have to do to become competitive on world markets are impossible. America does not have to circle the wagons and retreat into a defensive, falling dollar, second-class protectionist society. Others have done what was necessary to make themselves competitive. Americans can become competitive. They simply have to realize that becoming competitive is now necessary for their survival as a country with a world-class standard of living.

The Eckstein-DRI volume has a set of recommendations that will also be examined in the chapter on industrial policies, but even more important than its recommendations is its sense of urgency. Since Otto Eckstein knew that he was dying as the *DRI Report* was being written and that it was his last chance to speak to Americans, let him say it in his own words.

"To assure a more successful development of U.S. manufacturing industries, an industrial viewpoint should be introduced into economic policy decisions. . . . Industrial development must become an explicit objective of economic policy."[25]

"The trade deficits are real and will lead to further damage to our industries. The capital flows that will be needed to offset these trade deficits will generate future interest payments that will be a burden. . . . The United States now experiences a 'structural' trade deficit in the $40 to $60 billion range."[26]

"A nation that casually surrenders leading industrial positions through policies of neglect will find it difficult to stage a comeback, particularly if the period of non-competitiveness stretches for more than a few years."[27]

"The danger lies in too slow an adjustment process. If the present situation is allowed to continue, more markets will be lost and the damage to our trade position will become irretrievable. The present problems will not keep: in the absence of improvement in the current decade, they will become insoluble by the next one."[28]

DANGERS ON EITHER SIDE

To become competitive America will have to sail between the Scylla of protection and the Charybdis that "left alone, the market will take care of it." Either notion seems like the seductive easy answer, but if America steers toward either it will eventually run aground and destroy its chances of having a world class economy.

Protection is not the answer.[29] This springs not from altruism and the desire to help the rest of the world but from direct self-interest and the American desire to have a high standard of living second to none. Politically, protection is sold on the grounds that it is necessary to give local industry breathing time to become competitive. But it never works. Examine the industries that have been given protection in the United States. Not one of them has remade itself into the world-class industry that it promised to become when given protection. This is true of steel, this is true of autos, this is true of garments and textiles, this is true of consumer electronics. It is a simple fact of life that industries that do not have to compete won't compete. Competition requires sacrifice and change. These are too hard if there are any other options.

Protection can temporarily move an industry such as autos from the loss column to the profit column, but no one in the industry will make the changes that have to be made as long as they know that they will be protected from the competition. In the four years that the American auto industry has been protected some positive things have been done, but no progress has been made in reducing the cost differential between it and its Japanese competition. In the words of retiring Ford Chairman Philip Caldwell, "The gap is in the $2,500 range according to our most recent numbers—as big as it's ever been."[30] Protection has not led to the competitiveness to which it was supposed to have led.

Such a cost gap cannot be closed with better technology alone. The American auto industry will never again have a 25 to 30 percent productivity advantage over its Japanese competitors. The American industry can improve its productivity, but the Japanese will be working just as hard to improve their productivity. Since American auto wages and salaries are far above those in Japan and those in the rest of American industry, they will have to come down if the industry is to be competitive. This simply won't happen as long as protection exists. Despite that $2,500 cost gap, in 1984 large bonuses were paid to managers ($8,000,000 to Mr. Caldwell alone) and not surprisingly in the aftermath of these large bonuses the most recent auto contract saw wages rising 7 to 8 percent in the first year—far above the pattern in the rest of American industry.[31] Since auto salaries and wages exceed those of the average American, auto quotas result in a relatively poor group of auto consumers being asked to subsidize a relatively rich group of automobile producers. That is not fair.

With protection as a live option, going back to Washington to extend protection is always easier than doing the research and development, building the new factories, acquiring the new skills, altering wages and work rules, and selling the new products that would be necessary to become competitive. Where was the auto industry in the spring of 1985 after promising to become competitive in 1981? In Washington asking for an extension of protection. It didn't get it in Washington, but Tokyo kept the quota, although at a higher level.

While America can protect its domestic markets it cannot protect its markets in the rest of the world. If American products are not competitive in America, they certainly won't be competitive in the rest of the world. Without sales somewhere, Americans cannot buy what they want to buy to have an "American" standard of living.

Protection leaves weak industries weak, but it also weakens the healthy industries that depend upon them. If cheaper or better quality foreign steel is kept out of America, then firms who use steel such as autos or machine tools find themselves at a competitive cost disadvantage. With higher input costs, they lose market share at home and abroad, eventually become uncompetitive, and have also to be protected. As the waves of protection spread, the economy becomes ever more uncompetitive.

Ultimately foreign products cannot be kept out. Foreign firms develop the new products such as video recorders that Americans cannot produce but want. When these new products are let in, as they inevitably will be, the sales of old American industries (record players) decline. Jobs are lost in the old industries but not gained in the new industries. The economy becomes sicker with fewer good job opportunities.

There may be a limited role for protection in restoring an industry to competitive economic health, but protection by itself is never the answer. It always has to be combined with explicit quid pro quos as to what the industry will do in exchange for a period of protection and have a definite time when it will end, whatever the then health of the industry being protected. By itself protection is simply the road to long-run economic decline.

Real competition is painful. Americans are feeling that pain, but competition also serves as a spur to make us perform better than we otherwise would. In many ways the best thing going for America is the fact that it for the first time since World War II has equal economic and technological competitors who will force it to improve faster than it otherwise would.

America likes to think of itself as the leader of the free world. If it is, and wishes to exercise its responsibilities as a leader, then it cannot circle the wagons and retreat into protection. If it does so, the rest of the world will do likewise. Each country prohibits imports, and as a necessary consequence everyone's exports fall. Since countries tend to export what they do best and import what they do worst, everyone loses a few jobs in their best industries and gains a few jobs in their worst industries. As in the case of limiting Chinese textiles, low-wage textile jobs were gained in South Carolina and high wage aircraft jobs were lost in Seattle. At the end of the process everyone's economy is sicker than it was at the beginning; everyone's income is lower than it was at the beginning.

If the leader of the free world declares an economic war on its military and political allies, then it should also not find it a surprise if it no longer has military and political allies. America and its allies can compete and still be friends, just as football rivals can still remain friends. But America cannot declare economic war on its allies and still remain friends.

Any trade war also inevitably leads to the collapse of the third world. Third-world debt problems are not solvable in the third world. Countries such as Brazil can only earn the foreign exchange necessary to pay their debts if they are allowed to sell their products in the industrial world. Yet in early 1984 the United States and Europe both proposed limits on Brazilian steel exports. How was Brazil to pay its American and European debts if it could not sell its goods in the United States and Europe?[32] Whatever the dangers of communist subversion in Latin America they are greatly enhanced in a world economy of protectionism and economic collapse.

To raise productivity and gain real competitiveness a country must eschew protection but it also must go beyond this and learn to compete in foreign countries.[33] Just as the only good defense is a good offense, so the only good protection economically is the ability to compete in foreign markets. If foreign firms invade the American market but American firms do not invade foreign markets, foreign firms will use their secure home markets as bases from which they can pick off American firms in the American market. American firms will occasionally be defeated at home and will have no compensating foreign victories. In the world economy ahead of America, a firm that cannot compete successfully in foreign markets will not survive in the American market.

In many ways it is a mistake to think of Americans buying Japanese cars. Americans buy cars specifically designed for the American market that happened to be built in Japan. Some of them are even products of American design studios. In contrast American firms almost never design products to meet the specific needs of foreign consumers. They design things for Americans, and then if the rest of the world happens to want precisely what Americans want, American firms are glad to sell it to them. That was a viable strategy when America had a huge technological edge on the rest of the world and could sell its products because of that technical edge, but it is not a viable strategy in a competitive world. Foreigners can now get the latest technology adapted to their specific needs and desires and do not have to accept American needs and desires just to get the latest technology.

The president of Nippon Telegraph & Telephone Company complains that major American suppliers try to sell him equipment that is incompatible with the existing Japanese phone system—presumably assuming that it is a Japanese duty to shift to the American system. If America had superior products they might, but we don't and they won't. In a similar manner American businessmen often talk as if it were the duty of foreign countries to restructure their economies so that American firms could enter their markets without having to change attitudes or practices. This is not going to happen. Americans are going to have to learn to do business in Japan as the Japanese do and in France as the French do.

The phrase "export orientated" captures what must be done, but it includes a lot. It begins with a willingness to learn foreign languages, but it extends far beyond.[34] Foreign history and culture must be known, appreciated, and understood. Different legal systems have to be accommodated. Management has to be malleable enough to deal with government banks in France and administrative guidance in Japan.

In the era of American supremacy American firms could follow a multinational strategy of simply buying successful firms in foreign markets. Since America had the ability to infuse these foreign firms with superior technology and capital, they were worth much more to American buyers than they were to their local sellers. Takeovers were permitted by foreign governments to gain the benefits of that superior American technology and capital.

Since much of the industrial world is now as wealthy as the United

States and has higher savings rates, it no longer needs Americans to provide capital. Without superior technology, fewer and fewer foreign firms are going to be more profitable for Americans than they were for their original owners. From now on Americans will have to learn how to invade foreign markets with exports from America or to construct successful firms abroad. Neither is going to be as easy as the old strategy of simply buying an already successful foreign firm.

While a successful strategy cannot be forged from protection, "Leave it to the market!" leads to an equally unsuccessful strategy. Market principles and forces have to be used, but "leaving it to the market" is a recipe for failure.

To be successful in the world market a country must organize itself to win. Those who organize themselves to win with high-quality inputs and good strategies beat those who simply "wing it." There is nothing intrinsic in the American character or forms of social organization that guarantees that Americans will be market winners simply because they are willing to play the game. For a society which loves team sports, with all of their organization and preparation before the game begins, it is surprising that Americans won't recognize the same reality in the far more important international economic game. Without high-quality inputs, preparation, and a well-thought-out and well-executed strategy Americans will simply be losers in the world marketplace.

The view that a market economy takes care of itself without government help springs from the postulates of competitive economic theory. To understand the need for social organization and institution building, it is important to understand where these postulates fail to describe reality. In the economist's standard model of free trade in a world of competitive supply and demand, there is no room for social organization, no need for coordination or strategic vision. A country simply inherits its comparative advantage based on natural resource endowments and factor proportions. If a country has copper deposits, it will export copper. If it has a lot of labor relative to capital, it will export labor intensive goods. Reverse the factor endowment and it will export capital intensive goods. Given these initial endowments and factor proportions, there is no way for government to intervene that will not incur more costs than it would produce benefits in the simple economic model.

According to the conventional economic theory taught in most introductory economics classes, all countries have access to the same technology and competition is self-limiting. Everyone is assumed to be operating on the same rising cost curves. To increase production, one must incur rising costs. That is why supply curves are always drawn with an upward slope. But this upward slope means that those firms who on the margin expand production always have higher costs than those firms who are already in the industry. As a result, it is impossible for a country to deliberately conquer any industry using industrial policies. To attempt to expand an industry would be to confront higher costs than one's competitors.

While certainly the standard view within the economics profession and often elevated into a religious belief in Fourth of July speeches on the virtues of capitalism, it unfortunately isn't true. The standard view is based upon a static view of the world where the only source of efficiency is getting to a fixed production frontier. There is no such thing as dynamic efficiency and making the production frontier move more rapidly outward with research and development expenditures or other improvements in efficiency. In contrast to the static assumptions of the conventional model, the real world is full of economies of scale and learning curves that overwhelm the rising costs of simply expanding factor inputs. Those who expand production are, as a consequence, often the low-cost producers and not the high-cost producers. They race down the learning curves with new technologies and force old producers out of business.

In reality comparative advantage is not simply something that one inherits. It can be created as the Japanese have done and as America itself has done in the past in farming and with process inventions such as interchangeable parts (See Chapter 9). The essence of comparative advantage is not static relative factor endowments or natural resources, but the creation of dynamic technological or efficiency advantages.[35] The United States used to have enough such technological edges. It no longer does. The only relevant question is how to regain them.

The rest of the world has demonstrated that by coordinating research and development and then sharing the information widely it is possible to cut the costs of technological advancement and increase the speed with which new technologies show up in the economy. If such coordination were not efficient, one would have to ask why large American firms always worry about coordinating their various divisions. None of them let the market do their coordination for them.

Just as a firm can, within limits, pick the industries in which it would like to compete, so a country can, within limits, pick the industries in which it wants to compete. One of the factors leading to the rise and fall of firms, and countries, is in fact their skill in choosing where they wish to compete.

It is also well to remember that while market economies take care of themselves under the standard assumptions, some market economies will be the winners and others will be the losers in the economic ball game. And nothing in the standard postulates say that America will always be a winner. America can be the market loser as it now is with its large trade deficits and slow productivity growth.

In any case, the problem for a company or a country is not "the market" versus "planning," but how strategic coordination can be used to improve one's market performance. There is a world market, and America's market performance leaves something to be desired. Whatever the "right" theoretical model, empirical evidence indicates that "success" is not occurring with the present modes of American behavior.

5 / A Perception of Fairness

Americans are uncomfortable when it comes to talking about equity or economic fairness. They are willing to help those in need, but they don't like to think about economic justice in a larger context. Taking from one and giving to another somehow feels wrong. Basically Americans wish that the issues of economic equity would go away and hope that the market will turn up an acceptable (no one feels too aggrieved) distribution of income. Perhaps because of this strongly held desire, Americans of all income classes tend to believe that the distribution of income and wealth is more equal than it is.

As the income of the middle class has declined, the American distribution of income has become noticeably more unequal. Between 1969 and 1982 the income share going to the bottom 50 percent of all American families has fallen from 23 to 20 percent of the total (see Table 5), the income share going to the next 40 percent has fallen from 48 to 47 percent, while the income share of the top 10 percent of the population has risen from 29 to 33 percent of the total. As officially defined ($10,178 for a family of four in 1983), poverty is now rising rapidly and about half of the people being added to the poverty roles are children.[1]

While slow productivity growth, recessions, demography, and trade deficits played a role in these adverse trends, the programs of

TABLE 5
SHARE OF FAMILY INCOME[4]

Income Decile	Percent of Total Income		
	1969	1976	1982
Lowest 10 percent	1%	1%	1%
Second	3	3	3
Third	5	4	4
Fourth	6	6	5
Fifth	8	7	7
Sixth	9	8	8
Seventh	11	10	10
Eighth	12	13	13
Ninth	16	16	16
Highest 10 percent	29	32	33

the Reagan Administration have contributed to these changes. According to the Congressional Budget Office, Reagan programs added 557,000 people to the poverty rolls, and the Urban Institute estimates that Reagan programs subtracted $281 from the average income of those in the poorest 20 percent of all families while adding $598 to the average income of those in the richest 20 percent of all families.[2,3]

If one looks at the distribution of wealth (net worth), inequalities are larger and growing more rapidly than those of income. While the top 10 percent of the population receives 33 percent of total income, they own 57 percent of total net worth.[5] Almost 20 percent of all American families have zero or negative net worth.

Given the prominence of stock market reports on the evening news, one would expect that most Americans owned shares in corporate America. In fact only 19 percent of all American families own any shares whatsoever (down from 25 percent in 1977) and only 40 percent of this group own shares in more than one company.[6]

If one were writing an income distribution motto for America it would have to be "The top 10 percent gains; the bottom 90 percent loses." That is not a motto I believe that most Americans want written over their society, and it is certainly not a motto that the Democratic party should help write.

While Americans prefer not to think about inequalities, they are also uncomfortable that they exist. The discomfort starts with our religious heritage. Not many of us would want to explain to Saint Peter why we allowed children to go hungry and did nothing about it.

It goes to our vision of what makes America great. In the words on the Statue of Liberty: "Give me your tired, your poor, your huddled masses yearning to breathe free, the wretched refuse of your teeming shore . . . I lift my lamp beside the golden door." At a more self-interested level it is simply nicer to live in neighborhoods and cities without poverty and hunger. At the most self-interested level, there are few examples of democratic societies that have managed to survive while tolerating extreme disparities in income and wealth.

American interest in fairness is confirmed by the fact that not many politicians want to defend hunger or poverty as fair. When confronted with hungry children our leaders may look the other way, pretend that these children do not exist, or argue that the market mechanism is the most efficient and best way to eliminate their hunger, but few are willing to argue that hungry children are part of a good society, a good America. For most Americans to allow such conditions is to demean themselves as well as to permit real deprivation among those unable to help themselves.

The problem of economic justice is not going to go away as long as black males earn significantly less than white males (58 percent as much in 1983),[7] as long as women earn significantly less than males (64 percent as much in 1983),[8] and as long as the gaps between rich and poor are growing as they now are. Income distribution problems may for a while be superseded by other problems and lie dormant, but they will inevitably reappear. Democracies that profess to believe in political equality live only uneasily with rising economic inequalities.

Historically it has been the role of the Democratic party to work for economic justice. This is a role it cannot and should not attempt to jettison. Almost without notice, however, there has been a shift in the perceived strategy for dealing with economic injustice. Today the Democratic party is tagged as the party in favor of welfare—income transfer payments. Such an identification is recent and in some ways not fair. Not so long ago welfare programs were seen by Democrats as a second-best temporary solution to a problem that required a first-best permanent solution.

In 1964, armed with a brand-new Ph.D. in economics and having just gone to work for the President's Council of Economic Advisers, I was given the task, at what I was told were the direct personal orders of President Johnson, of going through the *Economic Report of the President* and making sure that the words "welfare" and "income transfer payments" never appeared and never were associated with President Johnson's Great Society programs. In President Johnson's view the Great Society programs (more education, more manpower training, less discrimination, more jobs) were to help people earn their own incomes. They were not income transfer payments designed to give anyone an income without work. At the time I remember thinking that I had been given a rather silly task. I no longer believe it was.

Looking back at Roosevelt and the New Deal, the same beliefs were firmly held. It was all right to provide relief for those who could not work (the elderly, the handicapped, the sick) and it was all right to give temporary relief to those who had previously been working and who had been thrown out of work (unemployment insurance), but permanent general welfare programs were never part of the New Deal ideology. Instead jobs were provided. In 1938, 4.3 million people were employed in agencies such as the Works Projects Administration (WPA), the Civilian Conservation Corps (CCC) and the National Youth Administration.[9] To employ the same fraction of the labor force today more than 9 million jobs would have to be provided.

In both the New Deal and the Great Society the first-best solution was always jobs. Whenever income transfer payments were to play a permanent role they were structured so that those who received the transfer payments (the elderly, the unemployed) had a hand in paying for them (Social Security and unemployment insurance taxes) and those that paid the most taxes got the most benefits, linking effort and benefits. There was always a welfare element in the system (relatively speaking, the poor got more back than they paid in) but no one was excused from payments and no one was eligible for the system unless they had contributed.

The Democratic party needs to go back to its first-best solution and deal directly with labor market problems. It is possible to create a full-employment society without business cycles where the distribution of earnings is significantly narrower than it now is. If anyone doubts that this can be done, they need look no further than the Japanese. The Japanese run an efficient economy with essentially no involuntary unemployment and half America's inequality. The American economy cannot be run as the Japanese economy is run, but it can be run just as well. To settle for less is to settle for less than can be had—second best.

The efficacy of existing welfare programs can be defended economically. The Institute for Research on Poverty finds that transfer payments reduced the pretransfer poverty population by 47 percent in 1982.[10] The rising incidence of poverty is caused not by transfer payment programs that encourage people to become poor to become eligible for benefits (benefit levels are so low in most programs that few would want to live on them), but by an economy that did not perform in the late 1970s and early 1980s.[11] Job training programs failed to stem the rise in poverty not because they failed as training programs but because they were too small to make any significant difference in national statistics and because there were no jobs to be filled in the period between 1979 and 1982 anyway.[12]

Welfare programs, however, are an area where myth is more important than reality. People believe what they want to believe and someone is always willing to tell them what they want to hear. According to opinion surveys, for example, the public believes that only 48 cents out of every dollar collected in taxes goes to Social Security recipients.[13] In fact 98.7 cents out of every dollar collected is paid to recipients. If one believes that welfare programs have failed, however, one does not need to feel guilty about hurting people when those programs are cut back or eliminated.

If one asks why the Democratic party shifted from being a party with an emphasis on jobs and an opening up of opportunities for higher earnings to being seen as a party identified with higher welfare payments, there is an interesting story to be told. While one would think that there would be less political resistance to job programs than there would be to welfare programs (and that is true for the general amorphous public), precisely the reverse is true when it comes to special-interest groups. Most of these special-interest groups are producer groups, and they are much more willing to see general tax revenue go for expanded welfare programs than they are to see government actively working to create jobs or working to alter the distribution of earnings. Producer groups pay only part of the higher taxes necessary to finance more welfare payments, but any restructuring of the economy to produce more jobs or a more equal distribution of earnings directly threatens their current positions.

As a result an implicit compromise was worked out during the Nixon Administration. Programs would be expanded to help the poor, but they would be welfare programs and not programs that required any fundamental restructuring of the economy. After correcting for inflation, income transfer payments to persons rose 156 percent in the eight Nixon-Ford years—more than twice as much as they had risen in the eight years of the Kennedy-Johnson Administration.[14] After correcting for inflation, income transfer payments actually fell 9 percent under President Carter. Despite these statistical facts of life the Democrats were tagged as the party in favor of putting people on welfare. Congressional Democrats had voted for the increases and President Reagan, not being willing to extend the implicit compromise made by Presidents Nixon and Ford, make attacks upon a welfare mentality a central theme of his campaigns.

While welfare can be defended economically, it cannot be defended politically. To want to reform the welfare system to make it into a better, more humane system is politically seen, or can easily be made to be seen, as a policy advocated by those who want to put more people on welfare. Politicians placed in that position usually lose. Americans do not want to put people on welfare. Nor should they. No one should want to put people on welfare. The best that can be said for welfare (and it is a lot) is that it is better than having a society full of hungry people. But it is a second-best solution.

Welfare has a role to play. Its permanent role is for those who cannot be expected to work (the elderly, the ill) and those temporarily out of work (the unemployed) but they should help finance their systems with earmarked taxes. Welfare also has a temporary role to play helping those in genuine need (the hungry) until the economy can be restructured so that they themselves can earn what they need, but jobs are the real answer to hunger and poverty.

Democrats should focus their attention on first-best solutions—a restructuring of the economy to provide more jobs and a more egalitarian distribution of earnings. The time is ripe for such a shift, since the economy needs to be restructured anyway if productivity growth is to be enhanced and international competitiveness restored.

Fortunately the changes that will be necessary to make the economy more efficient are congruent with what needs to be done to make the economy more equitable. In this case efficiency and equity go together. All of our major international competitors have found this to be true. None have slower productivity growth; all (with the possible exception of France) have a much more equal distribution of income. While the ratio of average incomes between the top and bottom decile of incomes is 14 to 1 in the United States, it is only 6 to 1 in West Germany.[15] What can be achieved in Germany can be achieved in the United States.

In an economy with rapidly growing productivity it is possible to argue that equity questions can be pushed to the back burner. If everyone's income is going up, then equity is being enhanced—at least for those who believe that equity is best measured by looking at absolute incomes or the percentage of the population that cannot afford some minimum standard of living, such as the American poverty line. It isn't possible to avoid equity questions, however, in an economy with low productivity growth where the relevant question is not "How should the economy's growth dividend be allocated?" but "From whom should the resources be taken to provide the funds necessary to restore productivity growth?"

If investment in plant and equipment must go up to be competitive, then the funds necessary to make such investments must be taken away from someone. When the new production facilities come on line, consumption standards of living can resume rising, but there is an interim period where someone must be bribed or forced to consume less. Who should that someone be?

When the Reagan Administration designed its 1981 tax and expenditure cut package, it claimed that the supply-side response to the tax cuts would be so rapid that no one's income would decline. As predicted by others it did not work that way. Families with incomes below $40,000 had their incomes reduced; families with incomes above $40,000 had their incomes enhanced.[16] Explicitly the Reagan Administration denied that it was making equity decisions, but in fact it made a very unfair equity decision to load the costs of raising the American savings rate (the announced reason for the tax cut package) on low- and middle-income Americans. Since the American savings rate did not go up in the aftermath of the 1981 tax cut, the tax cut package was inefficient as well as inequitable, but that is a later story (see below). Democrats need to replace such equity decisions with a better understanding of what economic justice is all about.

I believe that those who argue that democracies cannot impose sacrifices on their citizens for the sake of the common good without the impetus of a major war are wrong. When I talk to different groups about the structural changes, such as the need for more savings and investment, that America will need to make to restore productivity growth, I do not get a negative response. Instead the response goes something like this: "I don't like what I hear. I wish it weren't true. But I can understand that low productivity growth and big balance of payments deficits are not viable in the long run. I would be willing to make some of the sacrifices that will be needed to restore U.S. competitiveness *if you could convince me that everyone else was fairly sacrificing and carrying his or her share of the load at the same time.* I do not mind being part of a marching army restoring the American economy, but I do not want to look back and see no one else marching behind me."

A perception of equity is central if sacrifices are to be imposed in a democracy. Sacrifices don't have to be identical, but they do have to be equivalent if they are to be voluntarily made; and in a democracy they must in some collective sense be voluntarily made. No one wants to sacrifice while someone else reaps the benefits. Everyone wants to be fairly treated when society is handing out the good things of life. Conversely, most Americans are willing to accept the concomitant responsibility that they have an obligation to carry their fair share of the sacrifices necessary to get those good things flowing again. Americans are smart enough to understand that different groups will be asked to shoulder different burdens, but they want to be fairly treated when those sacrifices are assigned and assured that every other group will be carrying its proportionate share of the total burden. A sharing of burdens where the top 10 percent wins and the bottom 90 percent loses is not acceptable.

If a sense of economic justice can be generated, it just might be possible to make the large number of changes that will be necessary to restore U.S. competitiveness, even though each of the individual changes evaluated one at a time would be called politically impossible. What is needed first is a sense of crisis—the U.S. faces a competitive fight for its economic life. Second, public education, in the best sense of that word, is needed to convince most Americans that the changes are necessary; and third, leadership is necessary to fashion a package of sacrifices where all end up feeling that they are carrying their fair share of the necessary burdens and that no one is escaping from his fair share.

EQUITY—AN INESCAPABLE ISSUE

In a democracy fairness is doubly important. It helps create the common bonds that hold us together politically, but it is also necessary if markets are to be allowed to operate. Whatever the efficiency of free markets, in a democracy the majority or even substantial minorities can effectively vote to stop the market from working freely if they feel that the market is treating them "unfairly." If markets are to be allowed to work, voters must feel that they are being fairly treated.

Most often anyone who is a market loser, regardless of his previous religious attachment to the virtues of free markets, feels that he or she is being unfairly treated. Industries threatened by international competition, for example, invariably run to Washington for protection—right-wing Republican businessmen hand in hand with left-wing Democratic unions. Many groups have gotten such protection —dairy products, autos, steel, textiles, processed meat, motorcycles; many other groups want such protection—machine tools, semiconductor chip manufacturers. Demands for protection are not peculiar; they are the rule. Only market winners want to let the market work unfettered by government intervention.

Market forces can be and should be harnessed to help us restore American prosperity, but if market forces are to be used society has to have a clear standard of what is fair and unfair so that it can judge the validity of any group's claim to be exempted from the results of market forces. One can argue that a specific standard of fairness is unnecessary, because all claims to be exempted from market results should be rejected a priori, but this is politically naive. Such a position is never going to be adopted in a democracy, nor should it be. For a democratic government does what its citizens want—even if they happen to want something that interferes with the market. To use market forces to help solve the problems of productivity and international competitiveness it is necessary to have a clear standard of fairness and to be willing to implement that standard.

Standards of fairness become central when an economy needs major restructuring if it is to remain successful. Any restructuring requires sacrifices on the part of someone, and in most cases such sacrifices cannot simply be ordered. People will vote against any restructuring that requires sacrifices on their part unless they feel that these sacrifices are fairly shared. Even in wartime sacrifices cannot be commanded but have to be volunteered in a cooperative effort to achieve victory.

To address major problems that require temporary sacrifices and changes in ways of life Americans must feel (1) that they have something to lose if the problems confronting society are not solved, (2) that it is not possible to solve those problems unless everyone is willing to be mobilized, and (3) that such a mobilization can only occur if all

Americans feel that they are being fairly treated in terms of the sacrifices asked.

In the case of low productivity growth and diminishing international competitiveness, America faces just such a wartime situation. Everyone, even the most favored groups, has something significant to lose. Consider adult white males—the most favored group in the American labor market. The hammering that American industry is taking in world markets is being administered to precisely the industries where they have traditionally been employed. Males accounted for 65 percent of the more than 5 million people who had been working for more than three years but lost their jobs between January 1979 and January 1984.[17] Three million of these job losses could be attributed to America's trade deficit. Not so long ago (1981) adult men had unemployment rates significantly below those of adult women. Today the reverse is true. Of the 5 million people who lost their jobs, 40 percent have not found new jobs. Of those who have found new full-time jobs, 45 percent are earning significantly less than before. Another 7 percent have suffered large income losses, since they have only been able to find part-time work.

If the only problems facing America were discrimination and low earnings for blacks, Hispanics, and women, white males could opt out. They cannot opt out from the problems of productivity and competitiveness, however, since they are losing their jobs at an even faster pace than the groups that have traditionally been at the bottom of the labor force. Successful foreign competition won't drive Americans from their bad jobs. Foreigners don't want those jobs. The competitive pressures will come precisely in those jobs Americans want to have.

In this particular case equity or fairness is even more important than the feelings of fairness required for a democracy to force itself to make sacrifices. If one examines what must be done to bring each of the major inputs going into the American economy up to world-class standards, it is clear that Americans are going to have to rediscover teamwork. No one, however, can build a successful economic team if the individual players on the team feel unfairly treated.

THE NONEXISTENT "BIG TRADE-OFF"

Conventionally equity and efficiency are seen as mutually con-
flicting goals—the "big trade-off" in the words of the late Arthur
Okun.[18] In economic theory the free market in its search for 100
percent efficiency generates a particular precise distribution of income. Technically every worker or unit of capital used in production
is paid in accordance with individual (marginal) productivity. To in-
terfere with the market distribution of income in any attempt to generate greater equity reduces efficiency. Any factor paid less than its
productivity warrants works less or saves less than it otherwise would,
so that the total output to be divided falls. Efficiency suffers. The
greater the interventions to promote equity, the less efficiently income is generated. As a result there is only a limited amount of equity
that any society can afford to buy—or so the argument goes. Conservatives argue that American economic problems spring from too
much equity. More efficiency demands less equity.

This conventional view *is incorrect*.[19] As has been mentioned, all
of our major industrial competitors with the possible exception of
France distribute income both before and after tax more equally than
the United States. The world is full of empirical evidence that efficiency does not require less equity. Quite the contrary, to obtain the
efficiency the United States needs, it is going to have to promote
equity.

Equity is often incorrectly used as a synonym for equality. Equity
does not arise when everyone is treated equally regardless of circumstances or contribution but when everyone is treated "fairly." Fairness
is a social phenomenon. What any population is willing to regard as
fair depends upon history, institutions, and values. It also changes
over time.

With the onset of World War II, for example, social standards of
fairness changed. Because many Americans were risking their lives in
combat, those at home were convinced that civilian earnings were
unfair relative to the sacrifices on the front lines. As a result wage and
price controls were deliberately used during World War II to narrow
the distribution of earnings. The sacrifices of those directly fighting
the war required more fairness in the domestic economy, and those
indirectly fighting the war willingly gave up their unfair wage differentials.

According to conventional economic wisdom such efforts to promote fairness should have led to less efficient military production. But they didn't. The American economy enjoyed enormous gains in both output and productivity—up 22 percent from 1940 to 1945.[20] The perception of fairness created a feeling of teamwork and esprit de corps that contributed to efficiency and output rather than subtracting from it.

The results that would have been predicted from conventional economic theory were wrong because of three words—motivation, cooperation, and teamwork—that do not appear in the "big trade-off" view of equity and efficiency. To fight a war successfully requires motivation, cooperation, and teamwork. They produce what might be called "soft" productivity. In wartime a feeling that everyone is being fairly treated is at the heart of any effort to attain greater motivation, cooperation, and teamwork. Any major peacetime initiatives to restore American competitiveness will require the same feelings.

Present peacetime economic problems are not all that different from those experienced in World War II. Americans must mobilize to increase the quantity and quality of the products that they produce, and this requires a widely shared perception of fairness. Just as an army can move only as fast as its slowest unit, so the economy can only be as good as its poorest motivated, least cooperative component. As with an army, the economic problem is teamwork—obtaining sacrifices from everyone, getting everyone to march faster and work together better.

Consider the "hard" solution to one of the minor sources of low American productivity growth alluded to earlier—those 602,000 private security guards who add to hours of work but since they are guarding old ouput add nothing to new output. The conventional "hard" solution is to see crime simply as a problem of costs and benefits. Crime occurs when the benefits of crime (higher incomes) are greater than the costs (the income lost by being thrown in jail). The hard solution to the crime problem is to increase the number of policemen, locks, burglar alarms, and jails until the costs of crime exceed the benefits, but all of this produces a society with even lower productivity growth, since all of these measures absorb resources that could otherwise be used to produce more output. A really efficient society solves the crime problem not with these hard techniques but with the "soft" techniques of inculcating different values and a different structure of opportunity so that its citizens voluntarily do not commit crimes even though they face specific situations where the expected benefits clearly exceed the expected costs. The economic costs of raising the costs of crime are high and ultimately lead to a less efficient society than one where each individual citizen voluntarily abjures participation in criminal activities. In this case the "hard-headed economic" solution is a "non-economic inefficient" solution.

Similarly real efficiency does not result from the simple enforcement of rules and regulations on a sullen work force. Everyone is familiar with instances where workers do not strike but withdraw their voluntary cooperation and "work to rule." In the Boston subway system, for example, the rules say that a train cannot leave the train yards without its window wipers in working order. Normally the rule is ignored on sunny days, but when working to rule, it is not. Within a few weeks of working to rule a few years ago the whole subway system essentially ground to a halt for a lack of operational equipment. A society or a firm that depends solely upon the enforcement of rules and regulations is an inefficient society or firm. All societies need voluntary cooperation to be efficient. Such cooperation only occurs in societies where most citizens feel fairly treated.

THE MYTH OF THE LONE RANGER

Americans like to view themselves as economic descendants of the Lone Ranger. It was "rugged individualism" that made the American economy great. Or was it?

Social myths are important. True or false they are part of what we are. They color how we see ourselves. More importantly they create a set of blinders so we see only part of our own history and only part of the vista before us. As a result, we are apt to act without a complete view of who we are and where we are going. Not surprisingly those who act in partial blindness are apt to make blind mistakes.

Consider *Fortune* magazine's Business Hall of Fame. What rugged individuals hang on the walls? Henry Ford. What did he invent? The assembly line—a form of social organization where production workers worked together in more efficient ways than they had before. Alfred Sloan. What did he invent? The committee system—a form of social organization where managers and white-collar workers learned to work together more efficiently in planning company operations.

In America's mythological past, what were in fact improvements in social organization often get described as if they were examples of rugged invidualism. Ford and Sloan were bright individuals, but their genius was not found in Lone Ranger solo activities. Their genius was found in their ability to get other individuals to work together in more productive ways.

Since economies are almost by definition social organizations it is not surprising that economic genius almost always involves the ability to organize a society better; but any society that insists on describing its own history as if it were a product of rugged individuals and nothing else is apt to underestimate the importance of social organization and focus too little of its attention on improving social organization. And if there has ever been a society that has fallen into this trap, it is America.

"Liberate the entrepreneurs" is a popular political battle cry. In 1981 it was heard in the defense of lower taxes for high-income individualists, and in 1985 it was the answer given by President Reagan's Commission on Industrial Competitiveness. There may be ways in which entrepreneurs need to be liberated, but America is not being beaten on the productivity front and in international competition by societies who have liberated their entrepreneurs and emphasized rugged individualism.

The Reagan Administration and much of the economics profession believe that social institutions and structural arrangements either don't matter or take care of themselves. "Get the government out of the economy and off of the backs of the people." Underlying this political battle cry is the belief that competition forces the best possible institutional arrangements to the fore. "If it wasn't efficient it wouldn't exist. If it does exist, it must be efficient. If there was a better way to do it, that better way would automatically drive the inferior way now in use out of existence." Therefore, as the syllogism goes, societies don't have to make deliberate social changes in their institutions and the ways in which they organize themselves. Instead of trying to improve the ways that society is organized so that it works better, as President Roosevelt did when the American economy failed to recover from the Great Depression by itself, Americans have merely to stand aside and "let free enterprise do its thing."

Social organization matters.[21] The most efficient forms of social organization do not automatically come to the fore. Economies that need only cope with two recessions since World War II (Japan) beat economies that must cope with nine (the United States). Societies with 24 percent savings rates (Italy) beat societies with 5 to 6 percent savings rates (the United States). Such differences don't happen by accident, they have to be created.

Social choice is important. The societies that win economically are the ones that pay attention to improving their social organization. Efficient modes of social organization may always drive inefficient modes of social organization out of existence, but the efficient modes may be found in Japan while the inefficient ones are found in the United States. Nothing found in the doctrine of free markets says that America must be a market winner. If America wants to be a market winner it must organize itself to win.

In international trade precisely the opposite is happening. The rest of the world is organizing itself to make America a loser. Our bilateral balance of trade deficit with Japan is so large as to be embarrassing. Polite people simply don't talk about the actual numbers in public. Whatever one thinks about the causes of Japanese success, it cannot be attributed to rugged individualism. If there was ever a society that de-emphasized rugged individualism and emphasized social organization, it is the Japanese.

Industrial societies need brilliant individuals, but they succeed or fail depending upon the average quality of each of the components going into the economy, and a high average almost always requires social organization. A society where everyone can read and write beats a society where most are illiterates but a few are geniuses. This is why our forefathers invented mass public education and required that everyone be educated. They understood that they could not be successful unless all of their neighbors' children were well educated and capable of being productive members of the work force.

In the late nineteenth century and the early twentieth century, when the United States was overtaking Europe, America had mass education on its side while Europe had elite education on its side. Economically, mass education beat elite education. Today the reverse is true. Americans win more than their share of Nobel prizes, but the average Swedish high school graduate knows twice as much math as the average American high school graduate. Based on America's own history, it should come as no surprise that America is simultaneously dominating in elite education while falling behind in mass technology. In the past it happened to Europe; today it is happening to America. To improve American education, and it will have to be improved if we are to succeed economically, will take a lot of social organization and very little rugged individualism.

The interesting thing about America's love affair with the Lone Ranger myth is not that the Lone Ranger did not in fact exist. It is that he could not have existed. The American West was not settled by Lone Rangers. Precisely the opposite, it was settled by wagon trains and community barn raisings—social organization. Individuals alone on the high plains of Montana in 1840 or 1870 weren't successful— they were dead. What was in fact a social triumph is mythologically described as if it were an individual triumph. Moreover, even the Lone Ranger had helpers who were forever rescuing him from trouble —Tonto, Silver, and Scout.

Evidence for the importance of teamwork is all around us. Each of us knows that her own individual wages will be higher if she plays on a successful economic team (IBM) than if she plays on an unsuccessful economic team (Braniff Airways). Economics professors in the United States make more money than economics professors in the United Kingdom.

Firms that can inculcate a feeling of teamwork do better than those that cannot. Such individual experiences are confirmed statistically in the learning or experience curves used in operations research.[22] Typically in the first two or three years after a new plant opens productivity rises 200 to 300 percent as workers learn how to work together as a team. Yet Americans often deny the obvious when describing what they do.

The poor American productivity performance comes not so much from less "hard" productivity (inferior technology) but from less "soft" productivity (poorer motivation, less cooperation, adversarial relations rather than teamwork). *Soft productivity is an untapped productivity vein of gold. America must tap this vein to create a winning economic team*—but this means doing the things that are necessary to generate motivation, cooperation, and teamwork.

Consider for a moment the single fact which Japanese businessmen would regard as the single most devastating fact that they had ever heard about the American economy. America's labor force turns over at the rate of 4 percent per month.[23] Within any one year the average American company loses about half its total labor force— about half quit and half are fired. If one ignores the importance of teamwork, high turnover represents high efficiency. From the perspective of conventional economic theory, unneeded labor is laid off and reallocated to more efficient uses while workers with better income opportunities are quitting to engage in more productive activities. In this reallocation process labor will be used more efficiently, so that the total output increases. High turnover simply reflects an efficient labor market allocating workers to the jobs where they are most needed.

But what worker or manager will sacrifice to make a company successful ten years from now if he or she knows that there is a high probability that they will not be around in ten years? Research and development, investments in production facilities, and marketing often take ten years or more for a major new product, but no one is going to work to insure success ten years from now if he or she knows the probability of being around ten years later is effectively zero. No one plants fruit trees if he doesn't expect to be around to harvest the fruit. Yet no one has fruit unless someone plants fruit trees.

Business firms are the social and institutional embodiment of economic teams. They are not simply statistical units where the more efficient automatically drive the less efficient out of business. Efficient firms are not a collection of elements but an organic whole. Individual members agree to make short-run personal sacrifices for the long-run common good. To do this individuals need to know that they will be on the team in the long run and that the team is being fairly run. Without both of these elements a willingness to make sacrifices for the future simply isn't there—on the playing fields, in the firm, or in the society. Fair treatment is central to a well-motivated, cooperative, high-quality economic team. Equity is the essence of efficiency.

Equity is one of the secrets of Japanese success. The gap in income between workers and managers is much smaller in the typically Japanese firm than in its American counterpart. As a result workers and managers feel that they are in fact playing on a common successful team. Japanese firms in America find that the same secrets work. In the American auto production facilities of Honda and Nissan in Ohio and Tennessee egalitarianism is emphasized.[24] Workers are not called workers but are "technicians" at Nissan and "associates" at Honda. Everyone from the boss on down wears the same uniform and eats in the same cafeteria. The office layout de-emphasizes individual rooms. Americans in those plants are quoted as saying that the "most impressive thing about the Japanese is their loyalty to the company and the way they work together and help each other."

THE TRICKLE-DOWN SOLUTION

There is no "trickle-down" solution to the problem of productivity growth. President Reagan's argument that fairness is not an issue cannot succeed economically. Unequal distributions of income do not automatically lead to more efficient societies but to the opposite. Even if "trickle-down" policies could be imposed in our democracy and did not lead to class warfare or widespread obstuctionism, they would still fail.

The necessary resources simply aren't there. Consider investment. In 1982 American fixed capital formation (a measure that includes investment in housing) was 15 percent of the GNP, while the Japanese were investing 30 percent of their GNP. Clearly America cannot compete investing one-half as much.[25] In trickle-down theory the solution is to encourage the rich to save by reducing their taxes and to force the poor to save by slashing their income transfer payments. The theory was put in place in 1981, but empirically it did not work. Personal savings rates went down—not up.

More importantly the plan could not have worked even theoretically. If both earnings and transfer payments are included, the poorest 20 percent of the population has 4 percent of total personal income.[26] To compete with competitors such as the Japanese on an investment-per-worker basis, a lot more than 4 percent of personal income would have to move from consumption to investment. One could deprive the poor of all of their income, indeed starve them, give all of their income to the rich, and even if the rich were willing to save 100 percent of that extra income, America would still not have gotten even halfway to closing the investment gap with the Japanese.

Most of the necessary cuts in consumption are going to have to be allocated to America's upper classes for the very simple reason that they have most of the income. The richest 20 percent of American households have 44 percent of total income, which means that these households are going to have to pay at least 44 percent of the total cost of rebuilding America. Realistically, since a minimum level of private subsistence expenditures is also essential, the upper quintile is going to have to be willing to pay quite a bit more than 44 percent of the total bill if America's problems are to be solved. What President Reagan's Budget Director, David Stockman, called "trickle down" does not work any better arithmetically than it does sociologically.

THE "THROW THEM OVERBOARD" SOLUTION

"Every man for himself—jump overboard and swim to safety" is equally a non-starter. In this strategy individual industries or firms decide that they can win without creating a winning American team. American banks will become world banks and service the winning foreign manufacturing firms. American firms will become multinationals, maintaining top jobs for Americans but with manufacturing and most of the low- and middle-wage jobs located abroad. High-income Americans maintain their favored position by throwing the average American worker overboard.

As mentioned earlier in the case of banks, this strategy isn't realistic. British banks once thought that they were so good and so smart that they could maintain their world position without the aid of a healthy British industrial base behind them. They failed. New York became the world's financial capital after American industry achieved dominance over British industry and in a similar manner New York will be replaced by Tokyo if Japanese industry dominates American industry.

"Manufacture-it-abroad" is similarly not a strategy for survival. If American firms aren't successful at home it is only a question of time until foreign entrepreneurs drive them out of business. Americans have no insurmountable comparative advantage when it comes to managing Koreans. The manufacture-it-abroad strategy may also backfire on American managers. Instead of combining high-wage American managers with low-wage Oriental workers, we may combine middle-wage Japanese managers with middle-wage American workers as is now happening in Japanese-managed American automobile production facilities such as those of Honda, Nissan, and Toyota. It is easy to imagine a world in which the American manager, not the American worker, becomes extinct.

High-wage or low-wage Americans are on the same economic ship, in the same storm, on the same sea. Americans may occupy different classes and have different accommodations on the American economic ship of state, but they will all sink or swim together. Everyone will make it or no one will make it. Throwing some of the passengers overboard won't solve the problem. Unless there is a collective voluntary agreement as to who should do the tasks necessary to ride out the storm, everyone will drown.

In many ways the rest of the world is beating America by doing what Americans like to talk about—be more flexible and responsive than the competition—but somehow aren't. Americans are inflexible and unresponsive to rapid changes in world economic demands not because they are inflexible as individuals but because they have socially organized themselves in ways that make flexibility and responsiveness difficult. Americans have tied themselves into a workplace system characterized by a minute legalistic division of labor with thousands of work rules, job titles, and associated wage rates where firms cannot move labor speedily from area to area as they are needed or rapidly shift from one technology to another. While such inflexibilities are often blamed on unions, they are just as pervasive in non-union firms as they are in union ones. The secret of flexible manufacturing is not computers, robots, and high-tech machinery or union busting, but flexible workers and managers.

With militaristic top-down decision-making processes American firms cannot compete with foreign firms who can tap the ideas, initiative, and experience of their employees in the bottom-up decision-making process of quality control circles. The world where the foreman is the worker's representative to management (the typical pattern among our foreign competitors) is more flexible than the world where the foreman is management's instrument for giving never-to-be-questioned orders to workers (the American pattern). "Locked" numerically controlled machine tools where only skilled white-collar programmers have access to the programming (the American pattern) are less capable of adjusting to shop-floor bottlenecks than "unlocked" numerically controlled machine tools where the blue-collar workers who operate the machines are taught to do the programming (the foreign pattern).

If one asks why American firms lock their blue-collar workers away from their numerical machine tools, there is an interesting answer. In the words of *Iron Age*, a respected trade journal, "Workers and their unions have too much say in manufacturers' destiny, many metal working executives feel, and large, sophisticated Flexible Manufacturing Systems can help wrest some of that control away from labor and put it back in the hands of management, where it belongs." [27] In the eyes of management locked procedures tighten control over shop operations and prevent blue-collar workers from slowing the pace of production. White-collar programmers are more amenable than blue-collar programmers. Yet in most cases the locked procedures are less than optimal.[28] The person actually performing the work can make better small adjustments in the programming than anyone not right at the job site.

Class warfare is less efficient than class harmony even when the classes are working with computers and robots. If Americans want, or cannot avoid, class warfare, then Americans will simply be less efficient than those societies that have found it possible to eliminate class warfare on the shop floor.

While none of these rigid hierarchical characteristics are new to American industry, technology has made them into more of a handicap than they used to be. Computers, microprocessors, and robots are moving the industrial world away from fixed mass manufacturing where one can compete successfully by simply having low-skill workers on the assembly line turning the same screw year after year. To compete successfully workers have to be capable of readjusting the programming to shift the robots from one model of car to another within the same shift. Workers as participants are more efficient than workers as automatons.

While it may be accurate in some ways to pejoratively describe both Japanese and European industry as more bureaucratic than American, despite the fact that Japan has many fewer white-collar workers than America, there is an even more pejorative label that can be attached to America—it is an overly legalistic society.

"Administrative guidance" is the essence of a bureaucratic society. No formal rules, a need to consult before doing anything, lots of informal constraints, but everything is negotiable—and possible. Legalistic societies in contrast attempt to write detailed rules and regulations for everything (who does what work, who gets what job titles, who can be promoted up what seniority ladders, who may give an order to whom, who gets the largest office, which jobs are associated with which wage rates) and then use lengthy adversarial quasi-legal procedures (arbitrators, special masters, trials) to settle disputes. In a legalistic society nothing is negotiable. Everything must be settled in accordance with some prior written code of rules and regulations. In contrast with a system of administrative guidance, much is impossible in a legalistic society, and changing the rules and regulations is both hard and time consuming.

The American corporation has turned itself into a "do-it-by-the-rules" microcosm of our larger society. And "do-it-by-the-rules" just doesn't work very well. Americans may think that they are great at facing reality, being flexible, and taking individual initiative (they may even possess these virtues as individuals), but they have organized a society—an economy, firms—where they cannot exercise their supposed virtues. The current social organizations don't work and aren't going to automatically collapse simply because they don't work.

The more uncertainty an economy faces the more it needs flexibility. A world without OPEC oil shocks has less need for flexibility than a world with them. In a world without technologically equal competitors American firms have less need for flexibility than in a world where American firms face technically equal or superior competitors. The world is now full of economic uncertainty. America needs more flexibility than its institutions permit.

To the average American this is not yet visible. In the 1983–84 recovery the economy once again seemed to be working. But this is a temporary recovery based on borrowed dollars and America's ability to run a huge trade deficit. Such deficits simply aren't sustainable. At the point when the dollar starts to plunge, this will become obvious. Then the intellectual window will be open to selling the thesis that social organization matters and that effective social organization requires a fair degree of internal equity to be successful. It is the task of the Democratic party to be such a salesman.

Rebuilding The Foundations

6 / Constructing an Efficient Team

The United States did not always enjoy effortless superiority. America started off as a copier far behind the then industrial leaders when its industrial revolution began in the nineteenth century. New England's textile mills were started by hiring craftsmen such as Samuel Slater (we would now call them engineers) who had worked in or toured the British textile mills and had memorized or written down enough of what they had seen to copy those mills in the New World. American schoolboy history books remember this copying as a good example of Yankee ingenuity. British schoolboy history books see it in another light—theft. Americans stole the technology that had made Britain number one in the world. Viewed more dispassionately, America was simply doing what every country does when it is behind economically. It copies those who are ahead of it.

Throughout the nineteenth century American firms were famous for borrowing technologies. The great French observer of the American scene Alexis de Tocqueville described America as a land of copiers, but copiers who quickly made products better than the original. Ideas such as the Bessemer steel process were developed abroad—but brought to America and then tuned up to turn out slightly cheaper or better products than those produced in Europe. Starting from far behind, the American per capita GNP finally caught up with that of

Great Britain around 1900. From then on America had to invent new, more productive processes, such as Henry Ford's assembly line, rather than simply copying Europe.

The same is true in scientific leadership. One copies until one catches up, but as America's own history indicates it is possible to become an economic leader long before one becomes a scientific leader. While America became an economic leader at the turn of the century, it did not become a scientific leader until after World War II —almost half a century later. Until then any American physicist forced to give up either his subscription to the German physics review or the American physics review would have canceled his American subscription. Without World War II it is also doubtful that America would have caught up as fast as it did. The war destroyed Europe's basic scientific facilities in both physical and human terms and brought to America a generation of extraordinary scientists such as Albert Einstein and Enrico Fermi. Without the war American scientific dominance would have been much slower in coming.

America's own economic history of copying to catch up answers the complaint that other countries' efforts to copy and improve American technology are somehow unfair. Every country catches up by copying. It is popular to argue, for example, that Japan will eventually stagnate when it catches up with the United States because it will have no one to copy and will be culturally unable to enlarge its own fund of basic knowledge. The popularity of the argument (Japanese even make it in Japan) should not blind one to its falsity. When others have to, they will learn to do basic science just as Americans once learned. Like America they may also become the world's industrial leaders decades before they become the world's scientific leaders.

Unfortunately, Americans have forgotten their earlier practices— copying when behind—that led to success. In many ways this amnesia is not surprising. For two or three decades after World War II there was genuinely little to be learned industrially from the rest of the world—so Americans quit looking. But that time is now over. Now Americans must discover what others are doing, refine and adapt it to our own culture and institutions, and then use these modified techniques to outperform the originators of the idea. All good ideas do not originate in America, but all good ideas can be adapted, adopted, perfected, and used in America.

THE NEED FOR RISK TAKERS

Economic progress demands risks—the chance of failure. No one can prove that a new product or process will work either scientifically or economically before it is tried, but with a big post-World War II technological lead American firms did not need to be risk takers to be very succcessful. They could very profitably exploit their existing technological edge.

The route to success was not "betting the company" but "risk avoidance"—choosing to invest in marginal projects that promised high rates of return and that could not threaten the overall profitability of the company, even if they failed. Increasingly American firms ceased to be the leaders in the introduction of new products or production processes. The American steel industry was years late in adopting either the oxygen furnace or continuous casting technologies. The introduction of home video recorders was regarded as too risky by large American consumer electronics firms, so instead they became marketeers of foreign-made products. Countries that are behind economically, however, have to take risks, to leapfrog technologies, if they are to catch up.

While new breakthrough innovations are still being made in small American companies with little to lose if they fail, the American economy is too large to be sustained just by new small businesses. America cannot compete unless its large companies are good copiers, good innovators, and willing to take long-term risks. America needs the jobs and investments that only it has the size and financial muscle to provide. When Kodak decides to manufacture a new small video recorder abroad without even trying to manufacture it competitively in America, America loses jobs and the chance to explore new production technologies—opportunities it cannot afford to lose.[1]

Given America's large post-World War II technological lead, risk avoidance probably was the route to economic success in the 1950s and 1960s—for both individual firms and the economy at large. But circumstances have changed, and in the 1980s it is the route to economic failure. What works when an economy has a big lead in productivity and technology won't work when it is just one among equals. Some American firms will fail with a more aggressive stance vis-à-vis new products and new technologies, but the entire economy will fail in the long run under a general strategy of risk avoidance.

With foreign competition now armed with equal if not superior technologies, markets have objectively become much riskier and tougher for Americans. If it is to succeed, American industry is going to have to get used to employing strategies that would have been regarded as too risky twenty years ago.

CHANGES IMPOSED BY THE COMPETITION

While individual Americans can easily see the changes that foreign competition imposes on other actors in the economy, they not surprisingly find it harder to see the changes that they themselves will have to make. American managers, for example, are fond of pointing out that if auto workers make $13 per hour in Japan and $20 per hour in the United States and if productivity is equal in the two countries, then America can only have a successful auto industry if American workers are willing to reduce their wages to $13 per hour. Management is right; American labor is going to have to learn to keep one eye on foreign wages and the other eye on raising productivity.

American managers almost never mention, however, that they are paid almost three times as much as Japanese management.[2] Whereas blue-collar wages must come down by one-third, managerial wages must come down by two-thirds if America is to be competitive. In a world of international competition only superior productivity can result in superior wages for either management or workers

American capitalists often note the low profit rates in Japanese corporations without comprehending their significance. At a 1983 MIT conference the president of one of the divisions of Seiko Watch stated that their before-tax target rate of return on investment was 7.5 percent.[3] Rates of return on investment are the capitalist's equivalent of wages, and the standard American pre-tax target rate of return on investment is 20 percent. Yet in a competitive world American capitalists cannot get more than the competition unless they are more efficient—but the competition, as evidenced by Seiko, is now very efficient indeed. Capitalists, just like workers, must keep one eye on foreign rates of return and the other on raising productivity. Only superior productivity brings superior rates of return on investment.

In some American industries both wages and rates of return must fall if these industries are to stay alive. Their high wages and profits were a temporary result of the enormous technological lead that American firms enjoyed after World War II. Without that lead, Americans cannot command premium rates of return on their investments any more than they can command premium wages. In a competitive world those who are willing to work the hardest and the smartest set the allowable returns for everyone else—a painful fact but one which American capital and labor have no choice but to accept.

After thirty years of not being subject to the competitive discipline of real foreign competitors, however, it comes as a shock when it arrives. American businessmen like to give July Fourth speeches praising the virtues of competition, but when competition really arrives they complain. Real competition has a real downside risk—Americans can lose

A LACK OF HUSTLE?

In the inevitable human desire to find someone else to blame for America's economic problems, the amorphous American worker (not me, him) has been singled out as responsible for much of the problem. The decline of America is often seen as the decline of the American work ethic—among the young by the elderly; among workers by managers. In public opinion polls 63 percent of the American public believe that people do not work as hard as they did ten years ago and 69 percent believe that workmanship is worse than it was ten years ago. Seventy-three percent believe that work motivation is down, that Americans no longer want to work hard and that they are no longer willing to sacrifice for a successful economy.[4] A nation of eager beavers has turned into a nation of idle grasshoppers in the popular mythology.

If these opinions were true, the American outlook would be dire —idle grasshoppers don't succeed—but there is lots of evidence that the American work ethic is alive and well. Those same polls show that 76 percent of the public say that they feel a strong sense of dedication to their work. Nearly six out of every ten say that they have an "inner need to do the very best job I can, regardless of pay." Three out of four Americans would prefer to go on working even if they could live comfortably without working for the rest of their lives. Most workers want to produce high-quality goods. Sixty percent say that they would like to be more involved in efforts to get people to do their best on the job.[5] Those are attitudes that the American economy can capitalize upon.

Such polling results are confirmed in observed behavior. During the 1981–82 recession newspapers frequently showed pictures of thousands of workers lining up for a few minimum-wage jobs.[6] Most Americans of every race, color, age, and sex if given a chance prefer to work. In a two-and-one-half-year project the Manpower Demonstration Research Corporation found that among sixteen-to-nineteen-year-old black teenagers 63 percent were willing to accept and stay on a minimum-wage job that was offered to them with the condition that they return to high school.[7] There are lazy Americans, but they are a small minority.

The trends in labor force participation confirm these results. In the long sweep of history, higher productivity has led to demands for more leisure (or more accurately less time on the job) and more goods and services. From 1900 to 1960 the average American work year declined from 2,766 to 2,068 hours per year.[8] Yet productivity had risen so fast that workers could have more leisure and still afford a rising material standard of living. The decline in hours of work from 1900 to 1960 is not evidence that the American work ethic was on a long-run downward trend. Economically a rising desire for leisure is not evidence of a diminution of the work ethic. What counts is effort per hour of work, and one can work just as hard as one's grandparents even if one is working fewer hours per year.

But interestingly, today's American workers aren't demanding the additional leisure that their parents demanded. Since 1960, Americans have been working more, not less. A decline in male labor force participation rates of 6 percentage points has been more than counterbalanced by a rise of 12 percentage points among women. Hours of work per worker also have stopped falling. Males have stabilized at about 2,200 hours of work per year, and females' hours of work have risen steadily to about 1,800 hours per year. For the average American family there has been a dramatic increase in the total hours of work. Two-earner families are now the norm where they were once uncommon. Together sons and daughters are now working more than their fathers and mothers—a trend that has prevailed in good and bad times for two decades.

The average American workweek is 13 percent longer than the German workweek. The typical American firm has twenty-three paid holidays per year versus thirty in Japan, thirty-four in France and thirty-nine in Germany.[9]

While the facts are clear, the explanations for them are not so clear. Why is more work now more desirable than more leisure for the average American? Economic theory predicts the reverse. As productivity rises, potential incomes rise. Real disposable per capita income has risen 72 percent from 1960 to 1983.[10] Households are supposed to use some of this higher potential income for more leisure and some for more goods and services. Leisure is valuable in its own right, and extra time is usually necessary to enjoy more goods and services. Increasing hours of work as productivity rises is contrary to both past behavior and economic theory. From the perspective of conventional economic theory there is only one possible explanation —among American workers there has been a shift in preferences toward more work—i.e., the work ethic is up.

Other explanations are possible, but none of them vitiate the evidence they present for a healthy American work ethic. More paid work might simply be the mirror image of less unpaid work. With smaller families and increased household mechanization (washers, vacuums, microwave ovens), there is simply less unpaid household work to be done. As a result, housewives can enter the paid labor force and still have more real leisure than in the past. Real hours of leisure might be up even though measured hours of leisure are down. Studies of household work patterns, however, indicate that although working wives do indeed cut their hours of unpaid labor, they do not cut them anywhere near as much as they increase their hours of paid labor.[11] The working wife works far more hours (paid and unpaid) than the wife who does not join the paid labor force or the housewife of the past. When wives go to work it is a real and not just a statistical increase in the economy's hours of work. Husbands of working wives also slightly increase their hours of unpaid household work and show no tendency to reduce their own hours of paid labor.

Americans may also have discovered capital-intensive leisure. Each employed American has a choice whether he wants a month's vacation in a canoe or wants to work that month and enjoy his weekends in a much more elaborate boat. Does he cross-country ski for a month, downhill ski for two weeks near home, or go to Colorado for one week? As Americans move across this set of choices from cheap to expensive, they are not only choosing to have more capital-intensive forms of leisure (by the time they get to that Colorado ski vacation, they require not just skis and lifts but airplanes, airports, rental cars, hotels, and a wide variety of capital investments), they are choosing systematically to have less leisure and to work more to pay for the type of vacations they want. With capital-intensive leisure,

Americans have less leisure time, but a more enjoyable form of leisure. While the cause may be a desire for more capital-intensive forms of leisure, the result is a willingness to work more than in the past.

With an increasing proportion of skilled jobs, work may also be becoming more interesting and less onerous. As this happens, Americans systematically shift their allocation of time away from at-home leisure and toward work.

Each of these explanations for why Americans are working more may be partially true, but they all leave unchanged the basic conclusion that Americans are working more. Today's generation of laborers works harder and has more of the work ethic than their father's or mother's generation. Laziness among the young is not the American problem.

As Americans work more and their lives revolve less around family, church and neighborhood, however, it is not surprising that workers also expect more from their workplace—that it provide a substitute for some of the satisfactions that they used to get elsewhere. Widespread demands for more meaningful work are not surprising. People want to work, but what they expect from work has changed just as they have changed.

As people grow richer, they also naturally acquire different economic motivations. Hungry people will put up with almost anything for a job but as incomes move above subsistence, people work to buy the "good life" where the good life is defined in terms of straightforward consumer goods—a nice car, a fine house. At yet higher incomes, workers labor to buy the luxuries that make life fun—plane travel to a ski resort, eating out at a fancy restaurants, a concert. Eventually, however, they want work itself to be a source of pleasure.

The desire to make work self-fulfilling, less dangerous, cleaner, and more pleasant is not evidence of a declining work ethic. Given that Americans spend an enormous portion of their life on the job, it is natural that they wish to have a pleasant environment at work. Americans can work just as hard at a self-fulfilling, safe, clean, pleasant job as they do at a boring, dangerous, dirty, unpleasant job.

Historically, each generation believes that the generation following it has lost the work ethic. Negative comments about the work habits of the young go back as far as the written word itself. Times change. Children ride school buses rather than horses to school. When I was a boy growing up in Montana, the elderly regarded this as evidence of softness on the part of the young. But today's children can work hard mastering the computer in a way in which their elders cannot even imagine much less emulate. To say that work is different (there is certainly less heavy lifting by human beings) is not to say that the work ethic has declined.

As human workers move back from the edge of starvation, it should also come as no surprise that the economic stick wields less influence and that more resort has to be made to the economic carrot. Fear of starvation is a powerful motivator, but in a humane society it is a motivational technique that everyone should wish to minimize.

If American standards of living end up visibly slipping behind those of the rest of the world, America will probably return to old harsher forms of motivation. Envy may make Americans willing to do things they are not now willing to do, but such a return is not evidence of progress.

The American work ethic, far from being a handicap, should be a major source of productivity growth. In identical Ford auto assembly plants in Germany and the United Kingdom, German productivity was twice as high as Britain's.[12] Identical technology, capital equipment, and products were buried under the differences in motivation, cooperation, and teamwork. Perhaps general labor-management relations have deteriorated to such a point in Great Britain that no individual manager or set of managers can retrieve them (I personally doubt whether this is true), but this is clearly not true in the United States. There are many examples of companies (IBM, Lincoln Electric) with well-motivated cooperative work forces that produce a high-quality output with efficient economic teamwork in America. Firms without these attributes have only themselves to blame.

Such soft productivity gains can be seen in the dramatic improvements that have often occurred when Japanese firms take over the management of American facilities with American workers. In 1974 the Quasar television plant was under the management of Motorola.[13] For every 100 sets produced 140 adjustments or repairs were necessary to meet quality standards. Under its current Japanese management, Matsushita, defects are down to 7 per 100 sets—still below the Japanese rates of 3 defects per 100 sets, but an obvious improvement. The reasons for the improvement are not just motivation. The Japanese invested in new designs and equipment, but quality-control circles and other efforts to focus worker attention and effort on quality were a big part of the turnaround. American workers with Japanese mangers outperform American workers with American managers—hardly a commendation for American management.

In public opinion polls only 24 percent of the work force say that they are performing to their full capacity ("being as effective as they are capable of being"), yet only 18 percent say that they are not interested in improving their effectiveness.[14] The rest think that there is a large gap between what they are doing and what they could be doing—which suggests a major source of productivity improvement.

Workers do, however, want greater autonomy, challenge, and interpersonal contact. Eight out of ten report that they would do a better job if they were more involved in decisions relating to their work. Twenty-six percent of today's workers work to develop themselves as persons whereas only 10 percent of their parents were working for that reason.

The American work force wants to work, wants to produce a high-quality product, wants to be involved in making products and jobs better; yet America has organized a society where that work force often isn't working, is uninvolved, and produces a low quality product at what it regards as a low-quality job (more than half of the work force finds its current job unsatisfactory and would like to change job or occupation). Reducing the gap between these high aspirations and the reality of a poor performance has to be the major task of American management.

None of this is to say, however, that job security (the certainty of future income) or income itself has lost its motivational force. Sixty-eight percent say that job security is important. Motivation is just a more complicated business than it used to be when Americans were poorer and less well educated.

LEADING A HIGH-QUALITY TEAM

When a sporting team consistently fails, the first resort is to fire the manager, who is held responsible for the quality and training of the players, for supplying the right plays, and for hustle and teamwork. While slightly unfair, sporting practices nonetheless focus on a key ingredient in any successful team—the manager. Industry is no different. If American industry fails, the managers are ultimately accountable. To have a competitive team it is necessary to have the best players working with the best equipment under the best managers. The next two chapters will focus on producing the best players and acquiring the best equipment, but in accordance with sporting traditions, the remainder of this chapter will focus on the managers.

While America cannot fire all of its managers any more than it can fire its labor force, there is clearly something wrong with management. That "something" is going to have to be corrected if America is to compete on world markets. Some of the corrections can be encouraged by those in Washington, but most of the corrections are going to have to be made from within the private economy.

As has been shown in the earlier analysis of productivity growth, America's productivity problem lies not so much among lazy factory workers and featherbedding unions as among its non-union white-collar workers. Given a preponderance of white-collar workers, the key to productivity improvement lies not on the factory floor but in the office. Private bureaucracy is being added to the American economy at a rate which can only sink it.

Government rules and regulations are often invoked to explain the bureaucratic nature of American industry, but they don't explain what needs to be explained. The trend to bureaucratic white-collar employment in private industry continues regardless of whether there is or is not a surge in government regulations. Most of the regulations that business now complains about were enacted more than a decade ago and cannot be used to justify today's additional white-collar employees—especially given the Reagan cutbacks in regulation. Japanese companies find that they can operate in the United States under our rules and regulations with far fewer white-collar workers than their American counterparts. In the previously mentioned example at Quasar, Matsushita fired 25 percent of the white-collar workers when it took over.

The same results are visible in a study by Harbour and Associates of the $2,203 cost advantage that the Japanese had over their American competitors if they were both to have built the same car in 1982.[15] Lower Japanese wages and fringe benefits were important—explaining 25 percent of that $2,203 difference. American managers are right when they say that wages will have to come down if the industry is to be competitive—just as long as they remember that much of the labor cost differential comes from their own higher wages. Another 8 percent of the cost differential could be traced to adversarial union-management relations. Outsiders are right when they say that the auto industry is going to have to eliminate its long history of adversarial labor-management relations and restrictive work rules. But even if all of that is admitted and blamed on labor, 67 percent of the cost disadvantage comes from other factors under the sole control of management.

Three percent of the Japanese cost advantage comes from superior technology according to the estimates. It is management's job to insure that its work force is working with the latest technology. Twenty-five percent of the cost differential comes from Japan's just-in-time inventory system. Instead of incurring the costs of financing, storage, and tracking billions of dollars in parts, supplies are directly delivered to the assembly line as they are needed. In addition to cutting costs the just-in-time inventory system makes it much easier to trace the sources of defective parts and improve quality control. Inventory control is a management function. Why didn't American managers invent the just-in-time inventory system?

Another 39 percent of the cost differential could be traced to better management systems—basically, fewer white-collar workers. If management systems are inferior, management is by definition inferior. Reducing the white-collar labor force has to become a priority among American managers, but this means reducing their own numbers—a far more painful task than firing blue-collar workers or castigating unions.

Workers may be efficient or inefficient, but the quality of the product shipped to the customer ultimately depends on what management wants. Yet American products have slipped from a position of unsurpassed quality to something less. Whenever quality comparisons are now made, American manufacturers are less than number one. In a comparison of the quality of Japanese and American air conditioners, for example, the failure rates of the worst producers, all Americans, were 500 to 1,000 times greater than those made by the best producers, all Japanese. The average American manufacturer suffered seventy times as many assembly-line defects and made seventeen times as many service calls in the first year of service.[16]

Not surprisingly, given the widespread availability of such data, when a recent public opinion survey asked people what they would buy if all they knew about a product was that one brand was made in Japan and the other was made in the United States a majority of the American public said they would buy Japanese on the assumption that the Japanese product was of higher quality.

There are no mysteries in quality control. Consider the introduction of robots onto auto assembly lines. In the early 1970s robots did not meet rate of return on investment criteria in either Japan or in the United States. But in Japan they were introduced anyway—to improve working conditions and quality. Painting and welding are disagreeable jobs on an auto assembly line, and few workers can consistently turn out high-quality work hour after hour, day after day. Quality control was considered more important than short-run rates of return on capital in Japan, while the opposite was true in the United States.

In the long run, however, better quality control leads to market dominance. By being the first to use and build robots in large numbers the Japanese gained a tremendous economic advantage from being the first to go down the learning curve. Robots now pay for themselves in less than two and a half years. As a result the Japanese raised production from 2.5 million cars in the early 1970s to 11 million cars in the early 1980s while still employing the same 450,000 workers. By making quality control a secondary consideration to short-run financial performance, the American auto industry and much of the rest of American manufacturing lost their markets. American firms ended up showing huge losses (until they were given protection from Japanese competition) while the Japanese competition made fat profits.

The problems are clearly seen in Motorola's explanations for the improvements in productivity and quality when Quasar shifted from American to Japanese management. When asked to comment on the differences before and after the sale of Quasar, the president of Motorola said that he had deliberately reduced capital spending in Quasar, "allowing it enough investment to remain viable, to build up the Quasar name, but not enough to lead us into the new wave of the future . . . I wanted the business to be healthy so that it would be salable." He went on to say, "We're winning vis-à-vis the Japanese in the businesses we chose to stay in."[17] According to this explanation, Quasar was being milked as a "cash cow" and deliberately allowed to run down while management concentrated on other more profitable activities. That may be "smart" management in the short run for a single company, but such "smart" management is exactly what leads customers to think that American products are inferior. In the end this is "dumb" management as far as the economy as a whole is concerned.

With such attitudes industries fall behind technologically. The American steel industry built its last open-hearth furnace eight years after the Japanese had given them up.[18] Nine percent of America's steel is still made in open-hearth furnaces, but virtually none is made that way in either Europe or Japan. While 85 percent of Japanese steel is produced by continuous casting, only 25 percent of American steel is produced in that way. If an industry gets that far behind in its own technology, it has no chance of winning. In the case of steel there is no evidence that the American firms even want to catch up. From 1975 to 1980 the American steel industry invested only 0.6 percent of its revenues in research and development and less than 20 percent of this small amount was channeled into basic research. What little modernization is done as a consequence has to rely on foreign technical guidance. Obtaining foreign assistance is fine, but how can one get a competitive edge if one isn't willing to use this assistance to develop one's own technical capabilities?

It may be rational for the U.S. steel industry to demand protection from foreign competition, use the high profits generated by protection to buy into other industries, and gradually leave the steel industry, but it is not rational for the entire economy. Present U.S. steel companies may leave the materials business, but the American economy cannot afford to do the same.

The failure to innovate is not peculiar to steel. Despite mounting foreign technological competition, American firms cut their new research-and-development spending by a factor of two in both real and money terms in the two years between 1980–81 and 1982–83. R&D cuts were the easiest to make in a recessionary period and the goals of short-term profit maximization completely dominated the long-term needs to keep up with the rest of the world in new technologies. While Japan was increasing R&D spending from 1.2 to 2.6 percent of the GNP between 1960 and 1983, the United States was reducing spending from 2.9 to 2.3 percent of the GNP.[19] Not surprisingly the result is short-run success followed by long-run failure.

When American industries first started to fall behind their foreign competitors, the phenomenon was dismissed as isolated cases of stupidity or bad luck. The American steel industry just happened to be slow in shifting to oxygen furnaces and continuous casting. Consumer electronics just happened to miss the significance of the transistor or the video recorder. But as the list of industries that have lost out or need government protection to survive has grown longer it has become increasingly obvious that something is systematically wrong.

A Starting Point

America's biggest handicap is found in its inability to generate an environment where the labor force takes a direct interest in raising productivity. A high-quality well-motivated work force interested in working together as a team to raise productivity is ultimately the major source of productivity growth. Constructing such a team is a direct management responsibility.[20]

Yet the difficulties of doing so should come as no surprise in the American context. New labor-saving machines that lead to improvements in productivity typically mean layoffs in American firms. Who is going to work to raise productivity if it means that he or his friends are going to be fired?

Consider a comparison between Germany and Japan that could easily have been replicated in America. When workers were asked "Is an increase in productivity good for you personally?" 74 percent of the German workers said no but 87 percent of the Japanese workers said yes. When asked "Does an improvement in company profitability benefit you personally?" 74 percent of the Germans again said no while 94 percent of the Japanese said yes.[21] Which set of responses is apt to lead to the productive profitable companies? To ask the question is to answer it. Yet the essence of any manager's job is to make sure that the players feel that their individual welfare is congruent with the success of the team. If that does not happen, management is at fault.

American management has also let the time over which investments must pay for themselves grow so short that they will not undertake the basic research and development, make the necessary investments, or build the service networks necessary for long-run survival. While teaching at the management institute of one of America's largest corporations, I was told that the average time horizon of the 30 divisions represented in the room was 2.8 years. Is it any surprise that new products and new production processes are increasingly introduced abroad and that the construction of completely new "greenfield" industrial facilities has almost stopped in America? No one can build, much less recoup the cost, of a major new facility in 2.8 years. No one can introduce and build a mass market for a new product such as video recorders in 2.8 years. Firms that demand such quick payoffs will simply lose out to those with longer time horizons.

Management time horizons are short not because Americans are impatient or stupid but because America has created an environment where it is individually rational for everyone to have a short time horizon. With high turnover and everyone on his or her own when it comes to economic success, how could anyone expect the American corporation to do otherwise? Corporate time horizons are set by individuals who themselves expect to be with the firm for only a brief time and have, as a result, a short personal time horizon.

The problem is compounded by merger mania. In 1983 mergers and acquisitions, excluding leveraged buy-outs, absorbed sixty-nine times as much capital as net venture start-ups. Nineteen eight-four saw the two largest acquisitions in U.S. corporate history (Chevron's purchase of Gulf and Texaco's purchase of Getty), and *Fortune's* list of the fifty largest deals doubled in total value from 1983 to 1984.[22]

In this context it is not surprising that a chief executive officer worries about quarterly profits lest his stock decline and a hostile takeover bid be aimed at his company. When ITT announced on July 11, 1984, that it was cutting its dividend by nearly two-thirds so that it could afford heavy investments in the U.S. telecommunications business, the stock price dropped by roughly a third in one day, making ITT a prime takeover target with a book value of $39 per share and a stock price of only $21 per share.[23] Yet the decision to cut the payout promised to help ITT's long-term competitive position and did not make it either richer or poorer than it previously was.

What happened to William Agee, president of Bendix (fired within a year of being taken over by Allied), happens almost always to top executives who are "taken over." At Bendix the less controversial nice-guy second-in-command was also fired by Allied. Within a year of taking over Getty, six top officers (the chairman, the president, three group vice presidents, and the vice president and general counsel) were removed by Texaco.[24] It makes no difference whether the takeover is supposedly friendly or hostile—good guy or bad guy—top management goes.

No one likes to be fired. It is partly a matter of money but more a matter of goals, power, and prestige. Executives become executives because they want to run things, and few will become successful at finding jobs with equal power and responsibility if they are fired in a takeover.

Most CEO's also get a bonus based on current profits that will end up being a very substantial fraction of their lifetime incomes, yet they are typically CEO's for only five or six years. Suppose that you have been a CEO for three years and have three years of your tenure left. What are you going to do? What short-term CEO will take a long-run view when it directly lowers his own income? Only a saint, and there aren't very many saints among top management. Normal mortals are going to maximize the hell out of the next three years and forget the long run.

In many corporations middle-level managers have also been set up as independent profit centers and are promoted or demoted based on quarterly profits. Is it any surprise that middle management also has short time horizons? All of the middle level managers at the management institute previously mentioned agreed that a 2.8-year time horizon was too short, but they were all going back to their divisions to manage on the basis of that 2.8-year standard upon which they were going to be promoted or demoted. Most managers would have done likewise in their circumstances.

The charge is also made that American industry has too many new MBA's who are taught that the short-run bottom line is the only thing. As one who does some of his teaching in the Sloan School of Management at MIT, I believe there is some truth in the charge. Not in the sense that any business school professor has ever stood up and said, "the short-run bottom line is the only thing," but in the sense that it is easier to teach the quantitative methods that are applicable in short-run profit maximization where most of the parameters of the problem are known than it is to teach long-run profit maximization where risk, uncertainty, and the unknown dominate. Once on a job where short-run pressures are already intense, the new MBA quite naturally wants to use what he or she has just been taught to get on the "fast track" to the top.

In America young managers typically get on the fast track by some brilliant piece of short-run profit maximizing that brings them to the attention of top management. Once on the fast track the best advice is to avoid any risks that might lead to mistakes which would knock one off the fast track. For those who don't quickly make the fast track within the first three years, the best advice is to quit and go find a different job where they have another shot at the fast track.

Compare this with the incentive structure facing the new Japanese manager. Knowing that he will remain with the same firm for the rest of his career and that the "fast track" does not begin until his early forties he is interested in the long-run success of the company and in gaining the experience that will bring him to the head of his age cohort twenty years later. If he makes a mistake, there will be time to compensate for it. A slow start is not a permanent defeat.

Successful companies require hard work by everyone and not just by the brilliant few. Few people will work as hard knowing that they have missed their opportunity to reach the top as they will work if they think that they still have a chance to make it. Those who ultimately won't make it will work harder longer in the Japanese system, since they won't know they have missed the fast track until they have been at work for twenty years. To maximize the incentives of the few while minimizing the incentives for the many with an early start of the fast track is to court defeat.

Mental laziness also contributes to short corporate time horizons. It is simply easier and safer to invest based on short-term criteria than it is to figure out what products will be successful ten years down the road. To research, design, and build the products that may be needed ten years from now is to take risks and court failure. The manager has to be willing to live with ten years of uncertainty as to whether he has made the right judgments.

Any board of directors, no matter how inept, can hand out bonuses to top management based on current profits; but to know whether top management has positioned the company well for the long haul requires real skill. Mechanical judgments of middle-level managers based on the earnings of their profit centers generate no controversies. Such judgments favor managers who may be making good profits now but who should be investing to make much larger profits later, and discourage managers who are doing a good job in areas where the external environment makes profits difficult or impossible to obtain.

During the 1981–82 recession I was told that the aerospace executives in a firm which also makes auto parts were to get big bonuses because their profit centers were making money on the defense budget, while the auto executives were to go without bonuses because their profit centers were taking losses, although everyone agreed that the auto managers were doing a terrific job. They were losing money, but nowhere near as much money as everyone else in the auto industry. Yet in 1981 a management idiot could have made money in defense while a management genius would have lost it in autos.

To reward people in such a way is to set up enormous long-run distortions. Managers are told that if they are managing a losing area they will be penalized regardless of whether they are losing $6 million or $60 million. To win the management game you must have the good luck to be in a growing area. If your firm assigns you to a losing area, bail out and go with another firm in a growing area. Yet neither firms nor economies can work in such a manner, for good management in shrinking and difficult-to-manage areas is even more important than good management in rapidly expanding markets.

The impacts of corporate mergers extend beyond those of personal job tenure. To play the merger game, either defensively or offensively, firms must have ever rising quarterly profits and high P/E (price/earnings) multiples to make takeovers expensive (defense) or cheap (offense). With the recent megamergers, all but the biggest industrial fish can be taken over by someone.

The usual argument against mergers that they absorb investment resources is simply false. When U.S. Steel buys Marathon Oil it borrows money to pay the Marathon stockholders, who then return the money to the financial markets. The purchase and sale of existing assets doesn't reduce the funds available for new investment. The real argument against mergers is that they distort time horizons, absorb scarce management talent and time, and distort management perceptions as to where the real road to success lies.

Instead of engaging in the lengthy process of growing and fine-tuning new products or processes at home, top managers come to feel that they can get rich quick and expand their company with a well-timed takeover.[25] Thinking that there is an easy route to success, firms do not undertake the difficult time-consuming work of developing new products or processes and do not work out the links between new products or processes and old ones. Instead they wait for other firms to do the hard work and then try to take their economic candy away from them. A "successful" American manager doesn't plant or harvest—he is simply a Viking raider.

Why should anyone develop new products or processes if there is a high likelihood that those developments will be taken over by others? Those taken over sometimes get rich, but most of them went into the business of developing new products for more than just money. If they just wanted money, there would have been no need for a hostile takeover bid in the first place.

In most of the recent merger cases in the United States there isn't even the pretense that the acquirer is going to manage the assets better than they were being managed. The acquirer simply thinks that the stock market was undervaluing the worth of the acquiree's assets.

Even when an old corporation acquires a promising new growth area that it can manage better than the original management, however, a perverse set of economic signals go out. Managers are told that the big payoffs go not to those managers who develop new products or processes but to those adept at arranging mergers. The manager who will make the most money for himself and his firm is not someone who understands how to produce a high-quality product but the lawyer or accountant (40 percent of America's largest firms have CEOs with law or finance as a background) who understands the merger game.[26] Ambitious young managers are explicitly or implicitly told to bail out of engineering and line management to get into the staff work that is the route to financial success. Technical competence suffers, and when a revolutionary change in technology occurs, such as the change from open-hearth to oxygen furnaces top management cannot judge what is going on and falls behind technologically, as steel did.

Conglomerate mergers and management by lawyers or financiers have arisen out of what is called "portfolio theory" in business schools. One buys a portfolio of companies the way one buys a portfolio of stocks. But this is to ignore the very real differences between financial firms managing portfolios of stocks and industrial firms managing portfolios of companies. A financial investor may well want to balance a portfolio with stocks of different riskiness and different cyclical properties to get the right average degree of risk and the right average profitability over the business cycle. Financial investors can do this for themselves by buying different stocks, however, far better than any conglomerate can do it for them. Financial investors need no technical expertise, but to be a successful industrial firm one needs technical competence in the industries which are being managed.

Ex-post mergers have not been the route to long-run success. In 1976 General Electric bought Utah International, a mining company, for $2.1 billion dollars because GE wanted to expand its international operations and have a natural resource hedge against inflation. Seven years later GE sold Utah International for $2.4 billion (only $1.5 billion in 1976 dollars) for the announced purpose of investing the money more profitably in rapidly growing high-technology companies.[27] Note that one of America's biggest corporations was not planning to invest the extra money in growing its own products or processes. When account is taken of taxes, the impact of inflation, the dilution of equity, and the funds generated by General Electric but invested in Utah International over the seven-year period, pre-Utah General Electric shareholders lost over $3 billion, or one-third of their then market equity—a disaster. Nor were they the only stockholders to lose as a result of such merger games—Exxon-Reliance,

Sohio-Kennecott, Atlantic Richfield-Anaconda, Mobile-Montgomery Ward, none of them examples of success.

When Conoco was attacked by Mobil, Seagram, and the ultimately successful Du Pont, with Texaco threatening to join in, the only benefit to the American economy at large would have been better management by the acquiring company—the new managers would have had to be able to use Conoco's assets more efficiently than Conoco itself had been using them. But there was no evidence that Conoco was more poorly managed than Du Pont, that Gulf was more poorly managed than Standard Oil of California, that the executives of U.S. Steel knew more about the oil business than those at Marathon, or that the mud-wrestling match at Bendix-Martin Marietta-Allied would lead to better management.

Suppose that the executives of U.S. Steel had not been allowed to buy Marathon Oil or diverisify outside of steel and its related industries. They would then have had to make their company successful in the materials industry or face bleak personal economic futures. Merger was an easy way to avoid the hard work of building a world-class materials science (powdered metals, ceramics, graphite composites, etc.) firm. Without the merger alternative U.S. Steel might have failed to become competitive, but it would at least have tried.

Unfortunately our current tax system compounds this merger mania with additional incentives to merge. The accelerated cost recovery system of depreciation allowances provides many corporations with tax credits which they cannot use, since their allowable deductions for depreciation are larger than their profits. With the abolishment of lease-backs or safe-harbor leasing (the buying and selling of tax credits) in 1982, firms are left with mergers as the only mechanism for using these unused tax credits.

As unused tax credits start to pile up, firms look increasingly attractive as merger partners, not because their real assets are undervalued in the stock market, not because they are badly run, not because they are synergistic with the activities of an acquiring firm, not even because they are good companies that would fit into a conglomerate portfolio of companies—but simply as tax shelters. The appropriate strategy will be to buy a firm with large unused tax credits, exploit the tax credits, and then dispose of the firm. The result is a great mechanism for tax avoidance but a poor mechanism for running an economy.

Industrial executives blame the problem on the financial markets.

ITT loses one-third of its value in one day because financial money managers have a short-run time horizon. ITT is not alone. In April of 1982 the stock market placed a value of $18.63 on Polaroid shares despite the fact that the company's current assets minus its short- and long-term debt were worth $19 per share and that it had $25 per share in plant and equipment and yet other assets in the form of patents and trade names.[28] More generally, in 1983 pension fund managers dumped 62 percent of the shares they had previously owned and replaced them with other shares.

In most cases a majority of a firm's shares are held by professional money managers and not those with patient long-term perspectives. When charged with distorting time horizons, financial executives respond that they manage other people's money, such as pension funds, and that if they fall behind the market averages for six months they get fired. From their perspective it is not what Polaroid is really worth that counts but what they think the market will think that Polaroid is worth. From the perspective of financial executives, the very same industrial executives who complain about the short time horizons of the financial markets insist upon just those horizons when judging which pension fund managers to hire or fire. If they bought Polaroid and it went down they would be fired even if Polaroid was a good long-run buy.

High interest rates compound the problem. In calculating rates of return on investment, future returns are discounted with interest rates that depend upon the firm's cost of capital. With a 5 percent interest rate, $1 in returns ten years from now is worth 61 cents today. As the interest rates rise to 10 and then 20 percent, today's value of a dollar to be earned ten years from now plunges to 39 cents and 16 cents. The higher the real borrowing rate the less willing firms are to invest in products where profits are far in the future. One reason Japanese firms have a longer time horizon than American firms is that the Japanese government does not permit real interest rates to rise to levels that our government is willing to tolerate. When American interest rates were above 20 percent in early 1982, the equivalent Japanese rates were 6 to 7 percent.

Short time horizons are produced by an economic environment where everyone responds rationally to individual incentives, but the sum total of those individually rational choices is social stupidity. Time horizons get shorter and shorter as each group (the board of directors to top management, top management to middle management, middle management to new management, industry to the financial community, the financial community to industry, interest rates to everyone) pressures the other for quick results. In such circumstances Americans are competing not just with foreign producers but with a self-imposed very fast-ticking clock.

BREAKING OUT

In business schools our future executives are taught that the corporation exists *solely* to maximize the net worth of stockholder equity. The stock market places the right net present value on the future stream of profits, and it is the job of the shareholders' agents, the managers, to maximize that stock market value. In this model the absentee owners are wealth maximizers—nothing more, nothing less. Similarly, employees wish to maximize the net present value of their earnings—nothing more, nothing less. The owners of a corporation and its employees are natural adversaries. Workers want to maximize wages and minimize profits. Owners and managers want to maximize profits and minimize wages. To fire redundant workers or to cut wages is a positive step from the point of view of managers—it directly contributes to higher profits and higher stockholder net worth.

It is not such a positive step from the point of view of labor. Workers wish to squeeze whatever they can out of the capitalists and have no long-run interest in the success of any firm. If any particular employer stupidly agrees to pay too much and goes broke, they will simply go to work for other smarter capitalists.

In such a system real interests diverge substantially. The introduction of robots may lead to higher productivity and greater profits for the corporation, but it leads to unemployment for the workers displaced. As a result those workers should rationally wherever and however possible resist the introduction of robots. While it is in the long-run interests of workers as a group to raise productivity, since general wages will rise with a rise in productivity, in each specific short-run instance it is in the interests of the workers who will actually be adversely affected to stop increases in productivity if they can.

High wages may make it impossible for the corporation to survive foreign competition but insisting upon them may make perfect sense for a sixty-year-old worker with a lot of seniority. He will not be laid off in the first shock of foreign competition and he will have retired long before the corporation goes broke.

From the individualistic perspective of the standard model of correct corporate behavior, no one should ever do anything that hurts his own income stream no matter how it may help the earnings of others. Neither side has any interest in the welfare of others. If labor isn't needed, it will be fired. If a better-paying job comes along, employees will quit.

If this view of the corporation were the only theoretical possibility or the only correct one, then Americans would be simply "blowing smoke" when they talk about eliminating adversarial labor-management relations. Adversarial relations can only be eliminated when there is a genuine community of interests. If no such community exists, then there is nothing to agree upon. Labor and capital are natural adversaries much as the viper and mongoose, and the firm is simply the battleground upon which their economic warfare takes place. The capitalists may win, the workers may win, they may arrange a temporary truce, they may fight each other into exhaustion, but there is no basis for cooperation.[29] There simply aren't any team goals congruent with those of the individual players.

Yet there is a bigger reality that teams don't win when everyone is out to set individual scoring records.

To build the motivation, cooperation, and teamwork necessary to construct a successful economy, America is going to have to shift its fundamental conception of the firm. The firm is going to have to become not a battleground but a partnership of labor, management, and shareholders collectively trying to maximize the firm's value added (value added is the difference between the selling price of products produced and the cost of supplies, materials, and components purchased).[30,31] In this conception shareholders are not the "boss" but silent partners providing capital to labor and management. Each partner provides something that the firm needs—capital from the shareholders, work from the labor force, direction from the management. Each partner is an owner with an interest in maximizing the value added of the firm, and as a partial owner each partner has a long-run interest in the survival of the firm.

As partners, the owners will divide the firm's value added in the way that profits are now divided in real partnerships.[32] The firm's value added, the gross income available to be divided, will be split into three parts, some to workers and managers, some to shareholders, and some to be invested in research and development or new plant and equipment to insure the firm's (and each individual partner's) future.

As a partnership, however, no one has the right in normal circumstances to fire the other partners or to make unilateral decisions. Partnerships grow and contract but partners don't fire one another. Decision making may be delegated to the managing partner, as it usually is in real partnerships, but the partners retain the right to take that decision-making power back if they feel that it is not being wisely used, and they certainly must be kept informed as to what is being decided and why. Only if the firm is heading for bankruptcy do the partners resort to beheadings.

Viewed this way a high return to each of the other partners is not a negative outcome but a positive outcome. A partnership that can pay high wages is better than one which cannot, but only highly productive partnerships can pay high wages. The aim of a successful partnership is not to minimize wages—as in the normal view of the corporation—but to maximize them subject to the basic constraints that wages must be consistent with productivity and future investment needs to insure the long-run success of the company.

Dividends from the perspective of such a view are not a capitalistic rip-off but a payment to a vital partner. Without an initial infusion of capital the partnership cannot be successful. Augmenting that initial investment, however, is a matter of concern not just for the capitalist partners. It is of equal concern to shareholder, manager, and worker. As partners all are willing to take somewhat less than their maximum income cut from the partnership to assure the future healthy survival of the partnership.

In hard times, on the other hand, partners have to accept their share of reduced earnings. Instead of allocating all of the income cuts to a few workers—to those fired—everyone takes a share of these cuts, usually in the form of work sharing and smaller bonuses. The cure for redundant partners is not to fire them but to increase sales so that everyone's income can rise again.

Productivity becomes a common interest because labor is not fired when productivity rises. Higher productivity becomes instead a vehicle whereby each partner can potentially have a larger end-of-the-year bonus.[33] To realize this bonus, however, sales have to rise fast enough to absorb the higher productivity. The gains of higher productivity cannot be realized by firing workers. To get the necessary sales may require diversification into other markets if the firm's current markets are growing too slowly, but as a result better products and higher sales become a common interest rather than just a management interest. If higher sales can be realized with better products everyone's income can go up—not in some vague distant future or in some general sense—but now in the form of a year-end bonus for a specified set of workers.

Partners are smart enough to realize that although it may look as if the easy way to raise their own income is to throw some of the partners overboard, this is in reality a mirage. For if they do throw some of the existing partners overboard the remaining partners will know that the same can potentially happen to them; and the cooperation, motivation, teamwork and willingness to sacrifice for the common good that made the partnership successful will disappear.

Motivation, cooperation, and teamwork are not a matter of persuasion or company pep talks or even of better managers. Lip service in praise of quality-control circles without actual shared decision making won't work. If the corporate goal remains the traditional maximization of shareholders' net worth, there will be no fundamental improvements in soft productivity. Firms cannot fool even half of their workers even half of the time. Workers know when corporate goals are congruent with their own long-run self-interest and when they are not.

Motivation, cooperation, and teamwork require the establishment of a partnership agreement where everyone's interests will be taken into account and where everyone is secure in the knowledge that they will not be thrown overboard at the first convenient opportunity or at the first sign of difficulties. Realistically this means that firing labor becomes a last resort rather than a first resort when hard times strike.

There is no trick to breaking out of the vicious circle in which American industry now finds itself. American workers are as productive, as capable of taking individual initiatives to help the firm reach shared long-term goals as any others. Once the shift is made to the conception that firms should maximize value added rather than profits, it is easy to move on to specific arrangements that will dramatically alter the structure of the corporation and its ability to engender motivation, cooperation, and teamwork.

A Bonus System

The place to start is by altering the present structure of salaries and wages. Instead of receiving straight wages or salaries, with all of

the residual profits allocated to the capitalists, as is true in partnerships, part of each worker's or manager's income should come in the
form of a bonus based upon increases in value added per hour of
work. During the transition to a bonus system all normal wage increases would be allocated to bonuses until bonuses account for
about one-third of total labor income. While the exact formula determining the size of the bonus would differ from industry to industry
and from firm to firm, some bonus system is important to stimulate
interest in raising productivity. If bonuses are an important component of everyone's—blue-collar workers', white-collar workers', man-
agements'—annual income, everyone immediately shares a common
interest in higher productivity and success.

Profit sharing is one answer, but the American experience with it
has not been highly successful. Profits depend upon so many items
beyond labor's control—interest rates, foreign competition, national
economic policies—that labor sees little connection between its efforts to raise productivity and the profit share received. Labor also is
rightly suspicious of the creative accounting that lies behind those
profit figures. Value added per hour of work is a much better index—
more closely related to what labor controls, less subject to accounting
distortions—to determine bonuses. To calculate a firm's value added
it is only necessary to know its gross revenue and the payments made
to suppliers of raw materials or components.

The tax system could nudge the private economy in the right
direction if bonuses were excused from payroll taxes. Since Social
Security, Medicare, workers' compensation, and unemployment insurance taxes are approaching 20 percent of payroll, both firms and
individuals would be eager to shift to such a bonus system free of
payroll taxes (see Chapter 8).

The bonus system should extend beyond the private profit-making
sector to include government and non-profit employees. Civil ser-
vants should be shifted to a bonus system where the size of their
bonus depends upon the average bonus earned in private industry.
The same for university professors. Such a system would do wonders
to remind those who are not directly dependent upon the success of
the private economy that they are indirectly dependent upon its success. The more productive the American economy is and the better
it competes in world markets, the higher incomes can be for all Americans.

To lengthen everyone's time horizons bonuses should also extend to retirees in their first ten years of retirement—on the grounds that what they did helped prepare the ground for the company's success in the first ten years after they retired.[34] Suppose that today's chief executive officers, rather than getting a very large bonus based on current profits, as now happens, got a bonus which depended in larger part upon the success of the firm in the ten years after they retired. If CEO's (and everyone else) were paid based on the long-run value added of the firms they manage (or work for), the internal structure of the firm would soon change to lengthen the time horizons of everyone concerned. Such a system would also contribute to less turnover. Those who left would be abandoning their share of those future bonuses.

Delayed bonuses can be particularly helpful in reducing management turnover among executives who have learned that to bail out is to move up. In 1981 over 20,000 executives making over $50,000 changed jobs. One in six was paid more than $100,000. Over 80 percent of all firms with 500 or more employees recruit from the outside.[35] This creates a whole set of perverse incentives. When a big salary premium leads an executive to jump companies, the other executives at both ends of the line become dissatisfied with their salaries and start to think about jumping ship too and in the meantime operate on the premise that "if he is so smart and paid so much, let him solve the problems." When executives come to believe that the way to advance is to go elsewhere, the recipient team learns by implication that its own members aren't considered good enough for the top jobs, while the team left learns that one of their best members believes that his old team is inferior. Hardly attitudes that encourage future success.

When delayed bonuses are suggested to today's CEO's it first brings a smile and then an objection. They point out that their successors would load all of the costs of achieving success in the interval ten to twenty years from now into the interval zero to ten years from now and deprive them of their bonus. By believing this, top managers merely confirm the perversity of the current system. If the next generation of managers would distort the optimal time path of investments to maximize their future bonuses then this generation of managers is distorting optimal investment time paths to maximize their current bonuses. And if there has to be a distortion, a distortion toward the long run is precisely what American business needs.

A future-oriented bonus system would also promote investments in human skills and encourage short-term sacrifices to promote long-term success. With lower turnover rates, company training programs would have a bigger payoff. A sacrifice today would mean a bigger bonus tomorrow. What is irrational from the point of view of self-interest in one social system becomes rational in another.

Cooperation becomes rational not only between labor and management but among workers. With seniority firing provisions and generous unemployment and pension benefits to those near retirement, it is rational for older workers to refuse economic concessions—even when such a refusal leads to the demise of a firm or plant. Fifty-one percent of the labor force usually feel, often correctly, that they will not be the ones fired. And even if the plant is closed they will get generous termination, unemployment, and pension rights. In case after case—a Schlitz brewery in Milwaukee, a Ford parts plant in Sheffield, Alabama, an Interlake steel pipe plant in Newport, Kentucky—older workers have essentially voted to unemploy younger workers by demanding wages that guaranteed a plant shutdown.[36]

The dual wage systems that are now being negotiated in industries such as airlines, where much lower wages are paid to new employees than to old employees doing the same work so that the firm can be competitive, are going to exacerbate this problem. Today's entrenched workers preserve their high wages and fringe benefits at the expense of new workers. While such systems may work for a while, new workers will eventually become the majority, and then watch what they do to old workers. When the old eat their young they can expect to be savaged in turn—hardly a high-productivity environment. Dual wage systems are yet another easy short-term solution to a long-run problem—the need to cut labor costs—that is going to come back to haunt any chance of long-run success.

To increase training, strengthen teamwork and mutual loyalty, and lengthen time horizons, American corporations are going to have to adopt management practices that dramatically cut turnover rates. If America wants a loyal labor force interested in raising productivity, layoffs have to become the last, rather than the first, resort in difficult times. Incentives have to be structured to reward those who do not hop from job to job. Outside recruiting should be a last resort, and benefits should be given to those who stay and withheld from those who leave.

"Every man for himself" is not the route to economic success.

Ending the Merger Wars

Hostile mergers are less frequent in foreign countries because most foreign countries have what are called merchant or investment banks. These merchant banks own controlling positions in most large corporations and take an active role in management, such as sitting on boards of directors. Since the merchant banks own large blocks of stock, firms cannot be taken over without their approval, and normally their approval is not given. They simply have no incentive to approve outside takeovers. If they wanted different management or a different corporate strategy, they would simply change managers, using their power on the current board of directors. Mergers are not needed to meet cash-flow problems, since merchant banks exist to provide such funds. No merchant bank wants to lose a good captive customer for its lending and investment activities. Today's precise stock market values are irrelevant, since the merchant bank can make informed inside judgments as to the long-run worth of its investments rather than relying upon the outside judgments that determine stock market values from day to day. Unlike pension funds, which, to carry out their fiduciary role, must sell to whoever offers them a price higher than today's stock market value, merchant banks are under no legal pressure to sell simply because someone has made an offer. As a result they can play the role of real institutional capitalists rather than that of financial speculators.

Merchant banking is a hard fortress to storm in the merger wars. As a consequence foreign managers do not have to spend time worrying who may be plotting a hostile takeover and can worry less about quarterly profits and daily stock market prices.

For most of its history the United States had merchant banks. They became illegal in 1933 with the Glass-Steagall Act. The current Wall Street firms that today call themselves investment banks, such as Morgan Stanley, are not merchant banks with major sources of equity finance but brokerage firms that match investors and savers. They cannot accept deposits from the public to make equity investments. Nor can they sit on boards of directors where they are financially involved or take a hands-on long-run interest in the success of industrial firms.

Merchant banking was abolished for reasons that were both wrong at the time and now irrelevant. When the Glass-Steagall Act was passed, the House of Morgan was being blamed for the Great Depression, and merchant banks were abolished as punishment for their perceived crimes. The causes of the Great Depression, however, were much more fundamental than the speculations of the House of Morgan, and by now these causes are in any case irrelevant. If the rest of the world uses merchant banks effectively, as they do, then the United States will have to relearn to rely on them too.

To a limited extent merchant banking has been reinvented in the United States under the name of "venture capitalism." Venture capital financings have risen from essentially nothing in the mid-1970s to something over $3 billion in the mid-1980s, but venture capitalists cannot undertake major investments, such as the next generation of new integrated steel mills—each one of which might cost $5 billion— since they have no way to tap really large sources of funds. Apple Computer began with only $26,000 in equity, but the next major growth industry is very unlikely to be as kind to America as electronics when it comes to low initial capital requirements. If the next new industry arrived with large capital requirements, it would not be apt to be an American industry. America would simply have no way to finance it if it did not happen to fall in the domain of one of our existing large firms and had to be started on a new-venture basis.

J. P. Morgan within a few years set up the United States Steel Corporation, General Electric, and International Harvester and in a short period after World War I lent the equivalent of $12 billion in today's dollars.[37] Given a much bigger economy, there is no reason to believe that the need for investments on that scale is any less today.

After World War II America's lack of merchant banking was not important. Industry could essentially finance itself through internal profits because of its huge economic and technological lead. In 1983 American business savings, $455 billion in the form of undistributed profits and capital consumption allowances, exceeded the $341 billion in non-residential business investment.[38] But 1983 was a recovery year with little need for new investment. The era of self-financing is nearing an end.

In the past American firms had higher savings rates than their foreign competitors because they had higher profit rates, rates produced by a technological lead that is now disappearing. In industry after industry, foreign competition is driving profit rates down, and American firms find that they can no longer accumulate the funds necessary to build the next generation of production facilities. The effects of this trend can already be seen in the American semiconductor industry, where firms are in the process of shifting from technologies with relatively low demands for capital to those with much higher demands for capital.[39] The traditional American way to make this transition would be to borrow some of the necessary money (typically 20 to 30 percent) and to finance the rest out of earnings retained from high profits earned on current products. But this time those profits aren't there.

In contrast the Japanese semiconductor industry will use debt capital up to 95 percent of total capital to build new factories before profits are earned on old products. Simply by building plants ahead of demand rather than behind demand, the Japanese are able to preempt markets. Prices are aggressively set to expand production rapidly so that firms can quickly go down the learning curve. The rest of the industry sees enormous excess capacity in Japan, knows that prices will erode because of that excess capacity, and decides not to build new capacity in the face of existing excess Japanese capacity. Just this situation existed in semiconductors in early 1985. When demand rebounds, only the Japanese have the on-line capacity to meet it. Just such an availability gave the Japanese their initial market position in 16K and 64K RAM chips. Two or three such cycles, and the Japanese have effectively taken a dominant position in the market. The same strategy has been used in shipbuilding, consumer electronics, and steel; and they will do the same in the knowledge industries—the announced Japanese industrial targets of the 1980s.

In the steel industry the few big American companies that might be able to finance the next generation of materials plants have essentially abandoned the industry and have become technologically backward in any case. It may or may not be smart for these firms to leave the steel business, but America cannot afford to abandon the industry, because materials science is one of the three hot scientific areas along with electronics and biogenetics that are and will be leading to major new industries in the next two decades. Powdered metals, metal ceramics, graphite composites are a sunrise category within the metals industry that America cannot afford to ignore. But the large investments necessary to get into full scale production are probably beyond the capabilities of today's venture capitalists.

The reinvention of merchant banking is not going to eliminate the capital cost handicap faced by American industry (the cost of capital is three times as high in the United States as it is in Japan),[40] but it can help reduce it. There are multiple reasons for this difference in the costs of capital—America's lower savings rates, Japan's policy of low interest rates—but the higher debt-to-equity ratios permitted by merchant banking is one. In Germany the debt-to-equity ratio is now 4 to 1—equity capital now accounts for only 20 percent of total investment.[41] This is possible under merchant banking, since there is no sharp line between debt and equity and no one has to worry that debt capital will suddenly be withdrawn. The equity investor, the merchant bank, is also the debt lender. Being able to use more debt, foreign firms can profitably invest in new technologies faster than would be prudent in the United States.

Merchant banks allow foreign firms to build new facilities before they earn large profits, to go quickly down the learning curve with those new facilities, and to price aggressively so that American firms cannot finance the investments necessary to stay in business. American industry can no longer rely on profits from today's products to finance tomorrow's new investments. More and more often those new investments are going to have to be financed with new equity investment. Venture capitalists are a step in the right direction, but they need to be augmented with merchant or investment banking to handle the full range of investments and to raise equity investments to the scale that will be necessary to compete on world markets.

Merchant banking plays an important role in new sunrise industries, but it also plays an important role in restructuring sunset industries to save those parts that can be saved. Compare what happened to Chrysler in the early 1980s with what happened to Mazda after the 1973–74 oil shock. Mazda had been gearing up to conquer the auto world with the rotary engine car and might have succeeded if the one weakness of the rotary engine car had not been its bad fuel mileage. Suddenly the company's sales plunged. For all intents and purposes it was broke. What happened?

Workers and managers responded with 50 percent wage cuts. Mazda earned their loyalty with no layoffs, but they also knew that if Mazda died their economic future would be severely curtailed. They could not bail out. Since Mazda's investment bankers had billions at stake they took an active role in rescuing the company. They responded with billions of yen in loans to redesign and retool for a conventional piston engine car. Within a few years the company turned itself around and once again became a powerful international competitor. Government helped, but during the crisis the company was carried by its investment banks. When a similar situation arose at

Chrysler, there were no investment banks with their equity at stake. The commercial banks simply walked away from Chrysler and the government had to come to the rescue.

America needs to break down the walls between industrial and financial institutions. Investment banks should be able to invest in industrial firms; industrial firms should be able to own bank shares. American industrial and financial firms all live in the same economy and will succeed or fail together, but this de facto reality needs to be legally acknowledged. Merchant banking is simply the best way to get financial and industrial institutions to work together.

Current financial mergers, such as those undertaken by Sears, American Express, and Prudential, are essentially attempts to skirt banking regulations and recreate the large financial firms that existed in America prior to the Great Depression. Far better to change our banking laws and then let firms merge than to leave the laws intact and promote mergers that are only sensible given silly laws. By changing our banking laws the present financial merger movement could lead to the supermarkets of investment finance that America needs rather than the supermarkets of consumer finance that America does not need. With its low savings rate the last thing America needs is a better banking system for consumer finance.

Different Management

When America had a big technological lead it could concentrate on activities such as mergers that paid off quickly in higher stock market values. With a huge technological lead, production took care of itself. Without that lead, however, American industry faces a very different world. The best salesman in the world cannot sell a technologically backward product. The best merger in the world cannot make a successful company from two companies that are technologically inferior. The best financier in the world cannot finance an obsolete technology successfully. To reap superior returns one has to have new unique products or new processes for making old products more cheaply.

To regain their technological edge American firms are going to have to recast their personnel policies to reduce the proportion of top managers who come up through marketing, finance, or governmental relations and to increase the proportion who know how to build high-quality products efficiently. Today about two-thirds of American chief executive officers are lawyers, accountants, and advertising executives by training. In contrast, over two-thirds of Japanese firms are headed by chief executives who are engineers and scientists by training.[42]

One of the ways to do this is to return to the days when everyone who wished to get to the top was expected to spend some time in on-line production management. Since no one can be a quick success in on-line management in the way in which one can be an instant success in finance or advertising, it will take the average executive longer to acquire the experience required to reach the top, but it will also mean better management if the fast track to the top begins later. There are simply too many American managers who do not know enough about the technologies that they themselves are supposedly managing.

One of the ways to address this problem while at the same time alleviating a scarcity of engineering talent is to go back and redesign new career ladders for engineers. Since America needs more engineers, while having too many low- or middle-level managers, and since many middle managers have engineering backgrounds, the obvious solution is to keep engineers in engineering longer. In America many engineers are sucked out of engineering into staff positions before they have exhausted their engineering talents. Many bail out of engineering earlier than they themselves would like. They are afraid that if they do not leave engineering early they will miss the management "fast track" and the chance for high wages, responsibility, and power. When they bail out, however, society loses the very scarce engineering talent it needs. By making it possible for engineers to get on the management fast track at a later age and by often paying engineers more than the managers who supervise them, the Digital Equipment Corporation has proven that engineers can be kept in engineering. Just as professional basketball players are paid more than their coaches, so engineering comes first. Managers are essentially facilitators to insure that the engineers have what they need to work efficiently.

Often new products and processes mean undertaking activities where no one can prove that the investments meet traditional rate of return on investment criteria. The hard information necessary to make such calculations with any confidence simply isn't there. It is a judgment call depending upon dynamic developments, even if the decision is dressed up with fancy financial calculations, and only those who are thoroughly familiar with the technology can have the necessary intuition and be expected to make good judgments.

Robots are a case in point. Careful financial accounting led Americans to reject robots on auto assembly lines when they were first invented. They did not meet the necessary rate of return on investment requirements, since they were more expensive than the people that they were to replace. The Japanese did use them despite similar negative calculations by their accountants and as a result got such a head start down the learning curve in both an old industry (auto production) and a new industry (robot manufacturing).

Almost by nature lawyers, accountants, financiers, and economists are not risk takers when it comes to new technologies. Only the engineers who understand a new technology can believe in it, and as a result they are much more apt to be risk takers with new technologies. There is always the danger that engineers are too much believers in new technologies and plunge ahead when they should hold back, but from a social perspective if one is to fail it is better to fail by attempting too much than by attempting too little. Financial resources are wasted if one attempts too much, but whole industries (video recorders) are missed if one attempts too little.

Soft Productivity

Foreign economies have become more successful not because they have better individual entrepreneurs or because their tax laws or government regulations are better than those in America but because they have been able to create an environment where workers are interested in working together to improve productivity. Unless American managers can stimulate a similar interest in "bubble-up" productivity, the American economy will remain unsuccessful regardless of the wisdom of the tax laws enacted in Washington or the brilliance of America's individual entrepreneurs.

Bubble-up productivity requires individual workers interested in team productivity. Think of the quintessential American game—professional football. The Pro Bowl team, the all-stars, has individual players who are superior to the players on the Super Bowl team, the league champions, yet no one doubts that the Super Bowl team could easily beat the Pro Bowl team, for a team of good individuals who have played together is simply better than a team of superior individuals who have not.

The same is true in industry. Individual workers need time to polish their production skills and to learn to work together effectively. When new plants are opened, labor costs (man-hours per unit of output) typically fall dramatically over the first four or five years of operations as workers learn to work together and perfect their skills. Learning curves are not automatic, however. They differ dramatically from country to country and between companies within the same industry.

Excessive turnover is one of the reasons for such differences. In some statistical studies of industrial experience Steven Sheffrin of the University of California at Davis and I found that a 50 percent reduction in the turnover rates raised productivity by almost 30 percent over five years.[43] Less turnover would have a major positive effect on American productivity. None of this is to say that the optimum turnover rate is zero. Just as a Super Bowl football team wants to introduce a few new players each year so that the team does not become old all at the same time, so an economic team has an optimal rate of turnover that will insure its long-term success, but that rate of turnover is far below the rates now prevailing in the United States.

To get loyalty, firms will have to prove that they deserve it. In the aftermath of the 1981–82 recession, it became a hot topic of debate as to whether firms should supply medical care for their laid-off workers who had lost their health insurance. The refusal to do so was almost unanimous. Given current operating procedures this refusal was both expected and consistent. Under American doctrines firms have no responsibilities to former workers. Yet a mutual interest in each other's health care is one of the ways that human groups create a feeling of social solidarity. If firms don't care about workers when they are sick, why should workers care about firms when it is the firms who are sick?

The willingness of Japanese workers to sacrifice on behalf of their companies and to accept new technologies is always commented upon by American business observers, but the commentators pay little attention to the reciprocal side of that relationship. Firms provide a strong private social safey net for their workers. They often run hospitals. Being willing to provide such support may in fact be one of the ways firms create a well-motivated, cooperative, economic team with a high degree of loyalty—even if it means some sacrifice in short-term profit maximization.[44]

Historically the United States has tried to meet the legitimate human demands for economic security through government social welfare programs—unemployment insurance, old-age pensions and assistance, medical care for the indigent and elderly. Viewed from a welfare perspective, it makes little difference whether Americans pay for a public social safety net with higher payroll taxes (and hence higher prices for the products they buy) or whether Americans pay for a private social safety net with higher prices for the products they buy. Either way Americans pay for the social safety net in the form of higher prices. Viewed from the perspective of productivity and team spirit, however, there may be a lot of difference between a private social safety net and a public social safety net. One engenders team loyalty; the other does not.

The demand for economic security (income certainty) is not going to disappear. Economic security is to modern man what a castle and moat were to medieval man. When public opinion polls ask what workers want, economic security always takes top place—well above higher pay. One can preach the doctrine that market losers should be thrown out in the cold in a system of rugged free enterprise, but few are willing to practice the doctrine when they are the market losers. Every group when it feels its economic security slipping away turns to government for protection regardless of how loudly it may have preached the virtues of rugged free enterprise. The list of groups now being protected is almost endless. These groups are not villains. They simply want what each of us wants—economic security.

Such groups usually demand protection from foreign competition, but protection freezes the economy into sick industries. History demonstrates that protected industries almost never really work to become more efficient. They do not risk investments in new products and processes. It is simply much easier to retreat to the protection of government. As we will see, there may be a role for protection as a temporary quid pro quo in an overall recovery strategy, but simple protection is always a failure. Yet it is the path on which America is now embarked as more and more industries become protected from the rigor of international competition and become what might be called quasi-government enterprises.

America's choice is not between security and efficiency. An environment can be built where Americans have security and efficiency simultaneously. According to free market theory, economic insecurity is supposed to promote economic change. Hunger forces workers to adjust to new technologies and new conditions. The facts are precisely the reverse. Workers who fear economic uncertainty and hunger thwart economic change at every opportunity. As foreign examples demonstrate, the rest of the industrial world has more economic security and is changing faster—that is what those higher foreign rates of productivity growth measure. Economic change is only to be had by building an environment where workers are willing to accept new products and processes precisely because they know that they will not be thrown out of work by these innovations.

On a recent trip to Japan I asked businessmen, large and small, when they had last fired someone and what were considered adequate grounds for dismissal. Without exception in big corporations and small companies everyone that I talked to said that he had never personally fired anyone. I also asked about the existence of workers who simply were not doing their jobs. Every manager that I talked to admitted that he had some bad workers who were not performing adequately. They were described in very unflattering terms and according to company officials immense social pressure was brought to bear upon them to get them to start working. But they were not fired even if they had "not worked in years," largely because management did not entirely blame them for their failures. As the Japanese see it, the entire system somehow shares the blame for inadequate individual performances: Either it has not provided the right job for the individual or it has failed to motivate him properly.

These talks reminded me of parents desperately trying to find a way to reform a son who has failed. They feel that somehow they have failed to bring him up "right." Whatever the son does and whoever he is, however, he is still part of the family and will not be thrown out. This is the only social attitude that can lead to success. American failures remain American. Free market doctrines fail to come to grips with this reality, since they literally assume that market failures will die of starvation and exit from the society.

Think of an American worker and a Japanese worker facing the introduction of some new labor saving technology. The Japanese worker goes at it armed with a guaranteed lifetime job, a bonus based on productivity, and a wage rate that attaches to him as an individual and not to the particular job that he happens to be doing. A new labor-saving machine presents nothing but opportunity. He will not lose his job or be forced to take a wage reduction. The innovation can only raise his bonus.

In contrast for the American worker the new machine is a potential threat. It may abolish his job or reduce his pay. Long-held and expensively acquired skills may disappear overnight and the company has no obligation to help him acquire new skills. The potential benefits of new technology, if they exist at all, are distant and indirect. Wages will eventually go up with higher productivity, but there is no direct immediate linkage between the new technology and a higher income for affected workers. Rational workers knowing that they have a high probability of leaving the company before the higher wages are actually paid will also heavily discount those future wage gains.

In the American theory of the firm, productivity is solely a management function. Workers have no responsibilities to help raise productivity. Yet each worker is apt to know better ways of doing his or her own job. But who is going to mention those new ways to the boss when to do so is to reduce the number of workers that the company is willing to hire in one's own job category. Even if the initiator keeps his own job, he certainly does not get praise from his laid-off compatriots or those who may be laid off as the result of his next "good" idea. To make the most of a new technology every worker must feel that he or she will benefit from it. Too often this does not happen in the United States, and the result is a failure to harness the individual initiatives for which Americans are supposedly famous.

It is a fact that American workers are interested in restrictive work rules (formal or informal) and resist technical change. Anyone who has ever worked in an American mine or factory knows that as a new employee you are informed as to the informal work quotas. Violation of this informal quota first brings warnings from one's fellow workers and then stronger measures of social control that can often end up in physical intimidation. Given the American system of incentives, workers would be stupid to do otherwise. Enforcing such informal quotas is individually rational yet socially stupid. Everyone ends up sacrificing the higher productivity that permits higher real standards of living.

Meanwhile at the Yamazaki Machinery Works manless factory robots are busy working by themselves on the graveyard shift.[45] Only the night watchman prowls the floor with his flashlight. "Robot-making robots" is the catch phrase. Who could say about an American plant what Mr. Yamazaki said about this work force: "There is no one here among our work force that resisted this at all"? Yet such an answer would not be a surprise in America if no workers were threatened with losing their jobs as they weren't at Yamazaki. The extraordinary willingness of Yamazaki's workers to accept new technology springs from the system of lifetime employment (workers do not fear that the robots will take their jobs) and from highly trained workers (at Yamazaki 43 percent of the workers are college graduates and most of the rest are graduates of technical high schools) who know that they have the fundamental skills to benefit from an extensive system of formal on-the-job training and retraining.

When managers (foreign or American) talk about American unions, their complaint is not so much with the average wage level but the constraints that unions impose on their ability to design jobs, assign workers, or utilize equipment in a productive way. The standard American procedure is to negotiate hundreds of different job classifications and wage rates.[46] The problem is not so much inefficient work rules initially associated with different jobs but that the rules are static. As firms progress down the learning curve and learn how to better operate their current technologies, the old work rules prevent them from fully exploiting the potential learning curve ahead of them. When technology changes or someone has a better idea it is very difficult to change old job definitions and move on to the new technologies.

Different wage rates for each job make it hard to rotate workers across different jobs. No one wants to rotate into the low-paying jobs, but such rotations are an efficient way to gain flexibility, to generate a more skilled labor force, and to keep people from becoming bored with their work. Very few human beings can turn the same screw on the assembly line week after week and do a high-quality job every time.

In many other countries unions do not freeze production technology at the same level of detail. German unions practice co-determination, worry about investment decisions and the selection of technology, but they do not worry about detailed job classifications. French unions restrict layoffs and push for lengthy notification and generous severance pay if layoffs do occur but do not negotiate detailed job classifications. English unions do negotiate detailed work rules, but they merely illustrate the American problem in an even more extreme form.

With the introduction of more flexible computer-aided design and manufacturing processes it is clear that the penalty for inflexible labor forces is going to increase. As a result American industry, especially unionized industry, is going to have to move to a more flexible system of wage and job determination. The old system makes America un-competitive now, and it will make America only more uncompetitive as time passes.

American unions, like dinosaurs, will disappear if they do not adjust to the new competitive environment and realize the real need for flexible labor forces. The disappearance process is now well under way. Union membership as a percentage of the total work force is falling rapidly. Previously unionized industries such as construction, trucking, and airlines are becoming increasingly non-union. Union firms are starting to set up non-unionized subsidiaries. In other indus-tries, such as steel, unionized firms are being driven out of business by non-union firms (the mini steel mills) and by more flexible union-ized foreign firms. With lower labor costs from more flexible work forces, non-union organizations can squeeze out union ones even if they pay the same wage rate.

As a result both unionized businesses and union leaders have an incentive to design a very different wage determination system and shop floor labor-management relations. What is needed is a system where there are specific individual incentives (the value-added bonus system talked about earlier) to encourage individual workers to be interested in promoting technical change and where wages are tied to individual skills and seniority and not to the job that the worker hap-pens to be doing at the moment.

Bonuses give workers a direct immediate interest in raising pro-ductivity. To be effective, however, everyone must be on the bonus system. The goal is not a two-class system where some workers are dependent upon productivity for their incomes while others are not, but a one-class system where all employees have a direct interest in cooperating to raise their own productivity and that of their co-workers.

In many ways the changes that are required are not as radical as they first seem. Most American workers are now promoted up a de-tailed job-classification ladder based on seniority. Seniority is the basic determinant of most workers' wages and the job-classification ladder is simply an instrument to this end. From the point of view of worker flexibility straightforward seniority pay is far better than a sys-tem of detailed job classification.

Lifetime employment, like seniority wages, seems revolutionary at first glance but in reality isn't all that different from current American practices. Given the prevalence of seniority hiring and firing in the

United States, the percentage of the American work force with de facto lifetime employment is probably just as large as the part of the Japanese labor force with de jure lifetime employment. Many Americans with de facto lifetime employment, however, don't realize it and fear for their jobs anyway. The Japanese seem to get something back (higher productivity) in exchange for granting lifetime employment overtly, while we Americans get nothing back by giving it covertly. Since overtness beats covertness, Americans should shift to an overt system of employment guarantees.

If some variant of lifetime employment were combined with an individual wage structure that rose rather steeply with seniority and a system of productivity bonuses, the American labor force could become as self-motivated and flexible as any in the rest of the world. If American rhetoric is true and Americans are good at taking individual initiative, then there is no reason why America could not have a work force second to none.

A long time horizon, bubble-up productivity, loyalty, and a willingness to sacrifice for the common good all depend upon a work force that expects to be around for a long time. A seniority wage system can help reduce turnover. The steeper the seniority wage gradient the greater the price of movement. In Japan if the wage of the average twenty-to-twenty-four-year-old is set at 100, those from thirty to thirty-four will make 153, and those forty to forty-four years old 194. Wages essentially double over the first twenty years of seniority.[47] In such a system to move is to face a large cut in income.

Since the Japanese have introduced variants of lifetime employment in many of the American facilities that they now manage, the necessary experiments have been run. The system can be made to work. When Kikkoman Foods in Wisconsin found that its American workers were worried about job security, they agreed to resort to layoffs only when uniform cutbacks in wages and salaries, including those of top management, failed to lead to the necessary results. The company has ten applicants for every job and as partial compensation for this policy can select a very high quality labor force.

To avoid layoffs in a cyclical economy, wages must be flexible as is the case at Kikkoman. Instead of forcing those laid off to bear the entire burden of the economy's cyclical behavior, the burden is shared, with everyone taking a wage cut to help the company through hard times. Social solidarity replaces economic homicide as a survival technique. There is also mounting evidence that social solidarity has enough positive effects on productivity to make it a better long-run survival technique than economic homicide.

Some American firms—Eli Lilly (no layoffs in 107 years), IBM (no layoffs in forty years), Hewlett-Packard, Digital Equipment, and Delta Airlines (no layoffs in over thirty years)—shun layoffs just as much as their Japanese competitors.[48] The short time horizon of much of American industry precludes such policies, however. Without layoffs there are periods of time when profits are going to be lower than they would be with layoffs.

In the long run a loyal, well-motivated, high-quality labor force interested in the success of the company is the only permanent comparative advantage a company can acquire. Everything else—technology, better equipment, natural resources—can be bought in the open marketplace. A high-quality economic team in contrast is something that money cannot buy. It must be created.

With less turnover, less rigid job classifications, and more open channels of communication, opportunities for talent to move up open up and there is also a better sharing of information. Fellow workers are not just competitors for limited job openings and higher wages. Foremen can become group leaders and pipelines of information up and down the organization rather than serving as middlemen squeezed between superiors blindly giving orders about they know not what and workers adhering to their traditional work norms regardless of impending disaster. What is often visible to one side (This job isn't designed so that a human being can do a quality job) is often invisible (This company is about to be crushed by foreign competition) to the other. And even if explicitly told about the other's problem, the level of distrust is so high that neither side believes the other.

Individuals, companies, and countries can commit economic suicide, with all parties arguing about their traditional rights and privileges as they all march over the edge of the cliff together, but it isn't necessary.

Participatory Management

According to public opinion polls American workers feel that their companies are not really interested in high-quality products. Companies have spoken too often about improving quality without evidencing any willingness to put in the resources and time necessary to get a high-quality product. Poor quality control is often seen as a reflection of a poor work ethic when in fact the connection is exactly the reverse. Inadequate quality control leads to a poor work ethic, for few people can work hard at producing what they know to be a low-quality product. To improve work ethics one has to demand high-quality performance. The "zero defect" goal of the Japanese engenders a better work effort than the "acceptable" quality level used by many American companies.

Jobs are more than money. Positive values are associated with good work. Man is by nature a tool-building animal and the workplace is where he expresses his creativity in using those tools. Most of us want a chance to be an "empire builder" even if only in our own little domain. Given this desire, participatory management can simultaneously contribute to both equity and efficiency. What is needed, however, is not some representative laborer on the board of directors —what the Germans call co-determination—but a willingness to make workers part of the local management team, to share information, and wherever possible to replace managers with workers who manage themselves.

The changes necessary can be seen in the traditional American procedure for ordering a new piece of capital equipment, say a drill press. Some industrial engineer typically looks at the tool catalogues, talks to the salesmen, places an order, and one day a new drill press appears on the shop floor—often as a surprise to the workers who are expected to operate it. Consider the differences if the workers who will eventually operate the press are allowed to look at the catalogues, talk to the salesmen, and sign the purchase and sales agreement. Much of the time workers will end up ordering the same piece of equipment that the engineer would have ordered, but even if they don't, the differences in the quality of equipment from one manufacturer to another are more than offset by the extra motivation created in the labor force. The equipment is *their* equipment and *they* have to prove that *they* have made a good decision. When the inevitable glitches arise, instead of standing aside and saying, "Let the bastard fix it, he ordered it," *they* will feel responsible to solve the problems that have arisen.

Since workers need to feel important, require variety, and enjoy making decisions, they do a better job on the production line or in the office when they can make important local decisions. Firms also find that they do not need to "waste" expensive engineering time making decisions that can be better made by someone else.[49] By using such techniques Lincoln Electric reduced its managers and supervisors to one for every hundred workers—far below the American average.

This change is what the quality-circle approach to management attempts to engender. If I may exaggerate a bit, the old-fashioned General Motors theory of management was "Don't think, dummy, do what you are told." With Buick City and its quality of working life program, GM is trying to engender a very different theory of management: "Think, I am not going to tell you what to do." Nothing could be more fundamental to American success than this shift and nothing is going to be more difficult to do.

To make such a system work, however, managers have to share information and goals with their labor force so that workers feel that the company goals are their goals and so that workers can make local decisions that are congruent with the firm's strategic posture. Workers in turn have to share local production information with managers so that they in turn can make the right decisions without the current reporting systems and without the large staffs of white-collar workers necessary to man those reporting systems.

When shifting to such systems the difficulties arise not so much with workers but with middle managers. Top management may decide that less hierarchy and fewer authority/status relationships are a good thing for productivity, but the idea scares middle managers. They are the ones being asked to give up authority and status. They know that successful participatory management will mean fewer supervisors and managers. They, not top management, risk being laid off or not being promoted. When the Gaines Dog Food plant of General Foods at Topeka, Kansas, went to self-management, the major stumbling blocks were to be found not among the work force but among middle management.[50]

CONCLUSION

If the foundations of the American economy are to be rebuilt, the rebuilding must begin with a reconception of the theory of the American firm. Conceived as a partnership, structured to promote common long-run goals, and operated to push decision making to the lowest possible echelons—the American firm can succeed. Operated as it is now operated, it can but fail.

While a few of the changes such as the bonus system needed in the reconception of the American firm can be encouraged by shifting the tax structure, most of the necessary changes have to come from within the private sector and cannot be imposed by government. Major elements of the Democratic party, such as the labor movement, however, can encourage business firms to move in the desired direction in their bargaining.

Just as importantly, since private enterprise produces most goods and services in America, the Democratic party has to have an intellectual conception as to how these firms should be run. The importance of such a conception can be seen in the uses to which Reagan Republicans have put their conception—"Get the government out of the economy and off of the backs of the entrepreneurs." It provides an organizing framework for looking at problems on the supply side of the economy. Although the Republican conception is often violated, as when the Reagan Republicans talk about free trade and practice protection, as a conception it is still important politically.

The flaw in the Republican conception is that it implicitly assumes that Americans will always be winners in any free market competition and that social organization is not important in creating a winning team. Neither assumption is true, as I have just tried to show in the case of the firm and will show in the case of labor, investment, and government in the next three chapters. Americans won't be winners unless they improve their social organization in all four of these areas.

Today's Democrats have no conception as to what should be done to make the market economy work better. Historically the Democratic answer was to focus on antitrust and government regulation to prevent monopolistic abuses. While there is still room for laws preventing predatory pricing by American or foreign firms, to a great extent that old Democratic conception is simply out of date. In the new world economy American firms are going to face strong foreign competition with active government backing even if they are very large and dominant relative to other American firms.

The obsolete thinking that still imprisons Americans was well illustrated in a January 1985 *New York Times* article "The Daunting Power of IBM."[51] The headline, all of the graphs, the data, and the first fifty-three paragraphs focused exclusively on IBM's strengths relative to its American competition. Only if one was willing to work one's way through more than one full newspaper page of dense printing did one finally learn that there were Japanese competitors to be considered.

The one paragraph that mentioned the Japanese as competitors never pointed out that the Japanese competitors were IBM's equal technologically and financially and that they are systematically reducing IBM's market share in Japan and the rest of the world. After this one paragraph the article then went on to make the argument that IBM was so weakening other American competitors that the Japanese success was due not to Japanese strengths but to the weakness that IBM was causing among these other American competitors. The article then returned to comparing IBM's strengths relative to American producers and ended with a quote—"Four years of unfettered growth for IBM at this high-growth stage of technology may be an extravagance that the country cannot afford"—taken from an industry magazine.[52]

What Americans cannot afford is such thinking. Big companies do sometimes crush small companies, but far better that small American companies be crushed by big American companies than that they be crushed by big foreign companies. Every American firm, big and small, was crushed in the video recorder industry before they got started. That is not a happening Americans can often afford.

When talking about supply-side problems the Democratic counter to "liberate the enterpreneur" should be "improve social organization." What America needs is not more government rules and regulations but better social organization. Within the firm this means partnership, value-added maximization, the bonus system, and a shift away from detailed job classifications. For other major inputs into the American economy it means a systematic effort to insure that all of these inputs are at world-class levels.

7 / A High-Quality Work Force

When the United States was overtaking Great Britain as the world's economic leader between 1860 and 1900, America had the best educated, most skilled labor force in the world. Mass high-quality compulsory public education was an American invention and America rode it to economic success. Where America once had the best-educated labor force, it now, however, has a labor force that does not stand comparison with most of the industrial world. Foreign firms with American production facilities have started to complain about inferior educational and job skills among their American workers and to attribute lower productivity in their American facilities to defects in the quality of the work force. They have every right to complain. Whenever and wherever quantitative comparisons are made, Americans do not show up well.

In 1981 one out of every two people who took the examination to become telephone operators in the city of New York flunked.[1] This should not have been surprising given that 8 percent of New York City youths between the ages of fourteen and twenty-one test out as functionally illiterate (i.e., they cannot read at a fifth grade level).[2] Most of these youths have left school and will not become literate in the future. While comparable figures are not available for other cities, officials at the National Center for Education Statistics believe that the proportions are similar elsewhere, since dropout rates and reading achievement levels in other urban school systems resemble those in New York. Using slightly tougher definitions of functional illiteracy, as much as 20 percent of the entire American work force may be functionally illiterate. In comparison less than 1 percent of the Japanese labor force is functionally illiterate.

In a national assessment of mathematics abilities only 17 percent of the thirteen-year-olds and 29 percent of the seventeen-year-olds could correctly answer the question "George had 3/4 of a pie. He ate 3/5 of that. How much pie did he eat?"[3] In an international study of mathematics ability for eighth and twelfth graders, Americans were not above average in anything.[4] The eighth graders ranked in the bottom tenth internationally and the twelfth graders were "markedly lower" than the international average in all seven of the areas tested. In another study of first and fifth graders where from a statistical point of view there should have been an equal number of Americans in the top and bottom group, there were four Americans in the bottom group for every one in the top group among first graders and sixty-seven Americans in the bottom group for every one in the top group among fifth graders.[5]

The problem is not just finding work for the functional illiterate in a high-tech scientific society that does not need functional illiterates but how society itself is to survive competitively if so much of its work force cannot effectively contribute. Poor educational performance is not just an individual problem. It is a national disaster. If left unattended, the unsuccessful pull down the successful.

Unfortunately the problems are not just concentrated at the bottom of the educational distribution. From 1966 to 1981 average test scores on the Scholastic Aptitude Test given to college bound high school seniors declined from 478 to 424 on the verbal part of the test and from 502 to 466 on the mathematics part of the test. Scores at the top of the distribution declined even more. While verbal scores were falling an average of 11 percent and math scores 7 percent, the number of students scoring over 600 (out of a total score of 800) declined 39 percent on the verbal exam and 19 percent on the math exam.[6] Since 1965 the average test score on the Graduate Record Examination given to college seniors bound for graduate school has declined 10 percent. Performance is falling faster at the top of the education distribution that at the bottom, and for some inexplicable reason test scores are falling substantially faster for women than they are for men.

When 19 different achievement tests were administered to students in different countries, Americans never ranked first or second, and if comparisons are limited to other developed nations only, the U.S. ranked at the bottom seven out of nineteen times.[7] Mean scores placed Americans in the bottom half of the rank-order distributions thirteen times and in the top half only six times. Comparison with students from underdeveloped countries were even more shocking. Iranian students passed Americans in vocabulary at age fourteen; students from Chile did so at age eighteen; Thai students scored closer to us in science at age eighteen than we scored relative to the next worst developed country. Given falling achievement scores within the United States, the educational gap with our economic competitors can only be wider in the early 1980s than it was in the early 1970s.

These results cannot be excused on the grounds that America has a more egalitarian education system with higher retention rates at the bottom of the educational distribution. After the data are corrected for higher retention rates and a more egalitarian distribution of opportunities, Americans are still at the bottom. As stated in a review of the international evidence, "The plain truth appears to be this: In the late 1960's and in the 1970's, American students did not perform as well as most of their peers in other developed nations, and their poor showing cannot be attributed mainly to egalitarianism that makes us encourage large majorities of our students to finish high school."[8]

There are some encouraging signs. The SAT test scores seemed to have bottomed out and maybe started up again. In the 1980 to 1983 period test scores quit falling, and in 1984 the average verbal score went up by one point while the average math test score was going up by three points.[9] Test scores in the bottom half of the educational distribution seem to have been improving in the lower grades in recent years.[10] In the math examinations given by the national assessment program students are tested at ages nine, thirteen, and seventeen. From 1973 to 1978 test scores declined for all three age groups, but from 1978 to 1982, nine- and seventeen-year-old test scores remained constant while thirteen-year-olds were improving 4 percent. Black and Hispanic students, while still below the mean, made a substantial 7 percent improvement.

No one knows, however, whether American education has hit bottom and is now headed up or merely temporarily pausing on the route to general illiteracy. Even if America has hit bottom and is slowly heading back up, however, there is no cause for self-congratulation or a feeling that the American education problem has been whipped. There still is an enormous gap between American workers and foreign workers when it comes to educational performance.

Once on the job such differences show up in what workers can be taught to do. The "just-in-time" inventory system works better abroad because the assembly line workers can be taught the simple operation research techniques necessary to implement it. They know enough mathematics to learn what must be learned. Foreign numerically controlled machine tools can be "unlocked" since blue-collar workers can be taught to do the necessary programming, while American machine tools are "locked" partly because blue-collar workers cannot easily be taught the necessary programming.

Math and science instruction has suffered as math and science teachers abandon our school systems in droves for better-paying industrial jobs. In 1982–83 thirteen times as many math and science teachers left teaching as entered teaching.[11] In 1981–82 half of the new math and science teachers hired were unqualified, hadn't taken enough math or science, to teach those subjects.[12] In the last ten years the numbers of people studying to be math teachers fell 79 percent and those studying to be science teachers fell 64 percent— and only half of those students actually end up being teachers.

The reasons are not hard to find. New teachers make $12,000, while new math or science graduates make more than $20,000 in industry. The same problem is now spreading to our colleges and universities. Over 40 percent of all science Ph.D. candidates are foreign students.[13] At the present rate there will be no "next generation" of science and math teachers in high schools or colleges.

Given the lack of qualified teachers, it should come as no surprise that the proportion of high school students enrolled in a science course fell from 60 to 48 percent from 1960 to 1980. Only one-third of all high school students will take three years of math and only one-fifth three years of science. Among college freshmen in New Jersey 61 percent cannot do simple algebra problems. Two-thirds of American high schools do not even teach calculus.[14]

Without good science instruction it is not surprising that out of every 10,000 workers twenty choose to be lawyers, forty accountants, and seventy engineers in the United States while in Japan the numbers are one lawyer, three accountants, and four hundred engineers.[15] With twice as many engineers on the payroll of the average Japanese firm, it should come as no surprise to learn that Japanese products are better engineered than those in America.

Nor is the contrast simply with Japan. While 6 percent of American undergraduate degrees are awarded in engineering, the comparable figures are 35 percent in the Soviet Union and 37 percent in West Germany. The next few decades will be a time of tough international competition in high-tech products. Clearly America cannot compete without math and science personnel.

From a public policy perspective any specific education or training program can be labeled a failure, but the basic goal, a well-educated labor force, cannot be abandoned regardless of the number of failures. Every failure simply has to be replaced with another attempt. One can be hard-nosed about illiteracy but the hard-nosed fact is that the functionally illiterate are going to be part of our society for the rest of their lives, and their children may carry on where they leave off. The functionally illiterate cannot be thrown overboard when the economic ship of state leaves the dock. They are on board for the duration. Without a well-educated labor force, enough engineers, and strong science education in our school systems, none of us is going to have a successful economy in the high-technology era ahead of us. To work, modern economies need a mass well-educated labor force. An educated elite does not suffice. Illiteracy hurts the literate.

This is particularly true if America moves to some of the participatory management techniques for improving its productivity performance outlined in the last chapter. To be used efficiently blue-collar workers have to be taught to program robots, and in the office of the future every clerical worker is going to have to be taught some of the functions of a computer programmer.

Social welfare programs may be a matter of ethics and generosity, but education and training are not. I am willing to pay for, indeed insist upon, the education of my neighbors' children not because I am generous but because I cannot afford to live with them uneducated.

This is a fact that President Reagan forgets at America's peril when he says that the student loan programs "defy common sense, insult simple justice, and must stop." [16]

SOURCES OF THE PROBLEM

While behind at high school graduation, Americans have comforted themselves with the idea that things do not look so bad at college graduation. Higher education is better in the United States than it is in Japan or Europe. While probably true, some of the problems that have been bedeviling elementary and secondary education are now spreading into higher education.

From 1984 to 1996 the number of Americans eighteen to twenty-two years of age will fall 28 percent.[17] Even under optimistic assumptions about increasing participation rates, enrollments are going to fall by one-fourth. Given such a fall, one way or another there is going to be a corresponding decline in university teachers. Without students to be taught someone has to be fired, even if all educators were super teachers and super scholars.

What happens when institutions do nothing but fire people for a decade? The best and the brightest with alternative job opportunities bail out first. This has been happening in our elementary and secondary schools for the past fifteen years. Smaller colleges are already suffering a disappearance of their math and science teachers. With the best leaving, the average quality of those who remain goes down. In the case of elementary and secondary school teachers the average Scholastic Aptitude Test scores of those choosing to go into teaching have been falling for more than a decade and are now thirty-two points below the national average in verbal abilities and forty-eight points below the national average in mathematical abilities.[18]

This phenomenon will be replicated in colleges and universities as enrollments fall. As enrollments fall, there will initially be a surplus of warm bodies and in accordance with supply and demand salaries will fall. Young people quite rightly decide that there are better things to do than become a university teacher. Who wants to be paid very little and then take a chance on being fired regardless of job performance? With seniority firings and few new entrants, the work force becomes older and more ossified.

Where there is only one question—"Who gets fired this year?"—morale and esprit de corps plummet. With no opportunities for promotions there are no positive rewards to be distributed. If good teaching doesn't pay off, why do it? Intellectual rigor is replaced with intellectual, sociological, and administrative rigor mortis. Instead of focusing on education, teachers quite naturally focus on self-survival.

It is nearly impossible to manage dying industries well. Think of other industries with declining sales. Such industries are never well run. The industrial landscape is littered with the wrecks of industries such as railroads or steel with declining sales. It is very difficult to run an efficient firm when there are no positive rewards to be distributed regardless of whether it is a private firm or a public agency—and education is no exception. Educational bureaucracies become worse, not better, in their death throes. Yet America cannot afford to let its education and training systems rot.

Private universities are going to find themselves caught in a squeeze between falling enrollments and cheaper state institutions. Unless they have something unique to sell, their only possible response is to lower standards and take students they would not previously have admitted. With falling enrollments it isn't realistic to expect universities to help raise elementary and secondary school graduation standards by increasing their own college admissions requirements.

State universities have been overbuilt in all but a few places. The rational efficient solution is to close one-quarter of the campuses and to run the remaining ones at capacity, but few states are going to be rational and efficient. What town wants its university closed down? The standard response will be to put enrollment limits on the popular state university campuses to force students to go to the unpopular campuses so that state legislators are never confronted with almost empty campuses. This is a policy of killing the best to save the worst, yet it is a policy already under way in at least one state.

Since the enrollment decline is behind elementary and secondary education, one can imagine a rebound in quality at this level. Institutions are going to be shifting from a negative to a positive mode with expanding enrollments and opportunities in front of them. This automatic turnaround is not going to get America to where it needs to be in terms of quality, but it is a step in the right direction and is going to make improvements much easier to make.

At the university level the only question is damage control. What America has to do is clear, although how America becomes tough-minded enough to do it is not clear. Instead of cutting every institution back by one-fourth, some technique has to be found to force the system to eliminate entire colleges or universities. Good departments have to be moved from bad universities and bad departments in good universities shut down. Across-the-board cutbacks are the easiest politically, but they are a long-run educational disaster.

This is very easy to say but very difficult to do. It can be done only if those making the decisions are willing to make some very unpopular decisions as to which of the institutions under their jurisdiction are their best institutions or departments. If those in charge aren't willing to make such decisions, then quality is going to decline.

How does a society most efficiently drive the worst firms out of an industry? There is no good answer, but consumer choice is one answer and restrictions on that choice should be vigorously resisted. If students don't want to go to some university, there are usually rather valid reasons as to why this is true. Enrollment restrictions should be resisted wherever they appear in our state systems. Those making charitable contributions to private universities should resist giving to institutions where enrollments are falling rapidly. However illustrious their history, they aren't providing a competitive product today.

Damage control isn't fun. It wasn't effectively carried out as enrollment declines rolled through elementary and secondary education, and today Americans are paying a price for that failure. As hard as damage control may be, it is much harder to rebuild institutions than it is to save them from decline. Effective damage control is going to be necessary in higher education if Americans do not want the rot in elementary and secondary education to spread to higher education at precisely the time they are acting to improve elementary and secondary education.

Beyond demography the problem, to put it bluntly, is "us." In the long run the public schools are us—they give us what we want. If Americans want tough, rigorous education, Americans will get it. If Americans want life adjustment and baby sitting, they will get it. Basically, Americans are too easily satisfied with what they get from their schools. In a comparative study of Sendai, Japan, and Minneapolis, roughly comparable cities, mothers were asked to evaluate their children's schools.[19] Despite the fact that the poorest performer in the Japanese group was well ahead of the best performer in the American group the Minneapolis mothers consistently thought that the schools were just fine, while the Sendai mothers were worried that their children were not performing up to potential. American mothers were willing to explain away the failures of their children in terms of lack of ability, while Japanese mothers saw failure as a lack of effort by someone—child, mother, school.

Schools sometimes seem out of touch with public opinion, but this is only because of lags in the adjustment process. Public opinion simply changes faster than the public schools can change. The public may want a more rigorous education system than the schools are delivering—our rhetoric, but not yet our resources, seems to indicate that is so—but it is important to recognize that today's schools reflect what Americans wanted yesterday. Low-quality public education was not a conspiracy foisted off on an unwilling public. If there is blame to be allocated, it must be allocated to ourselves and not to those that work in the classroom.

From 1963 to 1983 the average American household upped its viewing of TV 36 percent to more than seven hours per day.[20] Teachers report that they cannot assign homework because the students won't do it. Homework is precisely what it says it is—"homework." Homework may be assigned by teachers, but only parents can force students to do "home" work. If the parents won't play their role— inquire as to what work is to be done, turn off the TV set, make sure that the work is done—no teacher can succeed in the classroom. Without such parental support and parental reinforcement for the idea that the most important business of children is education, no education system can deliver a high-quality product. If two out of every thirty students fail to do their homework, school punishments may succeed in dealing with the problem, but if twenty out of thirty students fail to do their homework no school system can deal with the problem.

The Viet Nam war was a critical turning point of American education. Because hostility to the Viet Nam war seemed to be centered in American universities, the educational system was seen as vaguely unpatriotic and not worthy of support. Students did not appreciate what they had, and therefore what they had should be taken away from them. Paradoxically education also suffered the general loss of respect for authority that occurred when it became clear that our political leaders had lied to us and that the war would not turn out as Americans had been promised. Whatever its anti-war views, education was part of the establishment and should be punished for the failures of the establishment.

No one suffered a faster or greater decline in authority and respect than the public school teacher. Where supportive parents once felt that the teacher was better educated than they and hence the right person to make educational decisions, they were now unsupportive and felt themselves better educated than the teacher. Almost by definition teachers were vaguely incompetent. Not surprisingly almost 50 percent of today's teachers report that they would not choose teaching as a career if they had it to do over again. Superimpose the problems of declining enrollments, and there was an almost complete loss of educational self-confidence.

Most teachers and many parents can no longer look their children in the eye and say, "I know that mathematics is more important than pottery. You have to take mathematics." Formal educational requirements declined. Fewer than half of the nation's public high schools now require more than a year of science and mathematics. Even more important was a decline in parental and peer requirements. Fewer than one in ten high school students now study physics. Rigorous vocational and academic enrollments have declined. Those registering for less rigorous general education rose from 12 percent in the late 1960s to 43 percent in the late 1970s.[21] There is room in every student's curriculum for a few courses the equivalent of pottery making—but not many. "Potting" societies are in the end poor societies.

UPGRADING EDUCATION

The solutions are as clear as the problems. America knows how to upgrade its education system. After Sputnik, a rather minor but spectacular scientific defeat, the United States embarked on a program to upgrade human skills. Programs such as the National Defense Education Act led to improvements in science education, language skills, and basic literacy. For a decade after these programs were adopted SAT test scores rose. In some ways it is unfortunate that the United States reached the moon first and most of the education and training programs were then abandoned in the aftermath of what was also a rather minor, if spectacular, scientific victory. Once again "number one" in their own eyes, Americans abandoned the very educational efforts that allowed them to catch up with the Russians in space.

In the 1980s a much less dramatic but much more important economic defeat requires a similar but more sustained effort to upgrade the quality of the labor force. A high-quality school system begins with a public that wants a high-quality school system, gives high-quality education its total support, is willing to provide the necessary financial resources, and refuses to tolerate low standards. Unless these conditions exist, there is nothing that can be done inside the classroom that is going to improve American education.

The foreign countries that outperform America educationally all have three characteristics—a longer school year, a system of quality control, and a well-paid, respected teaching corps.

Among our competitors the school year and day are much longer. Foreign students work harder. In the United States the average school year is 180 days, runs five to six hours per day, and the average student is absent twenty days per year. In contrast Japanese schools run 240 days per year and six to eight hours per day with minimal absences. Many Japanese students also go to after-school classes to better prepare themselves for the examinations necessary to get into college.[22] The net result is almost twice as many hours in school per year in Japan as in the United States. European countries typically have a school year of 220 days. The 180-day school year is a hangover from an agricultural society that needed students on the farms in the summertime. That society no longer exists and Americans don't even know what to do with their children in the summertime, yet America still has the 180-day school year.

Given such differences in hours of work, it is a surprise that American students are not farther behind the international competition than they are.

The standard American response to proposals for a longer school year is to argue that Americans should learn to more efficiently use the current 180 days before they worry about adding more days. Such a response is to get the whole problem backwards. Instead of starting with what is easy to do—work longer and harder—Americans start with what is very difficult to do—work smarter. The argument is also a form of implicit American arrogance. Americans think that they can learn in 180 days what the rest of the world takes 220 to 240 days to learn. It also forgets that the rest of the world is trying to use its 220 or 240 days more efficiently.

To be effective, more work must be combined with a system of quality control. Abroad, students typically must pass a national achievement examination to graduate from high school. French children struggle with their baccalaureate examinations. The British have their A and O levels, and similar examinations occur across the industrial world. The nation knows what it wants and sets a high standard that local schools and students are expected to achieve.

Quality control is a universal American problem. It pervades our industrial establishments as it does our school systems. Yet if Americans won't set quality control standards in their education system why should anyone find it surprising that America won't set high-quality standards in its factories. The "no educational standards" society is a "low industrial standards" society.

Arguments against achievement examinations are often couched in terms of states' rights and not letting "big brother" in Washington run everything. That is a phony issue. Achievement examinations could be set at the state level, at the city level, or at the level of the local high school. National examinations are not the heart of the issue. Setting quality-control standards—somewhere, anywhere—is the issue. If such standards aren't set, everyone is kidding himself. Students think that they are high school graduates, they have diplomas, but functionally they are not high school graduates. They cannot do the work that foreign high school graduates can do.

Culturally biased testing is the other phony argument behind which Americans hide when talking about competency testing. There certainly can be subtle cultural biases in testing but that is not the issue in exit testing. Students are not being tested as to their IQ's so that they can be slotted into the school system. They are being tested as to whether they can demonstrate the skills that employers will demand that they demonstrate if they are to become successful workers. Can they do what is necessary—math, science, read and write the English language, know any foreign languages—to be economically successful? Those skills are culturally determined in the sense that they will be needed in the American economy in the coming decades, but that culture is precisely the culture in which all American students are going to succeed or fail. If exit tests focus on the skills people will actually need to be successful, there is nothing biased about such tests, even though they are culturally determined. All of us, for example, are going to live in a more mathematical society in the computer age, and the math is going to have to become more a part of each of our cultures.

While exit requirements could be set by the local school board, they are not likely to be. It is rational from the viewpoint of every local community, but not the nation, not to solve the problem. The solution is going to require money, many of the children are going to move away and work in some other community, and if the community really needs skills for local industry they can be hired from somewhere else—or so the belief goes. If local school boards were going to solve the problem they would have done so long ago. They watched it develop and did nothing. When Americans had a national disaster such as Sputnik they didn't leave it to the localities to confront it. They can't and they won't. The current educational disaster is no different.

Abroad, teaching is a well-respected, well-paid profession. Japanese teachers make an above-average wage; American teachers' wages are near the bottom for those with a college education.[23] Historically, American teachers have never been well paid. When women were forced to be schoolteachers for lack of alternative economic opportunities, American education could survive paying less than competitive wages. Most of us probably remember that good teacher, and for most of us she was probably female. "Good people" could be gotten without "good" pay. But that captive supply of teachers has been liberated and is no longer there. That good female teacher each American remembers in his own education now works for IBM. From now on schools are going to have to pay competitive wages if they want to get a competitive high-quality labor force.

In 1982 the median year-round, full-time male college graduate earned $30,000. Why should an average-quality American work as a teacher for less? If America wants superior qualities in its teachers it will have to be willing to pay more. Yet today's average teacher makes $20,000.[24] Teaching salaries are going to have to rise to be competitive with industry, not because there is a shortage of warm teaching bodies, there isn't, but because America needs high-quality people with the right skills in its classrooms.

With a competitive salary scale, America can demand competitive standards of performance from its teacher work force rather than having to accept the inferior standards of achievement it now accepts. To talk about raising teacher standards without raising wages is to talk about the impossible. In a capitalist economy Americans get the quality that they are willing to pay for. Today Americans are not willing to pay for quality. America spends 26 percent less on its school system than its leading competitor, Japan.[25]

No one can or should, however, pay competitive full-time, year-round wages for part-year work. The 180-day school year represents part-year work. No industry pays full-time wages for 180 days of work. The average full-time year-round American works more than 240 days per year. To get a competitive wage teachers must work a competitive year.

If the need for higher pay to get and keep better teachers is put together with the need to lengthen the school year so that our children can work longer and harder, there is a compelling case for a much longer school year. The school year should be lengthened from 180 to 240 days per year, students should be required to be in school a full five days per week (no half days off for teacher preparation or meetings), and the school day lengthened to seven or eight hours per day for those in high school. Within this lengthened school year, students should be required to complete a much larger number of courses leading to math, science, writing, and verbal sophistication.

In 1983 it would have taken $20 billion to raise teacher salaries from an average of $20,000 to $30,000 per year. (For how this is to be financed see Chapter 8.) A high-quality educational system won't come cheap. If Americans are not willing to pay such a price, Americans are not going to have a world-class educational system or a winning economy.

It is always interesting to see how each society can easily find the flaws and propose remedies for problems in other societies but not its own. Forty percent of all Soviet fruits and vegetables are produced on the 2 percent of the land area that is in private plots. Given their tremendous food shortages, the standard American response is to note that the Russians could solve their agricultural problem if they would just increase the land area in private plots by a small amount. But given Russian ideology and historical practices, this is very difficult to do.

Similarly it is just as obvious to an outsider that if starting salaries are $12,000 for new math majors in teaching and more than $20,000 in industry, few will go into teaching. American schools will have to pay more to get good teachers and are going to have to pay those in short supply (math and science) more than those in surplus supply (English and history). But this obvious and necessary solution is against our ideology (all teachers should be paid the same regardless of subject taught) and historical practice (schools are a part-time job). Americans and the Russians fail for the very same reasons.

Beyond a 50 percent increase in general salaries, the Federal government should establish a system of temporary salary bonuses paid directly to teachers where there is a national shortage in a particular specialty such as mathematics. These bonuses would rise and fall as shortages develop and are eliminated. Such bonuses are discriminatory, but they leave local government with an egalitarian wage scale that will be re-established once enough people have been attracted into the shortage areas. Any teacher can also earn the bonus by being willing to retrain and become certified in the shortage skills.

Unfortunately President Reagan has turned what should be a serious dialogue on what can be done to improve American education into a trivial dispute about the virtues of merit pay for super teachers, often known as master teachers.[26] Whatever you believe about the merits of using some criterion to designate a small group of master teachers, merit pay alone is not going to solve problems emerging from a lack of parental support, a declining enrollment, collapsing intellectual self-confidence, a short working year, a lack of quality control, and a general salary structure that needs a lot more than a few small bonuses to a few workers to become competitive.

Good teachers should be rewarded, but to do so with a system of merit pay for those who are held to be super teachers violates every principle that industrial psychologists have learned about motivating workers to do a high-quality job. American industry is learning that workers can be motivated with narrower pay differentials and a more egalitarian structure of fringe benefits. Good students require a steady sequence of good teachers. To say that 15 percent of the teachers are going to be called master teachers and get a premium wage may raise their performance, but what happens to the performance of the 85 percent who are not designated master teachers? To get good schools America needs good teams of teachers, not a few stars. Given current wage scales, the bonuses would also have to be very large just to give the stars a wage competitive with average workers in the rest of the economy.

Suppose someone came into your place of work, evaluated everyone's performance, labeled a few of you "master workers," and gave such workers a 50 percent wage premium. Would productivity in your place of work go up or down? To ask the question is to answer it. The result would be disruptive and reduce average performances. No private industry pays people in such a manner.

In my career as a university teacher I have taught in two economics departments. Both were equally famous for their research. But one was famous for its good teaching while the other was infamous for its bad teaching. There were no significant differences in the ways that people were paid or in the size of the salary differentials. Both thought that research was important, and neither promoted people based upon their good teaching. The department that taught well believed that good teaching was a central responsibility and it was rewarded with peer respect. The other department did not respect good teaching and engendered no feeling that it was your number-one responsibility. Lately the department with poor teaching has significantly upgraded its performance, not by widening salary differentials but by changing its ethos of what is important.

Before the Reagan cutbacks in support for education occurred, the Federal government was spending $6 billion per year on elementary and secondary education. Since the longer school year will cost about $20 billion per year, Federal expenditures should rise to $20 billion so that the Federal government is essentially paying for the longer school year. Half of this money should be distributed to school districts as a bribe to get them to lengthen the school year to the 240-day, seven-to-eight-hour norm suggested above. No local government would have to lengthen the school year, but they would not be eligible for their share of the $10 billion in local aid if they did not.

The remaining $10 billion in Federal aid should, however, be allocated in a very different manner so as to promote quality control. Basically the system should be structured so that quality control is seen as a group responsibility and so that all can be a winner if they improve the quality control of their group. To do this the remaining $10 billion should be allocated based on the performance of the school district's high school seniors on national competency examinations. No school district would be required to take the national competency tests, but no district would be eligible for any of the $10 billion unless it did.

Any reform of the educational system has to start with the realization that educational performance is to a great extent dependent upon the family and not solely upon the schools. Children from different income, educational, and family backgrounds are *initially* going to have very different average scores on any achievement examination. But that is not a valid excuse for producing a poor product at graduation or for the conclusion that national achievement examinations cannot or should not be used to judge how well a school system is doing.

Given any competency examination, it is relatively easy to work out how well the children of any school could be expected to score given the income, education, and ethnic backgrounds of the students in that school. States should set minimum standards for graduation, but the Federal examination should be used to judge a school's performance relative to the expected norms for schools with students of the same background. The $10 billion in Federal aid should be awarded to schools based upon how well the children in that system scored relative to the norms for their peer group. Thus a suburban school district with an expected norm of 90 and an actual score of 85 would get very little while a slum school district with an expected norm of 40 and an actual score of 50 would get a lot.

While some of the $10 billion might be used to expand education programs, most of the money should be used as bonuses for teachers. Teachers who work in school systems where students end up doing well relative to the norms for schools of their type should be paid more than teachers who work in schools that perform poorly. Schools should be judged and teachers paid based on the quality of their output. Merit pay should exist, but merit should be based on measurable output and paid on a team basis.

National achievement tests can also help restore the esprit de corps, self-confidence, and authority of the teacher. The willingness to set such examinations indicates that our society knows what it wants and needs to be successful and that it is willing to reward those who produce a high quality product. Teacher authority would be enhanced, since teachers would have a society behind them willing to say that without the ability to read and write, to do mathematics, to understand basic science, to have a knowledge of history, and to speak foreign languages, it is the considered judgment of society that both the student and the society will fail. It is not the test against the student but Americans as a national economic team versus failure.

Academic achievement can lead to increased spirit and self-confidence among students just as much as athletic achievement.[27] Everyone loves to win, and there is no reason why each school district cannot outscore the historical norms for schools of its type. Schools that have shifted to stiffer requirements report that better discipline is one of the side effects. A high-quality standard raises the work ethic for students as well as workers. Both students and workers like to have a goal worth striving for, to know what is expected of them, to receive feedback on their progress, and to receive rewards and praise when they succeed. Soft productivity in the workplace is not all that different from soft productivity in the school.

In the last two or three years a number of reports have heightened America's concerns about its school system. There are now limited efforts under way to correct the situation. As yet, however, the efforts are not commensurate with the problem. Education has been a Democratic interest for decades. This an old tradition that should be refurbished by Democrats at every level of government.

At the college level President Reagan's budgetary attack on student grants and loans must be resisted but only after rethinking the purposes of those grants and loans. The President proposes to focus grants and loans on a very small number of low-income families.[28] In a narrow economic sense this is the efficient cost-effective thing to do, but in a more general political sense such a focus is equivalent to killing the programs. With the beneficiaries limited to a small and politically powerless group, it will be easy to completely kill the programs in the next budget cycle.

More importantly, college grant and loan programs are not solely for the benefit of those getting the grants or loans. They are designed to create an American work force that can compete with those in the rest of the world. That is a national goal, not just an individual goal. The subsidies going to college education are equivalent to the compulsory attendance laws for elementary and secondary education. They both embody the idea that there is a national interest in education that goes beyond mere personal choice. It isn't appropriate to require attendance at a university, but it is appropriate to offer a bribe.

The balance of grants and loans should also be rethought. Here again in a narrow economic sense it makes sense to use subsidized loans. A given amount of money simply goes a lot farther. It may not make sense, however, in a more general social sense. What happens when a nation graduates a generation deeply in debt as it leaves school? Students rightly worry about those large debts. To repay them quickly one must earn "big bucks." Such loans may create a materialism among the young which is both unattractive and socially disruptive. They focus on maximizing their own income and forget about their larger social obligations.

All of today's polling evidence points to a very materialistic and self-centered generation of college students. In little more than a decade the proportion of college students who report that they are going to college primarily to earn more money has risen 40 percent.[29] Economically in the long run it makes no difference whether each generation pays for its own education with loans or whether each generation pays for the education of the generation following it—its children. Socially, however, it may make a large difference in basic attitudes. No one knows for sure how attitudes are formed, but I would lean toward a college aid system where the mix of loans and grants is heavy on the grants side of the ledger.

The Non-College Bound

Whatever their ultimate quality the American economy is not going to succeed based on the skills of the one-half of the work force who enter college or the one-third who eventually graduate from college. The skills of the non-college bound are just as important yet America does not even have a system of post-secondary skill training for them.

Historically, Americans have relied on an informal system of on-the-job training where skills are casually passed from worker to worker. In the early 1960s the President's Automation Commission found that 80 to 90 percent of working skills had been learned in such an informal process. A good secondary education was an important background characteristic, making it easier to learn working skills, but by itself it usually did not produce adequate working skills.

During recessions America's failure to train enough skilled non-college workers is hidden, but shortages become apparent whenever unemployment falls. What do employers complain about in tight labor markets? Certainly not an inability to hire unskilled workers or college-educated labor. Complaints almost always focus on shortages of skilled blue-collar workers—machinists, tool and die makers, etc.

These complaints are authenticated in earnings data. Relative wages should rise in shortage occupations, and this is what is found. The earnings of year-round, full-time skilled blue-collar workers have risen from 72 to 88 percent of those of professional workers between 1972 and 1981.[30] Skilled blue-collar workers are becoming increasingly valuable because they are becoming increasingly scarce.

Much of this scarcity is produced by frequent recessions. In recessions informal worker-to-worker skill training essentially stops. New half-trained workers are laid off and often move on to other jobs where they must start over learning new skills. With a seniority system of job allocations, new workers are bumped back down the job queue to less skilled jobs. In these less skilled jobs they are no longer in a position to learn new skills and their old skills atrophy from disuse.

When the economy enters its next expansion phase, it runs into bottlenecks created by the failure to train skilled workers during the previous recession. Production cannot expand as fast as demand because of skilled labor shortages. As rising demand presses in on limited supplies, prices rise. In a collectively self-defeating effort to get the skilled blue-collar workers they need, employers begin to raid one another for labor. Wages soar. Foreign firms, such as the Japanese in the machine tool industry, step in under such circumstances to take that part of the American market which American firms cannot service. Once entrenched they are hard to dislodge. With wages and prices rising from skill shortages, monetary and fiscal authorities step on the economy's brakes to prevent inflation from accelerating. In a vicious circle, recession-induced shortages of skilled workers produce recessions, which further increases the shortages of skilled workers.

Since skilled blue-collar workers have essentially reached full employment while there are still millions of unemployed unskilled workers, the national unemployment rate must be held at very high levels to prevent inflation. In 1978 many observers felt that the economy was operating at its non-inflationary capacity, although it was using only 84 percent of its manufacturing capital and 94 percent of its labor force.[31] If 16 percent of the existing capital stock must be idle to stop inflation, however, companies have little incentive to invest. With depressed investment productivity, growth slows further and the economy becomes even less competitive on international markets.

In an increasingly technological society skilled non-college blue-collar workers become more and more important. New machines and products may be invented and designed by college workers, but they are built and maintained by skilled non-college workers. On a visit to an Arizona copper mine and smelter, I was told by the manager that he had more than twice as many workers in maintenance and repair as he had in production. Robots may build the cars of the future, but skilled human beings are going to maintain and repair those robots. In the office of the future the skill mix will shift in the same direction. There are going to be fewer unskilled production workers who keep the paper flowing and more skilled workers who operate and maintain the machines that keep the paper flowing.

At full employment there are endemic shortages of non-college skills. The American economy is producing plenty of economic generals and too few skilled economic combat troops. The American machine tool industry, for example, is rapidly losing ground to its German and Japanese competitors, partly because it cannot service either its domestic or international markets during periods of robust economic growth. The skilled workers that it depends upon just don't exist and aren't being trained.

Traditionally firms have been much more prone to lay off non-college than college workers in recessions. While craftsmen and skilled operatives accounted for 26 percent of the work force, they suffered 62 percent of the unemployment in 1982.[32] While white-collar workers had a 5 percent unemployment rate, skilled blue-collar workers had a 10 percent unemployment rate. Most striking, in the

1981 to 1982 recession 90 percent of the firms that laid off blue-collar workers laid off not one white-collar worker.

Such a system is unfair but it is also inefficient. High unemployment rates for skilled blue-collar workers send an incorrect market signal to both individuals and companies. Individuals are implicitly told that they should not choose these occupations—that they are in surplus supply. They are also told that the occupations are very risky. If they acquire the skills, there is a high probability that a recession will intervene to make it impossible for them to employ their skills. No one willingly chooses economic insecurity, given the lifetime nature of investment in skilled trades. The normal human desire is to be very risk-averse when it comes to our own standard of living. In this context it is not surprising that repeated recessions lead to greater reductions in skilled labor supplies than would be warranted if one simply looked at earnings averaged over some long period of time. The fact that employed skilled blue-collar workers make 88 percent as much as professional workers is of little solace if one is unemployed.

Companies are implicitly told that they should not invest in training programs and that they can, if desired, simply hire already trained workers. And during recessions or periods of slow economic growth they indeed can. But while it is rational for any one employer to think that he can simply hire skilled workers from the pool of already trained workers if they are needed, what is possible for any one employer is impossible for the economy as a whole. When the next boom comes, the skilled workers aren't available and economic growth grinds to a halt.

Recessions tend to be analyzed in terms of lost production and the associated individual privation of unemployment. Important as these issues are, they are probably less important than the adverse long-run impacts on efficiency and competitiveness. To adopt an anti-inflationary strategy of frequent recessions is to adopt a strategy of destroying the economy in order to save it. Part of the better performance abroad since World War II is found in a history with many fewer recessions. While America was having nine recessions Japan was having two. That meant nine cutbacks in American on-the-job skill training and two in Japan.

Historically, many of America's skilled blue-collar workers have been attracted from abroad, especially Germany, because of higher American wages. With the ability to earn an American standard of living without having to live in America increasingly available, this supply of skilled workers is gradually fading away at just the time that a competitive world economy is making those skills ever more essential. From now on America is going to have to design and operate a system of training its own skilled non-college workers, or they simply will not exist.

Basically, the problem lies in an institutional structure where no one has an economic incentive to take responsibility for insuring that enough skilled workers exist. Government is involved in manpower training programs for augmenting the earning abilities of low-income individuals, but it has stayed out of the business of training middle- or high-income skilled non-college workers, with the exception of some limited apprenticeship programs in the construction trades. In West Germany, government solves the problem with elaborate apprenticeship training programs for those who do not go to college. These programs are jointly financed by government and industry, involve formal education as well as substantial on-the-job experience, and start at age fourteen or fifteen. In Japan with its lifetime employment where workers cannot easily quit (no one would hire them since a worker who quits is by definition not a good worker), companies train their own skilled blue-collar workers. They know if they don't train, they won't have any skilled workers, since raiding others is impossible. Conversely, they also know that they will get the lifetime use of any training that they do give to the work force. No one is going to raid them. In the jargon of the economist, the job market has been structured so as to internalize the externalities of training. The benefits of training can be captured by firms doing the training, and therefore they have an incentive to train.

In contrast American industry does not want to train skilled blue-collar workers, because they are expensive to train, are apt to quit for a better job before an employer can recoup the costs of training, and are not needed during our more frequent recessions anyway. The externalities of training have not been internalized, and therefore no one does enough training.

Even in an expanding economy acquiring skills by osmosis is not the best method. In many cases it is very difficult to even tell someone how they could acquire certain skills. For example, suppose that someone wanted to be a skilled machinist. They must get an entry level job with a firm that employs machinists and then hope that the firm will expand so that skilled jobs will open up and that they will be in a position where other workers will offer them the chance for informal on-the-job training. Workers formally trained in Germany or Japan are more skilled than workers informally trained in the United States, and just as with engineers or mathematicians America will not compete with inferior skills.

Much of what must be known to run successful manpower training programs is known from previous experience. Manpower training programs can only be effective when the trainees know that if they perform satisfactorily during the training process there is a definite job waiting for them. As a result the training process must be closely linked with and often run by private employers. No one works hard in a training program if there is a high probability of not finding work in the desired trade at the end of the program. It is also rational for anyone to drop out of a training program whenever an alternative job appears if jobs are not directly connected with training. Everyone needs income, and a definite bad job today is simply worth more than the uncertain probability of getting a good job tomorrow. Without job certainty at the end of the successful completion of a training course, dropout rates are very high. If this occurs costs are very high, since much of the training is wasted on those who do not complete the training. In recognition of this reality, income support grants were added to manpower training programs in the 1970s. When the Reagan Administration cut these income support grants in 1981 as unneeded luxuries the Reagan Administration was guaranteeing a big increase in dropout rates and per capita costs so high that they could then argue that the programs should be abolished in 1985.

To be a competitive world economy and to make America into a real equal-opportunity society, America should start investing in the human capital of its non-college citizens to the same extent that it now invests in its college citizens. The Democratic party should lead in this effort.

In 1983 the Federal government spent $7 billion and state and local governments $40 billion on higher education.[33] About $11 billion of state and local government expenditures were recouped in tuition and fees, but this still leaves a total net expenditure of $36 billion. Assuming four years of education, this amounts to a per capita subsidy of almost $12,000 per person over a four-year period of time.

A similar subsidy should be given to the non-college bound in the form of a skill voucher that they could gradually cash over their working lifetime at any approved employer training program. Employers could design training programs that they themselves ran or that they ran in cooperation with local schools and colleges. Students would pay for these training programs using their training vouchers. Sometimes such a system is referred to as an individual training account. Each individual worker would have a $12,000 bank account upon which he or she could draw to pay for training over a working lifetime.

To eliminate unscrupulous employers who collect payments without offering training the programs would have to be government certified just as colleges must now be certified. To collect what the student was willing to pay, the employer would have to keep the worker in training and employment for the same four-year period of time that it now takes to complete a college education. Given the prevalence of seniority hiring and firing it would be very difficult for any employer to fire these newly trained workers at the end of four years. Even if he did, however, as long as the training is real and not fraudulent, the new worker has something to take with him to the next job.

Such a program would be both more equitable and more efficient than what we have now. Equity—equal education investments in those going and not going to college—can be used to create efficiency —a more productive economy.

While an extra $14 billion for elementary and secondary education and a $36 billion program for training the non-college bound sounds very large, there really isn't any choice. Americans can do it and compete in world markets with a high-quality labor force or Americans can refuse to do it and not be able to compete. If the latter occurs, America loses a lot more than $50 billion per year.

Such a buildup in American education is much smaller than the buildup in the Defense Department ($115 billion) enacted in the first four years of the Reagan Administration. It is a buildup that should be proposed by Democrats, financed with a new tax system that will be outlined in the next chapter, and enacted by Democrats when they next win control of the political process.

8 / More Investment and Saving—Public and Private

Conservatives tend to see inadequate investment as the sole cause of America's productivity problems and lower taxes on capital investment as the sole cure for America's productivity problems. Neither the diagosis nor the prescription is correct. As seen earlier, American investment in plant and equipment has gone up, not down, over the past fifteen years. Baby-boom demography is the major cause of the decline in the capital-labor ratio, and the capital-labor ratio can at most explain no more than 25 percent of the observed slowdown in productivity growth.

In 1981 the Reagan Administration essentially abolished taxes on new capital investment with its accelerated cost recovery system, yet investment remained essentially unchanged—11.5 percent of the GNP under President Carter and 11.4 percent of the GNP in the first four years of President Reagan. Personal savings rates actually fell from 6 percent of disposable income under President Carter to 5.5 percent of disposable income in 1983 and 1984, when Reagan's personal income tax cuts were fully in place. The Republican prescription was taken, but lower taxes on capital did not lead to more savings and investment.

Inadequate investment is not the sole cause of America's competitive problems, but Democrats need to realize that it is one of the causes. If America is to be competitive and American workers are to have the latest technology to match that used by workers abroad, capital per worker must grow at least as rapidly in the United States as it does in the rest of the industrial world. For this to happen America must invest much more than it has been investing. To do this, however, it is not necessary to construct a regressive tax system with lower taxes for rich capitalists and higher taxes for the average working person.

In 1983 the United States invested 17 percent of its GNP in plant and equipment, housing and inventories (see Table 6). Only the United Kingdom invested less. Japan was far ahead, investing 28 percent of its GNP. Since the United States enjoyed a booming economy in 1983 while the rest of the world was still mired in or slowly recovering from the 1981–82 recession, Americans in a very good year were being out-invested by the rest of the world in a mediocre year.

TABLE 6
SAVINGS AND INVESTMENT

	Percent of GNP	
	Personal Savings Rate[1]	Gross Fixed Capital Formation[2]
Country	1982	1983
United States	6%	17%
Italy	24	18
Germany	14	21
Japan	18	28
France	16	20
Canada	13	20
United Kingdom	11	15

The plant and equipment investment gap is also larger than the gross investment gap, since Americans tend to invest more in housing. There is nothing wrong with housing investment, but the funds to finance it cannot be taken from business investment if America is to remain competitive.

LOW AMERICAN SAVINGS RATES

If Americans are to invest more, they must save more. Some investment funds can be borrowed from abroad, some investment funds can be generated by internal corporate savings or government savings (see below), but high-investment countries all have high personal savings rates. In 1982 America's personal savings rate was essentially one-half that of the next worst industrial country and only one-fourth that of Italy—the world's leader in personal savings (see Table 6).

Since government deficits represent funds borrowed from private savings to finance public consumption, deficits represent a subtraction from savings. To get the net flow of funds provided by the rest of the economy to the business sector it is as a consequence necessary to subtract government dissavings (deficits) and expenditures on new housing. If this is done, the net savings flowing into the business sector from the government and household sectors was actually an outflow (negative savings) of 0.8 percent of the GNP under President Carter. Internally generated business savings were diverted from plant and equipment investment and used to finance housing and the government deficit.[3]

In the 1980 election campaign President Reagan rightly charged that this was unacceptable and that Americans saved too little. In 1981 President Reagan proposed and enacted corporate and personal income tax cuts biased toward high-income groups on the theory that such a bias would provide more disposable income to those able and willing to save. It didn't work. In the first four years of the Reagan Administration personal savings were down and government deficits were up. As a consequence the negative savings rate rose and 2.5 percent of the GNP was diverted from business investment to housing and the government deficit.[4] In 1984 individuals saved $157 billion, and state and local governments saved $52 billion, but the Federal government deficit absorbed $176 billion and housing absorbed another $154 billion. No country can compete and grow under such circumstances.

If one inquires as to why the rest of the world saves so much and the United States so little, the answers are not to be found in ancient samurai traditions or mysterious Italian frugality. There are only three reasons why people save—they are misers, they wish to die rich, or they wish to buy something in the future that they cannot afford out of current income. While there are a few misers and a few who wish to die rich, most saving occurs because people want to buy something in the future.

If it is possible to get what they want without saving, however, this is precisely what they will and ought to do. If the goal is a $30,000 recreational vehicle that can be had with no down payment, that individual is not just a zero saver, he is a negative saver, for $30,000 must be borrowed from the pool of savings to finance his consumption. Conversely if he must save to pay for the recreational vehicle before he gets it, industrial firms can borrow his savings for industrial investment until he gets enough together to afford his recreational vehicle.

Personal savings rates measure not the gross amount that individuals save, but net savings—personal savings minus personal borrowings to buy consumption goods. The difference between low American savings rates and higher German or Japanese ones is not so much in differences in our gross personal savings rates as in the amounts that Americans are permitted to borrow back to finance consumption.[5] In 1982 consumption lending absorbed 66 percent of gross personal savings in the United States.[6] Savings would have more than doubled if there had been no consumer credit.

The rest of the industrial world saves more because it is more restrictive with consumer credit—down payments are larger, repayments must be faster, and interest charges are not tax deductible. America's industrial competitors don't allow consumer credit to eat up 66 percent of their gross personal savings. The "no down payment" society may be individually rational, but it is socially irrational. In a "no down payment" society there is no one left to finance the industrial growth that America needs to remain competitive and to have a rising standard of living. When Americans were richer than the rest of the world and had a big technological lead, they could afford the "no down payment" society—they could get by investing less—but that time is past.

Americans are like everyone else. They will save if they cannot get what they want without saving, and they won't save if they can get everything that they want without saving. It's that simple. Saving is not an end in itself anywhere. It is a means to an end—future consumption—everywhere.

The Reagan Administration tried to stimulate savings with individual incentives (lower income taxes, more generous tax-free savings accounts—IRA's, Keoghs, etc.), but the strategy did not work. Savings did not go up.

Raising savings is a matter of social organization. One organizes a society where saving is individually rational. Consider what our industrial competitors have done to make it rational for their citizens to save.

In Canada mortgage interest payments are not tax deductible. In Germany consumer interest payments are not tax deductible. Both make it more expensive to borrow money to finance housing or consumption. In Japan a 40 percent cash down payment is required to buy a house. The saving necessary to do this can be borrowed by industry until the family reaches that 40 percent goal. Austrians are subject to a value-added tax (a tax on consumption) that is 15 percent on necessities and 30 percent on luxuries, with cars being classified as luxuries. Buy a $10,000 car, send $3,000 to the government. Don't buy the car, don't send the money. A rather strong reminder that "thou shalt not consume."

In Japan about one-third of earnings come as a twice-a-year bonus. Human beings of all races tend to adjust their standard of living to their monthly or weekly income and save more out of a bonus than they do out of their regular income.[7] Japanese savings rates, for example, are only high in the months in which they get their twice-a-year bonus (see Table 7). The Japanese also often get a large lump-sum cash settlement at retirement rather than a monthly pension.

TABLE 7[8]
JAPANESE PERSONAL SAVINGS RATES

Month		Savings Rate
September	1982	11.2%
October	1982	10.5
November	1982	10.0
December	1982	47.4
January	1983	3.2
February	1983	12.4
March	1983	5.0
April	1983	1.3
May	1983	5.0
June	1983	41.6
July	1983	30.0
August	1983	10.8

What would happen to the American savings rate if Americans lived in a society where all of these provisions were in effect? No one knows whether the American savings rate would go up to the 14 percent of the Germans or the 24 percent of the Italians, but everyone knows that savings would go up dramatically. For it is just such social incentives that have generated the much higher foreign savings rates that are making it difficult for America to compete.

The difficulties in moving from the current forms of social organization that discourage savings to forms of social organization that encourage savings are easily found. While almost everyone agrees that America needs more savings, almost everyone wants to keep the consumption breaks that benefit them. Think of the Washington lobbying that would occur if a President were to propose measures such as those just listed. Sears and General Motors would be there to testify against removing the tax deductibility of consumer credit. The housing industry would mobilize to defend the tax deductibility of mortgage interest. The labor unions would probably come out against bonuses. The insurance industry would want to retain monthly pensions. Each of these groups would say that they were for more savings and investment, but not these particular savings incentives that hurt them. Yet higher savings mean less consumption for someone and fewer sales for those who make their consumption goods.

Mathematically more saving is just another way of saying less consumption, and Americans won't really be serious about raising savings until they confront this reality. If each particular savings incentive is blocked on the grounds that it hurt some specific group, then no savings incentives will ever be adopted and America will never be able to rebuild its industrial structure. Americans can understand this reality, but they will only do what must be done if it is possible to construct a set of incentives such that the reductions in consumption are fairly shared across the income distribution. Equity is central when it comes to allocating sacrifices.

Not surprisingly, the real cost of capital is lower abroad, where there are more savings to be borrowed. In 1983 the real interest rate (the cost of funds minus the rate of inflation) was 2.1 percent in West Germany but 6.9 percent in the United States. With a lower cost of capital foreign firms can profitably invest in projects that would be unprofitable for Americans. Foreign workers can afford to work with equipment that Americans cannot afford.

By historical standards American savings rates are only slightly below their long-term norms. Personal savings averaged 6.7 percent of disposable personal income from 1945 through 1982.[9] For most of this time, however, America had a per capita income that was far above that of its competitors. A 6.7 percent American savings rate with a per capita income of $6,000 yields savings equal to a 20.1 percent Japanese savings rate with a per capita income of $2,000. Because of higher incomes lower American savings rates did not formerly mean less machinery per worker, but with little or any income gap remaining, lower savings rates now mean less savings. What was once viable is no longer viable.

Historically, low personal savings rates have been partially offset with high business savings rates. In 1983 businesses saved $455 billion or 13.7 percent of the GNP in the form of undistributed profits and capital consumption allowances.[10] This exceeded the same year's $341 billion in nonresidential business investment. American industry essentially ended up providing all of its own savings, financing a portion of housing investments, and underwriting all of the government deficit.

This system cannot continue. It provides too little savings for business investment now and is apt to provide even less in the future. High business savings rates were produced by high profit rates, and these in turn were produced by a technological lead that is disappearing. Foreign competitors are driving down American profit rates and in the future will be depressing business savings.

American firms need more investment funds, but they also need patient long-term equity financing as their traditional sources of internal finance dry up. This problem is compounded by other changes in our financial markets. Redemptions, policy borrowings, the difficulty of selling life insurance as an investment vehicle in an inflationary economy have all forced insurance companies to look for quicker returns and have all but dried up this traditional source of long-term industrial finance. Pension funds are growing, but pension fund managers are imposing shorter and shorter time horizons on their investments. The net result is an acute shortage of long-run equity investment funds to finance new activities.

Other countries are aggressively infusing new industries with capital at faster rates than has been occurring in the United States. For a while funds can be borrowed on world capital markets, and Americans are now doing so at record rates. It is only this lending that has stopped the Federal deficit from crowding private investment out of the capital markets, but no economy can forever exist on foreign debt capital. At some point the lending stops. When it does, private American investment will essentially stop with it. The Federal government will have to drive interest rates ever higher to get the money it needs to finance the Federal deficit, and private firms will not be able to profitably invest at those higher interest rates.

To raise American investment, the personal savings rate has to go up and government borrowing has to go down.

HOW MUCH MORE SAVINGS?

In a competitive world one has to save and invest as much as one's most aggressive competitor. Japan is probably that competitor, but Japan is still behind the United States in terms of per capita GNP and average productivity. As a result it is not yet necessary to keep up with the Japanese. It is, however, necessary to keep up with the investment rates in the European countries that are already equal to or slightly ahead of America in terms of productivity. Since America's work force is growing more rapidly than Europe's work force, for capital-labor ratios to grow at the same rate America's investment has to be somewhat higher than that in Europe.

To keep capital per worker rising as fast here as there it is easy to work out what fraction of the GNP America will have to invest. In 1982 Americans invested 11 percent of the GNP in industrial plant and equipment. Given potential hours of work growing at 4 percent per year, America has to invest 13 percent of the GNP just to keep its capital-labor ratio constant. To keep America's capital-labor ratio growing at European rates would have required an investment of 20 percent of the GNP in 1982. And if Americans want to invest a normal amount in housing, another 5 percent of the GNP would have to be invested for an aggregate investment rate of 25 percent.

As a result America should set itself the goal of increasing gross fixed investment to 25 percent of the GNP in seven years. Relative to 1984's gross investment rate of 18 percent, investment would have to rise 7 percentage points or 1 percentage point per year. Since our economy's potential growth rate exceeds 1 percent per year, absolute standards of living do not have to be reduced to meet this goal. Social discipline in the form of less consumer credit is necessary to limit consumption's growth below where it otherwise would be, but no one has to have a falling standard of living.

To reach this goal Americans will have to raise their personal savings to something like 15 percent of disposable personal income or 11 percent of GNP and convert the Federal government from a dissaver into a saver. Instead of running a deficit equal to 5 percent of the GNP, the Federal government should be running a surplus so that government (state, local, and Federal) contributes 2 percent of the GNP to the pool of savings.

Raising savings rates *only temporarily* means a slower growth of consumption. Permanent reductions in the growth of American standards of living are not required. Quite the reverse, with more capital per worker productivity growth can accelerate, earnings can rise, and even though a higher fraction of these earnings must be saved, consumption can grow faster than it is now growing. All that is needed is a temporary period when consumption standards of living do not grow as fast as they otherwise would.

Once the transition to higher savings rates is made and the new plant and equipment comes on line, consumption can grow at a much faster rate than it is now growing. If the output available to be divided is growing at a 1 percent rate, consumption can only grow at this rate. No one can divide what isn't there. Suppose that with a 15 percent savings rate to increase investment and productivity, output started to grow at 2 percent. Once the transition has been made to that 15 percent savings rate, personal income can be divided into two parts, an 85 percent consumption part and a 15 percent savings part, each growing at 2 percent per year. There are no sacrifices, only gains to be had once a society has made the transition to a high savings rate.

Paradoxically, permanent sacrifices result only if Americans are not willing to make temporary sacrifices. Given a negligible productivity growth from the first quarter of 1979 to the last quarter of 1982, for example, the per capita GNP fell 4 percent. This negative trend will return once the current cyclical recovery is over unless Americans provide the investment resources necessary to make the economy competitive.[11]

Americans face a very simple choice. They can make temporary sacrifices in the rate of growth of their consumption standards of living today to provide the resources necessary to put that standard of living back on a rapid upward path tomorrow, or they can refuse to sacrifice today and find that tomorrow they are forced to sacrifice because there is less to be divided among Americans. It would be nice if there were a better choice, but there isn't.

Essentially this is what the Japanese and Germans were forced to do after World War II. When General MacArthur took over Japan, everything was blown up and no one had any income. Yet for a period of time he had to build factories to produce the materials necessary to build more factories. Once this process had been completed Japan could let consumption rise. Given devastated economies, Germany and Japan had no choice but to hold personal consumption down until they had rebuilt their capital stocks. Once rebuilt, they were smart enough to keep in place many of the forms of social organization necessary to promote the recovery from World War II.

America's capital stock has not been blown up, but much of it needs to be modernized and expanded if America is to compete. Americans have to force themselves to do what Germany and Japan were forced to do after the war. In the past Americans have prescribed it for others. Now they have to take the same medicine.

THE TRICKLE-DOWN SOLUTION

"Trickle down" was President Reagan's solution to the savings and investment problem. Taxes would be cut for the rich, and these cuts would be financed with cuts in social welfare spending for the poor. Eventually the higher savings of the rich were to have provided more investment and hence more jobs for the poor. The strategy did not work, and while it is important to understand why it did not work, it is even more important to understand why it could not have worked.

It did not work because higher after-tax incomes do not automatically lead to more savings. Saving is not a goal by itself but a means to having more consumption in the future. *If individuals can reach their consumption goals without saving, that is precisely what they should do.* And it is what they do. In 1981 America's high-income citizens were given large tax cuts and large increases in after-tax disposable income, but they consumed most of it. Trickle-down economics can work theoretically, but only in a society without plentiful consumer credit where high-income individuals have a high propensity to save out of additional income.

But even if the rich were to have had high marginal propensities to save, trickle-down economics runs into another arithmetic problem. Suppose, for example, that households with incomes below $23,000 per year (the bottom 60 percent of the population in 1982) saved nothing and that households with incomes over $55,000 (the top 5 percent of the population) saved 100 percent of any additional income they received. To raise personal savings by 5 percentage points of the GNP government would have to take $154 billion from the zero savers (the bottom 60 percent of the population) and give it to the 100 percent savers (the top 5 percent of the population). With such a transfer the bottom 60 percent would suffer a 26 percent cut in their after-tax incomes while the top 5 percent would get a 49 percent increase in their after-tax incomes.[12] The actual income transfers would also have to be much larger than this, since the bottom 60 percent do some saving while the top 5 percent could not be expected to save 100 percent of their extra income. To raise savings rates by 5 percent of the GNP would require such huge shifts in the distribution of income that they simply are not realistic in a democracy.

Trickle down hasn't worked in America and it also isn't the source of higher savings rates abroad. Foreign countries have not found the route to success by cutting social welfare payments for the poor so that they would be forced to save more and work hard to protect themselves against the hardships (unemployment, illness, old age) of life. While Japan spends a smaller fraction of its GNP on government than America, it now spends a greater percent of its GNP on social welfare activities. Lower defense spending more than offsets higher civilian spending. The Germans simply spend more. In the United States, governments (state, local, and Federal) absorb 32 percent of the GNP but in Germany almost 50 percent.[13] And this does not include the spending of Germany's nationalized firms and industries —railroads, utilities, telephones, and a number of partially or totally government owned companies such as Volkswagen. If they are included, the German government controls far more than 50 percent of the GNP.

Foreign countries have not found it necessary to widen income differentials to encourage individuals to save. If wider income differentials were the key, the United States should have the second-most successful industrial economy in the world, for only the French have more after-tax inequality. In the United States there is an 11 to 1 gap between the average income of the top and bottom quintiles (20 percent) of the population; but the Germans run an efficient economy with a 7 to 1 gap, and the Japanese run an even more efficient economy with a 5 to 1 gap.[14]

Neither is it possible to argue that somehow Americans are just different and require more inequality than foreigners to save and work hard. There is a 5 to 1 income gap in the distribution of earnings between the highest and lowest quintiles for fully employed white American males. What is still the dominant work group works hard with approximately the same earnings gap that keeps the Japanese working hard. Among the rest of the American population the earnings gap is 27 to 1. Unless Americans believe that fully employed white males are brought up in a different culture with a different set of values than everyone else, the income gaps that keep white males on their economic toes should be adequate to keep other Americans on their toes as well.

A SERIOUS PROGRAM FOR RAISING PERSONAL SAVINGS

Restricting Consumer Credit

To raise personal savings America must begin by eliminating the "no down payment" society. In the spring of 1980 the Carter Administration placed restrictions on the use of credit card credit. Consumption purchases almost instantly fell. Since the restrictions were not combined with a program to raise investment by easing interest rates and cutting taxes, however, President Carter's restrictions simply produced a recession. But his actions demonstrated the effectiveness of limits on consumer credit if lower consumption is desired.

The sudden elimination of consumer credit, however, would be too great a shock for the American economic system to absorb. American consumers would have to go through a transition period where they were still paying off old debts and have not yet had time to accumulate the savings that would allow them to start purchasing the consumer goods they would purchase in a world with less consumer credit. What is needed is a gradual five-year program for reducing consumer credit.

The program would start with a five-year phaseout of the tax deductibility of consumer credit. In the first year only 80 percent of consumer interest charges would be tax deductible, in the second year only 60 percent, and so on until no consumer interest charges were tax deductible in the fifth year. At the same time minimum down payments would be raised 5 percentage points per year—5 percent the first year, 10 percent the second year, etc. Consumer credit tax deductions would fall and down payments would rise until the

American personal savings rate reached the target level—15 percent. If this occurred before the tax deductibility of consumer credit had been completely eliminated, consumer credit would remain partially tax deductible.

Since such a change is not a marginal change in the incentive structure facing individual American consumers, no one knows, or can know, exactly how restrictive consumer credit provisions must be to meet national savings objectives. As the program gets under way, however, it will be possible to see how savings rates respond to tighter credit provisions and to estimate how tight the limits would have to be to reach a 15 percent personal savings rate.

While eliminating the tax deductibility of consumer credit will be attacked as hurting low-income consumers, it does no such thing. It in fact affects upper-middle-income consumers, since they are the ones who itemize their tax deductions and use consumer credit. Low- and lower-middle-income taxpayers seldom itemize their tax deductions and thus gain nothing from the tax deductibility of consumer interest. Low- and middle-income households would, however, be impacted by higher minimum down payments. As a consequence a broad spectrum of consumers would face significant pressures to hold down their consumption.

Similar provisions should be imposed on mortgage credit. Since many people bought their current home with the understanding that mortgage interest payments were tax deductible and probably could not afford their present home if mortgage interest payments were not tax deductible, however, it isn't possible or fair to retroactively eliminate the mortgage interest deduction. This does not mean, however, that all of the burdens of restricting mortgage credit should be on those that have not yet purchased their first home.

Restrictions should begin by limiting the tax deductibility of mortgage interest to one house per family. America has a public interest in seeing American families well housed, but it has no public interest in giving tax subsidies for second homes. No tax deductions should be allowed for the purchase of new second homes, and the tax deductibility of interest payments on existing second homes should be phased out over ten years. Ninety percent of such interest payments could be deducted the first year, 80 percent the second, and so on until no such interest was deductible in the tenth year. This is a restriction that hits hardest at the upper-income groups that can afford second homes.

The limit of one tax deductible home per family should be combined with a limit on the size of the allowable deduction for one's first home. Interest on loans over this amount (I would suggest $250,000) could not be deducted from gross income when purchasing new homes, and interest on loans over this amount on old homes should also be phased out over ten years. Here again society has no interest in subsidizing the ownership of mansions, and the burden of the change would fall only on upper-income groups that buy expensive housing.

Minimum down payments should also gradually rise, beginning with the re-establishment of a 20 percent minimum down payment, and continuing with an extra 2 percent minimum down payment per year until the personal savings rate reaches the 15 percent target. This provision and only this provision impacts the average moderate-income first-time home buyer.

Together these changes represent a balanced package of sacrifices where everyone will be making some sacrifices. Upper-income groups can obviously buy the household durables and cars they want without consumer credit easier than low- and moderate-income groups, but low- and moderate-income groups will find no increase in the costs of their housing, while upper-income groups will find housing costs substantially increased.

Moving to a Bonus System

As the Japanese demonstrate, the bonus system plays an important role in raising savings rates. Families save more when their income comes in large lumps rather than small frequent increments. Thus the need for more savings and the need for greater labor-management cooperation would both seem to call for the establishment of a bonus system in America.

While it is not desirable for government to impose a bonus system legally, it can nudge the entire system in that direction by changing its tax laws so that it does not collect payroll taxes on earnings which come in the form of bonuses as long as bonuses constitute less than one-third of total earnings. Since payroll taxes are approaching 20 percent of payroll, with about half coming from workers and half from businesses, both business and labor would have an incentive to shift to the bonus system. Those who don't move to the bonus system would pay substantially higher payroll taxes than those who do.

Here again it is impossible to accurately predict just how much of an increase in savings would occur with the establishment of the bonus system. The change is not a marginal one. If bonuses have a big positive impact on savings, then fewer restrictions will be needed on consumer and mortgage credit.

Liberalizing Individual Retirement Accounts

Individual Retirement Accounts (IRA's) should also be liberalized so that any amount of money can be deposited in them for any purpose and withdrawn at any time with normal income taxes due upon withdrawal. To make the system really work to increase savings, however, it is necessary to close a loophole that vitiates the savings incentives of the current IRA law. Individuals can now move money out of old savings accounts into IRA's and gain the resulting tax advantages without saving out of current income. If tax-free savings accounts are to encourage savings, the accounts must be restricted so that only new savings are eligible for the tax advantages. This means that those claiming tax-free savings status must be forced to provide the accounting records necessary to establish that they are in fact real savers and have not simply moved money from one savings account to another.

If such institutional changes were made, America would have a serious and equitable program for raising savings and investment. To be effective, however, it would need to be combined with a serious program for converting government from being a dissaver to being a saver.

A SERIOUS PROGRAM FOR RAISING PUBLIC SAVING

With a government deficit over $200 billion it is simply not possible for America to invest what it needs. If America is to reach a 25 percent investment rate, government will have to contribute at least 2 percentage points of the total. Since state and local governments have had to save to fund their pension programs, they have already become reliable savers. In 1984 they contributed $52 billion (1.4 percent of the GNP) to national savings. As a result, to reach national goals for public savings the Federal government has to convert its current 5 percent of GNP deficit into a roughly 1 percent of GNP surplus.

Such a shift from deficit to surplus is important for three economic reasons. First, surpluses are necessary if Americans are to have the investment funds they need to be competitive in world markets. Second, eliminating large deficits is necessary if inflation is not to break out once again. Deficits represent Keynesian stimulus. They are appropriate in the midst of recessions, but become less and less appropriate as economies move back toward full employment. Third, deficits make it difficult to practice countercyclical fiscal policies when recessions break out. Given huge deficits, countries are reluctant to make them worse, but without the political ability to increase deficits it is very difficult to break loose from the grip of a recession.

For Democrats the shift is doubly important. Facing large deficits, the political party that believes that government has a positive role to play in making America a better place to live is permanently on the defensive. It must spend all of its time defending programs that are already on the books and has no resources that can be used to fund creative new experiments.

To convert the Federal government from dissaver to saver there are only two options—cut spending or raise taxes.[15] Everyone is in favor of eliminating waste in the Federal government, but there is very little waste in the Federal budget. There are programs that may not be wise, but they benefit particular groups. A large part of the Grace Commission's waste, for example, was found in what it considered excessively generous Federal pensions. Federal employees don't consider their present pensions waste.[16]

Realistically, taxes will have to rise and expenditures will have to fall. Even a cursory analysis of budgetary arithmetic reveals that it is not possible to reach the desired goals by cutting expenditures alone. To eliminate a $200 billion deficit by cutting defense spending, the defense budget would have to be reduced by two-thirds. If Social Security and Medicare benefits were to be cut, then these programs would have to be cut by 75 percent. And if one exempts defense and Social Security from the cuts and remembers that interest on the national debt is a legal obligation that cannot be cut, then one would have to essentially shut down the rest of the Federal government (no roads, no FBI, no Congress, no national parks, no President, no weather bureau) if $200 billion in budget cuts were to be found. For all of the rest of the Federal government together only spends about $200 billion.

Whatever one believes about cutting government budgets, major tax increases will be necessary to eliminate the current budget deficit and generate the budget surpluses that are needed if America is to save what it needs to save. But the American tax system has reached the point where the problem cannot be solved with simple surtaxes. To eliminate a $200 billion deficit by raising personal income tax rates, for example, would require an increase in effective tax rates of two-thirds under the current system. That isn't possible or desirable. The entire tax system will have to be revamped if it is to do what must be done.

A NEW TAX SYSTEM

Construction of a new tax system has to start with an examination of the corporate income tax and the payroll tax. Neither tax is capable of bearing the burdens that are being placed upon it. The economic distortions built into the existing corporate income tax are so large that they will destroy the efficiency of our capital markets. The payroll tax is simply being asked to carry a rising revenue load that is beyond its capacity.

The Corporate Income Tax

Americans often talk as if corporations pay taxes, but corporations do not pay taxes. They simply collect taxes from someone—the owners of the corporation who receive lower dividends because some of their profits are taken in taxes, the customers of corporations who must pay higher prices because taxes are included as an extra cost in the prices of what they buy, or the employees of corporations who receive lower wages because their employer has less after-tax income to pay them—and pass what they collect on to government.

The economics literature on tax incidence disagrees as to where the actual short-run burden lies, but in the long run the tax must be shifted forward onto the consumer in the form of higher prices. The reasons for this are simple. Savers demand an after-tax rate of return on their savings equal to the rate at which they are willing to defer consumption today to have consumption tomorrow (what economists call the rate of time preference). A person who is willing to give up $1 in consumption today for $1.10 in consumption in a year has a 10 percent rate of time preference and demands an after-tax 10 percent rate of return on his savings. If he does not get it, he will simply stop saving and start consuming.

Suppose, for example, a corporate income tax were imposed and reduced rates of return below the required 10 percent level. The saver simply cuts back on his savings by consuming more. As he does so, he reduces the savings available for investment. With less savings and the same demand, the before-tax rate of return to savings rises. Firms who must borrow this now more expensive money find themselves with higher production costs and raise prices to compensate for their higher costs—shifting the incidence of the tax forward onto the consumer. With less savings the capital stock falls and eventually it becomes small enough to raise the pretax rate of return to the point where the after-tax rate of return on capital has been restored to the necessary 10 percent. If the corporate income tax were 50 percent, savings would have to be reduced enough to raise before tax rates of return to 20 percent. In the process, however, the saver—the corporate shareholder—has been eliminated as a real taxpayer. He gets his required 10 percent after-tax rate of return regardless of whether there is or is not a corporate income tax. Efforts to tax the rich by taxing corporate income are ultimately self-defeating. What looks like a tax on wealthy corporate shareholders is in fact a disguised sales tax.

Moreover, even if the corporate income tax were paid by shareholders, it is an unfair tax. Every shareholder, rich or poor, is taxed at the same rate, about 46 percent. There are much better, fairer ways than the corporate income tax to tax the rich if this is what Americans wish to do. While there are some political advantages in seeming to impose a progressive tax upon the rich while actually collecting a regressive tax from the average consumer, there are no ethical or economic advantages in such an arrangement.

The problems with the corporate income tax go far beyond those of equity, however. They start with revenue. In 1950 the corporate income tax yielded 25 percent of the revenue raised by the Federal government, but by 1986 the corporate income tax will raise only 7 percent of Federal revenue.[17] The American corporate income tax is being gradually eliminated, but America is failing to fill the revenue gap left behind. If the corporate income tax is to be abolished, something must replace it.

Efficiency is even more important. An efficient corporate income tax would raise revenue with the fewest possible distortions—the pattern of investments with the tax would be similar to the pattern of investments without the tax. Yet America has created a monster of a corporate income tax with enormous distortions. The distortions are so large that if the current tax incentives are allowed to continue for any length of time they will burden the economy with an inefficient pattern of investments that will severely handicap America's efforts to compete with the rest of the world.

Different firms and industries simply pay very different tax rates under the current law (see Table 8). This means that instead of investing where the returns are the highest (before and after taxes),

TABLE 8
EFFECTIVE CORPORATE TAX RATES[18]

Industry	1981–83 Effective Tax Rate	Firm	1981–83 Effective Tax Rate
Aerospace	7%	General Electric	− 4
Beverages	23	Boeing	− 18
Broadcasting	14*	Lockheed	0
Chemicals	− 5	General Dynamics	− 8
Computers	26	Columbia Gas System	− 11
Construction	8*	Dow Chemical	− 29
Electronics	13	Transamerica	− 15
Financial Institutions	2	Grumman	0
Food Processors	28	American Financial	0
Instruments	27	Mitchell Energy	− 10
Insurance	2*	Greyhound	− 15
Investment Companies	15*	Centex	− 6
Metal Products	23*	Champion International	− 5
Paper and Wood Products	7	Singer	− 12
Petroleum	20	U.S. Home	− 99
Pharmaceuticals	32	Carnation	41
Railroads	0	Sherwin Williams	41
Retailing	21	K-Mart	41
Rubber	29	SuperValu Stores	42
Soaps and Cosmetics	34	Interco	42
Telecommunications	3	Foster Wheeler	42
Tobacco	34	Ralston Purina	42
Trucking	39	Raytheon	45
Utilities	11	UF Corp	45
Wholesalers	35	Whirlpool	46

* 1982 and 1983 only

investment patterns are distorted toward those industries that have the most favorable tax advantages rather than the most favorable investment opportunities.

Among industries, effective tax rates ranged from minus 5 percent for chemicals to plus 39 percent for trucking. Among individual firms, the differences are even greater. Some firms (Whirlpool) paid taxes at the maximum rate (46 percent), while others (U.S. Home) were getting a rebate which almost doubled their net earnings. In the current tax code investors are told to invest in railroads (no taxes) but not in instruments (27 percent tax rate); in Dow Chemical (-29 percent taxes) but not in Foster Wheeler (42 percent taxes). In any one year or even over a few years such distortions are not a disaster, but if they are allowed to continue over long periods of time, they yield a very inefficient pattern of investment—a pattern of investment with which America cannot afford to live.

The distortions implicit in the corporate income tax code began long before the Reagan Administration took office, but they were grossly enlarged in the Accelerated Cost Recovery System (ACRS) enacted by the Reagan Administration in 1981. Essentially the ACRS is a system of accelerated depreciation allowances in which the time over which an investment may be depreciated is much shorter than the length of time over which the investment will actually be used. If the period of depreciation is short enough relative to the actual length of life of an asset, effective corporate tax rates can be reduced to zero or even to negative rates—in effect a subsidy.

Suppose for example that a firm invests in a machine that costs $1 million and that will last ten years. The machine earns $100,000 per year after all expenses (including the $100,000 per year that must be set aside to replace the machine when it wears out or to repay the loan) have been paid. If the firm borrows the $1 million and is paying a 10 percent interest rate, no taxes would be owed on the $100,000 in annual earnings, since they would be given to the lender and as interest payments are tax deductible. With economic depreciation no taxes would also be owed on the $100,000 per year that is set aside to replace the machine or to repay the loan, since this amount would be allowed as depreciation, given the ten-year life of the machinery. As a result this project just breaks even. It repays the lender but there is nothing left over for the entrepreneur.

Now suppose that the government allows a 10 percent investment tax credit on new investment and permits the same machine to be depreciated in two years rather than its ten years of actual life. The $100,000 in annual earnings is still a tax-free interest deduction. But the investor now gets a $100,000 tax credit and a $500,000 deduction from taxes in each of the first two years. If the investor has other taxable income, these deductions can be used to shelter it. The two years of depreciation deductions are together worth $955,000 in net present value (the number is not $1,000,000, since today's value of $500,000 one year from now is $455,000 with 10 percent interest rates) and the investment tax credit another $100,000. If the investor puts his $1,055,000 in tax-free income to work at 10 percent, he will have $2.7 million at the end of ten years. He repays the $1 million loan and is left with a profit of $1.7 million. What was a break-even project is now a very profitable project.

Such a subsidy system certainly encourages more investment, but it also induces investors to misallocate capital because they can now make money on projects that do not earn the competitive (10 percent) market rate of return.[19] What is worse, if the length of time over which an asset can be depreciated relative to its actual useful economic life differs for different types of assets, the tax system offers very different subsidies for different kinds of investment in different industries or firms. Reagan's ACRS, for example, allows a larger subsidy for long-lived assets such as steel mills than for short-lived assets such as equipment in an electronics factory. The result is an incentive to invest in too many steel mills and in not enough electronics equipment. As a result the pattern of investment is distorted away from those activities that would have the greatest output-enhancing potential.

ACRS also distorts incentives between profitable companies and unprofitable companies—which is often the same as the distinction between new and old companies. Tax credits and tax deductions have no value unless the firm has other taxable income it can shelter. As a result if General Motors is profitable and Ford is not, General Motors but not Ford gets the subsidies implicit in ACRS. Similarly new, rapidly growing firms are unlikely to have enough other income to use their allowable credits and deductions. In contrast a stagnant firm with a substantial cash flow can use its tax credits and ends up paying lower taxes than the new progressive firm.

To cure these problems the Reagan Administration enacted lease-backs along with the ACRS system in 1981. Lease-backs were basically a way for temporarily unprofitable firms or new firms to sell their unused tax breaks. Thus in 1981 the Ford Motor Company sold a significant fraction of its unusable tax subsidies to IBM. (Technically it sold some of its factory equipment to IBM, who could use the tax break, and then leased this equipment back from IBM.) In the market that developed for tax breaks the seller usually got about 90 cents for every dollar of tax reduction gained by the buyer. Ford got 90 percent of the tax breaks it would have gotten if it had been profitable, and IBM was able to reduce its tax bill by 10 percent.

In the process of solving one problem, however, this legislation created others. Firms with taxable profits such as IBM were not paying taxes to the Federal government but were essentially paying taxes to other private firms such as Ford. Efficient profitable firms ended up subsidizing inefficient firms. The resulting furor led to the 1982 repeal of lease-backs, but nothing else was done to eliminate the distortions lease-backs were designed to cure.

Without lease-backs ACRS generates long-run tax incentives for mergers and acquisitions. Profitable firms buy up unprofitable firms with large unusable tax credits, use the tax credits, and then sell off the firm that has just been acquired. While there is nothing intrinsically wrong with mergers and takeovers, there is quite a bit wrong with mergers and takeovers that are done solely for tax reasons. Time, effort, and money go into a sophisticated system of tax avoidance rather than into producing a better or cheaper product.

Given that the corporate income tax is in the long run a regressive consumption tax, the national need for investment incentives, the small amount of revenue being collected under current laws, the huge legal and bookkeeping costs of administering the present system, and the mess created by ACRS, it is clear that the corporate income tax should be abolished. There are simply better, fairer, more efficient ways to raise the revenue that the Federal government must raise.

The Payroll Tax

While the corporate income tax has been gradually fading away, the payroll tax has been growing from 12 to 35 percent of Federal revenue.[20] Social Security and unemployment insurance payroll taxes together now exceed 16 percent of payroll and will be well above 20 percent before the turn of the century. Current laws also understate the future tax increase that will be required. Within months of the 1983 tax increase, which was supposed to solve Social Security financing problems for the rest of the century, discussions had started as to how to raise the revenue necessary to finance Medicare.

Unemployment insurance is a federally mandated system dependent upon payroll taxes that is also clearly underfunded. More than half the states ran out of funds in the early 1980s and were borrowing funds from the Federal government to pay current unemployment insurance benefits. At some point not far in the future, payroll taxes are going to have to be raised to repay those loans and to pay future benefits.

Liberals traditionally object to payroll taxes on the grounds that taxes paid go down as a fraction of total income as incomes go up, since payroll taxes are not levied on all of earned income or on income from investments. It is incorrect, however, to look only at taxes to determine burdens when these taxes are paid into a trust fund and used to finance a particular set of expenditures. One must look at both taxes and expenditures together before equity judgments can be drawn. If expenditures are distributed so that low-income individuals get more benefits than upper-income individuals relative to their incomes, a progressive expenditure pattern can more than offset a regressive tax pattern.

Such is the case in both Social Security and unemployment insurance. Because of the minimum monthly benefit, the ratio of benefits to taxes is higher for low-income individuals than it is for high-income individuals in Social Security. Similarly in unemployment insurance the greatest benefits go to those with the highest probabilities of being unemployed. Since the probability of being unemployed goes up as one's income goes down, unemployment insurance is also a system where a progressive benefit structure more than offsets a regressive tax structure.

The real objection to payroll taxes is not equity, but efficiency. Since payroll taxes raise the costs of hiring labor, they create an incentive to reduce costs by substituting machines that do not have to pay payroll taxes for people who do. The effect is most dramatic in the case of a firm deciding whether it is most profitable to hire a robot or a worker. If it hires a robot, it pays no payroll taxes. If it hires a human worker, it pays an extra 8 percent in payroll taxes. Not only does the robot not have to pay a payroll tax, the purchase may lead to an actual tax subsidy via the Accelerated Cost Recovery System. Employers get paid by government to use robots but must pay government to use human workers.

From the perspective of a political party that worries about unemployment and seeks to represent workers, the payroll tax represents a perverse set of incentives. The Democratic party should place the reduction or elimination of the payroll tax high on its political agenda. In this case both political self-interest and economic efficiency work in the same direction.

Luckily this conclusion fits with the previously outlined need to shift the wage structure toward a bonus system. By passing a law stating that bonuses up to one-third of earned income would not be subject to the payroll tax, the payroll tax would be on its way to elimination.

If the elimination of the corporate income tax and the reduction of the payroll tax are viewed together, they have desirable equity and efficiency properties. Low- and middle-income Americans no longer have to pay a disguised sales tax and no longer have to pay as much in payroll taxes. Efficiency is served in that the distortions now implicit in the corporate income tax are eliminated and in that firms are no longer told to acquire capital and eschew labor because of the gap between the corporate tax on capital and the payroll tax on people. In a similar manner a lower payroll tax reduces distortions in the optimal labor-capital mix and creates incentives to hire more workers.

In 1984 the corporate income tax raised $70 billion, and exempting one-third of earnings from payroll taxes would have cut payroll tax collections by about $75 billion. If these tax reductions are combined with an existing $200 billion deficit and the need for a Federal government surplus equal to 1 percent of GNP, some other taxes will obviously have to be raised.

The Value-Added Tax

To ask what tax could possibly be raised to yield such a large sum of revenue is to come up with one and only one answer—the value-added tax. Value-added taxes, common in the rest of the industrial world, are determined by subtracting a firm's purchases of materials or components from its gross selling revenue and levying a tax upon the difference—the firm's value-added. If a firm bought supplies worth $10 million and sold products worth $18 million dollars, it would have a value-added of $8 million. With a 15 percent value-added tax, the firm would owe $1.2 million in value-added taxes, and these taxes would be built into the price of whatever the firm sells.

Value-added taxes (VAT) are widely used abroad because they raise large amounts of money while simultaneously creating incentives to consume less and save more. Instead of being taxed upon what one puts into society (the income from work and savings) one is taxed on the consumption one takes out of society. With a 15 percent value-added tax a person who buys a $10,000 car must pay an extra $1,500 in value-added taxes when he buys the car but can completely avoid those taxes if he instead saves the $10,000. The incentive effects of value-added taxes work in favor of what society wants—less consumption—rather than against what society wants—more savings and work—as is the case with higher personal income taxes. As a result value-added taxes are an integral part of any program seeking to encourage more private saving and to transform government from a dissaver into a saver.

Value-added taxes also make it possible to tax illegal underground activity that is not now taxed. The Florida drug smuggler may pay no taxes when he sells his cocaine, but must pay the VAT when he buys his Mercedes. Millions of Americans who are illegally evading income taxes would be caught when they spend their income. The greater a country's problems with tax compliance (the U.S. Treasury estimates that Americans are now illegally evading $90 billion in taxes that they should be paying), the more imperative the value-added tax becomes.[21]

The value-added tax is also partially self-enforcing. To cheat on the value-added tax, a firm must under-invoice its sales or over-invoice its purchases of materials to reduce its value-added. If sales are under-invoiced the firm's customers have fewer purchases of materials which they can subtract from their gross sales revenue and they must pay more taxes on a larger value added. If purchases are over-invoiced then a firm's suppliers have larger sales, a higher value-added, and must pay more taxes. Firms are less likely to cheat either their suppliers or customers than the government; and even if they do so, the government is not left without its rightful share of the revenue.

Value-added taxes also have an advantage in international trade. The value-added tax is rebatable under the rules of international trade where other taxes are not. Thus when Germany exports a car to the United States, German car companies get a tax refund, say $2,000, from their government. When German cars are exported to Japan this refund makes no difference, since Japan also uses value-added taxes and the German car exporter will have to pay $2,000 in value-added taxes when the car arrives in Japan. But it makes a difference when the car is exported to a country like the United States which does not have value-added taxes. The rebate is still given in Germany but there is no countervailing levy that must be paid in the United States. Thus German companies are selling cars that do not have to pay German taxes when they are sold in the United States.

In contrast when an American company exports a car it cannot get a $2,000 refund for the corporate income or payroll taxes which it pays and must upon arrival pay the foreign value-added tax. American cars when they are sold abroad essentially pay two sets of taxes— the American payroll and income taxes and the foreign value-added taxes. This creates a $2,000 handicap for American car manufacturers in export markets and a $2,000 advantage to foreign car manufacturers in the United States. This is an advantage America can no longer afford to give. The only solution is to establish a value-added tax as large as that used in the rest of the industrial world.

While Sweden has a 25 percent VAT, America could probably get by with the 15 to 20 percent that is common in most of the rest of Europe. In 1984 a 15 percent value-added tax would have raised $447 billion in America.[22]

Since the VAT is essentially levied upon consumption and consumption falls as a fraction of income as incomes rise, VAT tax payments fall as a fraction of total income as incomes rise. Fortunately there is an easy way to convert a regressive value-added tax into a progressive one. The value-added tax is levied at some flat rate on all goods and services, but a per capita refundable tax credit is given to offset the effects of the tax on the poor. Suppose, for example, that America had a 15 percent VAT and a refundable per capita tax credit of $375. A family of four with an income of $10,000 (approximately the poverty line) would pay $1,500 in value-added taxes when it spent its income but would get that $1,500 (4 × $375) back in the form of a refund. On a net basis it would not be paying the value-added tax at all. A four-person family spending $20,000 would pay $3,000, get a $1,500 refund, and pay a net value-added tax of $1,500. Similarly a four-person family spending $50,000 would pay $7,500, get the $1,500 back, and be a net payer of $6,000. And so on up the income ladder. Such a system of refundable credits can be used to make the value-added tax as progressive as anyone desires.

By integrating the refunds into income tax withholding tables, the rebate can be effectively returned to the taxpayer as it is paid. A large rebate also forces the millions of people who now evade taxes by simply not filing the necessary forms to file. Unless they filed they would not get their rebate. As a result income tax compliance would also go up.

If America had had a 15 percent value-added tax that excluded state and local government spending with a $375 refundable tax credit in 1984, $89 billion would have been refunded in credits and the value-added tax would have raised $385 billion on a net basis.

Since value-added taxes are included in the prices of the products bought, any increase in the value-added tax shows up in inflation as it is usually measured. If wages or other prices are indexed to the measured rate of inflation (a common situation in labor union contracts and in contracts with suppliers), higher value-added taxes would cause higher wages or prices and hence even higher inflation than the value-added tax would have warranted by itself. In Britain in the late 1970's Margaret Thatcher forgot about this effect to her regret. She enacted a major increase in the value-added tax and then saw it show up as a huge increase in the rate of inflation as wages and prices rose in a sickening spiral.

When the value-added tax is designed to replace two other taxes (the payroll and corporate income tax) that also raise the costs of production, there should be no big inflationary effect, but whatever the size of the effect it should be kept out of the cost-of-living indexes. This easily can be and should be done by those constructing the index. If taxes are to be included in cost-of-living indexes, then it is necessary to include the value of government goods and services received, since taxes are used to buy government goods and services. A cost-of-living index should either include all taxes and government benefits or no taxes and benefits. Since the existing cost-of-living index includes neither income taxes nor government benefits, the index should not include other forms of taxation either.

Sometimes the value-added tax is portrayed as an infringement on the ability of states to collect their traditional sales taxes. On the contrary it is a vehicle to cut the costs, increase the collections, and raise the efficiency of state sales taxes. State sales taxes could easily be converted to piggy-back value-added taxes added on to the national value-added tax. A state would simply notify the Federal government as to the extra value-added tax it wished to levy in its jurisdiction. The Federal government would collect the higher tax and turn the extra money raised over to the state. State tax collection costs would fall, since the Federal government would be paying the costs of collection and enforcement. Collections would also be up because it is much harder to evade a national value-added tax than it is a state sales tax.

The U.S. Treasury estimates that it would cost $700 million to collect a value-added tax.[23] This is a modest sum, but if a value-added tax were imposed when the corporate income tax was eliminated it is clear that the total administrative costs of tax collection would fall for both government and firms, since the corporate income tax as it is now constituted is a much more costly tax to administer for both the payer and the payee.

Conservatives sometimes objected to value-added taxes on the grounds that they made it too easy for politicians to raise revenue and to spend it on their favorite projects. With current deficits this is simply not today's problem, but what is a drawback to conservatives should be an advantage for Democrats. Selling the value-added tax will not be easy politically, but it will be a lot easier than living with the current deficit and tax system for the foreseeable future. Realistically the current deficit and tax system place the Democratic party in a losing position. It is the party of new ideas, but it cannot champion any new ideas in the current fiscal environment.

In the 1960s the United States had an annual fiscal dividend. Tax revenues at full employment rose faster than government spending. In the 1980s the United States has a perpetual fiscal deficit. Tax revenues at full employment rise less rapidly than government spending. Given this situation, it is not surprising that the 1960s were a Democratic decade and that the 1980s are a Republican decade. To reverse the situation, Democrats will have to reverse the fiscal situation and this can only be done with a value-added tax.

The Personal Income Tax

The truth about the Federal personal income tax is not that it is on average progressive or regressive but that it is unfair. Some people with high incomes pay high taxes; others pay low taxes.[24] Several hundred Americans with incomes of over $1 million per year pay little or no tax, yet there are other high-income Americans who pay at the statutory maximum.

Hoping to conserve energy, help charities, promote investments in cattle and scores of other things, the Federal personal income tax system has acquired so many legal loopholes that it is like cheap Swiss cheese—more holes than cheese.[25] Most of these loopholes benefit investors (rich or poor) and not wage earners (rich or poor), but almost everyone ends up with a few dollars' worth of loopholes. The result is a structure of legal loopholes that favors the rich on average but is very hard to alter, since most of us are beneficiaries of at least a few dollars.

The problem with such a system is not just that it unfairly assesses different taxes on individuals with the same income but that it sets up a corrosive social system. When historians report that the decline and fall of Rome was set in motion by corruption from within rather than conquest from without, they are not talking about Nero fiddling while Rome burned or Caligula making his horse a member of the Roman Senate. Those were but external manifestations of a more fundamental corruption. Rome fell because Romans lost their civic virtue.

Citizens manifest civic virtue by meeting the letter and spirit of their public obligations. One of those obligations is the duty to pay taxes. In all of the talk about shifting to modified flat taxes and raising taxes to reduce budget deficits, something is missing. What is missing is the realization that the United States tax system is rapidly decaying from gross abuse.

Illegal underreporting of income has reached epidemic proportions. And it isn't just those illegal heroin smugglers who are cheating on their income taxes. For every dollar of tax not paid on illegal income the Internal Revenue Service estimates that $9 of taxes are not paid on legal income.[26] Unreported legal income reached $250 billion in 1981. Two or three decades ago Americans used to make fun of the French cheating on their income taxes. Today Americans are in no position to point a finger at anyone else.

Even our government promotes tax evasion. To encourage foreign citizens to buy more U.S. government bonds, the U.S. government quit withholding taxes on interest owed to foreigners in 1984 and started issuing bearer bonds, where no record is kept of ownership. Essentially the U.S. government is helping foreigners cheat on their taxes. But if the U.S. government helps foreigners cheat on their taxes should it be surprised when Americans also cheat?

Tens of billion of dollars in interest and dividends are not reported on U.S. tax forms. When the Federal government attempted to institute withholding to prevent such cheating a couple of years ago, it was successfully opposed by the banks, who did not wish to see funds now held in bank accounts diverted to taxes. In a very narrow interpretation of their self-interest, bank managers were unwilling to help the Federal government use the only efficient technique for collecting taxes owed. Civic virtue was nowhere to be seen in the banking industry.

The corruption is now spreading to wage earners. Wage earners have discovered that they can also cheat by raising their number of claimed dependents to a level where nothing is withheld from their income, and then just not file their annual income tax forms. The action is illegal, but if millions of others are doing it, and they are, the chances of getting caught are small.

The problem with a system of tax loopholes is not just that it unfairly assesses different tax rates on individuals with the same income but that it sets up a corrosive social system that destroys civic virtue. The average citizen without loopholes sees President Nixon paying no taxes because of special legal loopholes for gifts of personal papers to libraries (this loophole has now been closed and probably was closed before President Nixon made his gift). If the "big guys" can give themselves legal loopholes, the average citizen thinks that he will build himself some illegal loopholes. The U.S. Treasury now loses more in illegal loopholes ($90 billion) than it does in legal ones ($65 billion).[27]

In the United States whole industries such as farming or real estate have become tax scams. Consider farming in 1980—a year in which net farm income totaled $22 billion according to the Department of Agriculture. Slightly more than 1 million farmers reported net incomes of $9.9 billion but another 1.5 million farmers reported net losses of $11.7 billion. Farmers reported less than half of their total net income. Those sheltering urban income overwhelmed those who reported profits, and on a net basis $1.8 billion in urban income was sheltered behind farm losses—much of it phony accounting losses on pleasure farms. If America had simply abolished taxes on farming and prevented farms from being used as tax shelters, more taxes would have been collected than were collected.

In collecting revenue both the perception and reality of fairness are necessary, since without them there is no efficient way to collect taxes from a hostile non-cooperative citizenry. Every dishonest taxpayer and special loophole essentially raises the taxes that must be paid by the honest taxpayer without loopholes. These people eventually begin to see themselves as "suckers" paying what others should be paying. When they do, we reach the point historians focus on in Rome. Internal corruption destroys civic virtue and the republic falls.

No tax system can work without honest voluntary compliance on the part of the vast majority of citizens. The Internal Revenue Service can collect taxes from the dishonest few, but it cannot collect taxes from a dishonest majority or even a large minority. When everyone begins to feel that he is a "sucker" if he pays taxes, it is only a matter of time until the tax system collapses. America is very close to this point, yet no society can long run without an efficient fair way to collect the revenue that it needs to operate. Both the perception and reality of fairness are necessary, because without them there is no efficient way to collect taxes from a hostile non-cooperative citizenry.

To rectify this situation the United States must move to a fairer personal income tax. The Bradley-Gephart bill is the best embodiment of this approach.[28] Most loopholes are eliminated, tax rates are reduced, yet America is left with a progressive tax system where high-income families pay more taxes than low-income families. Enactment of the Bradley-Gephart tax bill should be a prime Democratic priority.

In Bradley-Gephart the zero bracket amounts are raised to $6,000 for married couples and $3,000 for single persons from the current $3,400 and $2,300. Income above this level is taxed at 14 percent until adjusted gross income reaches $40,000. Income above this level is taxed at 26 percent until adjusted gross income reaches $65,000. Above this level adjusted gross income is taxed at 30 percent. All exemptions and deductions are reduced in value, since they are only deductible at the minimum 14 percent rate, but Bradley-Gephart maintains those for health care, mortgage interest, state and local taxes, charitable contributions, and IRA contributions.

With very minor modifications the Bradley-Gephart proposals can be turned into a progressive consumption tax rather than a progressive personal income tax and made more politically defensible.

With the establishment and extension of tax-free Individual Retirement Accounts, savings are gradually being exempted from taxes. The average American family already faces a consumption rather than an income tax, since their annual savings are less than their maximum limits on IRA contributions. This is a trend that Democrats should further. If, as was recommended above, the existing IRA's were expanded so that individuals could save any amount of money for any purpose for any period of time without paying taxes but where taxes would be due whenever funds were withdrawn, the present personal income tax would become a personal consumption tax. Any income saved becomes a deduction from taxable income and as a result the income tax would become a tax on comsumption (income minus saving).

If people were prohibited from moving old funds from taxable to the new tax-free savings accounts (the loophole that vitiates today's IRA's as an incentive to save), such a change would be an efficient way to stimulate savings. If Americans don't save, there is no loss of tax revenue. To gain a $1 tax reduction, a taxpayer would have to be willing to save $7, for example, if he was in the 14 percent income tax bracket. In such a system individuals would end up paying taxes on their income up to the amount that was consumed. If they earned, say $30,000 and saved $3,000, they would pay taxes on $27,000. Or if they earned $30,000 and borrowed $3,000 for consumption purposes or reduced their tax-free savings account by $3,000, they would pay taxes on $33,000.

As it stands, one of the weaknesses of Bradley-Gephart is that there is no economic rationale for the loopholes that they retain. These loopholes are retained simply because those benefiting from them have too much political power to be disturbed. If Bradley-Gephart is viewed as a consumption tax, however, there is a rationale.

Since gifts to charities are not personal consumption, they could still be made and deducted from total income to get taxable income. Similarly state and local taxes are not personal consumption and would be allowed as deductions from total income. Since housing expenditures are partly consumption and partly investment, a limited mortgage interest deduction is consistent.

It also becomes easier to resist some of the current pressures to modify the proposal. Lower tax rates for capital gains, for example, are defended on the grounds that they are necessary to stimulate investment. With unlimited tax-free savings, special capital gains provisions are not necessary, since income from the sale of appreciated assets would not be taxed if it was reinvested in other assets. If consumed, however, it would and should be taxed at normal rates.

The personal income tax needs a thorough reform of the Bradley-Gephart variety, but as the authors themselves realize, reforming the income tax does nothing to raise the extra government revenue that is needed. Other taxes will have to fill that function.

A *Gasoline Tax*

Outside of North America every industrial democracy has a tax on gasoline of more than $2 per gallon.[29] The rest of the world pays high gasoline taxes and has become just as dependent upon the automobile as the average American. A high gasoline tax does not mean the end of driving. It just creates an incentive to plan one's driving more carefully. Few drive to the store for a pack of cigarettes.

The case for a gasoline tax is simple and compelling. America is a major oil importer with a huge balance of payments deficit that cannot afford to import what it is now importing. Militarily the United States also cannot afford to be hostage to the whims of Middle Eastern politics. Arranging the American economy so that it does not need Middle Eastern oil is much easier than paying for and protecting a Middle Eastern oil supply which it desperately needs. A large gasoline tax which reduced consumption and cut America's dependence on world oil supplies would be both cheaper and more effective than the rapid deployment force that is now being planned for the Middle East.

A gasoline tax is also a big revenue raiser and would go a long way toward eliminating the Federal deficit. An extra $1 per gallon tax on gasoline and diesel fuel over and above the tax now collected to finance highway construction would raise approximately $116 billion.[30] Here again it is not easy to sell gasoline taxes, but for Democrats the option of living with a large deficit is worse.

FEDERAL REVENUES

Together a 15 percent value-added tax with an offsetting income tax credit and a $1 per gallon gasoline tax could raise enough revenue to pay for the elimination of the corporate income tax, the reduction of the payroll tax, and to produce a Federal surplus equal to 1 percent of the GNP. The old and new looks in Federal revenues are shown in Table 10. Instead of a deficit of $176 billion, the Federal government would have a surplus of $123 billion. The $123 billion is more than 1 percent of the GNP, but if the extra spending recommended for research and development, education and public infrastructure (see Table 9) are included, as well as the extra revenues that would be earned by moving to lower unemployment rates, the Federal government would have a structural surplus approximately equal to 1 percent of GNP.

TABLE 9
FEDERAL REVENUE 1984[32]

	Existing Law	Proposed Law
Personal Income Tax	$315 billion	0 Personal Consumption
Tax	0	$315 billion
Corporate Profit Tax	70	0
Indirect Business Taxes	56	56
Social Insurance Taxes	263	188
Value-Added Tax	0	358
New Gasoline Tax	0	116
Total	$704	$1,013
Expenditures	$880	$ 880
Surplus or Deficit	−$176	+$ 123

The United States is not a high-tax society. When all local, state, and Federal taxes were aggregated, the United States stood fifteenth in 1982 in terms of tax revenue as a percent of GNP.[31] While the United States collects slightly more than 30 percent of the GNP in taxes, most of the rest of the industrial world collects between 40 and 50 percent of the GNP in taxes. Only Japan and Spain collect fewer taxes. Even with the tax changes suggested above Americans will still be well below average in terms of tax burdens.

The time has come to start over and build a new American tax system.[33] I am well aware that none of the tax changes just outlined are now politically feasible. They are necessary, however, and the political ground must be prepared to make them politically feasible. For if one asks how Americans are going to solve their problems within the constraints of current political feasibility, the truthful answer is that they are not going to solve their economic problems. There are no solutions that lie within the bounds of current political feasibility. Those bounds have to be widened.

REVAMPING OUR EXPENDITURE SYSTEM

On the expenditure side of the budget the Federal government undertakes a surprisingly limited number of activities. Basically it pays for national defense (33 percent of total spending), pays interest on the national debt (14 percent), writes checks to raise individual incomes (34 percent), and writes checks to state and local governments (11 percent). Housekeeping functions such as the President, the Congress, and the courts take 2 percent; and everything else—education, training, the weather bureau, the national parks—takes only 7 percent of the Federal budget (see Table 10).

TABLE 10
THE FEDERAL BUDGET 1982[35]

	Dollars (billions)	Percent
Defense, Space, Foreign Affairs, Veterans	$241*	32%
Interest Payments	85	11
Transfer Payments Excluding Those for Defense Purposes	278	36
Grants-in-Aid to State and Local Governments	84	11
All Other	76	10
Total	$764	100%

* Includes pensions of retired military personnel and civilian employees of the Defense Department.

The social programs other than Social Security and Medicare are too small to make much difference (one year's cost-of-living increase for Social Security is larger than all of the expenditures on AFDC— Aid for Families with Dependent Children—the major program for the poor), have already been squeezed by the Reagan Administration, and are vital to the quality of life for many Americans. Consider food stamps as an illustration. Food stamps began in 1967 because a team of medical specialists found widespread malnutrition, especially among black children in the south. By 1979 a similar group of doctors could find no evidence of systematic malnutrition. But by 1983 malnutrition was once again recurring. Doctors at Boston City Hospital reported that three times the expected number of five-year-olds were at the bottom of their growth charts.[34] Infant mortality rates are up to 33 out of every 100 children born in Detroit and 55 out of every 100 in the Avalon Park section of Chicago.[36] One-third of the elderly in St. Louis are in need of supplemental nutritional assistance.[37] One million poor children no longer get the school lunches that provided as much as half their daily nutrition.

Grants-in-aid to state and local governments can easily be cut at the Federal level, as President Reagan proposed in his fiscal 1986 budget, but Americans are just kidding themselves when they do so. For most of the functions have to be done, and this means financing them at the local level. A cut in grants-in-aid which shifts the locus of budget deficits from the Federal government to state and local governments does not help. A deficit is a deficit and a subtraction from national savings wherever it occurs. The whole issue of federalism and what should be done by whom and who should pay for it needs to be rethought, but a new division of authority is not going to solve the deficit problem. That can only be done by raising taxes or cutting expenditures—not by reshuffling the "old maid" card of the deficit back and forth between different levels of government. Since interest on the national debt is a legal obligation, any serious budget cutting must focus on either defense or Social Security.

Defense

It is often said that defense is an issue where economics is not and should not be paramount. A country decides what is necessary for its defense and then goes about raising and spending those funds in the most efficient possible way.[38] That is certainly correct and worth saying as long as it is recognized that it is equally true with respect to domestic necessities such a well-educated skilled work force. If one looks at history, few large countries have ever been conquered from without before they have rotted from within. In the long run a strong vibrant domestic society is a much more important defense than any number of missiles. Domestic and defense spending stand on the same base. Well-run societies decide what must be done and then figure out how to finance it.

In deciding what must be done in defense, the prime focus must be on the nature of the threat and what it takes to nullify that threat. Having said that, however, there are some general economic principles that need to be applied.

First, defense budget comparisons with the Soviet Union are always irrelevant in determining what the United States should be spending on defense. Relative prices of people and equipment are so different in the two countries that it simply isn't possible to make useful comparative estimates of their military spending. Since people are cheap and equipment is expensive in the Soviet Union, one gets an enormous Soviet defense budget *in dollars* if people and equipment are evaluated at American prices, where people are expensive and equipment is, relatively speaking, cheap. Conversely, if the American defense budget is evaluated *in rubles*, it becomes enormous because all of our equipment must be evaluated at a very high ruble price. Depending upon how the translations are done, one can show that the United States is outspending the Soviet Union or that the Soviet Union is outspending the United States.

One judges Soviet military power not by the rubles they put into the system but by the outputs (tanks, divisions, aircraft, missiles) that come out of the system. Higher Russian outputs may require more American defense spending, but higher Russian inputs do not. Any argument that the United States should spend more on defense because it is being outspent by the Soviet Union should be rejected categorically. No one knows or can know whether the United States is being outspent, and even if the United States were being outspent the conclusion is irrelevant. What counts is being outgunned not outspent.

The absurdities that budget comparisons can lead to were seen in the mid-1970s when the CIA increased its estimates of Soviet defense spending but not Soviet military power. The estimates went up because the CIA decided that Soviet military production was less efficient than previously thought. Higher Soviet defense spending was used as an argument for higher American defense spending, but if the CIA estimates were correct, the higher Soviet defense spending should have been seen as evidence of Soviet weakness and not evidence of Soviet strength. The Soviets were having to spend a larger fraction of their GNP on defense than Americans previously thought; and since they had no more military power than they were previously thought to have, they were obviously economically weaker than they were previously thought to be. What was in fact a mark of Soviet weakness was used as if it were an indicator of Soviet strength.

Secondly, since both the Soviet Union and America have allies, it is a mistake to look at Soviet or American military forces in isolation. America's allies spend less as a percent of GNP on defense than either America or the Soviet Union and its allies; but they are very rich countries, and 1 percent of the Japanese economy devoted to defense is a lot more than 8 percent of the GNP devoted to defense in Eastern Europe.

In this context it is also well to remember that America's allies are old sophisticated countries used to taking care of themselves, who cherish their national independence. They are not about to roll over and play dead for the Soviets. Any arguments that America must spend money on weapons to bolster European or Japanese psyches should also be rejected categorically.

Yet these were precisely the arguments used by the Reagan Administration to place intermediate-range missiles in Europe. Any Soviet target could be hit just as well using American long-range missiles, but the Europeans would feel more self-confident and be more resistant to Soviet influence if those targets could also be hit with intermediate-range weapons based in Europe. Just a slight knowledge of European history makes this a less than convincing argument. Expenditures made for such psychological reasons are wasted expenditures.

Third, crude missile or warhead counts are also almost always misleading. If a country has enough missiles and warheads to completely destroy another country, it has enough missiles and warheads regardless of how many missiles and warheads the other country may have. Any missiles or warheads above this level are simply going to make the rubble bounce and have no military value.

Psychologically it is hard to have fewer missiles and warheads than one's opponent, but to match him missile for missile or warhead for warhead is only to match his stupidity. America is also an old sophisticated country which cherishes its national independence, and its citizens are not going to be psychologically frightened into giving up their independence by irrelevant missile counts.

If the nuclear-winter hypothesis is correct, and it seems to be becoming a generally agreed upon hypothesis, then the number of warheads that are necessary to destroy one's opponents (and oneself) may be very small indeed.[39] The nuclear-winter hypothesis also means that there is no need to build second-strike weapons that can penetrate the opponent's air defenses. It simply isn't necessary for the warheads to land in the Soviet Union to destroy the Soviet Union (and everyone else). Warheads blown up in the United States will destroy the Soviet Union just as much as if they were dropped on the Soviet Union. The only difference will be the speed with which the end comes. And it is not clear that the last one to die is the winner.

Fourth, it is necessary to recognize the threats facing one's opponents when evaluating relative military strength. A larger Russian army, for example, is not a sufficient reason for expanding the size of the American army. The United States has no hostile land borders, while the Soviet Union has thousands of miles of potentially hostile land borders (China, Pakistan, Iran, Turkey).

Fifth, one should be skeptical of projections of Soviet military production. Historically, they have almost always been wrong. In the 1950s there was a potential bomber gap that never emerged. In the 1960s there was a potential missile gap that never emerged. In the 1970s there was a potential equipment gap that has come to be seen as a mirage. The CIA now admits that Soviet spending on weapons went down rather than up in the late 1970s.[40] Each of these gaps was based not on what the Soviets had or were building but on what they were planning to build. In each and every case the estimates were overestimates and the Soviets did not build what American estimates said they would build. Worry about real Soviet missiles; don't worry about missiles that the Soviets might build!

American projections of Soviet military production are inaccurate, because no one can know what the Soviets are going to do two or three years into the future. The reasons for this are simple. The Soviets themselves don't know what they are going to be doing two or three years into the future any more than the American defense establishment knows what it is going to be doing two or three years into the future.

Sixth, while arms control agreements can play an important role in stabilizing fears on both sides, past agreements have had perverse effects on defense spending. When limits have been placed on one or a few types of weapons, both sides have responded by putting more money into less cost-effective weapons systems that have not been proscribed in the agreements. Deflecting military spending from cost-effective systems to cost-ineffective systems is not a step forward from an economic perspective. Future arms control agreements should seek to reduce defense spending rather than deflecting it into more costly channels.

Whatever level of defense spending comes out of these considerations (the exact number is beyond the scope of this book and the competence of the author), there are some economic constraints that must be observed in doing what is necessary. Defense spending is a form of consumption. Neither an MX missile nor an automobile contribute to America's ability to produce more goods and services in the future. As a result if America needs to raise its defense spending, any increase in public defense consumption must be paid for by cutting private civilian consumption. If investment spending on people or machines is cut to fund defense spending, one is taking public consumption out of the investment funds that one needs to be competitive—and one should not then be surprised to find that one is not competitive. In paying for defense with a large government deficit as America is now doing, this is precisely the path being followed. Funds are borrowed from the pool of savings to fund public defense expenditures. Fewer funds are left for investment purposes.

Having essentially taken defense spending out of investment ever since World War II, the consequences have now caught up with America and produced an uncompetitive economy. If the 8 percent of the GNP spent on defense in the United States is compared with the 1 percent of GNP spent on defense in Japan, that 7 percentage-point difference would go a long way toward closing the investment gap between Japan and the United States. In the 1950s, when the U.S. was wealthier than the rest of its allies, it could afford to spend more on defense and from the point of view of equity should have carried more of the burden of allied defense spending. But as foreign per capita GNP's have caught up with those in America, what once was a fair distribution of economic burdens has become unfair.

One can be a success militarily and an economic superpower, but it takes some Spartan self-denial. Defense absorbs 8 percent of the GNP, over 30 percent of our technical manpower, and almost 40 percent of our durable goods production,[41] but its absorption of quality is probably even more important than its absorption of quantity. Defense research by its very nature is exciting scientific research. It is usually closer to the frontiers of what is scientifically possible than civilian research, since economic constraints are less binding. New weapons will be built almost regardless of costs, new cars will not.

Suppose a new MIT engineer is offered a job designing a better car and a job building laser space weapons. Which jobs does he take? To ask the question is to answer it. The laser space weapon is more exciting, and thus the "best and the brightest" are apt to go into military research and development. When the best of America are working on space weapons while the best of Germany are working on better cars, no one should be surprised that German cars are better than American ones. American missiles are better than the nonexistent German ones, but there is little market for the resulting product.

The quantitative competitive problem is in principle solvable. It is technically feasible for America to spend more on defense than Germany or Japan and still have a world-class economy if Americans are to raise taxes to cut civilian consumption. The qualitative problem, even in principle, is not so easily solved. If the very best of America's resources are in military research and production, the civilian economy is deprived of those resources. To stop this from happening one would have to limit the freedom of our very best technical personnel to take what they think are the best jobs open to them—and that Americans are unlikely to do. When it comes to the bottom line, there are unavoidable economic burdens if a country wishes to be a superpower.

While America is a superpower it is also a member of an alliance. An alliance is by its nature a cooperative relationship. That means agreeing with one's allies both as to the nature of the threat and as to the nature of the response. If they cannot be brought around to American views as to the nature of the threat and the amounts that should be spent to counter that threat, then America has to rethink. Perhaps they are right about the nature of the threat. Even if they aren't, perhaps America cannot afford to go it alone and have the massive solo buildup in military spending that it is now having.

Given its competitive position, America can no longer afford to spend much larger fractions of its GNP on defense, especially when much of this spending is used to pay for the defense of Europe and Japan. It is in America's self-interest to defend Europe and Japan from a Soviet takeover, but it is also in their self-interest. The problem is not for them to pay more or for America to pay less, but for all to agree on what needs to be spent and then to allocate the resulting burdens in ways that correspond to today's realities about ability to pay.

The Elderly

Social welfare programs immediately conjure up images of vast amounts of money being spent on the poor, but that is not in fact where the money is spent. Middle-class Americans tend to forget that most social welfare spending goes to programs designed to keep middle-class Americans from falling out of the middle class when they become elderly or unemployed.

America's unemployment insurance system is, however, already highly restrictive. Three percent of the Federal budget goes to unemployment insurance,[42] but with limited coverage (only 40 percent of the unemployed received benefits in 1982) and limited benefits (only 43 percent of weekly wages were replaced), it is clear that unemployment insurance expenditures cannot in good conscience be further cut by reducing coverage or benefits below current levels. The only real cure for high unemployment insurance expenditures is a prosperous low-unemployment economy.

Any serious civilian budget cutting has to begin with the problems of the elderly. In 1982, 35 percent of the entire Federal budget went to help the elderly in the form of pensions, welfare payments, or health care. As is true with military expenditures, America can afford to do what is necessary to keep our elderly (ourselves) from declining into a miserable existence as they (we) grow older. But what is the right level of expenditures?

The answer depends upon our views of intergenerational equity. How much should children contribute to the support of their parents? How much of a burden should parents impose on their children? For this is what Social Security is all about. Each of us on average is basically paying the benefits that go to our parents; each of us on average hopes to get benefits from our children when we are old. It is a system of intergenerational transfers.

Social Security is the crown jewel of American social legislation. If it did not exist, it would simply have to be reinvented. Left alone, many individuals simply won't save enough for their old age, and the rest of us are not willing to see them starve. President Reagan is just wrong when he says, "I am not sure that the benefits that you will receive when you come to the point of retiring from the work force will justify the amount of that [Social Security] tax." Social Security taxes do not disappear. They are paid to our own parents and grandparents. If the system did not exist, each of us would individually have to pay for our own parents or watch them squirm in poverty.

While Americans haven't eliminated poverty among the elderly any more than they have eliminated it among the non-elderly, great progress has been made. In 1967 the incidence of poverty among the elderly (29.5 percent) was more than twice that of the entire population (14.2 percent).[43] A just society does not economically discard its citizens simply because they have reached sixty-five years of age. As a result Social Security benefits were expanded to lower the incidence of poverty among the elderly. The programs succeeded. In 1983 the incidence of poverty among the elderly was lower (14.1 percent) than that among the population as a whole (15.2 percent).[44]

Similarly when Social Security was started there was sharp gap in living standards between the average elderly person and the rest of the population. In 1983 the per capita cash household income of the elderly slightly exceeded that of the entire population.[45] Since the young pay for their medical care while the elderly enjoy Medicare, and since the elderly have more wealth than the non-elderly, it is clear that the average elderly family now enjoys a standard of living higher than that of the non-elderly.

Much of this progress can be traced to Social Security. If Social Security and Medicare were to be abolished, the income of the elderly would be more than cut in half. Many elderly families depend entirely on Social Security for their standard of living.

America should hold a victory celebration. It has created a just society where the elderly are treated just as well as the rest of the population. That is something to take pride in. A victory celebration does not, of course, obviate the need to solve the system's financial problems.

Part of the problem is caused not by the elderly but by the performance of the economy. With no growth between the first quarter of 1979 and the first quarter of 1983, tax revenues did not rise as rapidly as expected. A stagnant economy inevitably leads to stagnant Social Security revenues. The correct solution is not to dismantle the Social Security system as President Reagan fitfully suggests but to improve the performance of the American economy. Sensible people don't cut off their hands if they fail to deliver food to their mouths because there is no food on the table.

Social Security also suffers from one of those good news–bad news dilemmas. During the 1950s, Americans who reached the age of sixty-five could expect to live an average of 14.1 additional years.[46] By 1980, a sixty-five-year-old could look forward to 16.4 years of life, with most of the increase occurring during the period after Medicare came into existence—good news. But an increase in life expectancy of 2.3 years raises system costs by 16 percent, since the elderly have to be supported for 16.4 and not 14.1 years—bad news.

In the long run the system also runs into problems after 2012, when the baby-boom generation starts to retire and must be supported by the baby-dearth generation.[47] With more retirees per worker, tax rates would clearly have to rise in a stagnant economy, but the extent of the rise in a dynamic growing economy depends upon how fast real per capita income (productivity) is rising. If productivity were to rise at a fast enough rate, Social Security tax rates would not have to rise even if there were more retirees relative to the number of workers. As a result, restoring economic prosperity is of relevance not just to the work force but to those who will then be in retirement.

One of the ways America can hedge its bets in this situation is to increase the probabilities of a prosperous American economy in the twenty-first century by building up a surplus in the Social Security trust funds that can be used now to make the investments that are necessary to re-create prosperity and can then be drawn down to ease the burdens on those who are working and paying Social Security taxes in the twenty-first century.

In 1982 President Reagan appointed a bipartisan committee that came to be known after its chairman as the Greenspan committee on how the Social Security problem should be solved. In the aftermath of the Greenspan report Congress placed a bandage (higher payroll taxes, a longer delay in cost-of-living increases, a later retirement age in the twenty-first century, included new Federal employees in the system, and taxed benefits for high-income—over $32,000—retirees) on the financial bleeding that will prevent any Social Security crises from emerging in the next few years; but long before the twenty-first century rolls around fundamental reforms will have to be made in Social Security.[48] The correct solution is not to bandage the bleeding but to fundamentally reform the financial base of the system.

As has been previously suggested, payroll taxes should be reduced by one-third, and any growth in Social Security expenditures should be financed with revenue from the new value-added tax. Such a change has a number of advantages. If a significant fraction of Social Security spending was financed through a value-added tax, those who saved (consumed less) would essentially be able to buy their pension benefits cheaper than those who did not save. By taxing consumption, capital income as well as earnings would effectively be partially taxed. High-income elderly people would also essentially continue paying retirement taxes after they had retired. As a result the system would end up being much less of a transfer from poor workers to wealthy retirees than it is now. The system would become both more efficient and more equitable.

Given that Social Security is a system of intergenerational transfers (not an insurance system), and given that the income of the elderly now slightly exceeds that of the non-elderly, the time has come to recognize that we are all Americans in the same economic boat subject to the same economic tides. If the tide is rising and national standards of living are rising, the standards of living of the elderly should rise along with those of active workers. If the tide is falling or rising more slowly, then the standards of living of the elderly must fall or rise more slowly. The standards of living of the elderly cannot rise while those of the rest of the country fall. That is neither fair nor economically feasible.

Since the average American income is governed by what happens to the per capita GNP, the standard of living of the elderly should be governed by the same factor. To accomplish this, Social Security benefits should be indexed to the per capita GNP instead of being tied to the consumer price index and periodically increased, as they now are.

Indexing the system to the per capita GNP neither raises nor lowers future benefits. It simply makes future benefits contingent on the degree of economic success. If the American economy is very successful over the next few decades, the elderly's real standard of living would rise faster tied to the per capita GNP than it would rise under the current system. If the American economy fails, then the elderly would get less. In the stagnant economy of the early 1980s, for example, such a change would have meant a July 1982 benefit increase of 4 percent rather than the 7.4 percent actually allowed under the present system. To do less is to be unfair to the elderly. To do more is to be unfair to the non-elderly.

The final problem is that of the retirement age. If Americans are living longer and remaining healthy longer, what was a reasonable retirement age (sixty-five) becomes an unreasonable retirement age—both in terms of forcing people to retire or in allowing them to retire. While ancient numbers seem to have an instinctive wisdom, a retirement age of sixty-five is not one of those numbers that have intrinsic wisdom. No one, for example, has ever presented health studies indicating that sixty-five is the age at which working abilities start to suffer a rapid deterioration.

Bismarck is usually given credit for picking sixty-five as the retirement age, but he actually chose seventy as the minimum retirement age in the first public retirement system in the nineteenth century.[49] The Germans lowered the retirement age to sixty-five in World War I. With a high retirement age and a short life expectancy, what looked like a generous social welfare system, and what was in fact with longer life expectancy later to become a generous social welfare system, cost very little at that time.

Realistically as the number of years of life expectancy at age sixty-five lengthens the retirement age is going to have to rise. Two factors have to be kept in mind as the retirement age rises, however. First, workers should receive plenty of warning as to when they are going to be allowed (or forced) to retire. Retirement takes prior planning in terms of being able to accumulate enough savings to supplement Social Security and have the retirement income that the elderly would like to have. Retirement plans cannot be changed on short notice. Therefore, workers should know at least fifteen years ahead of time what their own retirement age will be.

Given what has been happening to life expectancy at age sixty-five, the currently enacted increases in the legal retirement age—sixty-six in 2004 and sixty-seven in 2009—are unlikely to be large enough. Basically the retirement age should escalate with life expectancy, so that the average person can expect the sixteen years of retirement benefits that he or she now enjoys. Based on what has actually happened to life expectancy in the previous decade, the retirement age should be raised with a fifteen-year lag. Thus in 1985 Social Security would raise the retirement age in the year 2000 to sixty-seven if life expectancy had risen by two years from 1975 to 1985. Then in 1995 Social Security would again raise the retirement age in the year 2010 based upon how much life expectancy had gone up between 1985 and 1995.

As the retirement age rises, there may be a case for allowing earlier retirement in those occupations which are physically wearing. An increase in general life expectancy may leave one able to do desk work but unable to do heavy outdoor lifting. As someone who works as a college professor but who worked summers as an underground miner while going to college, it seems perfectly reasonable to me that at age seventy I would more likely be able to do the first job than the second. This is a problem to which medical answers could be found, and based upon such answers a system of differential retirement ages should be established that would allow individuals in certain occupations to retire earlier.

While changes such as those just suggested for Social Security do not save any money in the short run, they have a tremendous impact on reducing budgetary pressures in the long run. The goal should not be a year-to-year bandaging of the system but a major operation that puts the patient on its feet again for another half century. In doing so it is not necessary to cripple or dismantle Social Security. The necessary changes can make it into a better program than it now is.

Health Care

Health care is a related area where budgetary policy, or more accurately social policy, must be developed. The problem is not just a Federal government budget (Medicare and Medicaid) problem, not just a state and local budget (Medicaid, public hospitals) problem, not just a private health insurance problem, but a national problem however it is financed. Public and private expenditures on health care rose from 5 to 11 percent of the GNP between 1960 and 1983. While there is no magic precise limit as to what a country can afford to spend on health care, there is at the same time a limit. Every dollar spent on health care is a dollar that cannot be spent on something else. No set of expenditures can forever rise faster than the GNP. At some point health-care expenditures must slow down to the rate of growth of the GNP.

The United States is reaching this point sooner rather than later because of growing conflicts between the economy's performance, the need to increase international competitiveness, rapidly advancing and ever more expensive medical technologies, and inconsistent ethical principles.

If American productivity had consistently grown at pre-1965 rates, slightly above 3 percent per year, today's health-care spending would only absorb 7 to 8 percent of the GNP and there would be much less pressure to control health-care costs. But the slowdown did occur and America is forced to confront the fact that it cannot easily afford health expenditures that it could have afforded if productivity growth had remained on track.

International competition generates a related set of pressures. In terms of cash wages, American auto workers ($11.80 per hour) make only slightly more than Japanese auto workers ($10.27 per hour), but when fringe benefits are included the differential is enormous— $13.50 in Japan versus almost $22 in America. And at the Chrysler Corporation private health insurance accounts for $2.74 per hour of those fringe benefits.[50] If American companies cannot control their health-care costs, they cannot compete on world markets.

To be competitive America will have to cure its investment,

research-and-development, and educational deficiencies vis-à-vis the rest of the world; yet all of the cures require funds. Realistically, simply because of their size and rate of growth, resources that would otherwise be spent on health care will have to be diverted to solve some of these other problems. Americans cannot maintain the present rate of growth in health-care spending while simultaneously restoring productivity growth and increasing international competitiveness.

It has been traditional medical practice in the United States to employ treatments until they yield no additional payoffs, but with the development of more and more expensive techniques and devices that can slightly improve diagnoses or marginally prolong life, the expenditures that have to be made before this traditional stopping point is reached have grown to almost unlimited levels. To some extent this may be caused by the use of unproven or useless techniques, but to an even greater extent it is caused by employing techniques where the expected benefits are simply very small, statistically speaking, relative to large costs.

These new medical technologies require a shift in standard medical practice. Instead of stopping treatments when all benefits cease to exist, treatments must be stopped when marginal benefits are equal to marginal costs. But where lies the point where marginal costs equal marginal benefits? And who is to make this ethical decision—the patient, the doctor, some third-party payer? And how do we as a society decide that America cannot afford a medical treatment that may marginally benefit someone?

Ethically most Americans are simultaneously egalitarians and capitalists. None of us want to die because we could not afford to buy medical care, and as egalitarians few of us want to see others die because they could not afford to buy medical care. As capitalists Americans believe that individuals should be allowed to spend their money on whatever they wish, including health care.

This set of beliefs leads to an explosive chain reaction. A new expensive treatment is developed. In accordance with capitalistic principles, the wealthy are allowed to buy the treatment privately regardless of its medical effectiveness. Moderate-income individuals who cannot privately afford the treatment want it. They demand it. Being egalitarians, Americans do not have the political ability to say no to a middle-class person dying of the same treatable disease. Ways are found to provide the treatments through private or public health insurance. Being egalitarians, we have to give the treatment to everyone or deny it to everyone; being capitalists, we cannot deny it to those who can afford it, but since resources are limited we cannot afford to give it to everyone either.

In the summer of 1983 such a situation arose with heart transplants in Massachusetts. Regulatory authorities, to save money, were preventing Massachusetts hospitals from performing heart transplants. Some Massachusetts citizens could afford to fly to California to get transplants, others weren't but needed them just as badly. The media and the public essentially wheeled those needing treatment up on the state-house steps and dared the public authorities to let them die for want of treatment. Not surprisingly the public authorities relented. They altered state rules and regulations to pay for the California heart transplants and quickly began allowing a few Massachusetts hospitals to perform heart transplants.

Not having studied the question in detail, I do not pretend to know whether the costs and benefits of heart transplants have reached the point where Massachusetts hospitals should or should not be allowed to perform them, but I do know that this is the wrong way to make the decision.

As medical costs rise, it becomes less and less possible to live with our inconsistent ethical beliefs. The costs become too high. At some point, and the point is now, the inconsistencies have to be sorted out.

Insurance has been our traditional solution for individuals who cannot afford to buy health care, but it is not the answer here. Insurance is an appropriate remedy in situations where there is a small probability of a disaster which will incur large fixed losses. Fire insurance is the best example. Only a few of us will be unfortunate enough to have our home burn down, and the maximum loss is fixed by the value of our house. As a result we pool our risks and compensate those who actually suffer losses. Companies make money by being better at estimating risks and choosier as to whom they wish to insure.

While each of us has a small probability that his house will burn down, the probability that each of us will incur large health expenditures before death is becoming almost universal. In this circumstance insurance beomes not a pooling of small risks but an enormous distortion of incentives.

When an insurance system pays for future treatments rather than refunding previous losses, it appears to the individual as if prices are set below costs. Each of us makes a lump-sum payment, our insurance premium; and then when we use medical care, insurance pays all or a large part of the bills. This encourages each of us to consume more medical care. On the margin the care is cheap—but when we all do so we raise next year's lump-sum payments.

This is a problem, since we are not talking about losses that are fixed as in the case of the burned house but elastic, depending upon how we plan to treat our ailments. And since we are talking about our own life or our own health, each of us has an incentive to take the "don't spare the expenses" route. Unfortunately, with the development of new technologies that route is becoming more and more costly.

Each of us knows that if all of us use a lot more health care each of us will have to pay higher insurance premiums, but we also know that our own individual expenditures have essentially no impact on next year's insurance rates. As a result we each go ahead with our "don't spare the expenses" purchases and in the process collectively raise next year's insurance rates by a substantial amount. The system essentially becomes a pass-through system where the insurance companies are making money not by assessing risks and selecting their potential patients more carefully (we legally insist that everyone have access to health insurance) but by taking a management fee that depends upon total expenditures.

In these circumstances an insurance system ends up as a system without constraints. Insurance companies have an interest in higher health-care expenditures, since higher expenditures lead to higher corporate incomes. Doctors practicing in a fee-for-service system have a personal interest in prescribing services, since they raise their own incomes by doing so, and in an insurance system doctors know that they will not be directly raising costs for their patients if they do so. With insurance, patients have no interest in restraining their own health-care expenditures. The result, not surprisingly, is a system with exploding expenditures.

The health-care problem is not a federal or state budget problem. It is a social problem. The expenditure limits are the same regardless of whether the money is spent through the Federal budget or private insurance. Our basic problem is that somehow we are going to have to learn to say no.

Greater reliance can be placed on market mechanisms but this is basically to decide that the capitalistic part of our ethics is to dominate the egalitarian part. The market mechanism is often described as if it were a mechanism for producing less waste, but that isn't its prime virtue. It is a mechanism for saying no, but saying no in a very inegalitarian way. Since the richest 20 percent of all households have eleven times as much income as the poorest 20 percent in the United States, any efficient market mechanism will end up giving eleven times as much medical care to the top 20 percent as it gives to the bottom 20 percent.[51]

The present proposals of the Reagan Administration for higher deductibles and prospective rather than retrospective payment are good examples of the problem. To discourage use of expensive health-care facilities, the government announces that Medicare will pay less and users must pay more.[52] Private health insurance companies quickly announce that they will sell private health insurance to cover what is not covered by the government—thus undercutting the whole purpose of the larger payments that government is requiring of patients. Those with money can afford the co-insurance and do not face the market incentives for less use. Those without money cannot afford co-insurance and must face the incentives. But are we really going to say that patients who cannot afford the necessary private payments are not going to get medical care when they need it and others are getting it?

With prospective payment (known as the DRB system), hospitals are paid based on the disease diagnosed and not on how much it actually costs to treat the disease. What is likely to result? Hospitals will require more outpatient tests and procedures to reduce inpatient costs and will admit only those patients who are "low cost" patients in each diagnostic class. Once again this leaves the high-cost patients out in the cold.

These patients will be "dumped" as uninsured high-cost patients are now dumped. No hospital wants to treat patients without money and they are sent on to other hospitals—usually the municipal hospital in big cities. Boston City Hospital reports that it gets an average of four "dumps" per month.[53] It also spends twice as much on charity care ($148 million in 1983) as all of the other hospitals in Boston combined. But as city governments with their own budget problems attempt to restrain municipal hospital expenses, treatment at such hospitals increasingly becomes second class. To deny that this will happen is to deny that markets are efficient. Markets are precisely designed to encourage firms to segment, cream, and dump to find the most profitable niches while ignoring areas of low profitability.

Societies allow market mechanisms to work when buyers are knowledgeable or willing to live with their mistakes and when society is willing to distribute goods and services in accordance with the market distribution of income. In the case of health care neither of these two necessary conditions exists.

In the process of doing what markets do, they also create and alter values. In a market environment doctors and hospitals are income maximizers—nothing more and nothing less. They are to be seen and treated as such by their patient-customers. In a market environment cross subsidies cannot be extracted from the wealthy with minor ailments to help pay for the poor with major ailments. Every tub is on its own bottom.

No one is a real believer in the market mechanism unless he can honestly say that he would be willing to see some patients (including himself) die if they could not afford an available treatment that is being provided to wealthier patients. And if we can't really accept that then we simply won't let the market work when "push comes to shove."

The market approach also forgets that an egalitarian distribution of health care is one of the factors that create social solidarity, a feeling of community, and the non-monetary attachments that bind any society together. If health care is not part of the social glue that holds us together, what is?

If one is an egalitarian when it comes to medical care, as I will confess to being, what is the answer? One answer is for the third-party payers (In the United States private insurance pays for 31 percent of all health bills, the Federal government pays for 29 percent, state and local governments pay for 13 percent, and 4 percent is paid for with charitable contributions. Direct payments from those who receive services account for only 24 percent of the total.[54]) to write rules and regulations as to what they will or will not pay for and to prohibit their clients from buying what is not allowed under the private or public insurance systems. This is essentially how the British have kept health-care spending at half American levels.[55]

The British procedure works, but it works clumsily since no set of rules can be adjusted to the nuances and subtle differences of individual medical problems. Far better if American doctors would begin to build up a social ethic and behavioral practices as to when medicine is bad medicine—not because it has no payoff or because it hurts the patient—but because the costs simply aren't justified by the benefits.

To do this we are going to have to develop and disseminate better information on the cost effectiveness of alternative medical techniques for treating different ailments. Some small fraction of what we now spend on health care could better be spent on determining where limits on health-care spending should be drawn under different circumstances.

The medical profession now develops professional norms as to what constitutes bad medical practice. Those norms have to be expanded to include cases where large costs are not justified by expected benefits. If such norms were created and then legally defended against malpractice suits, it just might be possible to build up a system of doctor-imposed cost controls that would be much more flexible than any system of outside cost controls imposed by the third party payers can be. And if the medical profession fails to do so, then Americans will sooner or later move to a system of third-party controls. For something has to be done. But changes in social organization are to be preferred.

How much are we willing to spend (willing to sacrifice) as a society on prolonging life? The easy answer is "any amount," but that answer is neither true nor feasible. Like it or not, Americans are going to have to come to some social consensus as to the trade-off between costs and the life-extending benefits that result.

Health care costs are being treated as if they were largely an economic problem, but they aren't. To be resolved they will have to be treated as an ethical problem.

Infrastructure Investments

Simply put, America's bridges, ports, and roads are rotting from a decade of little new investment and even less maintenance. Such facilities are necessary both for a good society and for economic efficiency. U.S. Steel, for example, reports that one bridge around which they must detour their trucks in the Pittsburgh area is costing them $1 million per year in extra transportation costs. Those costs get added into the price of steel.

While one can argue as to the magnitude of the need (needs can easily be defined to become a wish list), there is no argument about the fact that some real need exists.[56] One-half of all of our water treatment plants are now working at capacity.[57] Forty-five percent of all of our bridges are obsolete or decaying—replacement cost: $48 billion. The interstate highway system has to rebuild 2,000 miles of highway a year and has a backlog of 8,000 miles that need rebuilding. Even assuming that only 20 percent of these are real needs still leaves America with lots of needs.

There is also no mystery as to how the problem arose. In the fiscal crunches starting with the Viet Nam war and extending into the slow-growth years of the late 1970s and 80s, governments at all levels simply found it easier to cut back on physical capital investments (repairs and new facilities) than to cut back on public consumption—either defense or entitlement programs. As a result spending on such facilities fell both absolutely and as a fraction of the GNP or government budgets. From 1968 to 1982 infrastructure spending fell from $37 billion to $22 billion (1972 dollars) after correcting for the impacts of inflation. If it took $37 billion in infrastructure investment to keep the country running in 1968 it clearly takes more now. There is no mystery as to why the bridges have started to fall down. They have not been maintained for more than a decade.

If America were simply to return to the spending levels of 1968, it would have to be spending $75 billion per year in today's dollars. As a congressional study recently found, America needs to double spending from $50 to $100 billion per year to meet the needs of a growing economy and a lack of investment in the past.[58] The needs have to be met and meeting them will require public expenditures.

A NEW BUDGET

The tax changes recommended in this chapter would have produced a $123 billion surplus in 1984. A doubling of physical infrastructure investments would, however, have added $50 billion, extra educational investments $52 billion, and extra R&D spending $8 billion to total spending. Lowering unemployment to 4 percent (the subject of Chapter 10) would, however, have added $24 billion to the surplus. The net result would be a $36 billion surplus—about 1 percent of the GNP.

If the recommended reforms in Social Security were adopted, the tax system would on a marginal basis be generating more than the needed amount of revenue in the future, and the country would return to the era when it had a fiscal dividend to distribute in the form of modest tax cuts or new programmatic initiatives.

While I also think that the military budget can be cut, no one should be allowed to propose expenditure increases that are to be financed by cutting programs favored by other Americans. If proponents aren't willing to propose accompanying tax increases that they themselves would have to pay, they simply aren't serious and their suggestions should be ignored. Following this dictum, I have proposed tax increases to match my expenditure programs.

While America has never been a high-savings, high-investment society, it can become one. There is nothing cultural about the high savings rates in the rest of the industrial world. The rest of the world is not more intrinsically frugal than America. They simply face a set of incentives where they cannot have what they want without savings. With social organization those same incentives can be created here.

Basically the Democratic party should lead the way to a higher-investment, lower-consumption society, but in doing so it should emphasize both public and private investment—not just private investment. Educational investments and infrastructure investments are just as vital to private free market efficiency as any investments in private plant and equipment.

9 / The Case for Industrial Policies

In America's mythological past "free markets" are seen as the secret to economic success. Some of America's first economic successes, however, were traceable to industrial policies, and America has often throughout its history relied upon industrial policies to make it great.

America's first unique contribution to industrial progress was the concept of interchangeable parts. Eli Whitney's 1798 system of interchangeable parts was developed under contract from the War Department to make muskets. No one in the private sector would take a risk on mass production, and the initial contract in fact paid Whitney more than it would have cost to buy the muskets hand-built from Europe. As the historian Daniel Boorstin records, "Government subsidy was crucial. The government's great power to invest and to wait for a return on its investment enabled Whitney to build his factory and tool up for mass production. This first great triumph of the American businessman was a government-sponsored and government-aided (but not government-run) venture."[1]

Half a century later the nation's railroads were built with the aid of government land grants. The nation's steel industry rose to prominence in markets closed to foreign imports when foreign steel producers were not allowed to build the rails upon which Americans would ride. The nation's civilian aviation industry was built on aircraft developed for military transportation. Government construction projects, such as the interstate highway system created the internal markets that allowed construction machinery manufacturers to gain the economies of scale that would allow them to dominate world markets for construction machinery. Computers were first built for and financed by the military—so were numerically controlled machine tools.

Free markets are important in explaining American success, but so is social organization. To win a free market game a country has to be organized to win—as well as willing to play.

In the past Americans have eschewed "industrial policies" while covertly carrying them out. This pattern is likely to continue in the future, but too often implicit industrial policies are inferior industrial policies. Far better to recognize what one is doing and attempt to do it well.

WHAT ARE INDUSTRIAL POLICIES?

Industrial policies are to a nation what strategic planning is to a firm. They outline the basic strategy the nation intends to follow in maximizing economic growth and meeting foreign competition. In both cases the aim is not a fixed, unchanging strategy that firms within an economy or divisions within a firm must follow but an elastic strategy that evolves in response to changes in the environment, that firms helped develop, and that they want to follow. Industrial policies are both an expression of and a vehicle for bringing about a strategic consensus among government, industry, and labor as to the basic directions in which the economy ought to be moving.

Such a strategic consensus allows each of the individual decision makers to undertake actions that will jointly increase the likelihood that all the economy's economic actors will be successful in reaching their desired collective and individual objectives. Business might, for example, promise new investment and labor changes in work rules if government were willing to help finance additional research-and-development expenditures in a particular industry. Or government might promise changes in the tax code which would make it easier to finance new start-up ventures if labor and business would agree to restrain wage and price increases.

The Japanese Ministry of Industry and Trade describes its industrial policies as "first" a matter of "vision." Industrial policies analyze how changes in technology and human needs are going to alter the industrial structure, and they attempt to clarify the problems that will be generated. Given such expected changes, a desirable industrial structure is deduced, but as the MITI says, "visions are not formulated by government alone. They are formulated through open discussions of councils composed of representatives from various quarters, including not just industries but also financial institutions, academia, journalism, labor, small business, consumers and local public entities. A daily exchange of views with corporate managers, careful analysis of industries and industrial structure, and opinions from the press, form the basis of discussions." The visions prepare "well arranged useful information pertaining to the industrial structure, and indicating the basic direction of medium- or long-term policy. Thus the uncertainties inherent in the market economy can be alleviated so that private enterprises may demonstrate their vitality more fully." It is, "however, up to business entirely to interpret or utilize a vision. A vision does not indicate (or dictate) corporate strategy. It must be determined by each individual corporation on its own responsibility."[2]

In addition to general tripartite consultation and bargaining, most industrial policies involve the use of three operating arms.[3]

1. A government agency is established to partially finance civilian cooperative medium-term industrial research on new products or new production processes. Projects are funded in a peer review process in much the same way that the National Science Foundation now awards projects to universities. If the projects prove to be profitable, however, government funds are repaid.

All of our international competitors have such an agency. The most elaborate such activities are found under the jurisdiction of MITI (The Ministry of Industry and Trade) in Japan. As an example of the problem, a recent report of the National Academy of Sciences warns that "the Japanese have a committed effort to develop vigorously and perhaps even to dominate the field of high-technology ceramics . . . They've targeted ceramics and are going after it just like they did with motor bikes, video cassette machines and other industries."[4]

2. Government systematically seeks to reduce the costs and increase the availability of capital to industrial firms. This might entail

the re-establishment of private and public merchant (investment) banking, but it also focuses on changes in tax laws or restrictions in consumer credit provisions to increase the supply of industrial capital. Whenever government credit is provided, however, government receives appropriate compensation in the form of equity (stock, warrants, etc.). All of our major international competitors permit private merchant banking and most have extensive public merchant banking. All have structured their societies to encourage (require) higher personal savings rates. The net result, as documented earlier, is a real cost of capital much lower than that found in the United States.

3. The government has some systematic procedure for dealing with what is essentially "industrial triage." If a sick industry such as steel or machine tools comes to the government asking for protection from foreign competition, government loans, or any other form of aid, the industry—the firms, the unions, the industry's banks, its suppliers—are first required to go away and come up with an industry-developed plan to remake the industry into a world-class competitor. Once this plan has been developed by industry—not by government—the government examines the plan to see whether it is workable and, if it is, what cooperative government actions are needed to complement those promised by industry and labor. If such a plan could not be developed or if the people in the industry were not willing to make the new investments, wage concessions, or whatever else was necessary to make the industry fully competitive, government would not be willing to extend any form of aid.[5]

Other industrial countries have regular procedures that have been worked out for dealing with sick industries. In Japan these procedures allow the establishment of a recessionary cartel. Only the United States relies on ad hoc measures designed after the crises arise.

The goal of industrial policies is not detailed central planning but a cooperative bubble-up relationship where government, labor, and industry can work together to create world-class competitive American industries.[6] Strategic plans become not documents that must be followed but plans that industry and labor helped develop, want to follow, and need help in implementing.[7] Above all, creation of an industrial policy is an educational process—a sharing of information, a foil for industry, labor, and governments—so that each can learn about the problems of the others and how they can mutually interact to solve their joint problems.

WHAT INDUSTRIAL POLICIES ARE NOT

Industrial policies are not a form of central government planning. At most, they are a form of cooperative coordination. They are not designed to slow down the workings of the market but to speed up the workings of the market and remove some of the economic pain and suffering that would occur if the market alone were relied upon.

In well-thought-out industrial policies there is no government agency doing centralized, detailed planning for the economy. No one picks winners or losers. In each case—research-and-development projects, investment projects, restructuring—the initiative must come from the private economy. No government agency has the ability to force any part of the private economy to do anything. If industries do not ask for help, no help can be forced upon them.

In no case can government do anything by itself. Since it can only pay for part of any research-and-development project or part of any investment project, and cannot force restructuring, those projects have to meet a market test. If private entrepreneurs won't put up at least 50 percent of the money or do not want to participate in restructuring, the projects do not get done—no matter how much any government agency may want to do them. Conversely, if aid were offered and taken—research-and-development funds, investments, tariffs, or restructuring assistance—the U.S. government and its taxpayers would always get some form of equity participation (stock, warrants, etc.) to compensate them for the risks undertaken or the costs incurred. The goal is to set up a process in which government, labor, and management are encouraged to work together within a market framework to take actions to strengthen market outcomes. The state becomes not a central planner but a cooperative market player.[8]

Above all, industrial policies are not a magic answer to America's economic problems. They are not substitutes for a good education system, adequate savings and investment, low interest rates, a competitively priced dollar, and better macro-economic policies. They should not be oversold as supply-side economics was oversold a few years ago. If America is to have a competitive world-class economy, it will have to bring each of the major components of the economy— labor, investment, technology, macro-economic policies, industrial policies—up to world-class standards. The only claim for industrial policies is that industrial policies can be a useful addition to these other factors and that if carried out in conjunction with improvements in these other factors can help restore America's lost economic eminence.

THE STARTING POINT

Industrial policies start from the observations that started this book. American industry is being beaten up in international competition, America's productivity growth rates are below those of the competition, and American industry faces a very different challenge in the next thirty years than it had in the last thirty years. For the first time in a long time America faces technologically equal, well-organized competitors backed up by foreign industrial policies. If American firms were coping with this challenge well as they are now organized and if there was not a faint whiff of the stench of economic failure about the American economy, no one would be talking about more explicit industrial policies.[9]

As previously demonstrated, the United States faces not a product cycle where old products are moving off to low-wage third-world countries, not a service revolution where industry is declining to be replaced by services, but the loss of its economic leadership. It is being challenged for economic leadership by other high-wage industrial countries.

Market principles should be used in the necessary restructuring, but markets by themselves are not going to solve American problems in the 1980s any more than they solved British problems at the turn of the century. Economic leadership does not come automatically in a market framework. Nations have to organize and struggle to maintain their positions of economic leadership. America can lose a fair economic game; and if America loses, the game is not automatically unfair just because America has lost. Just as good organization and teamwork lead athletic teams to be winners more often than those who do not have these attributes, so market economies with skillful industrial policies outperform market economies with unskillful industrial policies.

When failure appears, there are three options:

1. Accept the failure and learn to live with it. This means falling standards of living vis-à-vis the world's economic leaders and a loss of general American leadership. No country can be a political or military

leader for long while being an economic failure. I suspect that no American wants America to choose this option.

2. Hope that something magical will come along to reverse America's failure or that foreign competitors will suddenly start to stumble. Either might happen, but neither is likely, nor to be counted upon.

3. Since the old ways have failed, try new ways. Replace the inefficient implicit industrial policies which the United States now has with more explicit, more efficient industrial policies that match those found abroad.

WE DO IT NOW

The real problem is not "Should America have industrial policies?" America already has industrial policies. There is no such thing as a democracy without industrial policies. Every tariff (motorcycles, cheese, textiles), every trigger price (steel), every corporate bailout (Chrysler, Lockheed), every quota (autos, textiles), and any government allocation of private credit (in 1985 the Federal government will be involved in lending activities that total more than $1,000 billion and that are rising at the rate of almost $100 billion per year) is an implicit industrial policy.[10]

The only real question is whether America has effective front-door industrial policies in which it consciously attempts to design a strategy to give America a viable world-class economy, or whether it fails to recognize what it is doing and has back-door industrial policies with case-by-case ad hoc adoption of prop-up-the-losers strategies. By failing to admit what it is doing the American government is unconsciously designing a strategy for failure and lemon socialism where the government ends up owning all of the economy's losers.

The nature of the problem is clearly seen in the Reagan Administration—an administration that argues that America does not need an industrial policy, since all government has to do to guarantee economic success under capitalism is to get out of the way. Despite these views the Reagan Administration has an ad hoc industrial policy. In early 1983 it increased the tariffs on large motorcycles from 4.4 percent to 49.4 percent. How is a tariff on large motorcycles supposed to regain America's competitive edge in motorcycle production? In a good year the only American producer, Harley-Davidson, makes 50,000 cycles. In a bad year, such as 1982, it sold 32,400. In contrast, the Japanese make 7.1 million motorcycles and export almost 900,000 of them to the United States.[11] Given that Japanese motorcycle competition has been on the horizon for decades, why should anyone believe that another two or three years is going to make any difference? What is Harley-Davidson promising to do different from what it has been doing?

The problem with protection unaccompanied by any explicit quid pro quo is that it is always easier to come back for more protection than it is to do all of the tough things that must be done to become competitive on world markets. If the Reagan Administration comes to the rescue of a single firm with only 18,000 cycles at stake, it clearly isn't possible for the political process to resist the lure of bailing out the losers. The American steel industry has been protected since the late 1960s and it is less competitive today than it was then.[12] In late 1984 it had to come back to the Reagan Administration for another round of protection.[13]

The only protection from such a losing strategy is to recognize what America is now implicitly doing, to design effective front-door industrial policies, and to then insist that everyone seeking aid come in through the front door. Explicit industrial policies that set out to create world-class industries are America's only effective protection against implicit policies that only subsidize the inefficient.

One can argue that an explicit industrial policy will not successfully resist a bail-out-the-losers strategy, but even if true, nothing is lost. For that is what America now has. An explicit policy is apt, however, to have more powers of resistance. With an explicit charge to create competitive industries, someone has to explain the failures to do so. With today's implicit policies, no one is so charged and no one has to explain the failures in the steel industry. With explicit policies, where failure has to be explained America is apt to be a lot more successful than it is with implicit policies, under which no one is willing to admit what is being done, much less to explain or defend it.

Much of the controversy about industrial policies is theological (how much respect should be paid to the god of free enterprise) and has focused on the rather narrow issue of whether the United States does or does not need a public investment bank. Public investment banking is not the heart of the issue, and one can be for industrial policies without being disrespectful to the gods of free enterprise or being in favor of a public investment bank. If Ohio State hires a coach and develops a strategy to beat Michigan in football, it is not refusing to play football or playing unfair. It is simply organizing itself to win. Economies also need organization and planning to win. "Social organization" is not a four-letter word.

As far as Washington policymaking is concerned, industrial policies are essentially an attempt to increase the influence of the industrial community. An "industrial viewpoint" is to be brought to bear on decision making. Many people, especially liberals, complain about the excessive influence of the business community in policymaking, but it is important to remember that it is the financial community and not the industrial community that has influence. They are the ones represented institutionally by the Secretary of the Treasury and the Chairman of the Federal Reserve Board. They are the ones with clout. In theory the industrial community is represented by the Department of Commerce, but to mention its political clout in the same paragraph with that of the Treasury or the Fed is to be ridiculous. As Washington is now constituted, industrial firms would have little or no influence if it were not for the political clout of industrial unions.

A SUCCESS STORY

Until the dollar reached the stratospheric heights of 1984 and 1985, agriculture was the industry where America enjoyed its greatest competitive advantage in world trade.[14] Three percent of the labor force accounted for almost one-fifth of America's exports and would have accounted for even more if foreign markets were completely open to American products. It was also the industry with America's highest rate of growth of productivity—a rate more than three times as high as that in the non-farm business sector of the economy since World War II.

What Americans tend to forget is that American agriculture was not always a success story. In the nineteenth century, Russia, not America, was the largest grain exporter in world markets. From 1900 to 1940, U.S. agricultural productivity grew at less than 1 percent per year—with essentially no growth in the first two decades after the turn of the century. In the 1930s, agricultural productivity was far below that of the rest of the economy. American agriculture was an industrial loser—a sunset industry.[15]

After 1940, agricultural productivity grew at more that 6 percent per year and the gap between agriculture and industry quickly narrowed.[16] The shift from failure to success depended not upon good soil or good climate or hard-working farmers—all three were there during the period of failure—but upon an elaborate industrial strategy that heavily depended upon government funds and cooperative arrangements.

The strategy began with research and development. The Federal government put major amounts of money into basic agricultural research at our state agricultural colleges. The resulting research (new seeds, new procedures) was further developed at state experimental farms, and then county agents roamed the countryside explaining the new developments, providing technical aid, and attempting to persuade individual farmers, many of whom had been educated at those same agricultural colleges, to use the new discoveries. While some of the necessary elements (the land grant colleges) were in place before the Great Depression, none of them had a big payoff until they were coordinated and combined with the other necessary complementary factors in the 1930s.

Farming did not become an American success story because of the virtues of the unfettered free market. Farming was deliberately shifted from being a low-tech industry to being a high-tech industry with deliberate industrial policies. America did not inherit its comparative advantage in farming—it created it. Major investments were made in improving the physical infrastructure. Reclamation projects led to massive increases in irrigated farming. Time horizons were lengthened with Federal incentives to encourage conservation projects such as windbreaks and contour plowing—projects that would pay off in long-run productivity gains.

The Rural Electrification Administration (REA) was set up to bring electricity to every farm in America. Enormous productivity gains accrue when farmers can use electrical machinery for the first time. Imagine what today's farms would be like without electricity. Electrification was subsidized with low-interest-rate loans, and although most of us are not farmers, lots of us have benefited from the low-cost agricultural products those infrastructure investments made possible. Our real standard of living is up because the cost of farm products is lower than it would be in the absence of programs such as the REA.

Given problems with farm finance, a plethora of new financial institutions—some public, some quasi-public, some private but with government loan guarantees—were developed. Federal crop insurance, export credit, the Farmer's Home Administration—the list goes on and on. Many of those started with public money, like the REA, and are now self-financing. If one wants to see what happens to farming without these public finance agencies, one can go to any underdeveloped country and study the impact of private agricultural credit arrangements.

Efforts were made to stabilize incomes and output with price supports and acreage controls. The programs were not perfectly run—allowing grain reserves to get too high in the early 1960s and too low in the early 1970s—but they had an important effect, not just on the welfare of farm owners but on farm productivity. With more certainty in their incomes, farmers were willing to make heavy investments in new equipment, banks were willing to lend to finance new equipment, knowing that income to repay those loans was apt to be there, and farm machinery makers could gear up for massive production runs—reducing unit costs—and make large investments in developing new machinery for what was a stable market.

There were problems in our agricultural policies. Too little attention was placed on retraining and relocating those no longer needed in farming. But in agriculture what started out a desperate effort to prop up a very large, very sick industry in the 1930s ended up with an industry which is the world's most efficient. There is no reason why that feat cannot be duplicated elsewhere. There is an American success story.

In 1985 agriculture is again sick. Deprived of its export markets by the high-value dollar, the gains of the 1940s, 50s, and 60s are in danger of being lost. But that is another story best told in Chapter 11.

Similar stories could be told about the Erie Canal (backed by the State of New York), the western railroads (financed with Federal government land grants), and the TVA or Bonneville Power Administration. American history is full of examples where it has in the past made industrial policies work.

Historically the American Defense Department has often played the role of the Japanese MITI in the American economy. This role was cut back with the Mansfield amendment in the early 1970s (this law limited the Defense Department to a more narrow interpretation of what constituted military activities) but is now once again expanding.[17] The Defense Department has its fifth-generation computer project and its very large, very high speed semiconductor project to match those of the Japanese. The Defense Department has a Manufacturing Technology Program to encourage innovations in new production processes. The Defense Department has an Industrial Modernization Incentive Program to speed the installation of new process technologies once they are perfected. The Defense Department's R&D budget is up from one-quarter to one-third of total American R&D spending in the last four years. But, and it is a big but, 90 percent of the money goes to develop and test military projects "that mostly have no potential benefit in the civilian world."[18] A MITI hidden in the Defense Department is better than no MITI but it is not a substitute for a real MITI.

A RESEARCH-AND-DEVELOPMENT GAP

Total American research-and-development spending peaked at 2.9 percent of the GNP in the mid-1960s, fell substantially in the mid-1970s, and then recovered to 2.6 percent of the GNP in 1982. But much of America's spending takes the form of military research and development with limited payoffs in the civilian economy.

If one looks at civilian research and development, America's competitors are now outspending it. During the 1970s America spent 1.5 percent of its GNP on civilian research and development while Germany was spending 2.0 percent and Japan 1.9 percent of its GNP.[19] In the early 1980s the proportion of America's GNP devoted to civilian R&D expenditures was also eclipsed by that of the French. American spending has gone up in the mid-1980s, but most of the increases have been concentrated on defense. Little research is done in the United States outside of the areas where government pays for it directly (space, defense) or where government essentially guarantees that whatever is developed will be bought (health).

In contrast the Japanese government has just announced plans to raise its spending to 3.5 percent of the GNP in the next ten years.[20] Government spending will rise but a new high-tech tax credit has also been announced.[21] The marginal tax credit allowed on R&D will be increased from 20 to 30 percent for general research and be upped to 50 percent for basic research on new industrial materials for expenditures in excess of the average expenditures over the previous three years. The tax credit can be as large as 20 percent of taxes owed. There are no equivalent American plans. Since Americans are not smarter than people in the rest of the world, the R&D gap has to be reversed if America is to remain competitive in new products and processes.

With anything other than short-term development expenditures, government must take an active role to get adequate spending. R&D risks are often large and there is great uncertainty as to whether what will be found will match the characteristics of the firm sponsoring the research so that it can profitably use what was found. Empirically it is difficult for any one firm to capture all of the benefits of any break-through. There are very substantial externalities in R&D that call for government participation.

Once a new product or process is known, it is usually possible for others to invent around patents or simply use the device and litigate (as is now being done with the British patents for float glass). In addition, if something new is developed (hybrid corn), there is public interest in seeing that all of the potential users (farmers) get to use the new product or process as soon as possible. For that is what maxi-mizes American production and American standards of living, al-though it does not necessarily maximize the profits of any one firm. As a result, there is a strong case for using public money to finance research and development and to then rapidly spread the knowledge around the economy.[22]

The American problem, however, is not just too little spending. If one looks at the mix of spending, American firms do an adequate job of financing research and development that will quickly lead to mar-ketable products. The National Science Foundation and the Defense Department have kept us at the forefront in producing basic knowl-edge. Where America falls down is in intermediate-run industrial re-search and development that would lead to new processes for making old products or new products which are five to ten years from market-ability.

If one asks why American firms spend less in this area, there are two sets of answers. Externalities and short corporate time horizons have prevented private firms from financing such research. The par-tial government funding typically found abroad both lengthens time horizons (the firm pays only part of the bills) and reduces the exter-nalities problem (no one firm has to capture all of the benefits for the project to be successful). Government has been reluctant to fund such projects in the United States, since they are seen as a subsidy for one particular company. Cooperative efforts that are open to all firms willing to pay their share of the expenses eliminates the issue of subsidizing one firm and not another, but cooperative efforts have been illegal under American antitrust laws.

A lack of process research is in many ways America's most serious research-and-development failing. Process research often pays off for the economy much more than new products. New products are always small in relation to the total economy and they usually take decades to have a significant impact on national economic performance (think of the computer). In contrast, a new process for making old products can have a big impact, since the markets for many old products are already large. It is also usually easier to copy a competitor's new product (simply buy one and tear it apart) than it is to copy his new production technology. It cannot be bought, and he usually will not let a potential competitor look at it.

American firms have ignored process research and development for a number of reasons. Prestige went to those who developed new products rather than to those who were the cheapest producers of old products. Profit margins were thought to be higher on new, unique products than on old, competitive products. All of this was probably true in the past, but it is now clear that with equal technological competitors, those higher profit margins on new products do not last anywhere near as long as they used to. As the Japanese have shown, the long-term profits go to those with the lowest production costs and not to those who make the original discovery.

From a sociological standpoint, new process technology is also harder to manage. Managers have to confront formal or informal workplace norms of performance. Established routines and old rights and privileges have to be disrupted. With a new product, there are no old norms to disturb. Companies or countries with a more flexible, cooperative work force are going to find that process research and development pays off more for them than for countries with inflexible work forces and unalterable work rules.

Government has also been reluctant to finance process research and development. Process research and development, almost by its very nature, has to be done by some particular firm. The Defense Department has financed some process research, but the half-life of military products is so short that the Defense Department legitimately has only a limited interest in long-run process research on how to make its products cheaper. When the War Department financed Eli Whitney's musket with interchangeable parts, it expected to be making muskets for many years to come.

Historically, America's antitrust laws have discouraged cooperative process research and development efforts that would involve more than one company.[23] This handicap has now been essentially removed, but there still is a gap in the American research and development effort that needs to be filled with a civilian agency of industrial technology—a National Science Foundation for the business community.

Tax credits are often suggested to solve industrial research-and-development problems, but they are not an efficient vehicle for achieving the desired goal. The basic problem is that it is virtually impossible to draw a sharp line between industrial research and development and normal production expenses, especially when process research is involved. It is simply too easy for a company to take an engineer who is basically doing normal production engineering and reclassify that activity as research and development. Thus, tax credits end up costing the Federal government a lot of money without getting any additional research and development as far as the economy is concerned. While the Japanese give a tax credit for research and development, it is only a credit for expenditures over and above those done in the previous three years, to avoid paying for research that would have been done anyway and for "research" that really isn't research.[24]

A civilian ministry of technology or an industrial research-and-development foundation has several advantages. New information can be spread rapidly across the entire economy. Six different companies do not spend money inventing the same wheel. With outside peer review it is possible to insure that the project is a wise expenditure of government money. With more than one firm cooperating, firms also police each other to make sure that their money and the government's money do not become de facto operating subsidies for any one company. Government supervision becomes much less of a problem.

The American machine tool industry is a good example of both the need for such an agency of industrial technology and what it might do. The industry has always been highly fragmented, with little basic research and development. Germany has always been formidable competition in machine tools, but the Japanese are now threatening to drive both the Americans and the Germans out of the market with lower cost and superior-quality products. Yet machine tools are clearly a key linkage industry where the American industry should not fall substantially behind. No country can be fully competitive in new manufacturing industries if it falls behind in building the tools needed by low-cost manufacturers. Japanese manufacturers are always going to get first call on the productive capacity of the Japanese machine tool industry. A series of cooperative, partially government-financed research and development projects are clearly part of the answer to the problems of the American machine tool industry.[25]

In 1983 MITI announced a project with 50 percent government and 50 percent private financing to develop the unmanned garment factory. The idea was to connect a robotized computerized factory via telecommunications with retail stores where individual body measurements could be taken to produce made-to-measure clothes for the price of off-the-rack clothes. If the project succeeds, the Japanese gain an edge not only in garment making but also in the complementary production of garment-making machinery, textiles, and dyes. There is a small private American research project on the same subject funded at one-fortieth the Japanese level at the Draper Laboratories in Cambridge, Massachusetts, but given the scale of the two projects, it is not difficult to guess which is most apt to be successful.[26] What is the American answer to such competitive challenges? There has to be one.

To compete in the high-tech world economy of today and tomorrow America will have to establish a national science foundation for industry. To bring civilian research spending up to the level of our competitors would have required $17 billion extra research-and-development spending in 1983, but only half of this amount should come from government. To insure a market test of workability, government should never finance more than 50 percent of any industrial research-and-development project. Projects would be selected on a peer review process similar to that now used in the National Science Foundation and in general would go only to groups of companies working on collaborative projects. Exceptions might be made for very good projects where there is some valid reason as to why only one firm is willing to participate, but in these cases the outcome would have to be freely cross-licensed to other firms, with the government sharing in the license fees received.

THE INVESTMENT BANKING GAP

The case for private banking has already been made (see Chapter 6) Private investment banks can and should play an important role in both determining and implementing industrial policies. Their ability to mobilize capital can play a vital role in international competition. Strong financial banking allows firms to build the facilities they need, but it can also be used to stop competitors from building competitive facilities. If the Japanese semiconductor industry builds facilities ahead of demand, investors in other countries always see a market with excess capacity and potential downward pressure on prices if they also build new facilities. But as a result of having the financial ability to build facilities ahead of demand rather than behind demand an industry in one country can essentially block capital formation in another country.[27] Financial muscle ends up creating industrial muscle.

In creating such a synergistic relationship between financial and industrial power, there may be a role for public merchant banking as well as private merchant banking. The United States used to have a public investment bank—the Reconstruction Finance Corporation.[28] The RFC played an important and productive role in the American economy through the 1930s and 1940s. It financed, for example, the establishment of the aluminum industry, with the exception of Alcoa. It was abolished in 1953 because of minor scandals (its major fault was financing a casino in a more puritan era) and because it was seen in the context of the then virulent cold war as socialism. In fact most of its activities were not abandoned but dispersed to new agencies—the Small Business Administration, the Export-Import Bank, the Federal National Mortgage Association, and the Commodity Credit Corporation—with less controversial names.

Public investment banking is needed along with private investment banking for a number of reasons. First and foremost, government is now heavily involved in investment banking. That is what more than $1 trillion in loans or loan guarantees means. Given the credit allocation that is now being done by government, it would be far better to establish this function in an investment bank and bring government investment banking out of the closet. If this were done and public loans had to be publicly justified as part of an industrial strategy to create world-class American industries, the investment banking that America now does would be far more efficiently done.

But there are other reasons for public investment banks. In 1981 Japan had 14,000 programmable robots while America had 4,000. How did the Japanese get such a head start? There is an interesting answer. There is a fundamental problem for a firm wishing to produce robots. Initially, it is hard to sell enough robots to get the economies of scale that allow low per-unit costs. Potential buyers do not want to buy very many robots, because they are unsure as to how well they will work and how easily they can be maintained. They want to order a few to experiment, but they do not want to make massive investments.

Enter the Japan Development Bank, a government investment bank, and MITI, the Ministry of Industry and Trade. They organized a government-financed leasing company that guaranteed the producers a rapidly growing market and leased the robots on short-term leases to firms that might use them. Since the firms knew that they could return the robots if they did not work as expected and did not have to make major investments with their own money, they were willing to accelerate the initiation of robots into the production process. If the robots had failed, the Japan Development Bank would have taken a loss. What it did was to essentially socialize risk and speed up a market process. As robots did work, the net result was a new industry that has essentially been conquered by the Japanese before we in America ever knew that it got started.[29]

Question: If the American capital system is so efficient and can get along without public investment banks, why did the same process not happen in the United States? The answer is easy. No private bank has an interest in socializing risk, yet this is precisely what a public investment bank is chartered to do.

Questions: What is the American answer to the Japanese robot leasing company? If it is not a competitive public investment bank, what is it? If there is no answer, what is to stop the same thing that happened in robots from happening in every other new industry? (The same technique was basically used to prevent IBM Japan from dominating the Japanese computer market.) If there are no new successful industries in the United States, how does America succeed and grow in the future?

Public investment banking is also necessary to restructure sick industries. Any restructuring requires investment funds, and they have to come from somewhere. Public investment banks can insist on conditions (lower wages, faster state and local decision making, new managers, new private investments) that private investment banks cannot and will not insist upon. To get cooperation in restructuring, the government also has to have something positive to offer.

Public investment banks can also bring linkages into the analysis that will properly be left out by private banks. Why is it, given the success of the Rural Electrification Administration, that the activity had to be organized by public financial agencies and was not started by private banks? The simple answer is that the private banks could only look at immediate direct returns while the public investment banks could look at the total returns—i.e., increases in agricultural productivity.

Looking at foreign experiences with public investment banking, the major problem is not that they become back-door social welfare agencies (the normal conservative objection) making loans or equity investments that are not justifiable even when total returns are counted, but that they become banks that are indistinguishable from regular private investment banks. Public investment bankers want to be respected among their private investment banking friends—to be offered private job opportunities. As a result, public investment banks gradually move to a position where they are no more willing to take risks, no more willing to look at the long run, and no more willing to look at linkages than other bankers. The real problem is not to keep the public investment bank from being a social welfare agency but to keep it from forgetting that a public investment bank should not use exactly the same criteria as a private bank.

Non-economic loans, favoritism, special interests, and irrelevant geographic interests can be easily prevented with the requirement that no project can receive more than 50 percent of its funds (and its ownership) from the government. If private investors aren't willing to risk a substantial amount of their money, then the project simply does not get done.

The United States should establish a public investment bank with an initial capitalization of $5 billion to see if public investment banking can play a positive role in regaining American competitiveness. Given $1 trillion in outstanding lending and more than $100 billion per year in new government lending or loan guarantees, such a bank would neither constitute a noticeable extension of current government banking activities nor threaten the credit markets with its size. Such a bank should be chartered under a ten-year sunset provision, so that its successes and failures could be judged after a reasonable lapse of time. If successful, its life could be extended; if unsuccessful, it could be terminated.

THE PROBLEM OF INDUSTRIAL TRIAGE

In industrial triage the goal is to rationalize what is, save what can be saved, transfer unneeded resources to the rest of the economy with less pain, and to remake an industry into a viable international competitor. When it comes to dealing with large sick industries, there is no such thing as not having an industrial policy in a democracy. There are simply too many voters being adversely affected to let the market work. America's experience in textiles, steel, auto, farm products, and a host of other industries tells us that America is not willing to let the market work in such circumstances.

Even if America were to let the market work, there are problems with the market solution. The market will eventually drive unneeded firms out of the marketplace, but it is a crude instrument for reaching this objective. The order in which firms are driven out of business depends not primarily upon the quality of their work force, management, or plants—their efficiency—but upon their financial staying power. Firms that start with a lot of financial resources outlast those without financial resources.

Even if the firms get driven out of business in the right order based on their relative efficiency, there are still problems. Pieces of those firms driven out of business (the research and development team, particular plants, certain managers and workers) may be the most efficient in the industry. The long period of losses necessary to drive the least efficient out of business may also so weaken the ultimate surviving firms that they do not have the resources necessary to invest in new products and processes that they will need to stand up to the foreign competition that has not had to undergo such a protracted period of financial bloodletting.

If one wants to watch such a process at work, one has only to look at farm machinery, where a very sick International Harvester demonstrated incredible staying power while forcing John Deere and Caterpillar to suffer large losses. Eventually International Harvester went out of business but not before it had forced substantial losses upon everyone else.

In the rest of the world it would be completely normal to ask the members of a sick industry—the firms, the unions, the suppliers, the banks, the communities—to sit down and determine what part of the industry could be saved and how the industry could work together to strengthen itself. Competing firms might for example work out a shut-down of the most technologically obsolete facilities in such a way that it did not alter the relative competitive strength (market shares) of the firms being asked to shut down excess capacity.

In the United States any such conversation is a criminal conversation under our antitrust laws. While such laws need to be changed, it is also important to have a government representative at such meetings to make sure that they focus on strengthening the industry rather than exploiting the consumer. A government restructuring board is a way to have a government person in the room who can play a positive role and prevent abuses.

In most cases the problem of industrial triage is not a great mystery. Everyone knows what ought to be done to strengthen and restructure an industry. The real problem is putting together a politically viable package to get the job done. Consider the ingredients of an effective industrial policy for steel.[30] It would start with the realization that some part (low technology, standardized products) of the steel industry both should and will move offshore to low-cost foreign producers in Korea or Brazil.[31] Here the industrial policy problem is to help workers move out of these areas of production and into other good jobs.

Part of the industry is viable in the United States as mini-mills, but problems may exist as to siting and environmental regulations. Here the industrial policy problem is to get such decisions made more rapidly and to get the mills into operation faster.

Part of the industry is in the new high-tech sunrise category of powdered metals, metal ceramics, etc. Here the industrial policy problem is to make sure that the necessary research and development gets done in the United States first and to insure that the industry has access to the funds that a new high-tech capital-intensive industry would need.

Part of the traditional industry may be viable if two or three next-generation big integrated steel mills were built at coastal locations. Here the industrial policy problem is partly one of research and development, partly one of financing, and partly one of relative wage and work rules. Can those labor and social factors that must be changed to make new integrated steel mills profitable be changed?

In steel, America has had an industrial policy of protection since 1968, but the industry is competitively weaker today than it was then. To trigger pricing (the previously existing system of protection whereby tariffs and quotas are triggered if import prices fall below some trigger level), the Reagan Administration has added separate tariffs and quotas for specialty steel producers. American buyers of steel are now at a substantial handicap vis-à-vis foreign competitors which buy steel for hundreds of dollars less per ton. It is only a matter of time until the buyers of steel seek protection to offset the higher input costs imposed upon them by the American government.

No formal industrial policy could be worse than the informal industrial policy that America has in fact had in the steel industry. The same political pressures that now exist would exist with formal industrial policies, but those operating the explicit industrial policies would have to explain why they had undertaken policies that led to an American industrial loser. No one has to explain the failures of the current implicit industrial policies. No industrial policy board would have recommended protection without some quid pro quos on the part of the industry, its unions, its banks, and its suppliers. With protection and nothing else, it is simply too easy to slip into a comfortable position as a protected second- or third-class producer of steel, and that is exactly what the United States has done.

The first step in an industrial policy for steel would be to remove all protection and tell the industry that it would not be reimposed until they had come up with a concrete plan to remake their industry into a world-class competitive industry. I would be willing to bet that with such a spur the necessary planning could be done in less than a month. The problem is not "What should the American steel industry do?" but "Doing it is too painful!"

The answer is to put together a package of changes which share the inevitable losses that will have to be shared yet gives each of the major participants a chance to share in the gains that will come from a successful restructuring. In any such negotiations it is important for government to look out for the interests of the consumers, to contribute some of the ingredients that cannot be contributed by the private sectors (a short period of protection, part of the funds needed for research and development), and to serve as a guarantor that each of the parties will live up to its individual commitments.

The United States needs an industrial restructuring board that would be authorized to participate in such conversations. Without it industries that could be partially saved will not be saved.

OTHERS DO IT—THEREFORE YOU MUST DO IT TO REMAIN COMPETITIVE

In the end the case for industrial policies is simple. In a competitive world America has to do what is necessary to be competitive.[32] Competition forces America to do things that America may not want to do.[33] Most of our competitors use public investment banking and government funding of industrial research as two of their competitive weapons. The Japanese robot-leasing firm cited above illustrates the problem. What is the American answer to the cooperative labor-management-government efforts that seems to be succeeding abroad? The United States does not have to have the same answers as its foreign competitors, but it has to have a competitive response.

Suppose the Japanese target (as they have) and succeed in picking off the computer business (which they may well do) with programs such as MITI's fifth-generation computer project and the Japan Development Bank's robot-leasing company.[34] Suppose the French target and succeed in picking off the mass transit equipment industry (as they have). They win the bids for New York subway cars through their Canadian subsidiary. The Germans significantly increase government funding for industrial research (as they have) and attempt to pick off the newly emergent high-technology industry in materials science (powdered metals, metal ceramics, etc.).

At the same time some old American products will become low-wage low-technology projects and move off to the newly industrialized nations such as Brazil, Korea, and Taiwan. That transition is inevitable.

With both trends at work what is left for America? The obvious answer: not much.

There are a number of responses to the argument that in a competitive world the competition often forces America to do things that it may not want to do to remain competitive. One is to argue that foreign industrial policies are not the sole cause of success, especially in Japan.[35] The other is to argue that those in charge of foreign industrial policies have made mistakes.

Both of these are essentially reductio ad absurdum type arguments. Of course, Japanese industrial policies are not the *only* cause of their success. No one can build a high-quality economy out of low-quality components; and the Japanese success is due to many high-quality components—high investment; heavy research-and-development spending; a well-educated, well-motivated cooperative labor force; good management; and good macro-economic conditions. At the same time I know of no serious scholar of Japanese economic success who thinks that their industrial policies have had a negative effect.[36] Quite the contrary. Everyone thinks they played a positive role. The only disagreements are in the precise amount of the success to ascribe to industrial policies.

Similarly, any set of industrial policies will make mistakes. If it didn't, it would not be taking enough risks. The only relevant question is whether the successes outweigh the mistakes. For example, take the Japanese attempt to consolidate the car manufacturing industry in the 1960s.[37] Ex post facto, the attempt was a mistake, in the sense that the proposed consolidation was unnecessary. The Japanese auto industry achieved world domination without consolidation. It may also have conquered the auto industry with consolidation, but it did not need consolidation to achieve this goal.

That "attempted mistake" illustrates the heart of successful industrial policies. In well-designed industrial policies, no Washington bureaucrat would have the ability to force a private industry to take actions that the members of the industry did not feel were in their best interests, just as no Tokyo bureaucrat had the ability to force the Japanese auto industry to take actions that it did not feel were in its best interest. The bottom line of the famous Japanese industrial policy "mistake" is, of course, the fact that the "mistake" never happened. The firms saw the consolidation policy as a mistake and were unwilling to cooperate in a MITI-inspired consolidation. As a result the proposed consolidation did not occur.

At the same time members of the Japanese auto industry will also tell you that they think the "mistake" is part of their current success.[38] Each company knew that if it was not quickly successful on world markets unconsolidated, MITI would be back with a new consolidation plan at some later date. As a result they all worked doubly hard to prove MITI wrong and themselves right.

The attitude of many American firms isn't logically consistent when it comes to industrial policies. At one and the same time they complain about the inherent inefficiencies of government interventions in the American economy and the superefficiency of foreign government interventions to help their foreign competitors.[39] Witness the famous Motorola advertisement:

To many people, Japan is a land of cherry blossoms, gentle ways, and lifetime jobs. There is some truth in that. But, Japan is also the land of a style of industrial expansion which has changed the rules of free market trade.

The very term "free market" is an anomaly in Japan. While Japanese marketers are free to sell their goods in this country almost without restriction, many American and European goods have been virtually locked out of Japan.

Western industrialists prefer world commerce under regulations that permit individual companies to compete separately for markets.

But over two decades ago, Japan added the factors of centralized planning, financing, and control aimed at world-wide domination of certain industries. So, instead of individual companies engaging in market-determined competition, we have had a lop-sided situation. The government of Japan has directed and motivated the moves of selected companies like pieces in a giant chess game.

Once preselected companies have been assigned their roles, little national effort is spared to assist in the completion of the international missions. The government orchestrates; research is combined, and subsidies abound. Preferential loans are granted. Prices, specifications and standards have been collectively determined. Cartels can be, and are, formed.

These tactics, permitted by the government of Japan, would be considered illegal for American companies to engage in here. By targeting industries, Japanese firms are, in fact, selectively exempted from Japan's anti-monopoly laws.

How can the single American or European company compete? We have been spelling out some of the ways. But it is virtually impossible for many companies to combat these combined resources with traditional independent company efforts.

Make no mistake, Japan has not grown to the world success it is, by the normal "every-company-for-itself" rules of western business. Their industrial progress is substantially the result of extreme protection at home and collective efforts permitting targeting abroad. And it is folly to assume that this is a temporary condition. Japan's arrangement is ongoing.

Japan has waived the rules for the past 25 years. If America and western world continue to do nothing about it, Japan may go on to rule the waves for the next 25 years, and longer.[40]

One can argue that this description is a gross distortion of what happens in Japan. Many American firms—IBM, Texas Instruments, Procter & Gamble, and Motorola itself—have successful Japanese operations. Japanese industrial policies are not the top-down "Russian Gosplan" planning implied. They are more of a bottom-up consensus on where and how Japan can best compete in world markets. It is not obvious that MITI's role in the Japanese economy is larger than that of the Defense Department in the American economy.[41] The American government pays for a larger fraction of American research and development than the Japanese government (51 vs. 28 percent). Many foreign products—cheese, textiles, autos, steel—are kept out of the American market. No American producers of semiconductor chips were forced to produce a low-quality product, yet Hewlett-Packard in 1980 found that its worst Japanese supplier was six times more reliable than its best American supplier.

But leave all of that aside, assume for the sake of analysis that all of the charges are true, and think about the appropriate American response. Suppose that the American government were doing all of the things that the Japanese government stands accused of in the previous quotation. What would American businessmen be complaining about? They would be arguing that all of this intervention was destroying the smooth-running efficiency of the private economy.

American industry simply cannot have it both ways. If government industrial policies are inherently inefficient, then American firms should rejoice to see other countries "helping" their industries. Because regardless of how well-intentioned it might be, such "help" really hurts foreign firms more than it helps them; and if American industry is being beaten by those foreign firms hurt by "helpfulness," then American firms are doubly incompetent, for they cannot compete even though the competition is handicapped by a lot of ultimately harmful government intervention.

If foreign helpfulness is simply a subsidy to the inefficient, America should not worry about it. It is a gift to Americans that Americans should accept with the realization that the "universal" subsidy simply isn't possible. The resources to pay for permanent subsidies have to be collected from someone. The only possible someone is a country's taxpayers. If permanent subsidies are to be offered they can only result in a reduction in real standards of living in the country offering them and increase in the standards of living for those in the countries who buy subsidized products. Foreign taxpayers essentially pay taxes to subsidize products going to Americans.

Conversely, if "helpfulness" helps, then Americans are going to have to learn how to organize a helpful government and all of the interventions that "helpfulness" requires. Governments are supposed to take actions to help their economies become more efficient and more competitive.[42] If industrial policies succeed abroad, America will simply have to learn how to make them work in America—or quit complaining about their success and the resulting "unfair" competition coming from abroad.

Countries with industrial policies are not breaking any of the rules of the competitive ball game. Everyone is supposed to sell products at the lowest possible prices. In a similar manner those who invented the forward pass in football did not violate the rules of football. They simply improved upon what was done earlier and forced everyone else to learn how to make a forward pass.

IT'S ALL A MACRO-ECONOMIC FAILURE

Related to the view that good industrial policies have not contributed to foreign success is the idea that American failures are simply due to macro-economic mistakes. If America would just get its macro-economic parameters right—the value of the dollar, the level of interest rates, rapid growth rates—its micro-economic failures would disappear.

The evidence usually cited in favor of this argument is the fact that Americans added more manufacturing jobs than the Europeans or Japanese during the 1970s.[43] While true, this argument turns logic on its head. American manufacturers added more jobs than European manufacturers in the 1970s in part because American manufacturing had a much lower rate of growth of productivity than European manufacturing. The additional jobs were in fact an indication of weakness—not strength. If American manufacturing had had a competitive rate of growth of productivity, it would not have added more jobs than the European competition. As noted earlier, European manufacturers now have higher productivity and lower unit labor costs than their American competitors. American manufacturing declined relative to European manufacturing precisely because it was inefficient and added a lot of new workers in order to serve expanding markets.

To see the absurdity of the "more jobs added" argument, suppose that one were to learn that Indian manufacturing would have to add

3 million new workers to its payrolls to produce an extra $10 billion in output, while American manufacturing would have to add only 1 million new workers to produce the same $10 billion in extra output. Would that lead to the conclusion that Indian manufacturing was superior to American manufacturing? Obviously not.

It would be nice if America's only problems were macro-economic. Macro-economic problems are easier to solve than micro-economic problems. But unfortunately it is not true. The contrary evidence revolves around that twenty year decline in productivity growth. There is no evidence that this trend is caused simply by bad macro-economic parameters or would be reversible with good macro-economic parameters. It has continued through periods with good and bad macro-economic performance. Conversely, the rest of the world has suffered from a macro-economic environment that is just as bad as that in the United States, yet America's major industrial competitors still have very healthy productivity growth rates.

Here again it is important to understand that no one is arguing for industrial policies on the grounds that they can completely "solve" America's economic problems. America needs better macro-economic policies. No industrial policy can succeed with a dollar as grossly overvalued as that in early 1985. No industrial policy can succeed with real interest rates as high as they were in early 1985. No industrial policy can succeed with a stop-go economic cycle. Changes in all of these macro-economic variables is necessary, but such changes do not obviate the need for industrial policies. The basic problem of a low productivity growth rate would still exist even if all of America's macro-economic problems were solved. What does exist looks too much like permanent industrial decline to be casually dismissed.

PICKING WINNERS

Industrial policies exist not to pick the sunrise industries of the year 2000.[44] That is clearly impossible. No one knows what they will be, and the industries that are going to be important employers in the next two decades are already here.

The aim is to strengthen the industries that are now sunrise industries, to restructure old industries so that the parts which remain can exist as world-class competitive entities, to manage decline where decline must occur, and to finance civilian research-and-development projects with long- to medium-term payoffs. In coordination with other policies industrial policies can play a positive role in achieving this result. They are not "the" solution, but they are part of "the" solution.

The aim is not to fight the market but to speed it up or to create new channels in which it can flow. Comparative advantage is a dynamic concept where one's advantages must be created. The goal is not to subsidize capital or operating costs, but to absorb risks socially so that the private economy can move faster to exploit new opportunities.

CORPORATISM

Some object to industrial policies on the grounds that they would increase the power of big business or big labor and lead to the corporatist state. Technically, corporatism exists when public powers are delegated to private decision makers. Large private firms or unions exercise powers that rightfully belong to a democratically elected government.

In this sense, industrial policies are not corporatism. For all public decision-making powers will remain with the democratically elected officials who now make them, and all private decision-making powers will rest with the private decision makers who now make them. Neither side can force the other to make decisions that they do not want to make. As a result, industrial policies are neither centralized government planning nor private corporatism. With industrial policies, private and public decision makers get together to see if they can exchange information and coordinate actions so that each makes better decisions than if their decisions are made in isolation. Synergy is the aim.

While large national firms and unions will, it is hoped, participate with national government in national industrial policies, there is no reason why their participation should lead to the exclusion of small non-union firms or why industrial policies cannot be run in a decentralized way with equivalent local industrial policies being developed at the level of individual states, regions, or cities.

In American history there is a populist strain that maintains that the only good economic and political relationships are adversarial relationships. From this perspective if government, labor, and business get together to work cooperatively on any problem, they will end up screwing the common man. If an end to adversarial relationships is corporatism, then industrial policies are corporatism. Because bringing to an end such adversarial relationships is precisely what industrial policies are designed to do.

If industrial policies succeed in restoring productivity growth and in making the American economy competitive in international markets, they will end up helping, not hurting, the average citizen or the small firm. No one has more of a stake in such a goal than the average citizen. If America fails to meet this goal, it is the average citizen's standard of living that is at stake.

Industrial policies can also be structured so that they are of more aid to small new businesses than the present systems of tax credits or deductions. Research and development tax credits, for example, are only of value to large firms that have other sources of earnings. They are of no value to the new start-up firm. In contrast, a civilian technology agency could and would make some of its grants to groups of firms that included new firms. Small firms and unorganized workers would have to be represented in restructuring efforts, because in the end their voluntary cooperation would be necessary to make the restructuring work.

Finally, there are a couple of provisions that can be built into industrial policies to avoid relationships that become too "cozy." First, as in the case of Chrysler, whenever the government (we the taxpayers) provides aid of any sort, the government should get some equity participation back as compensation for the risks and costs that it incurred. This should also be the case when seemingly costless policies such as protection are used. These policies raise prices for the consumer (the taxpayer), who should be compensated with some equity participation in the industry if he or she is being asked to pay higher prices for protected products. To pay for protection, Ford and General Motors should have given warrants to the Federal government just as Chrysler did for its loan guarantees.

Second, as also was done in the case of Chrysler, the actions of current managers should be externally reviewed to determine whether these are part of the problem or part of the solution. Someone, presumably the current manager, has led that industry into disaster. People who lead other people into disaster should normally be removed from leadership positions. Existing managers should always be forced to prove that the causes of their problems were factors beyond anyone's reasonable foresight or control. Large executive salaries are justified on the basis of heavy responsibility, and those salaries should usually be lost when executives fail to deliver. In most cases the existing managers of firms who have gotten into trouble and need help should be replaced with new managers as they were at Chrysler.

PROTECTIONISM

While pressures for protection will not disappear with the introduction of industrial policies, the ability to resist those pressures should be strengthened. First, the government would not even be willing to talk about protection for an industry until the industry came up with a plan for remaking itself into a world-class competitor. Second, protection would have to be justified in the context of that plan and would not be adopted unless the industry could prove that it needed relief and was doing its share to become really competitive in terms of new investments or wage and work rule concessions. Third, as mentioned above, any protection would yield the U.S. taxpayer some equity participation.

Since explicit industrial policies mean that government has remedies other than protection that it can use to aid an industry (such as R&D funding), it is easier for government to make protection one of the last, as opposed to one of the first, options when requests for aid are being considered. In fact, the dangers are quite the opposite to those hypothesized. Without explicit industrial policies America is drifting very rapidly into protection. The public demands that something be done as American industries seemingly go off the cliff one after another. Not having anything else to do, protection is adopted as the only remedy in one industry after another.

WHAT CRITERIA?

What criteria should be used for research-and-development spending, for investment banking aid, and for implementing industrial triage? Opponents of industrial policies often charge that there are and could be no consistent criteria.[45]

They are both right and wrong. They are right that there can be no criteria that are universally valid across all three of these areas— R&D funding, investment banking, and industrial triage. The problems are too diverse. They are wrong in that consistent, rigidly held criteria as to what industrial policies should do are not what industrial policies are all about.

The National Science Foundation is now involved with picking the most promising basic research projects. Most observers would admit that they are doing a good job—more successes than failures. Yet no one in or out of the National Science Foundation could write down a list of consistent criteria that they use to distinguish between good and bad projects. It is a matter of peer judgment and consultation. The same would be true in a national science foundation for industry.

Yet the problem of what is a good project is easier to solve at the level of industrial research than at the level of pure research. Basic scientific parameters are known, and private industry has to be confident enough of its technological judgments to be willing to invest 50 percent of the money from its own funds. There is both a market test as to what should be done and more scientific knowledge than is usually the case with basic university-based research. The goal of both government and private research-and-development funding sources is to speed up the introduction of products into the market so that they become American products to be sold here and abroad rather than foreign products to be sold here and abroad.

While the goal is speeding up the market, the reduction of private risk and uncertainty is the method used for achieving this goal. A combination of government financing and cooperative financing among companies means that no one company has to carry the risks they would have to carry if they were to go it alone. With several companies involved and cross-licensing to recoup initial R&D investments, there is less uncertainty about payoffs. Even if a firm cannot use the technology itself, it can still get a return on its investment from those who can use the technology.

The same goals and mechanisms exist in the investment banking area. Investments should be made to speed up the market to enhance America's comparative advantage on world markets by reducing the risk and uncertainty faced by private decision makers. The Japanese robot-leasing company is a good example of what has been done abroad and what will have to be done here.

In investment banking there is another consideration. Some new industries, perhaps the new materials science industry that is now coming along, may be so capital intensive and so subject to economies of scale that it is difficult to get started without a consortium of private and public investment banks to share the risks and uncertainties with industrial investors. When it isn't possible to start small and grow large, private markets can become very risk averse—much more risk averse than is warranted from a national perspective.

In industrial triage the goal is to remake industries into industries that are capable of competing in world markets on their own. The criteria for doing this will differ from industry to industry or even within the same industry, as the steel case indicates—sometimes more research and development will be needed, sometimes new investments will have to be made, sometimes old facilities or weak firms will have to be shut down, and most of the time human resources will have to be retrained to move into new industries. The criteria that should be used for each of these possibilities are not those of immutable mathematics but those of judgment. The problem is to find a more efficient, less painful method than that of the market and a more efficient way than that now employed (usually protection with no quid pro quo from those being protected) to revive sick industries.

By sitting the principal actors down together it may be possible to come up with a negotiated package of proposals that would revive part of the industry. The problem is a political one of finding a balanced package of losses so that each actor is willing to quit vetoing change. One can also see this as a policy of reducing private risks and uncertainties—in this case those of decline. Economic actors become willing to make changes in declining industries because they know that their willingness to do so will not lead to their own economic extinction.

It is true, as the critics argue, that no one criterion (high value added per worker, linkage industries, future competitiveness, responding to other governments' industrial policies) is always right, but it is just as true that in certain circumstances all of those factors are germane. As the critics admit, "economies of scale, externalities, and the incentive-distorting effects of government policies furnish a valid basis for targeting—if the theoretical concepts can be turned into measurable factors in practice, and if one believes that the machines of industrial policy will actually work in the way we intend."[46] If good judgment is exercised, this can be done. If Americans have bad judgment, it of course cannot be done. And it certainly cannot be done following a set of formal rules.

In the end all of the critics of American industrial policies come back to that last comment. American government is incompetent and exercises bad judgment. Therefore even if industrial policies work abroad they cannot work here.

A Real Objection

I agree with the critics that this is the real objection. To be successful, industrial policies require that government participants have some ability to exercise discretion and judgment. These participants have to have some freedom from the geographic constraints that so often are built into American legislation. Thus it is possible to argue that although industrial policies have been made to work abroad and are needed in the United States, they cannot be made to work in America because American legislators would never allow the necessary discretion and would impose too many geographical restrictions. If Congress insisted that research and development funds or investment banking funds be spent equally in each congressional district, industrial policies could not possibly work.

The next generation of big integrated steel mills, for example, will have to be built at coastal locations to be economically viable. To be competitive these mills will have to be able to buy coal and iron ore wherever it is cheapest in the world and transport it to the mill at the lowest possible cost. This requires access to large ships. As a result, the next-generation steel mills could not viably be built at the locations of most of our existing old steel mills, and if Congress insisted on them being so built, they would be instant white elephants.

The way to stop Congress from exercising bad judgment, however, is not to pretend that America doesn't have an industrial policy for steel. Having no viable alternatives, Congress exercised bad judgment and gave steel an industrial policy consisting of simple protection. The result, as has been seen, is a steel industry weaker today than it was when the protection began.

Suppose instead that a government investment bank had the power to finance 50 percent of a big integrated next-generation steel mill. There would of course be political pressures to locate the mill at inland locations where steel mills used to be efficiently located, but the government investment bank would be in a position to demand that private sources come up with their half of the funds to pay for their half of the equity. Private investors might be willing to do that for a Baltimore location; they would not be willing to do it for a Pittsburgh location. Given a 50 percent private financing requirement, the government investment bank could say no to Pittsburgh much easier than Congress can now say no.

When America talks about establishing a government investment bank it is simply kidding itself. With over $1 trillion in government lending and loan guarantees, America already has government investment banking. It is simply called congressional investment banking. Those with congressional clout get loans; those without don't.

Instead of setting up a formal government bank where protection against political influence could be written into the rules and where the bank would have to defend itself against charges of political favoritism, Americans refuse to admit what they are doing and engage in congressional investment banking where each congressman brags at election time as to how much political influence he can bring to bear on government lending to help his district. If one wants to minimize political influence in government lending, a formal investment bank is much to be preferred over the present arrangements.

It is certainly true that to make industrial policies work Congress is going to have to exercise some self-restraint. America is not 435 congressional districts but one nation that is in collective competitive trouble. Solutions that benefit the nation as a whole will not benefit every congressional district equally. However, Congress has often acted with self-restraint in the past.

It is defeatism of the rankest sort to argue that members of Congress are so irresponsible that they would rather watch America economically sink than do something that would aid someone else's district more than their own. Anyone holding such views is essentially arguing that America is Rome in its period of decline. The political process has become so corrupt that it can no longer distinguish between the national interest and the immediate self-interest of each elected politician. I simply do not believe this to be true.

A CONTROVERSIAL TERM

If one examines the writings of the critics of government policy, it is clear that the term "industrial policies" is much more controversial than the substance. Those who come out attacking industrial policies end up proposing them in all but name.

Thus Robert Lawrence in the Brookings book previously mentioned in the chapter on international competitiveness argues against industrial policies but wants "an independent analytical agency [to] be established and [to be] charged with the responsibilities of maintaining records and issuing reports on government assistance to industries and firms in all sectors of the economy for the purpose of bringing greater coherence to the totality of policies . . . . Whenever new measures were undertaken, the agency would estimate the costs and benefits and record the objectives as stated by policymakers. All policymaking bodies would be required to file information on policy actions to the agency. In subsequent years, the agency would evaluate the efficacy of such policies."[47] This is a more centralized Washington-based approach than anything suggested by the overt proponents of industrial policies.

Lawrence proposes more government funding for industrial research and development. He also has his own program of industrial triage. Sick industries are to be rescued with vanishing tariffs that offer tariff protection for some limited period of time but grow smaller (vanish) over some specified period of time. Firms in sick industries are also to be allowed exemptions from antitrust laws if they wish to merge. Workers in those same industries would be given a trade adjustment assistance subsidy equal to 50 percent of the difference between the wages in the job they lost because of foreign competition and the job they now have. In cases of foreign targeting or assistance, American retaliation "should be confined to cases in which U.S. national economic welfare is clearly adversely affected and in which U.S. retaliation is likely to make the nation better off." Who could disagree? Matching credits are suggested in cases where negotiations do not lead to the elimination of foreign government aid for their industries. Vague political pressures are to be used to allow American firms to participate in Japanese industrial policy programs (Lawrence does not explain why anyone would want to participate if they never work) and to have open access to the Japanese market. Who could disagree? The only question is how?

These policies are not all that different from those advocated by Otto Eckstein, a proponent of industrial policies.[48] The *DRI Report* calls for lowering the costs of industrial capital with tighter budget policies, the end of preferential financing for non-industrial investments, and easier access to long-term debt capital for long-life assets. Although the means for the last objective are left unspecified, the reinvention of investment banking, public or private, is one option.

To preserve America's lead in high-technology industries, public policies must increase the supply of technical manpower and increase funding for research and development, according to Data Resources, Inc., since America now spends less on civilian R&D than its major competitors and less than it itself used to spend. Parity is to be the goal. International trade policies are to be focused on reversing the declining role of U.S. goods in world markets and to opening up foreign markets, especially those in Japan.

When it comes to what must be done, there is a lot of agreement between the Brookings and the DRI documents. Both propose an industrial policy, whatever words they choose to use.

So does the right-wing guru Kevin Phillips.[49] He proposes a new Department of Trade to coordinate our international economic policies and take a tougher line to open up foreign markets. Antitrust policies are to be changed to permit cooperative research. Tax credits and export interest rate subsidies are to be used to promote exports. Workers are to be retrained and the Federal government is to pump more money into research and development.

The words "industrial policy" are controversial. The substance is much less so. If the words "a competitiveness policy" are less controversial, let's all agree to use them from now on out.

THE BOTTOM LINE

Competitiveness policies are not a magic answer to America's economic problems.[50] If America is to have a competitive economy, it will have to bring each of the factors that go into the economy—labor, capital, management—up to world-class standards. By themselves competitiveness policies will do little, but in tandem with other world-class components they can help lead to a world-class American economy.

Compare America's competitiveness policy of propping up Harley-Davidson using high tariffs with the Japanese policy of subsidizing research and development on the fifth-generation computer. Which economy is more likely to succeed? To ask the question is to answer it.

PART FOUR

The Economic Environment

10 / Macro-Economic Conditions

In 1983, 1984, and 1985 the United States was in the "go" phase of "stop-go" economics. The economy was in its ninth expansion since World War II, but such a recovery provides no evidence that the structural parameters of the economy had been changed to reduce the expected number of recessions in the next thirty years. Quite the contrary. Unemployment hovered above 7 percent; inflation fluctuated around 4 percent. Stagflation was still lurking in the wings. Given the next surge in inflation, the authorities (Democrat or Republican) would once again be stepping on the economic brakes to create the tenth recession since World War II. America was still riding a self-constructed cyclical economic roller coaster.

In one sense the fiscal experiments of the early 1980s were comforting. Keynesian economics had once again been shown to work. In 1981 and 1982 there were arguments that it could not work because of "crowding out" and inflationary expectations. Higher public consumption would lead to higher inflationary expectations and as a consequence to higher interest rates that would lower private investment with no net increase in the GNP. Put to the test by the Reagan Administration, such a pessimistic scenario did not occur. The GNP boomed in 1983 and 1984, with investment reaching approximately the same levels that had occurred before the 1981–82 recession.

There was also an argument as to whether the United States was still large enough to practice one-country Keynesianism. According to some economists, imports would flood in as the American GNP expanded, the dollar would fall, and the authorities would be forced to stop stimulating the economy to protect the dollar. What was predicted happened to France when it tried to practice one-country Keynesianism at the beginning of the Mitterrand Administration, but these worries at least in the short run proved to be groundless for the United States. Imports did flood in, but the dollar did not fall, and the authorities were not forced to retreat to austerity.

If the problem is escaping from the quicksands of a major recession or depression, large Federal deficits can restart economic growth regardless of the level of interest rates. That is the lesson of recent history, and it is a historical lesson well worth remembering for the future.

The Phillips curve (the belief that higher unemployment leads to lower inflation) was also shown to be alive and well in the early 1980s. Pessimists had argued that inflationary expectations were so ingrained that high unemployment would not lead to a slowdown in inflation. If one examines the slowdown in inflation between 1980 and 1984, however, quantitatively it was just what one would have predicted given the level of unemployment and the behavior of price shocks in food and oil.[1] In the years after 1980 unemployment approached 11 percent, was held above 7 percent for four years, and was still above 7 percent in early 1985. High unemployment led to lower wage increases and less inflationary pressure, as expected. Instead of rising, food and oil prices were also falling. Neither the earlier rises nor the later falls were under the control of American policymakers. They were simply exogenous price shocks that the American economy could only weather. Good luck replaced bad luck.

After being reduced with unemployment and favorable price behavior in food and oil, inflation was at least temporarily capped by the high-valued dollar. Given the value of the dollar prevailing in 1984 and early 1985, American firms could not take advantage of the rapid recovery to raise prices without further eroding their market shares. If they had raised their prices, Americans would simply have bought cheaper foreign goods.

Historically, the relationships between inflation and unemployment have proven to be correct, although those who in the early 1980s were predicting the future course of inflation have been proven wrong. Those making the predictions simply did not believe that the policymakers would or could hold unemployment so high for so long and that food and oil prices would turn down as fast and as far as they did. Inflation fell faster than predicted not because the economic relationships were more favorable than previously expected but because the system proved to be more politically tolerant to high unemployment than anyone imagined possible.

Unfortunately, while under good control temporarily, the long-run inflationary problem persists like a dormant virus waiting for the right environment to break out. Eleven percent unemployment rates may stop inflation, but they validate a pessimistic Phillips curve in which very high levels of unemployment are necessary to stop inflation and inflation starts to accelerate long before the economy reaches anything resembling full employment. Experts differ as to how low unemployment could go without inflation accelerating, but the estimates range between 6 and 7 percent.

As it is now structured the American economy cannot operate at low rates of unemployment for long periods of time without the emergence of inflation. Localized exogenous price shocks (oil, food, a falling dollar) are quickly transformed into generalized inflation. If America is to be successful, that structure must be altered so that the economy can operate at full employment without inflation for long periods of time.

The Democrats practiced Phillips curve economics (step on the monetary and fiscal brakes when inflation occurs) under President Carter. Using the Phillips curve approach to curing inflation meant that President Carter had to deliberately engineer a recession when inflation struck in 1980. In doing so, however, he was deliberately raising the unemployment rates of exactly the groups that he supposedly represented right before an election. If these groups then didn't vote for him, as they didn't, no one should have been surprised. The Democratic party wasn't looking out for the welfare of those it sought to represent. Democrats lost, and should have lost, the 1980 election as a result.

The Democratic party cannot afford to practice Phillips curve economics under the next Democratic President. The minimum level of unemployment consistent with price stability, sometimes called the natural rate of unemployment, is too high. Too many traditionally Democratic voters have to be forced into perpetual unemployment to hold inflation in check and too many recessions have to be created.

Democratic leaders must find a technique for stopping inflation that does not rely on forcing Democrats and other Americans into unemployment.

More importantly, with a stop-go strategy of controlling inflation it is impossible to build a high-productivity competitive world-class economy. Who is going to invest in major new facilities when more than 35 percent of capital capacity is idle? No one. Who is going to pursue better education and training for the labor force when there are unemployed workers in every category from illiterate to Ph.D.? No one. Who is going to increase research-and-development expenditures when firms are going broke and corporate profits falling? No one. Who is going to be willing to build new cooperative labor-management relations in a context where managers are always firing workers. No one. In recessionary contexts everyone is going to focus on his own short-run economic self-interest and quite rationally not worry about long-run common problems.

To break out of stop-go economics is going to require changes in the structure of the American economy. As it is now structured, Phillips curve economics is the only game in town. Breaking out is not impossible. A better macro-economic performance is both necessary—and possible.

NO MAGIC MONETARY BUTTONS

For many years the monetarists told Americans that inflation was simply the product of stupidity. The monetary authorities were letting the money supply grow too rapidly. If only the money supply were to grow at the right rate, the economy could have full employment without inflation. Given an already existing inflation, a slowdown in the rate of growth of the money supply might involve some transition costs in the form of a recession according to some of the monetarists, but at most it would take a brief mild recession to correct the previous "imbalances" that had built up in the economy.[2] In the peculiar version of monetarism and supply side economics that came to be known as Reaganomics society was promised a transition to full employment without inflation with no intervening recession.

Given the conservative orientation of the economists that preached monetarism, one would have thought that Democrats needed no inoculation against the disease of monetarism, but it did not prove to be so. Monetarism actually began under President Carter with the appointment of Paul Volcker as Chairman of the Federal Reserve Board. As a doctrine it was put to the test between October 1979 (the date when the Federal Reserve Board officially proclaimed its allegiance to monetarism) and August 1982 (the date when the Federal Reserve Board abandoned monetarism) in the midst of the Mexican crisis mentioned earlier. In between it failed, producing a recession much larger and longer than anyone had anticipated.

Having been wrong about the extent of the recession that would be caused by tight monetary policies, the monetarists were equally wrong on the upside. When the Federal Reserve allowed the money supply to grow very rapidly in the year after August 1982, the monetarists confidently predicted rapid inflation in 1984 and 1985 as a result.[3] The predicted inflationary upsurge did not occur.

Theories have to be judged on the practical grounds of whether they do or do not work, but this only gets into the sticky question of what is meant by "work." Here one can only look at what the proponents of the theory claimed before the experiment began.

When it came into office the Reagan Administration claimed that monetarism in conjunction with supply-side economics could stop inflation without stopping the economy. Judged according to the predictions of what the Reagan Administration said would happen, monetarism is a failure. It did not live up to the predictions of those who designed it and supported it.

Monetarists have also always maintained that real interest rates (the rate of money interest minus the rate of inflation) did not depend upon the rate of growth of the money supply. A slow rate of growth of the money supply would not cause high real interest rates, in the theory. Yet real Federal Funds (overnight loans) interest rates were at record (7.9 percent) levels in the twelve months before August 1982. Why?

If predictions do not come true and practical men of affairs are forced to abandon the prescriptions behind those predictions, what is left? The theory is wrong. Or it has been poorly implemented. Not surprisingly, the proponents of monetarism came to the latter conclusion. According to these proponents monetarism failed because there was too much short-run volatility in money supply growth. The money supply was on target from year to year, but with too much variance from month to month. The short-term variance confused the public as to what the underlying trends were. Without the certainty of a slow future rate of growth in the money supply, the slow monetary growth policies from 1979 to 1982 did not have "credibility." And without "credibility" inflation was expected to rise in the future. Current interest rates reflected those high future inflationary expectations, but since current inflation was very low current real interest rates were very high.

Unfortunately this explanation simply isn't credible. Future inflationary expectations have nothing to do with short-term interest rates. The only rate of inflation that should be built into today's overnight loan rates is today's inflation rate.

To be useful, monetarism also needs a stable or predictable velocity of money. To set the right money supply the central bank must know how often per year the average dollar will be used to make a transaction. But in the period from 1979 to 1982, the velocity of money was highly variable and not predictable. Not knowing what needed to be known, no one could set the right money supply targets.

Just as importantly, the monetarists must explain why the Fed fouled up. Why didn't it run monetarism right? Was Chairman Volcker really a closet Keynesian out to discredit monetarism? Even the monetarists are reluctant to so charge. So far their explanations run in terms of "bureaucratic lethargy." The Fed was just too lazy to do it right. But is that really credible? The economy going down the tubes because some bureaucrats aren't willing to work hard and do it right. Hard to believe!

When it comes time to explain those high real interest rates to congressional committees, Chairman Volcker points at the Federal deficit. But it has always been an axiom of monetarism that government deficits don't matter. It is the Keynesians who believe that deficits are important. By the very fact that he points at the deficits the Chairman is indicating his own disbelief in the theories that he himself inaugurated at the Fed.

Moreover the monetarist promise of full employment without inflation was always more a sleight of hand than a real promise. Technically the monetarist only promised a stable inflation rate at the "natural" rate of unemployment; and this was a tautology since the natural rate of unemployment was defined to be that rate where inflation rates are stable. Monetarists never promised a zero rate of inflation—or anything close to it—and they never promised a low natural rate of unemployment. No one knows where the natural rate of unemployment is, if it exists at all, or if it is stable; but officials of the

Reagan Administration have placed the natural rate in the 7 to 8 percent range. More optimistic outside observers have placed the natural rate at 5.5 to 6 percent range. Whichever is true, neither constitutes an acceptable level of unemployment.

The evidence of history is clear. Monetarism did not deliver what it promised to deliver. Future Democratic presidents should avoid it like the plague.

Abandoning monetarism, however, does not solve the basic problem of keeping inflation in check. The public would clearly like a 3 to 4 percent unemployment rate, since this is the rate at which almost all of the unemployed are voluntary job changers. It would also like a 1 to 2 percent inflation rate, since at this rate what is measured as inflation is likely to be unmeasured improvement in product quality rather than real inflation. While desired and desirable, such goals are not now achievable in the American economy as it is now structured. To achieve these goals, it will be necessary to engage in some major structural changes. Democrats should lead in this effort.

WHOSE INCOME GOES DOWN?

The heart of the inflationary dilemma can be clearly seen in the second oil shock in 1979. OPEC doubled the price of oil and America's bill for imported oil rose from 2 to 5 percent of the GNP.[4] At the same time America's GNP was not growing. As a result, at the beginning of 1980 there was only 97 percent as much left to be divided among Americans as there had been at the beginning of 1979. An extra 3 percent of the American GNP had been given to OPEC. As a matter of simple arithmetic, the average American standard of living had to fall 3 percent. There were two ways to deliver the bad news.

1. If wages (and all other income) had fallen 3 percent, balance would have been restored between American incomes and the products left to be purchased by Americans. If wages had fallen, domestic prices could have fallen, counterbalancing the initial rise in energy prices and producing a non-inflationary economy.

2. Alternatively all could attempt to preserve their standard of living with a wage hike. This was the path actually chosen, and wages rose 9 percent in 1979. But without an equivalent gain in productivity, higher wages led to 9 percent higher production cost and 9 percent higher domestic prices. When compounded with the initial increase

in oil prices, the aggregate inflation rate rose to 12 percent. Real standards of living still fell 3 percent (prices were rising at 12 percent while wages were rising at 9 percent), but now America had to suffer both a 3 percent reduction in its standard of living and a 12 percent inflation rate.

No one wants to accept a fall in their standard of living, yet the fall is inevitable for the average American in circumstances such as those in 1979. Most Americans think that if they raise their wages faster than the rate of inflation then they can be the exception to the general rule. They are right, but as each of us seeks to become that exception, we only make the general inflationary problem worse. What is individually rational is socially irrational.

In the aggregate real wage rates cannot on average rise faster than productivity. No one can divide nonexistent output. If productivity is not growing, then the average real American wage rate will not grow regardless of how fast money wages are growing. If productivity is not growing, the only non-inflationary wage gain is "no" wage gain. In a world with no productivity growth if anyone's wages are rising faster than inflation then someone else's wages (income) must be rising slower than inflation.

The problem is not knowing such "facts of life." Most Americans know the "facts of life." What Americans do not know is how to deliver the bad news to themselves in such a way that they will accept it without making the problem worse. Inflation is simply the easiest way to deliver the bad news about slower productivity growth or a deterioration in America's terms of trade where more exports must be given up to buy the old volume of imports. With inflation, everyone can blame inflation on the government and not have to confront the fact that their wages are stagnant because their productivity is stagnant. Instead of an employer having to tell his employees that this year there are no wage increases because he and they have not learned how to work smarter, the employer distributes a 5 percent wage gain, all mentally congratulate themselves on their intelligence and hard work, and then bitterly complain when that 5 percent wage gain is taken away from them in the form of a 5 percent price hike.

The cure for inflation is not found in remedying stupidities at the Federal Reserve Board. If Americans want to live in a society without inflation they will have to discover an acceptable way to cope with bad news on the productivity or terms-of-trade fronts.

SOMETHING AMERICANS DO KNOW

While it is important to know what Americans do not know (how to run the economy at full employment without inflation), it is equally important to know what we do know. We know how to restart the economy's engines and that it is not necessary to tolerate prolonged recessions.

In the process of time President Reagan has become the ultimate Keynesian. Despite tough talk about holding down government spending, expenditures rose rapidly under President Reagan—up 48 percent from fiscal 1980 to fiscal 1984.[5] The extra spending has come in a form of public consumption called national defense but that does not make it any less government spending. The Reagan tax cuts were supposed to raise the personal savings rate, but as seen, they in fact reduced it. In 1983 the American personal savings rate was lower than it had been at any time in the previous twenty-five years. As a consequence, the tax cuts ended up stimulating demand rather than supply. When the authorities decided not to let Mexico default, the money supply, in correspondence with the dictates of Keynesian economics, grew rapidly at more than 12 percent in the following year.[6]

Consumption-oriented private tax cuts, increases in public consumption, a government deficit three times as large as that incurred by any previous President—that combination of policies is called Keynesian economics and it works. Keynesian economics was designed to lift the world economy out of the Great Depression. It worked then and the Reagan Administration proved that it works now.

The Reagan Administration is rehabilitating exactly the economic policies it pledged to bury when entering office, but it is also applying them more vigorously than any self-proclaimed Keynesian would have dared. Imagine what conservatives would be saying if a liberal Keynesian Democratic President had dared to run $200 billion deficits. The part of Keynesian economics that President Reagan is not practicing is the conservative part which calls for gradually eliminating government deficits as the economy approaches full employment. With the present structure of taxes and expenditures, the Reagan deficits will be larger at the end of the 1980s than they are in the middle of the 1980s.

The problem with the old Keynesian remedies, or the new Reaganomics if you prefer, is that they need to be combined with something else to be capable of running the economy at full employment without inflation. A Keynesian recovery starts with a demand-side stimulus, unemployment falls for both men and machines, but inflation breaks out long before the economy is fully employed, government steps on its monetary or fiscal brakes to stop inflation, unemployment rises, starting the stop-go economic cycle all over again. The real problem is not engineering a Keynesian recovery but being willing to make the structural changes in the economy that would allow America to break the stop-go cycle.

Income Flexibility

It is clear where structural changes are needed. A more flexible system of income determination (wages, salaries, dividends) needs to be built into the system. To run an economy at full employment without inflation, changes in incomes have to mirror changes in the rate of growth of productivity (output per hour of work) and changes in the terms of trade (the price of imports relative to the price of exports). If productivity falls and the terms of trade deteriorate, less output is being produced per hour of work and more of what is being produced has to be given to foreigners to buy needed imports, leaving less output remaining to be divided among Americans. If the necessary declines in real income are not to be delivered by inflation (prices rising faster than wages and salaries), wages and salaries have to fall.

The current stop-go strategy of using recessions or depressions to beat inflation out of the system is a failure. High unemployment can be used to repress inflation, but it is not a cure. America simply trades off one problem, inflation, for another problem, unemployment. Since when America goes back to low unemployment inflation breaks out in just as virulent a form as before, nothing is gained by being willing to tolerate high unemployment. However long Americans are willing to endure high unemployment, it never produces an economy that can simultaneously and persistently operate at full employment without inflation.

A recessionary strategy also entails enormous costs in both economic and human terms. When unemployment rises from 4 to 11 percent, America incurs a loss of more than $240 billion in annual GNP. Every man, woman, and child in America loses $1,000 in potential income. Those who are drafted into unemployment to be "Inflation Fighters for the U.S. of A." find both their careers and their self-respect shattered.

Medical researchers have found relationships between unemployment and increased blood pressure (hypertension), abnormal cholesterol levels, ulcers, respiratory diseases, hyperallergenic reactions, and alterations in blood chemistry. Age-adjusted death rates go up for the unemployed. Psychological evidence shows relationships between unemployment and feelings of aggression, anxiety, and depression. Sociologists link unemployment with alcoholism, suicide, homicide, mental hospital admissions, imprisonments, divorce, and child abuse.[7] In the last few years one had only to be a regular reader of newspapers to see specific human examples of all of these problems.

The drafting into unemployment is also done in a very uneven, very unfair way. Official unemployment rates for black teenagers were nearing 50 percent in late 1982; and if corrected for lower labor force participation rates among black teenagers than among white teenagers, total unemployment was over 70 percent. At the other extreme white professional workers had an unemployment rate of only 4 percent.[8] While the output of the auto industry fell more than 50 percent, the output of the health-care industry rose 10 percent.

The many may have benefited from lower inflation but the few have been asked to pay an enormous price. Politically the strategy has also reached a dead end. To control inflation in the decade after the first oil shock unemployment had to rise from 3 to 11 percent in the industrial world. Can you imagine our societies being able to take the social and political strains of going up a like amount in the next decade?

While it is probably impossible to evade every business cycle, it is possible to create a world where government does not deliberately create economic downturns. In this context it is well to remember that every recession since 1960–61 has been deliberately caused by government to stop inflation. There have been no accidental recessions. If government-induced recessions had been avoided, there would have been no recessions in the last two decades.

UNEMPLOYMENT AS A SOCIAL PROBLEM

Over the past two decades industrial societies have been willing to tolerate higher and higher levels of unemployment. Those who predicted revolution and social unrest in the wake of high unemployment have been proven wrong, but that does not mean that they were wrong to be concerned. Unemployment leads not to revolution but to social decay and individual disintegration. On any given day nothing terribly important seems to be occurring, but over time unemployment is a corrosive mixture.

Anyone who has been unemployed or who has had a friend who has been unemployed for a substantial period of time knows that it is almost impossible not to get "down" on oneself. What is in fact a social disease—there simply is not enough work to go around and someone is going to be unemployed—is seen as a personal disease: "I am economically worthless." This feeling is compounded in a society that uses work to measure worth. In 1982 I was told the story of a five-year-old whose father was going to take her to her first day of kindergarten. She asked her father to wear a suit so that the other children wouldn't think that he was unemployed. Suppose he had been unemployed. Think of the disgrace to both the child and the father.

Even if you do not personally know some good hard-working family whose lives have been destroyed by the 1979–82 depression, almost everyone has by now read about such people. Do they deserve what they are getting? They could be us. Yet we continue down the path of attempting to cure inflation by deliberately destroying their lives. There has to be a better way.

Bad as they are, official unemployment rates substantially underestimate total unemployment. In the last quarter of 1982 the official unemployment rate was 10.5 percent. But in addition to 11 million officially unemployed people there were 2 million discouraged workers (people who no longer met the test of actively looking for work and therefore were not counted as "officially" unemployed) and 6 million workers who were working fewer hours than they would like to work. Altogether, 17 percent of the population was totally or partially unemployed.[9]

The official "average duration of unemployment" was twenty weeks in 1983, not a trivial number, but that number also does not express what it seems to express—the length of time the average person will remain unemployed.[10] Suppose that every worker were to remain unemployed exactly forty weeks. A national snapshot of unemployment would find an equal number of unemployed workers in every week from one week to forty weeks with an "average duration of unemployment" of twenty weeks even though every unemployed worker would actually be unemployed forty weeks. In addition almost half of the jobless leave unemployment not because they have found work but because they drop out of the labor force.

Unemployment insurance certainly mitigates the economic hardship for those who get it; but in contrast with the extensive coverage typical in Europe, payments are made to a surprisingly small percentage of those unemployed in America. Only 4.3 million workers, less than 40 percent of those unemployed, were getting any unemployment insurance checks in 1982. And among that 40 percent unemployment insurance was replacing only 43 percent of their previous income.[11]

Prolonged stagnation and repeated business cycles end up reducing the quality of the labor force. The baby-boom generation (now twenty to thirty-five years of age) should be getting on-the-job training and integrating itself into the work force, but it won't if the opportunities for advancement simply aren't there because of repeated recessions. The decade from age twenty-five to thirty-five is the traditional period of gaining the skills used in later life, and no one knows whether a lack of training and job opportunities between twenty-five and thirty-five is remediable at a later age. Economically, swallowing anything as large as the baby-boom generation was bound to cause some indigestion, but it is important that the baby-boom generation be brought into the economic mainstream and given the set of economic opportunities open to everyone else. For if it remains undigested it is apt to give the rest of the society indigestion.

As unemployment has risen, I have repeatedly heard the sentiment privately expressed that it cannot really be that bad. After all, "They aren't rioting." Democracy was invented, however, to solve problems before they lead to riots and revolutions. Riots are a mark of profound political failure—not a statistical indicator that it is time for policymakers to address the problem of unemployment. Americans have all repeatedly seen those pictures of thousands of unemployed people lining up to apply for a few low-wage jobs in 1981 and 1982. In one sense those pictures are pictures of a profound national disgrace. In another sense Americans can take pride in the fact that American people are willing to line up peacefully despite their own personal problems and the desperation with which they need work. Their individual patience with the system, however, is not an excuse for social patience. A cure is needed *now*.

At one level job creation is trivial. Employment will grow in any economy where the demand for goods and services expands faster than the rate of growth of output per hour of work (productivity). If more jobs are needed, simply speed up the growth of demand. Americans know how to do that. Any society can speed up the growth of demand for its goods and services with lower interest rates, tax cuts, or increases in government spending.

If the question is "Can America provide jobs for everyone able and willing to work?," the answer is unambiguously yes.

If the question is "Has America provided jobs for everyone able and willing to work?," the answer is just as unambiguously no. Marxian predictions have been wrong on many fronts, but on one front Marx has been "right on." As he predicted, capitalistic economies have found it impossible to run continuously at full employment. The problem began with periodic recessions in the nineteenth and early twentieth centuries, exploded into the Great Depression of the 1930s with its 25 percent unemployment rates, continued with eight recessions between 1945 and 1975, and ended up with a mini-depression and the production of double-digit unemployment between 1979 and 1982. Viewed historically, unemployment crises are the norm and not an abnormality.

If the question is "Will America provide jobs for everyone able and willing to work in the 1980s?," the likely answer is also no. That negative answer springs from an examination of America's own history. In peacetime, America has never operated for any long period of time at full employment.

If one asks, "Why hasn't America created the jobs it could have created?," there is an equally simple answer. Unemployment is the only cure for inflation. Governments deliberately step on the economic brakes to control inflation with high unemployment. From a social perspective the unemployed are not unemployed but unpaid workers being used to discipline the wage demands of the employed.

One option if America wishes to enjoy a low inflation rate is simply to live with high unemployment for the foreseeable future. It is this option that is being recommended when economists or politicians start talking about the natural rate of unemployment.

Another option is to rebuild the structure of the economy so that it can operate with both low unemployment and low inflation. Here most of the difficulties are political and not economic. Structural changes could be made to make the economy much more inflation resistant. My MIT colleague Martin Weitzman has outlined an institutional arrangement whereby the economy can generate both full employment and low inflation in his book *The Share Economy*.[12] Essentially it is the bonus system seen earlier in the context of raising productivity and savings rates.

Suppose that instead of being paid a fixed per-hour, per week, or per-month wage, workers were to get a share of a firm's valued-added or gross selling revenue, which would then be divided among them. Wages would go up and down as selling revenue went up and down, and this would permit wages to mirror changes in productivity growth and the terms of trade—hence stopping inflation. Employers would want to hire new workers whenever unemployment existed, since new workers would be paid out of labor's share and would not cost the employer anything on the margin—hence preventing unemployment. The problem is not finding a cure for inflation and unemployment but persuading the public that such cures provide a better social structure than what they now have.

Social organization matters. The most efficient forms of social organization do not automatically come to the fore. Social choice is important. Societies can organize themselves efficiently or inefficiently. America can organize itself more efficiently than it is now organized.

Weitzman starts with a simple sociological observation that rests on an underlying economic foundation. In capitalistic economies sellers give gifts to buyers at Christmastime, but in socialistic economies buyers give gifts to sellers. Why? In socialistic economies the problem is production. There is a scarcity of goods at current prices and buyers need to ingratiate themselves with (bribe?) sellers. In capitalistic economies the problem is sales. There is a surplus of goods at current prices and sellers need to ingratiate themselves with (bribe?) buyers.

The reasons for the difference are simple. Modern advanced capitalism is marked by imperfectly competitive firms. Most firms are large enough that they cannot sell all that they can produce at current prices but must lower prices (or raise selling costs) to sell more of what they produce. This means that the extra revenue (what economists call marginal revenue) from an additional unit of sales is less than the price (what economists call average revenue) previously received. But if society wants firms to expand their production to full employment levels, then production costs must fall as sales expand. If production costs do not fall as output expands, firms will not expand production, since to do so would be to lose money. The falling revenue per unit of extra sales does not cover the costs incurred in producing more output.

Since labor costs typically constitute 70 percent of total production costs, labor costs must fall if total production costs are to fall. In the textbook world of classical supply and demand they do so. Full employment is guaranteed by falling wages. If unemployment breaks out, unemployed workers will bid for current jobs by offering to work for less than those employed and in the process drive wage rates down for those employed. With lower wage costs, employers will expand production. With production expanding, unemployed workers will be reabsorbed back into employment. In a perfectly competitive economy where every market worked as it is supposed to, unemployment would not exist; and if it were to break out for some unknown reason, it would be quickly absorbed by the expanding demand flowing from falling wages and lower production costs.

The unfortunate reality is that unemployment does exist and wages do not fall to reduce production costs. Despite unemployment rates ranging from 25 percent in 1933 to 17 percent in 1939, real wages rose during the Great Depression for the lucky ones who remained employed. From 1979 to 1982 average labor compensation rose 30 percent despite an unemployment rate which almost reached 11 percent. Wages should have been falling to reduce unemployment, but they weren't. Perhaps if America had been willing to let the Great Depression run for more than ten years and had been willing to let the recent maxi-recession run for more than four years, wage rates might have started to fall—but that remains a hope. In neither case were there any signs that the wage structure was about to crack. Within any reasonable period of time wages do not fall to do what has to be done.

Given this reality, Weitzman argues that America needs to change its social organization—moving from the current system of fixed wages (so much per hour, week, or month) to what he calls a share economy, where some portion of wages comes as a fraction of firm profits or revenue. In a share system if revenue per unit falls as sales expand, wage costs also fall per unit produced, and the firm has an economic incentive to increase production to full employment level. Until the firm runs out of extra workers to hire they will find that more production and sales always mean more profits. A share economy would eliminate unemployment, since wages would respond as they are supposed to respond and not as they do respond.

Similarly, inflationary shocks would be mitigated. If Weitzman's share economy had been in place in 1979, wages would have fallen as revenue fell because of higher imported oil prices. What should have happened would have happened. The Japanese, who are on a share system with their twice-a-year bonuses, sailed right through the second OPEC oil shock with hardly a blip on their inflation radar. Bonuses were drastically cut, leading to what was the equivalent of an 11 percent wage reduction.

For reasons which economists find hard to understand (in the conventional economic model a rational *homo economicus* is only interested in the bottom line of his paycheck and pays no attention to what part comes in wages or bonuses) but psychologists find easy to understand, homo sapiens seems much more willing to see a bonus reduced than he is to see his basic wage rate reduced. As a result it is easier, as the Japanese have found, to adjust bonuses up and down than it is to adjust basic wage rates.[13] No one likes a smaller bonus, but people are willing to accept it if the reduction is based upon a clear and well-understood system and if everyone else is upon the same system, so that no one sees himself as the victim of a double standard.

In a share system firms also have much less interest in raising prices. If the wage share was 70 percent of value added for example, a $1 price increase would end up adding 70 cents to wages and only 30 cents to profits. Few firms would want to raise prices under such an arrangement.

If bonuses up to a third of total income were exempted from payroll taxes, as suggested earlier, America would quickly shift to the bonus system. The problem is not what to do or how to get there, but being willing to change old familiar forms of social organization.

Given the wisdom of what Weitzman proposes, why don't we do it? Part of the answer is to be found in the dominant view that social organization does not require deliberate change, but part is to be found in self-interest and an unwillingness to confront reality. A share system hurts those who remain employed during periods of high unemployment. If unemployment exists because wages on the margin are too high, those who remain employed during recessions will receive less under a share system than they do now. Their share of extra revenue will not be as high as the wages they now get.

As with most problems the problem can be clearly seen by looking at it in someone else's back yard. In Belgium every employee must by law be given six weeks of paid vacation. Such laws are great for those employed, but they raise the costs of labor and make it unprofitable for employers to hire new employees. Those unemployed in a very real sense pay for the six weeks of paid vacation for those employed.

A share system also enlarges economic uncertainty for those who are sure that they will not be laid off during an economic downturn. With a share system they wouldn't know quite so surely just what their income will be in the upcoming year. Personal planning becomes marginally more difficult. Under a share system Americans would find it harder to kid themselves about reality. When something like the 1979 OPEC oil shock occurs, say a falling dollar, Americans would have to face the fact that their standards of living will fall as they give up more exports to get the old volume of imports. No one would be able to bail out of reality by thinking that he can get wage hikes higher than the rate of inflation.

The objections to a share economy are both minor and self-serving. A share economy would be a much better economy with a higher standard of living and better-operating properties (both less unemployment and less inflation) than America now has. Other societies have declined (Great Britain and the miners strike?) as they lost the ability to make social change. America may be another. It depends upon us. To say that the efficient beat the inefficient is not to say that America wins. By doing nothing Americans may collectively choose to be among the inefficient.

Democrats should lead the way toward a more efficient form of social organization that can transform the American economy so that it is capable of persistently delivering both full employment and low inflation.

None of this is to say that there isn't some structural unemployment in the United States. There are some people who have been laid off in industries that are unlikely to ever again employ them and who do not have the skills that would be necessary to become employed in the expanding parts of the economy even if there were such expanding parts. But it is important not to exaggerate the numbers. In every recession including the Great Depression there were those who were quick to say, "They are all structurally unemployed." In fact with not much more than a vigorous expansion of demand, that 25 percent unemployment rate of the 1930s was less than 1 percent in World War II.

Since no one knows exactly which industries will expand in the future, any counting of likely potential jobs versus actual people always ends up with too few jobs. Analysts know for sure that the people exist, but they cannot know for sure that the jobs will exist. Fortunately "counting" problems are often not real problems.

There is no remedy for structural unemployment in a stagnant economy. With what skills should today's unemployed be armed to make them employable in the future? In a stagnant economy no one can know what is going to be needed, because even the growth industries aren't growing. People can become more skilled; but if 11 million workers have to be unemployed to control inflation, then there are going to be 11 million unemployed people regardless of how many skills they have acquired. Training may reshuffle unemployment to different individuals, but it cannot change the final outcome.

America's reaction, or lack of reaction, to those pictures of long lines of patient people waiting to apply for work illustrates what is probably the major social value judgment that has to be made before any restructuring of the American economy is possible. What do Americans believe about the character of their neighbors?

An industrial psychologist by the name of Douglas McGregor once argued that people could be divided up into what he called Theory X People and Theory Y People.[14] Theory X People believe that man is by nature lazy and has to be driven to work with harsh economic sticks and large economic carrots. As in the nursery tale, man is an individual grasshopper who will improvidently starve in the winter if he is not forced to work in the summer. In contrast, Theory Y People believe that man is basically a communal beaver—a working, tool-building, social animal. Harsh whips and large carrots are not necessary to keep a colony of beavers busy building dams and storing food. One can of course screw up the situation so that even a colony of beavers won't work, but one needs to really work at it. McGregor went on to note that when Theory X People look at the world they always see a world full of grasshoppers, even though they may in fact be looking at one grasshopper in the midst of a colony of beavers—even though they themselves are often beavers.

McGregor put his finger on the central social judgment. Does a society restructure on the assumption that the world is mostly populated with beavers or does it restructure on the assumption that the world is mostly populated with grasshoppers? There are obviously lazy people. There are just as obviously hard-working people. The real problems revolve around the proportions of the two. I could attempt to present statistics showing the proportions of each in the population and demonstrate that Americans are mostly beavers, but if those pictures of thousands lining up for minimum-wage jobs during the 1981–82 recession haven't converted you, no statistical studies are going to convert you. You see grasshoppers where I see beavers. For I believe that our society can restructure itself on the assumption that most Americans—not all, but most—are beavers.

Republican policies basically assume that most Americans are grasshoppers and have to be driven to work with harsh punishments and large rewards. In contrast the Democratic party should base itself on the beaver hypothesis. There are lazy people, but the goal is not to punish them. The goal is to open up real opportunities for the overwhelming proportion of beavers among us.

ALTERNATIVE CHOICES FOR DEALING WITH INFLATION

The importance of social choice can be seen in indexing—the tying of wages to some measure of consumer prices. If a society chooses to index itself rather than to establish a share economy, it is choosing an alternative path with consequences. Since America is heavily indexed, since indexing is politically popular, and since it seems to be an alternative technique whereby the individual and groups of individuals can protect themselves from inflation, it is worth spending some time to understand why indexing is counterproductive if the goal is a non-inflationary economy.

Basically, indexing is a technique for living with inflation. If everyone and everything is indexed, inflation cannot hurt anyone. Adding zeros to the price of everything affects the value of nothing. Personally I have some sympathy with the idea of simply living with inflation, but most Americans don't. If the goal is price stability rather than arranging price increases so that no one is harmed, then indexing is counterproductive, as can be seen in the case of Israel—the country with the most indexing and the world's highest rate of inflation.

The nature of the problem can be seen in the oil price shocks. By itself a doubling of the price of energy (imported and domestically produced) raises American prices 10 percent. But something more severe happens in an indexed economy. With the average price level up 10 percent last year due to an energy shock, wages rise an extra 10 percent this year. With wages up 10 percent, industrial production costs rise 10 percent and hence industrial prices must go up another

10 percent. Indexing transforms an initial one-time energy shock into perpetual industrial inflation and a never-ending wage-price spiral. Every year wages go up this year because prices went up last year. Inflation can only be stopped in a world of 100 percent indexing if other import prices fall to offset the rise in energy prices or if productivity spontaneously accelerates without an equivalent increase in wages.

Whatever the level of unemployment necessary to control inflation in an unindexed world, it is clear that that level is much higher in an indexed world. Technically, in a completely indexed world unemployment, no matter how high, could not stop inflation. Indexing protects the individual or the firm from the effects of inflation, but it makes it difficult for the community to stop inflation.

As a consequence if the community wants to stop inflation, it must make indexing illegal. Any serious effort to cure inflation must begin by making, as Germany has done, all indexing illegal. This means removing indexing from all government programs (expenditures and taxes) and making it illegal for private industry to include indexes in either wage contracts or contracts with other firms. The elimination of indexation does not automatically prevent supply shocks from being converted into general inflation, but it slows down the process and makes it possible for government to intervene to attempt to prevent those bargains from being struck. Part of the better inflation performance in Germany is due to its social choice not to allow indexing.

Consider another social choice: the institutional framework—three-year overlapping contracts all negotiated at different times—in which American wages are set. In contrast the Japanese have chosen to set a time of year, the spring offensive, when all wage and supplier contracts are negotiated.[15] The value of such a choice is clear. Suppose that I am the head of the machinists' union and negotiating this year. Last year the electricians signed a three-year contract calling for 10 percent annual wage gains. Since my men work alongside those electricians, I must get at least the same 10 percent wage increase if I wish to stay in office. Essentially I have been economically imprisoned by their wage increase. Yet when the electricians next bargain they will also be imprisoned by the 10 percent wage increase that I negotiated this year for the machinists. With three-year overlapping contracts, it is very difficult to have a phase-down of wage increases if such a phase-down is necessary to stop inflation.

A spring offensive also allows the media and government to play an important role in informing the man on the street as to the facts of life. What is happening to productivity, how much of America's output is being taken away from it in the form of higher prices for imports, what is left to be divided among Americans? If wages rise at a 9 percent rate, then inflation must rise at a 12 percent rate. If everyone was bargaining at the same time, the media would have an interest in detailing this type of economic information, since every American would be interested in it. Important lines of communication would open up. Since all workers would be simultaneously negotiating their wages and prices for the succeeding year, it would be possible to have a national discussion as to what behavior is permissible and to educate individual members of our society as to what alternatives they and their country face.

Even more importantly, with simultaneous negotiations few workers would feel that if they negotiated an agreement that was compatible with low inflation they would be the suckers who sacrificed for the common good while others were ripping off the system. Agreements could be made contingent on what others were doing. Groups could be assured that if they moderated their income demands they would not be left out on an economic limb when other groups did not moderate their demands. Since everyone would be negotiating at the same time, everyone would be in a position to insure a fair distribution of the sacrifices necessary to prevent inflation. Such a period of common negotiations does not guarantee that people will make the right decision, but it at least makes it possible for them to make the right decision. Labor is in a position to insure that if it moderates its wage demands, producers will be charging prices that are consistent with those moderate demands.

Such a social choice is one of the reasons for a better inflationary performance in Japan. To prevent inflation America needs to make similar social choices.

Eliminating Price Shocks

While a system has to be built that can cope with price shocks, it is also necessary to reduce the magnitude of those shocks to the greatest extent possible. If the shocks are too large, nothing will be capable of coping with them. As a result the new share system of wage and price determination needs to be combined with efforts to prevent supply-side price shocks in the areas—energy, food, currency fluctuations—where they are most likely to happen and where they have the greatest impact on the costs of living. Dampening currency fluctuations will be left to the next chapter, but consider energy and food.

Since energy is heavily imported in the United States, its prices are not controllable by the United States. While prices fell from 1982 to 1985, no one can predict whether prices will go up or down. Given the right assassinations, one can imagine prices soaring through the roof. Given an end to the right wars, one can imagine large price reductions. The only good prediction is the basically unhelpful prediction that energy prices are uncertain.

Very large short-run fluctuations can be stopped by completely filling the strategic petroleum reserve.[16] This reserve should be full for political, military, and economic reasons. Private companies also should not be permitted to run down their private inventories to save money as they were doing from 1982 to 1985. Most foreign governments require oil companies to hold supplies capable of meeting their demands for a number of months as a condition for doing business in the country. America should have the same requirement.

To eliminate long-run fluctuations, America needs to continue working on alternative sources of energy. A temporary glut of energy does not justify gutting the synfuels program. In an environment of falling oil prices, America does not need massive investments in alternative sources of energy but it does need some efforts. This means a maintenance of research-and-development funds, but since many of the technical and economic problems are not laboratory problems but engineering problems encountered in scaling up to commercial operations, the government should be willing to enter into a limited number of contracts where it agrees to buy alternative energy at some price premium—let us say $40 per barrel in 1985. In the end the large costs of uncertain fluctuating prices can only be eliminated when America has achieved potential energy independence.

Grain prices present an opposite set of problems. America is not only self-sufficient in grain but the world's largest exporter of grain. Here our problems spring from that fact that the rest of the world is using us as a residual supplier. Foreign farmers are given a guaranteed local market at a predetermined price. If, and only if, local crops fail, Americans are then allowed to sell their products in that foreign market.

Essentially every country runs such a system. The only difference

between the "good guys" (Japan) and the "bad guys" (Russia or the
Common Market) is the frequency of bad weather and whether they
are usually large importers (Japan), erratic importers (Russia) or becoming large exporters (the Common Market). The problem with
such a system is that it throws all of the instability and associated costs
into the American market. While the rest of the world enjoys stable,
if high, prices, American prices soar up and down, creating problems
not just for our farmers but for industrial wages and prices.

Yet at the same time, given our comparative advantage in grain
production, it does not make sense to embargo agricultural exports
and become an unreliable supplier. Every time America has done so
it has hurt itself more than those it embargoed. In response to the
Nixon soybean embargo, Brazil became a major soybean exporter and
America lost a major part of its market. In response to Carter's embargo, the Soviet Union decided to place most of its orders for grain
in Canada, Australia, and Argentina. Export controls make the
United States into an unreliable food exporter and only strengthen
foreign arguments made that they should remain agriculturally self-
sufficient. American food-price problems cannot be solved with export embargoes. The United States produces far more grain than it
consumes even in the worst of years, and it needs grain exports to pay
for necessary imports.

Given its role as the world's grain supplier, the United States needs
a substantial grain reserve. America should never again let its reserves
get as low as they were in the early 1970s. Every inventory control
model shows that if one tries to run a business without inventories
the result is very erratic prices and occasional shortages. While America can certainly have too many inventories, no business can be run
without inventories, and America is in the grain business. As a result
some system of price stabilization and government-held inventories is
essential. The inventories must be government held rather than privately held as they now are, however, so that the inventories will be
released when prices rise and accumulated when prices fall. Holders
of private inventories have a financial incentive to do the opposite—
piling on trends rather than mitigating them.

Monetary and Fiscal Policies

The fiscal mix of the Reagan Administration could be characterized
as tight high-interest-rate monetary policies and loose large-deficit

fiscal policies. Democrats should choose the opposite mix—low interest rates, loose monetary policies, and tight budget surplus fiscal policies. The policy changes necessary to produce a budget surplus have already been outlined. If these policies were to be adopted, it would be necessary, however, to insure that the low-interest monetary policies were combined with them. Tight fiscal policies and tight monetary policies together would simply produce a recession. If budget surpluses are to be generated, monetary policies have to be aggressively run to encourage investment so that rising investment demands can counterbalance falling consumption demands.

In the years in which the economy hit bottom in the recessions from 1949 through 1975, the real interest rate (the rate of interest minus the rate of inflation) on Federal Funds (overnight loans between banks) was negative—minus 0.6 percent. That interest rate was not produced by accident but by deliberate policies on the part of the Federal Reserve Board. The economy did not die an inevitable high-interest-rate natural death in 1981 and 1982—it was murdered by its monetary policies.[17] The murder was justified by those who perpetrated it on the grounds that it was necessary to stop inflation, but whatever the validity of that justification, it was a justification that has been removed with the new system of wage and price determination outlined above. As a consequence the focus of attention at the Federal Reserve system must be redirected at what it can do—play a role in maintaining full employment—and away from what it cannot do—stopping inflation without stopping the economy.

The solution starts with a restructuring of America's monetary institutions. In most other countries, the nation's central bank is part of the finance ministry and subject to direct governmental control. If the bank fails in its appointed tasks, it is a failure of the administration in power. The administration cannot blame someone else. Yet the Reagan Administration spent the year 1982 ascribing the recession to a Federal Reserve Board that had not "eliminated erratic movements in the supply of money" and the year 1984 blaming the Fed for rising interest rates. Such a division between economic power and political responsibility must end.

Whatever its historical merits, the time has come to end the independence of the Fed and place it under the jurisdiction of the elected leader of our nation—the President. Independence was initially established on the grounds that the politicians were too incompetent or too untrustworthy to control the money supply. This argument is both wrong and irrelevant. If the President is competent enough to have his finger on the nuclear button, he is competent enough to control the money supply. If the Congress is competent enough to control taxes and expenditures, it is competent enough to approve changes in the rate of growth of the money supply.

But even if the President weren't competent, it is fundamentally anti-democratic to have such powers wielded by individuals who have not been elected by the people. If Americans elect incompetent or untrustworthy politicians they must live with them. Democracies have the right to make mistakes, but no unelected official has a right to make mistakes for them. Yet a majority of the Open Market Committee, the real policymaking group at the Fed, are presidents of regional Federal Reserve banks who owe their jobs to local bankers and have not in any sense been legitimized by a democratic appointment process. Although the seven members of the Federal Reserve Board have a quasi-democratic element in that they have been appointed by the President to fourteen-year terms and must be confirmed by the Senate, this process can easily lead to a situation where the appointees of defeated politicians are running the economy with monetary policies contrary to the wishes of the newly elected leaders of the country. Paul Volcker, for example, was appointed by President Carter yet served almost three years until August 1983 without President Reagan's approval. Whatever you think about President Reagan, he deserved to have his own person at the helm of the Federal Reserve from the beginning. If he wanted Volcker, he could have reappointed him at the beginning of his administration rather than in the summer of 1983.

Americans elect and defeat presidents and members of Congress on their ability to generate a prosperous economy. Those politicans deserve both the controls and the responsibilities that this implies. No President should be able to falsely hide his failures behind an "erratic" money supply beyond his control. And if the charge is true, no President should have to put up with an incompetent Fed.

The President now proposes changes in fiscal policies. Congress must concur, but once it has done so the President is responsible for carrying out the jointly determined mandate. Exactly the same system should exist in the monetary area. The President should propose an annual interest rate target. Once Congress concurs or modifies that target, the President should be responsible for managing the monetary system in accordance with that target, just as he is responsible for managing expenditures in accordance with the dictates of Congress. If circumstances change, he could always go back to Congress for changes, as is now done with spending programs that exceed their initial budget estimates.

While everyone talks about the independence of the Federal Reserve Board, it is a little known fact that it is only independent of the President. It is not independent of the Congress. If Congress wanted to start setting legally mandated monetary targets, it could do so without new legislation. It has just never chosen to exercise its legal rights. The time has come for it to do so.

Legislation should be passed, however, to give the President his normal role in determining what monetary policies should be enacted. To do this the Federal Reserve Board should be placed inside the normal government structure. Technically it matters little whether the Fed is placed inside the Treasury (the arrangement in other countries) or is a separate cabinet department.

More important are the substantive targets which the Fed ought to hit. While the failure of monetarism led to a de facto abandonment of monetarism, this failure is not an argument for going back to the Federal Reserve Board procedures for targeting interest rates that were in place from 1913 to 1979. The Fed made a serious mistake when it let real interest rates fall into the negative range in the mid-1970s (see Table 11). Instead of targeting nominal interest rates, the Fed should target real inflation-corrected Federal Funds rates.

The President would propose a range of real Federal Funds rates to Congress that he thinks would return the economy to full employment or hold it at full employment. If Congress concurred with the President's analysis or substituted its own analysis (the President having to concur, given his veto power), then the President and the Fed would be responsible for carrying out that jointly determined mandate.

To avoid the current situation where the Fed announces its money supply targets after they have been put in place, thereby giving the big investors who know how to ferret out that information an advantage over small investors, the Fed should announce its real interest-rate targets on Friday night after the financial markets have closed and direct its New York bond traders to start buying or selling short-term bonds to hold the Federal Funds rate at the desired level on Monday morning.

Interest-rate targets have an advantage in that they are much easier to hit than money supply targets. There is a market, the New York bond market, where they are set. The Fed knows what they are on a minute-by-minute basis. By their own admission they do not have the data necessary to successfully control short-term money supplies. They only know what those supplies are with a substantial time lag. If ignorance is the issue, knowledge is all on the side of targeting real interest rates rather than the rate of growth of the money supply.

There is also no doubt that the Fed can control short-term interest rates if it chooses to do so. Who is going to bet against a market player with an unlimited bank account who has just announced what he plans to do? Historically, the Fed held short-term rates below 2 percent from the outbreak of World War II to the end of the Korean war. What it did then it can do now. The relevant question is not whether the Fed can do it, but whether the Fed should do it. And the correct answer is that it should.

The 1983 *Economic Report of the President* details the Reagan-monetarist objections to real interest-rate targeting by the Fed, but none of their arguments are convincing.[18] It should also be noticed that they do not claim that it cannot be done.

It is true, as the *Economic Report* states, that the same real interest rate can be produced by many different combinations of money rates and rates of inflation, but investors and savers respond to real rates regardless of the particular combination producing them. Higher real rates of interest will always lower aggregate demand and dampen inflation to the extent that inflation is a product of too much aggregate demand. High real rates will continue working to restrict demand even though the particular combination of interest and inflation rates producing them is gradually changing as inflation diminishes.

The *Economic Report* notes that no one knows the future rate of inflation, but that would only be a germane criticism if the Fed were being asked to target long-term real rates of interest. The future rate of inflation is irrelevant if the Fed is supposed to target real short-term (Federal Funds) rates of interest. Borrowers and lenders know today's rate of inflation even if they do not know tomorrow's inflation rate, and only today's rate of inflation is necessary to set today's real overnight interest rates.

The *Economic Report* goes on to note that given the tax deductibility of interest payments, real interest rates differ depending upon investors' tax brackets and that it is real after-tax rates of return that are going to influence behavior. While it is true that different individ-

TABLE 11
INTEREST RATES[19]
1960–1984

Year	Nominal Federal Funds	Real Federal Funds	Nominal AAA Corporate Bond Rate	Real AAA Corporate Bond Rate
1960	3.2%	1.6%	4.4%	2.8%
1961	2.0	1.1	4.4	3.5
1962	2.7	0.9	4.3	2.5
1963	3.2	1.7	4.3	2.8
1964	3.5	2.0	4.4	2.9
1965	4.1	1.9	4.5	2.3
1966	5.1	1.9	5.1	1.9
1967	4.2	1.2	5.5	2.5
1968	5.6	1.2	6.2	1.8
1969	8.2	3.1	7.0	1.9
1970	7.2	1.8	8.0	2.6
1971	4.7	−0.3	7.4	2.4
1972	4.4	0.2	7.2	3.0
1973	8.7	2.9	7.4	1.6
1974	10.5	1.7	8.6	−0.2
1975	5.8	−3.5	8.8	−0.5
1976	5.0	−0.2	8.4	3.2
1977	5.5	−0.3	8.0	2.2
1978	7.9	0.5	9.1	1.3
1979	11.2	2.6	9.6	1.0
1980	13.4	4.1	15.3	2.6
1981	16.4	7.0	14.2	4.8
1982	12.3	6.2	13.8	7.8
1983	9.1	5.9	12.0	8.8
1984	10.2	6.9	12.7	8.4

uals fall into different tax brackets, the authorities know the average tax bracket of the average saver or investor. And that is all that is necessary to adjust the pretax real rate of interest to produce the desired average after-tax real rate of interest.

When it comes to tax effects, there is also no significant difference between money supply and interest rate targets. Tight money affects people differently, given their tax brackets and their pecking order in the queue of loanable funds. In terms of discriminating among individuals it is clear that interest-rate targets would lead to less discrimination than money supply targets.

Finally the *Economic Report* notes that no one can know for sure what real interest rate would lead to non-inflationary growth. True, but it is an observation that is equally germane with respect to the rate of growth of the money supply. No one knows precisely what rate of inflation will be produced by different rates of growth of the money supply. In both cases the rate will vary over time. Changes in the desire to hold money will lead to changes in the velocity of money and hence in the rate of growth produced by any given rate of growth of the money supply. Likewise, depending upon technical progress and shifts in demand, the same real interest rate can produce different levels of investment. In neither case is it possible to have a simple formula for the "right" real interest rates or the "right" rate of growth of the money supply. Judgment is necessary, and targets may have to be altered if those judgments happen to be wrong.

Real-interest-rate targets have a great advantage, however, in that investors and savers think in terms of interest rates and not in terms of the rate of growth of the money supply. Investors and savers can tell you how they would change their plans if interest rates should change, but they cannot tell you what they would do if the rate of growth of the money supply should accelerate or decelerate. As a result it is a lot easier for the monetary authorities to come to the right judgments about appropriate interest rates than it is for them to come to the right judgments about appropriate money supply growth rates.

When the objections of the Reagan monetarists to real-interest-rate targeting are reviewed, it is clear that none of them are substantive. The Fed should shift to real-interest-rate targets.

No one can be sure exactly how much long-term rates will fall if short-term Federal Funds rates were reduced, but they will fall (it is always possible to use a sequence of short-term loans to replace a long-term loan), and they cannot fall if short-term rates remain high (no one makes risky long-term loans at rates below what they could get on a sequence of riskless short-term loans).

While monetary policies can control short-term interest rates and have a major impact on long-term rates during recessionary periods, at full employment long-term interest rates are a product of the relative supplies and demands for savings. Easier monetary policies need to be supported by tighter fiscal policies at full employment. As a result, the government surplus outlined in Chapter 8 is necessary for both micro- and macro-economic reasons. It gives America the resources necessary to rebuild its economy, but it also permits the low real interest rates which will make sustained rapid full employment growth possible.

America needs a twist in its monetary-fiscal mix from tight money and loose fiscal to easy money and tight fiscal. It is possible to twist our monetary-fiscal mix.[20] Democrats should do so.

CONCLUSION

From the point of view of the professional economist the 1979–83 period was an interesting experiment. What happens when governments practice monetarism? What happens when a worldwide recession starts and governments do not come rushing to the rescue with easier monetary and fiscal policies?

No one knew the answers to these questions, since strict monetarism had never been applied, but the world now knows the answer. Monetarism does not work. It was a failure and had to be abandoned in August 1982. It was replaced with a vigorous Keynesian economic recovery, but however right a vigorous Keynesian recovery is in the short run it is not the right long-run solution. The long-run solution is only to be found in a change in the structure of wage determination so that monetary and fiscal policies can be adjusted to produce high growth and low unemployment without inflation. Democrats should lead in this restructuring. Social choices can be made which will recession- and inflation-proof the American economy.

11 / International Competition and Cooperation

When it comes to international competition, America wants to be a winner with a standard of living second to none. To win, America has to compete, but it also has to cooperate. To have a high standard of living America needs wealthy trading partners with healthy economies. Poor countries such as India or China are not good trading partners; they have a lot of unmet wants, but they do not have much income with which to purchase American goods. The best trading partner is a wealthy trading partner who both wants and can afford to buy a lot of American goods and who provides unique products that cannot be produced as cheaply in the United States.

To get the foreign exchange necessary to buy American goods, however, trading partners, wealthy or poor, must be allowed to sell their goods or services to Americans. It is a simple fact of life that America must buy if it wishes to sell in international markets. To put quotas on Chinese textiles, as America recently did, is to prevent China from earning the money it needs to buy Boeing aircraft and to force it to cancel its orders, as it recently did.

Without wealthy trading partners to provide a market for its goods America cannot afford to import the things that it cannot produce for itself (many minerals and 30 percent of its oil), the things that it can only with difficulty produce for itself (coffee and bananas), the things

where it has fallen behind in technology (video recorders and machine tools), and the things in which it is no longer competitive in
either price or quality (steel). If Americans wish to have a high standard of living they must take advantage of international specialization
and concentrate on producing the things that they produce best,
selling those things to the rest of the world, and buying from the rest
of the world those things that they are not very good at producing.

MACRO-ECONOMIC COOPERATION

While the Reagan Administration proved that the United States is
still strong enough to use Keynesian policies to restart the world's
economic engines, it is not clear how long it can pull the resultant
load.

Of the 3 million jobs lost in the 1984 deficit in the balance of
payments, Japan, Europe plus Canada, and the rest of the world each
received the gift of about 1 million jobs if bilateral deficits are examined.[1] When the internal demands generated by rising exports are
included, all of Japan's growth in 1983 and 70 percent of its growth in
1984 could be traced to its rising trade surplus.[2] The OECD estimates
that one-third of the growth in Western Europe in 1984 could be
traced to the American recovery and the high valued dollar.[3]

Despite this external impetus to their economic growth, however,
most of the rest of the world was still caught in stagnation in 1984.
Some countries had positive growth rates, but few countries outside
of the United States had growth rates strong enough to reduce unemployment. Without those jobs from America most of the rest of
the world would have still been buried in the recession that began in
1981.

There is also a real question as to how long the United States can
continue to provide such a Keynesian stimulus to the rest of the
world. America, like France earlier, is being inundated with rising
imports and falling exports. Between 1981 and 1984 imports captured
42 percent of the growth in domestic American spending.[4] Even such
a historically strong exporting industry as agriculture lost half its foreign markets between 1981 and 1984.[5] Imports of computers and office equipment soared 50 percent in 1984. Electrical machinery
imports were up 38 percent. Overall 20 cents out of every dollar spent
by Americans went into imports in 1984.[6]

The only difference was that the value of the dollar did not fall. In 1983 and 1984 foreigners were willing to finance America's trade deficits, and the inflows of capital paid for the outflows of funds necessary to buy all of those foreign-made products. This was possible since the United States was running a monetary policy where real short-term interest rates were being held at levels twice those in Japan or West Germany. America was simply a very attractive place to park money.

Such a combination of policies presents a number of short-run and long-run problems. While a large budget deficit can keep a recovery going in the face of high real interest rates, the high real interest rates discourage the economy from making the long-term investments it ultimately needs to be competitive. The recovery is consumption (demand) rather than investment (supply) orientated. What works in the short run (pump consumption into the system) hurts in the long run (there is too little investment).

While a large budget deficit can offset high interest rates and prevent a recession, a rising trade deficit requires a large and *rising* budget deficit. If the trade deficit were to be larger than the federal budget deficit, the two would represent a net subtraction of demand from the American system and in conjunction with high interest rates lead to a recession. As a result, ever higher federal deficits are required to offset ever higher trade deficits.

In the United States this requires a willingness on the part of both the federal government and the country to go ever deeper into debt. While ever larger federal debts are probably manageable (Americans hold both the assets, bonds, and the liabilities—taxes owed), an ever larger international debt is not. Foreigners own the assets; Americans hold the liabilities.

In just a few years the sums get so large that the rest of the world has neither the willingness nor ability to lend what must be lent even if interest rates remain high. Whereas America had net assets of $152 billion in 1982, it is estimated that it will have net debts of $700 to $850 billion by 1989 if the dollar remains high that long.[7]

A trade deficit financed by foreign borrowings represents a debt like any other debt, and no one can forever accumulate debts that grow faster than one's income. At some point the rest of the world will decide that it has lent America enough, just as America decided that it had lent Mexico enough, and the lending will stop. When this happens the value of the dollar will fall.

The United States will regain the 3 million jobs it is now losing but be hit by an inflationary shock in the form of much higher prices for imports. The rest of the world will lose 3 million jobs but be helped on the inflationary front with cheaper imports.

America, as France did earlier, is apt to apply a dose of austerity and a retreat from the goal of full employment and economic recovery. The rest of the world essentially becomes a train which the American locomotive could no longer pull uphill. As the American locomotive starts to slide backwards under the weight of its load, however, the rest of the train slides backwards even faster without those 3 three million jobs.

The current situation comes about for a simple reason. While the United States has been pursuing an expansionary fiscal policy of large and rising Federal deficits, the rest of the industrial world has been pursuing exactly the opposite policy. America expanded its structural budget deficit from 1980 to 1984, but the rest of the industrial world contracted theirs.[8] Conversely, the rest of the world has run a low-interest-rate policy while the United States was running a high-interest-rate policy. The net result has been a rapid recovery in the United States which fueled a weak recovery in the rest of the industrial world. Abroad the positive demand effects from the American trade deficit more than offset the negative demand effects from falling foreign government deficits. But unless one believes that the United States can forever run a large and rising trade deficit the macroeconomic underpinnings of the current recovery are unsustainable. Whenever the dollar falls and the American trade deficit unwinds, the recovery in the rest of the world stops.

Given the current degree of world economic integration, it is no longer possible to have uncoordinated national economic policies where countries attempt to go it alone. The major countries in the industrial world will either learn to coordinate their economic policies or they will sharply reduce the current degree of economic integration and return to the era when it was possible to have viable national economic policies. At the moment, the world is moving toward less economic integration and more viable national economic policies. The process is already under way as industry after industry—steel, shipbuilding, cars, consumer electronics—is withdrawn from real international trade and becomes a "managed" industry with formal or informal quotas or other government marketing arrangements. Protection will provide the vehicle for disintegrating the world economy and making national economic policies once again viable, but at an enormous economic and political price.

Without a vigorous worldwide recovery, economic warfare is almost certain. From the point of view of the individual voter, here and abroad, stagnation is too high a price to pay for economic integration. And they are right. There is no need to tolerate stagnation. As a result the industrial world is at a genuine turning point where the large industrial countries will either coordinate their economic policies or will return to economic nationalism. The world retreated once before into economic nationalism at the onset of the Great Depression with disastrous results. While the precise events will no doubt be different this time, they will be no less disastrous.

In theory the economic summits, held every June, were to solve the problem of economic coordination. They began in the aftermath of the 1973–74 OPEC oil shock. For the first time since the reconstruction from World War II the major industrial countries faced an economic problem that they could not handle on their own. The first economic summit, suggested by Helmut Schmidt, occurred at Rambouillet, France, in 1975. The aim was to have a quiet informal weekend where world leaders could get to know one another better and could exchange ideas on how to deal with world economic problems. If any acceptable ideas arose, they were to be worked out in detailed consultation and negotiations among countries after the summit was over. Agendas were simple, without a lot of prior staff work. Since all of the large industrial democracies were headed by leaders who could understand English and since many of them had previously been finance ministers with a detailed understanding of economics, quiet substantive dialogues were possible. At the Rambouillet summit nothing momentous happened, but nothing momentous was supposed to happen. Press coverage was minimal.

By the late 1970s and early 1980s the economic summits had evolved into something quite different. In the aftermath of the second OPEC oil shock in 1979 the world economy was hit first by inflation rates higher than it had seen since the 1920s and then by unemployment rates higher than it had seen since the 1930s. Everyone understood that these inflationary and recessionary storms could best be controlled if countries coordinated their national economic policies. If all fought inflation or recession simultaneously, each would find it easier to succeed than if half of the countries were deflating their economics to fight inflation while the other half were stimulating their economies to fight recession.

To have any chance of succeeding, however, agendas could not be left informal. Negotiations had to be undertaken prior to the sum-

mits to see if detailed agreements could be reached. Summit prepa-
rations became a year-round activity, and the statements to be issued
at the end of the conference were hammered out long before anyone
ever arrived at the summit. Since the problems were pressing and the
expectations high, press coverage rose from modest to gargantuan.

The aims were noble but ultimately unworkable. Agreements on
economic goals and policies could not be reached. In 1978 America
wanted easier monetary and fiscal policies to fight unemployment,
but Germany wanted tighter monetary and fiscal policies to fight inflation. In 1982 the Europeans with France in the lead wanted lower
American interest rates to fight unemployment, but America refused
to cooperate.

Since no country's leader can claim to be a world statesman if
summits end in failure and bickering, further evolution was predictable. No leader wants to be seen as a failure in front of his domestic
constituents. It is not good for one's re-election. In addition the world
leaders no longer had a common language (the only English speakers
in London in 1984 were those heading English-language countries)
and none of them had extensive knowledge of economics. As a result,
beginning with the 1983 summit in Williamsburg and continuing in
the London summit in 1984, the summits once again shifted their
tone and focus. To a great extent they became a photo opportunity
where incumbent leaders attempted to convince the voters back
home that they were international statesmen.

At the London summit the word "economic" was often even
dropped from the title. Instead of talking exclusively about economic
problems the summits were expanded to include discussions of the
Persian Gulf war between Iran and Iraq, international terrorism, dis-
armament, relations with Russia, and acid rain. It is simply easier to
get agreement on many of these topics. Everyone would like to see
Iran and Iraq fight each other into a state of mutual exhaustion where
neither was capable of invading its neighbors. Who could be in favor
of international terrorism? But there is also little that can be done at
a summit on most of these topics.

Despite the fact that all of the countries at the summit are democracies, have long been such, and are in no danger of changing, the
London summit issued a statement of "democratic values." The initial draft of this statement was described by a Reagan official as "so
platitudinous that it would be embarrassing if issued without change."
The statement actually issued was just as embarrassing. And it is

undoubtedly true that not one person in the world who did not believe in democratic values before the statement was issued believed in them afterwards. The statement had no purpose other than to make everyone feel self-righteously good.

In keeping with that spirit of good feeling, President Reagan assured the other summiters, each of which wanted lower American interest rates to speed their own slow recoveries, that our interest rates would fall. The President was undoubtedly right. Sometime before the end of time American interest rates would fall. But there were no promises to change the monetary and fiscal policies that would have to be changed if America was to have lower interest rates in some more immediate period of time. If the President had been serious about falling real interest rates, he would have had to announce that he was ordering the Fed to pursue different monetary policies and that he was going to raise taxes. When the French were asked why they did not push the President on these issues, they replied that they were not in the business of bothering presidents right before elections.

Not wanting to go home marked as failures, the other participants undoubtedly reported to their constituents that they had extracted a solemn promise of lower interest rates from President Reagan and would then attempt to blame their domestic failures on President Reagan's broken promises if American interest rates did not fall. At the national level such responses are politically sharper than openly confessing one's failure to alter the economic policies of the Reagan Administration, but in the long run it is highly destructive to a system of alliances. For now it is necessary to accuse the Americans of being dishonest as well as perverse.

The summits have become the mermaids of the economic world —beautiful to behold in the imagination of one's mind—nonexistent in reality. But in reality the world as it is now constituted cannot operate without some coordination. Summits cannot be abandoned because of past failures. New attempts have to be made, for if they aren't made the world will simply continue its current retreat into protectionism. Any new Democratic President should take the lead in this effort. What was not possible ten years ago may now be possible. The Europeans have ten years of stagnation under their belts and undoubtedly don't want another ten years ahead of them.

Coordinated policies begin with an agreement among the central banks of the major industrial countries to reduce real short-term interest rates. Here the problems lie almost entirely in the United States, since most of the rest of the world's central banks are running monetary policies that lead to much lower interest rates than those in the United States and would be delighted to go to even lower levels if American rates were reduced.

When it comes to fiscal stimulus, the problems lie abroad. Countries differ in their ability to provide short-term fiscal stimulus, but Japan and Germany are certainly in a position to do so. Both have been gradually moving to less fiscal stimulus and larger surpluses (or smaller deficits) in their full-employment budgets. While the United States full employment surplus fell by 3.4 percent of GNP between 1976–79 and 1979–83, the Japanese full-employment surplus rose by 3.9 percent of GNP and the German full-employment surplus rose by 0.8 percent of GNP. In 1984 both of these countries were moving to even greater fiscal restraint and larger full-employment surpluses.[9] No matter how much America is willing to step on its fiscal accelerator, it is unlikely that the world can enjoy a sustained economic recovery while Germany and Japan are stepping on the fiscal brakes. Given job creation problems, the Europeans should be cutting their payroll taxes to lower the cost of labor.

Whatever the right policies, however, they need to be coordinated so that some countries are not stepping on their economic brakes while others are stepping on their economic accelerators. Like it or not, all of the major countries are now sitting at the controls of the same world economy.

Such coordinated stimulus need not be inflationary. Leaving exchange rates aside for the moment, without oil or food shocks inflation is not going to break out in the immediate future. There is simply too much idle human and physical capacity. The appropriate policy is to step on the world's monetary and fiscal accelerators to avoid a collision with economic stagnation, and then ease up so that the world's economy does not ultimately exceed the speed limit necessary to contain inflation. To brake now to avoid a collision with inflation down the road is to prevent a possible future accident, but also to cause an even more disastrous current accident with high unemployment.

Beyond macro-economic coordination, however, each country will need to build its own micro-economic structure for operating its economy at full employment without inflation and without repeated recessions. What might work in America and does work in Japan—

the share system outlined in Chapter 9—need not be everyone's solution, but everyone has to have a solution.

Moreover if the world economy is to prosper, each major industrial country or group of countries needs to solve its own particular micro-economic problems. In the United States this means a cure for slow productivity growth. If American productivity does not grow at a rate commensurate with that of the rest of the industrial world, America will surely withdraw from the world economy and its position of economic leadership. Faced with low productivity growth and a permanently declining relative standard of living, Americans will retreat into protectionism.

In Europe the problem is jobs or, more accurately, a lack of jobs. European employment has not grown since 1970; unemployment has risen every year for more than a decade and is now well into the double-digit range. No set of democracies can tolerate such a situation for long. Europe's current slow withdrawal from the world economy will eventually become a flight into protection in a vain effort to create jobs, unless the employment problem can be turned around.

If one looks at the reasons for the differences between the United States and Europe on the jobs front, it is a good microcosm of the problems that the world economy faces and the solutions that will have to be developed. It is also a good illustration of how it is easy to solve the problems of others while remaining unable to solve one's own problems.

The European problem begins with macro-economic coordination. President Reagan proved that Keynesian economics still works, but President Mitterrand also proved that no country in Europe is big enough to practice Keynesianism alone. If demand is to be expanded, all will have to expand simultaneously. If such coordination cannot be arranged, the European Common Market simply isn't viable. What is true of the democratic industrial world in general is true of democratic industrial Europe in particular. Americans see the need for European coordination very clearly and cannot understand why it is so difficult to arrange it in Europe yet Americans do not see the need for world economic coordination and find it incredibly difficult to bring about when they do see the need.

Paradoxically each is easily able to solve the other's problem. While on a net basis there have been no new jobs generated in Europe since 1970, the American economy has in the same period of time generated more than 30 million net new jobs. From 1978 to 1983

American productivity growth was a dismal 0.6 percent per year while European productivity grew at a healthy 3 to 4 percent annual rate.

Both Europeans and Americans would like a simple technological fix for their problems. Facing a jobs problem, Europeans talk about a technological gap vis-à-vis Japan and America and propose increased expenditures on civilian research and development as the remedy.[10] Facing a productivity problem, Americans similarly call for more expenditures on research and development.

If there is a connection to the technological fix and expenditures on research and development, the connection is certainly not found in any simple correlation with R&D expenditure patterns. In the 1960s the United States spent a larger fraction of its GNP on civilian research and development than Europe, yet its productivity growth rate was about to start a two-decade decline. In the 1970s Europe expanded its spending while the United States was contracting its spending, so that by the end of the decade the situation was reversed —major European countries were spending more than America on civilian R&D. Yet the 1970s were a decade when Europe could not create jobs.

The answer to the paradox is found not in R&D spending but in very different labor markets. Relative to the price of capital, American wages were 37 percent lower in 1983 than they were in 1972.[11] This has not happened in Europe. Wages have risen relative to the price of capital.[12]

The relative price of capital and labor provides a key signal for capitalists making investment decisions. In Europe, where labor costs were rising relative to the costs of capital, firms were told to substitute capital equipment for workers wherever possible. Workers were becoming more expensive relative to machinery. Firms responded as they should to these signals, and the European capital-labor ratio rose 3 percent per year in the decade ending in 1983.[13] Firms, however, only add employees if their sales growth exceeds their productivity growth. Combine high-productivity growth with governments generally unwilling to pump aggregate demand into the system and European firms could meet their markets with the same or smaller labor forces. The net result was good productivity growth but bad employment growth.

In the United States capitalists got a very different signal. With labor costs falling relative to the costs of capital, firms were told to substitute workers for capital equipment wherever possible. The substitution of cheap people for expensive capital leads to a slower rate of growth of output per hour of work, however. The net result was a poor rate of productivity growth but a situation where much smaller increases in sales were necessary to persuade firms to add employees. Combine this with an American government generally willing to pump aggregate demand into the system, and the net result is good employment growth but bad productivity growth.

The relative movements in average wages also underestimate the real differences between the two economies. Legally mandated and socially expected fringe benefits are much larger in Europe than in America. By law, workers in Belgium get a six-week vacation. By law, no one gets any vacation in the United States and two weeks is the accepted social norm. While average wages are very different in Europe and America, there is much less variance (fewer low-wage workers) in Europe than in America. Minimum wages are also much closer to average wages in Europe than they are in America. As a result low-wage industries can thrive in the United States paying low wages (workers are available) whereas they could not pay low wages and survive in Europe (workers are not available). Much of America's employment gain has in fact been in low-wage jobs which the average European worker would reject as unacceptable.

It is easy for an American to tell Europeans to lower their wages, reduce fringe benefits, and relax legal or social minimum wages, but it is politically hard to do so in Europe. No one wants to give up those long vacations and generous fringe benefits. Similarly it is easy for Europeans to note that the American steel and auto industries are being driven out of business because their wages and salaries are out of line with wages in the rest of America. Getting them back in line, however, is no easier for Americans than it is for Europeans.

Europeans are often envious of the rapid growth of new firms in Silicon Valley in California or on Route 128 in Boston. Their response has tended to focus on subsidies for research and development and the need for a European venture capital industry to help new start-ups. Such activities are unlikely to solve the European jobs problem. What is needed is different forms of social organization.

New start-ups have one great advantage in America. Firms can easily fire unneeded workers. Advance notice need not be given; severance pay need not be paid. Firms simply do not need to carry the burden of unneeded workers if demand is not what was expected. Workers can be hired with the knowledge that if they are not needed they can be quickly fired. Recently this happened at Atari (the inventors of video games) and at Lotus, what was once America's leading software house.

In Europe firings range from difficult and expensive to impossible. Employees must legally be given several months' notice and then several months' severance pay. When labor is hired it is with the knowledge that it cannot easily be fired. This makes it much riskier and more expensive to go into business. What is a reasonable risk in America where labor is a variable cost becomes an unreasonable risk in Europe where labor is an overhead fixed cost.

America pays a price for its labor flexibility. If workers can be fired whenever they are not needed, workers will reciprocate by quitting whenever a better job comes along. The result is a labor force turnover rate that is vastly higher than that found in Europe. Among high-tech firms annual turnover rates in excess of 100 percent are not unusual. But with these turnover rates no one wants to make investments in human skills. Firms do not want to invest, since employees are apt to leave before the costs of training can be recouped in higher productivity; and employees do not want to invest, since they may soon be leaving and need very different skills with their next employer. The result is a much less well trained labor force.

To be successful every economy needs to be able to generate both new jobs and a healthy rate of productivity growth. New workers need new jobs if unemployment is not to continually rise, and everyone wants the higher standards of living that only higher productivity can bring. This means that both Europe and America need to find some way to gain the virtues of what the other has without losing the virtues of what they now have.

COORDINATING EXCHANGE RATES

Coordinating monetary and fiscal policies would remove some of the violent swings in exchange rates, but not all.[14] Flexible exchange rates are an area where members of the economics profession, myself included, were simply wrong. Back in 1971, when the world went onto the current system of flexible exchange rates, economists were sure that it would be impossible to have large fluctuations in exchange rates between major countries over short periods of time or to have currencies that were fundamentally over- or undervalued. Yet in the past decade both have occurred.

If changes in productivity, inflation, and nominal exchange rates are added together, the real dollar-yen exchange rate rose an amazing 70 percent over a few months in the early 1980s.[15] In 1983 the dollar-mark rate changed 5 percent within a single day. Between its low point in the third quarter of 1981 and the first quarter of 1985 the value of the dollar rose more than 85 percent relative to the value of all other currencies.[16] When the dollar does fall, it will almost certainly overshoot and become undervalued as it was in 1979.

With such violent swings in exchange rates, it simply isn't possible to run efficient economies. No one knows where economic activity should be located; no one knows the cheapest source of supplies; wherever economic activities are located they will be located in the wrong place much of the time. The result is a needless increase in risk and uncertainty, rising instability from protectionism, a shortening of time horizons as firms seek to limit risk and uncertainty by avoiding making long-term commitments, reductions in major new long-term investments, large adjustment costs as production is moved back and forth to the cheapest locations, the expectation of future inflationary shocks, with consequent instability in interest rates.

Consider the problem of building or operating a Caterpillar-type machinery firm.[17] At 277 yen to the dollar (the actual exchange rate in late 1982) a Japanese wage rate of 3,000 yen per hour translated into a dollar wage rate of $11 per hour. In comparison the wage rate was $18 per hour at Caterpillar. As a result of this and other cost differentials, Komatsu (Caterpillar's leading Japanese competitor) could sell a tractor for $50,000 that Caterpillar had to sell for $80,000. If such an exchange rate continues for a long period of time Caterpillar is systematically forced out of business both here and abroad. America loses one of its premier machinery manufacturers and one of its largest exporters. With that loss comes a decline in domestic sales, exports, employment, and income.

Although the dollar will eventually fall, some of the losses are permanent. If the high value of the dollar allows Komatsu to take domestic and foreign markets away from Caterpillar, Komatsu will get a chance to establish a worldwide service network, build customer relations, and achieve economies of scale that will make it impossible for Caterpillar to retain its old market share when the dollar eventually falls. Losses incurred in the effort to hold on to its market share will also prevent Caterpillar from having the funds necessary to develop the new products or production processes necessary to compete with Komatsu in the future. The dollar's exaggerated value is not an invigorating cold shower but a bad case of pneumonia that leaves the patient, American industry, in a permanently weaker condition.

In contrast at an exchange rate of 177 yen to the dollar (the actual rate in 1979) a 3,000 yen wage rate translates into a dollar rate of $17 per hour, and Caterpillar can maintain its position as a world-class competitive manufacturer of machinery.

The entire agricultural sector suffers from the same problem, and it perhaps best illustrates the price that is exacted when the dollar is allowed to become grossly overvalued. Agriculture is an export industry. From 1975 to 1978 it supplied 81 percent of world soybean exports, 40 percent of world wheat exports, 65 percent of world coarse grain exports, and 30 percent of world cotton exports.[18] The United States had a dominant position in world agricultural exports but it was also vulnerable in that it could not possibly consume all that it produced. Although exports were falling in the 1981–83 period of time, they still accounted for 54 percent of the wheat, 22 percent of the corn, 41 percent of the soybeans, 43 percent of the cotton, and 45 percent of the rice grown in America.[19] If American agriculture were to be cut off from its export markets it would have to shrink by very large amounts. Millions of farmers would be forced out of business and millions of acres taken out of production.

When Budget Director David Stockman, in his usual blunderbuss manner, asks why the American taxpayers should bail out farmers who have borrowed too much money, he is asking a question that deserves an answer. As posed, the question of course has a simple answer. Farmers who have simply borrowed too much money should not be bailed out by the American taxpayer. As posed, however, the question is also the wrong question.

Thirty to 40 percent of America's farmers were on the edge of bankruptcy in early 1985. Before anyone can answer what, if anything, should be done about this situation, one has to ask how it came about. If the problems were caused by individual stupidity, then no social remedy is necessary or desirable. If the problems were caused by circumstances that no individual farmer could reasonably have foreseen, then a social remedy may be desirable. Good societies don't willingly see efficient producers destroyed through bad luck or social mistakes if they can reasonably be saved. Communities, societies, and nations are designed to be mutual aid societies—helping each other so everyone can survive better than if each is on his or her own.

Stockman is partially right. Some fraction (probably something like one-quarter) of the farmers in financial trouble are in trouble because they were financial speculators who were betting that the price of farmland would go up when it in fact went down. That group of farmers—many of them aren't working farmers but absentee owners—does not deserve any aid at the expense of the taxpayer.

Most of the farmers in trouble, however, were not financial speculators. They were young farmers who had the bad luck to enter farming at the wrong time. When they entered farming, the price of farmland was soaring, since foreign demand for American farm products was soaring. Profits were high. Land values were exploding. In the last five years, however, that situation has completely turned around. Export markets have evaporated; the value of farmland is plummeting.

That turnaround by itself can turn a prudent farm borrower into an imprudent farm borrower. If land is evaluated at $3,000 per acre, the farmer has a lot of net equity and is a good candidate for new loans. If land is evaluated at $2,000 per acre, the farmer has no net equity and is a candidate for foreclosure.

Land prices fell by as much as 30 percent in 1984 because crop prices had fallen. With lower prices and profits farmland was simply an asset which generated lower profits and was as a result worth less. Farm prices had fallen because agriculture is an export industry and it had lost its export markets. In 1984 the agricultural trade surplus was just half its 1981 level and still rapidly declining. Americans do not begin to eat what they grow, and foreigners want to eat less American grain for a number of reasons.

The green revolution has worked.[20] With the exception of Africa south of the Sahara, grain production has soared in third world countries (China is now the world's largest producer of wheat; 20 to 50 percent increases in food production in the last decade are common), and as a result these countries need to import less.

Europe has shifted from being an importer of U.S. farm products to being a competitor on export markets. In the early 1970s the Common Market was importing almost 17 million metric tons of grain; in the early 1980s it was exporting 3 million metric tons.[21] The agricultural policies of the European Common Market (very high price supports) have given European farmers an excuse to produce like crazy and they have responded. Much of the income flowing from price supports has also been plowed back into new equipment, and European farm productivity is now growing faster than that in America. The level of productivity is still lower in Europe than in America, but the gap is closing rapidly and Europe will never again be the export market it once was.

The value of the dollar, however, is more fundamental. As the dollar has risen to undreamed of heights, it has cost all American exporters, no matter how efficient, their export markets. At the current value of the dollar, American farm products simply cannot be sold in world markets. Wheat, soybeans, feed grains, rice, and cotton are all to be had cheaper from other producers (Canada, Brazil, Argentina, Australia, Egypt, Thailand). The Soviet Union moved its grain purchases from the United States to Argentina in the aftermath of the Carter grain embargo, but it would have moved those purchases even without the embargo. Argentina's grain is now much cheaper than America's grain. No one buys expensive products when they can buy cheap products. Even Americans could eat cheaper if they were to buy Argentine grain and not Kansas grain. No one foresaw the huge rise in the value of the dollar, but it occurred.

The loss of export markets was compounded with high real interest rates. High interest rates clobber capital-intensive industries, and agriculture is a capital-intensive industry using a lot of land. Farm debts exceed $215 billion.[22] The importance of interest payments on that debt can be seen by comparing them with net farm income—about $30 billion in 1984. If interest rates go up by 1 percentage point net farm income falls by 7 percent. When today's farmers were borrowing money in the late 1970s, no one foresaw today's high real rates of interest.

Given all of these factors, let's once again pose the question: "What, if anything, should be done?"

Today's farm programs are clearly not the answer. These programs support the price of farm commodities, and most of the benefits go to the large farmers who are not in financial trouble. President Reagan is right when he proposes to phase out price supports. President Reagan is wrong, however, when he argues that America's farmers should simply be left to play the market game.

There is a case for doing something for those farmers who were not speculating but simply suffered from the bad luck of the high-valued dollar and high real rates of interest. Their problems have broad social and economic causes and are not the result of individual stupidity or sloth. Since government programs caused those high interest rates and the high-valued dollar, there is a case for government programs to alleviate the problem.

The long-run answers revolve around different interest-rate policies such as those outlined in the last chapter and the different foreign exchange policies that will be outlined in this chapter. Unless export markets can be recaptured, American agriculture will have to shrink drastically and many of the people in today's agriculture will be forced to leave the farm. Fundamentally there is no American-based solution to America's farm problem.

Until interest and foreign exchange policies can be reversed, palliative measures must be applied. Farm interest rates have to be reduced, loans have to be written down, and loan repayments have to be spread out over longer periods. Who should pay for it is not so axiomatically clear. It is a matter of social equity and social insurance. Basically the problem is loss sharing. What fraction of the losses should be borne by farmers, what fraction by financial institutions, and what fraction by the taxpayer?

One can argue that the taxpayer should pay for none of the losses, but that is not the right answer unless Americans are willing to argue that they themselves should not be helped when they are up against the economic ropes and that the United States is not a community or society willing to help its fellow members, but merely a statistical aggregation of completely self-interested individuals.

Left alone, the dollar will eventually fall. When it does, however, it will not slowly fall to an equilibrium point where exports equal imports but is apt to rapidly fall to being as grossly undervalued as it is overvalued in early 1985.

The German multinational treasurer who has moved his marks into the United States at three marks to the dollar knows that he will only get 200 million marks and not 300 million marks back when he tries to move his $100 million out after the dollar has fallen to two marks to the dollar. He also knows that foreigners will not forever be willing to add to the dollar bank accounts at a rate high enough to finance the American trade deficit. At some point they will have too many of their assets tied up in dollar investments and will stop investing more. As a result the treasurer and every other investor would like to be the first person out the door when the dollar starts to fall. As a consequence, the dollar is likely to fall very fast when it starts to fall. And given the history of the past decade, the dollar is apt to plunge right through its equilibrium point, shifting from being overvalued to being undervalued. If the dollar is on average 30 to 40 percent overvalued, a fall of 50 percent would not be surprising.

When this happens, the world rapidly moves from a situation

where it is coping with an overvalued dollar to a situation where it is coping with an undervalued dollar. Economies are disrupted both here and abroad. Production that has moved offshore moves back. This is good for recovery here but bad for recovery there. And if the dollar-yen exchange rate is going to move rapidly back and forth between 277 and 177 every few years, neither side knows where it is most efficient to locate production. As a consequence no one is willing to build major new facilities in either America or Japan.[23]

Anyone who believes in gravity and watches water run uphill has a fundamental problem. Facts are difficult to deal with when they conflict with theory. Before changing theories, most human beings will spend long periods of time pretending that the facts don't exist, hoping that the facts will magically go away, or denying that the facts are important. Only if the facts are very painful and very persistent will humans deal with the fundamental inconsistencies in their world views.

Nowhere is this more true than when it comes to the value of the dollar. For believers in the virtues of free unregulated markets, such as the Reagan Administration, it is simply impossible to have a persistently overvalued dollar. Free markets can't produce bad results. Yet there the dollar sits 30 to 40 percent overvalued.[24] Water is running uphill. The Reagan Administration sits hoping that the facts will go away, but the facts are very painful. At the 1984 value of the dollar most of American industry, well or badly managed, was not competitive. That is what a $123 billion trade deficit means.

It is true that no country has an unlimited ability to hold up the value of its currency. For America to hold up the value of its currency it must buy dollars, and this can only be done to the extent that it has previously acquired the foreign currencies necessary to buy dollars in international currency markets. When foreign exchange reserves are spent, America has no further ability to hold up the value of its own currency.

Countries have, however, an unlimited ability to hold down the value of their currencies, and fortunately this is what the United States needs to do. To hold down the value of the dollar, America must sell dollars; and there is no limit on the number of dollars that can be sold. America prints dollars. The only limit has to do with how fast a country wants its money supply to grow, and even here it is possible to offset adverse money supply effects with what is called a sterilized intervention.

The central bank sells dollars in international exchange markets to hold down the value of the dollar but keeps the domestic money supply under control by buying dollars (selling bonds) in the domestic money markets. To the extent that the central bank wants the domestic money supply to grow, the necessary funds are injected into the economy through the foreign exchange markets rather than through the domestic money markets as is the normal case. It has been done (the world was on a fixed exchange rate system from 1945 to 1971), it is being done (the European Monetary System limits fluctuations between European currencies), and it can be done.

To note that timid German interventions have not held down the value of the dollar in early 1985 is not to prove that a massive American intervention could not hold down the value of the dollar. Germany has a finite supply of dollars; America has an infinite supply of dollars. Traders also know that Germany is dependent upon its export surplus for its recovery and does not want big reduction in the value of the dollar. It only wants to stop the mark from dropping further. Many foreign currency traders will bet against timid German interventions; few would bet against massive American interventions.

There is also a fundamental difference between interventions designed to hold a currency above levels consistent with its productivity and interventions designed to prick a speculative bubble and force a currency down to its appropriate level. Any announcement that such a policy was under way would send corporate treasurers and currency speculators rushing to sell dollars.

In a little more than a decade the prevailing intellectual fashions have gone from "governments can stop any and all movements in foreign exchange rates" (that is the belief required to operate a fixed exchange rate system) to a belief that "governments can do nothing about foreign exchange rates." Neither is true. No government can forever hold its currency above the levels dictated by wage rates and relative productivity, but it is equally true that no government has to accept a grossly overvalued currency or a wildly fluctuating currency.

The market will eventually correct the value of the dollar. "The higher she rises the faster and the farther she will fall." But the market will not eventually correct the problem of currency fluctuations. To move from an overvalued dollar to an undervalued dollar is not to solve the problem but merely to change the nature of the problem.

The origins of the current problem are not mysterious. The overvalued dollar was produced by the fiscal and monetary policies of the Reagan Administration. If the rest of the world holds its interest rates down while the United States is holding its up, funds flow into the United States to get those high interest rates. To move funds into the United States one must buy dollars and sell local currencies, leading to a rise in the value of the dollar. When the dollar appreciates there are capital gains to be made by buying dollars, and others move their funds into the United States to get both high interest rates and the capital gains from the rising dollar. The more people move their funds into dollars, the faster the dollar rises, the greater the profits to be made, and the more people move their funds into dollars. Such a cycle can continue for a substantial period of time.

But eventually it will reverse. A few people move their funds out of dollars because they are worried about the future value of the dollar. International debts are piling up, the trade deficit is too large to be sustainable. As they move their funds out of dollars the value of the dollar falls. Capital gains are replaced with capital losses. To avoid these losses others rush to sell dollars and in the process further drive down the value of the dollar and magnify the capital losses. An orderly retreat from the dollar becomes a flight from the dollar and eventually a panic.

If the Japanese central bank can hold overnight interest rates at 6.4 percent and the German central bank can hold them at 5.0 percent, the Federal Reserve Board can hold its overnight interest rates at something less than 11 percent. If not, America can import some foreign central bankers to run the Fed. High interest rates are a man-made disaster. What man makes, man can unmake.

The difficulties in lowering the value of the dollar do not revolve around technical details but around the attitude that free markets can do no wrong. That belief, if sustained, is going to "do wrong" to American industry in very major ways.

If one asks how far the dollar would have to fall to eliminate the 1984 bilateral deficit of $37 billion with Japan, the dollar would have to fall drastically, let's say for the sake of a concrete number 125 yen to the dollar. The 125 yen to the dollar exchange rate has not occurred and will not occur for a simple reason. If any such rate threatened to occur, the Japanese government would intervene in the market to prevent it from happening. The world may have a system of flexible exchange rates but it does not have a system of "cleanly floating" exchange rates where governments never intervene in the market. Only the American government has self-imposed any such handicap upon itself. Most governments actively buy and sell their currencies in what is called a "dirty float."

The problem is to achieve some coordination in the "dirty float." Since holding down the value of one's own currency is equivalent to holding up the value of a neighbor's currency, it is clear that governments working together can prevent rapid fluctuations in exchange rates. France cannot hold the franc up but the United States can hold the dollar down.[25]

Without cooperation, America leaves it to foreign governments to set the value of the dollar. America may not believe in intervention but they intervene. Foreign countries do not want grossly undervalued currencies, since they have to pay more for imports, making inflation worse and standards of living lower, but they have an incentive to get a competitive edge by maintaining slightly undervalued currencies. With lower prices in foreign markets, what is gained by larger sales more than offsets the small losses that are suffered on imports. But when other governments intervene to undervalue their currencies this leaves the dollar systematically overvalued.

With the early 1985 value of the dollar, American industry cannot be competitive. One will simply kill American industry if it is whipped too long with a high-valued dollar. The only choice is to participate in the "dirty float" or more preferably to construct a managed system of floating exchange rates if one wants to protect America's industrial base.[26]

The reasons for the economics profession's mistaken 1971 predictions of exchange rate stability are clear. Economists assumed that large interest-rate differentials could not exist for long periods of time and that there were currency speculators with two- or three-year time horizons who would iron out the fluctuations in exchange rates caused by temporary factors such as different interest rates. If foreigners wanted to buy and hold dollars because interest rates were temporarily higher in the United States than abroad, or wished to move their money from Latin America to the United States because of political unrest, the speculators would enter the market to sell dollars and keep exchange rates near their long-term equilibrium levels.

This did not happen, because there are no speculators with those hypothesized two- or three-year horizons. Speculators have two- or three-month, if not two- or three-day, time horizons. They pile on cycles and amplify the magnitudes of the swings rather than eliminating them.

In early 1985 everyone recognized that the dollar was grossly overvalued. American exports, manufacturing or farm, could not be sold anywhere. Given actual and prospective deficits in the American balance of payments, everyone agreed that in the long run the dollar was going to plunge. But in the short run it rose. The problems are those of timing. When does the movement start? But that question is everything. Real speculators want to pile on trends once they have started, but do not want to bet against the dollar and find that they have even temporary paper losses as the dollar rises in the short run.

Why? The answer is clear. In terms of having "big bucks" the speculators are not the gnomes of Zurich, but the treasurers of major multinational companies. Given their size and extensive lines of credit, multinational companies can move enormous amounts of money from country to country instantly. They dwarf all other short-term foreign exchange movements.

Multinational companies have much less risk than ordinary speculators. Since they are earning money and have lines of credit in each country, they can repay loans out of local earnings or credits without having to worry that their loans will come due at a moment in time when foreign exchange rates have moved adversely and large cash foreign exchange losses would be suffered if they had to move money into a country to repay loans.

Decisions as to where to park company money dominate speculative short-term flows in foreign exchange markets. Corporate treasurers play an active short-term role in the foreign exchange markets, but not the long-term stabilizing postulated by economists. The short-term perspective starts with the incentives facing the average corporate treasurer. His job is to make money for the corporation by earning the highest possible interest rate on unneeded funds. Treasurers find themselves judged as money managers on a quarterly, if not more frequent, basis. As a consequence they do not want their quarterly accounts closed showing them holding large paper losses on foreign exchange transactions, even if they are personally very certain that they will make money for their company in the long run.

This desire is reinforced by top management. The purpose of the company is not foreign exchange speculation. Top management is willing to make money in limited foreign exchange speculations but does not want to see its successes in the normal part of the business

washed away in even temporary foreign exchange losses by the corporate treasurer. Who wants to report quarterly losses even if they are
composed of real quarterly profits and short-term paper foreign exchange losses?

Most companies quite rationally are not willing to tolerate long-
term foreign exchange exposure—no matter how potentially profitable. The treasurer of the company may be an expert in foreign
exchange movements, but the heads of the company are not. Given
their own lack of expertise CEO's do not want to bet the future of
their company on their own judgments about foreign exchange fluctuations; and given the size of the risks involved they are not about to
delegate such a decision to the corporate treasurer. As a result CEO's
are willing to see their treasurers piling on trends when those trends
are firmly established and only small risks are involved, but they are
not willing to see their treasurers betting against market trends, no
matter how temporary the factors underlying those trends or how
certain the eventual reversal of those trends.

This leads to a world where those stabilizing speculators of economic theory do not exist and where fluctuations in foreign exchange
rates are so rapid and large that they threaten the stability of the entire
system. What has happened should not have happened, according to
economy theory, but it did happen. And when events conflict between theory, the theory has to change.

This does not mean going back to the fixed exchange rates that
existed from World War II until 1971—that is neither possible nor
desirable—but it does mean an international agreement to dampen
wild fluctuations. The obvious answer is some system of crawling pegs
where an attempt is made to isolate the changes needed in foreign
exchange rates to accommodate changes in countries' long-term
competitiveness—their relative rates of inflation and productivity—
from the temporary factors that cause capital flows from one country
to another. No one can make these judgments perfectly but almost
anyone can produce a better result than those now occurring.

Under a system of crawling pegs there would be a band, say 10
percent, within which currencies would freely move without government intervention, but governments would intervene in foreign exchange markets in a cooperative way to keep fluctuations within this
band and to let the band itself float up or down as seemed warranted
given differences in inflation and productivity. If no special factors
were disrupting foreign exchange markets, the 10 percent band might

normally be readjusted every six months using inflation, productivity, and trade surpluses or deficits as a guide.

Authorities would permit greater movements in cases where there were gross disparities in inflation or productivity rates. If, for example, the United Kingdom and Germany started from a position of equilibrium in their balance of payments, authorities would allow the mark to rise 20 percent vis-à-vis the pound if inflation was 20 percent per year in the United Kingdom versus 5 percent per year in Germany (inflation is pushing production costs up 15 percent per year faster in the United Kingdom than in Germany) and productivity growth was 6 percent in Germany versus 1 percent in the United Kingdom (productivity growth is pushing production costs down 5 percent per year faster in Germany than in the United Kingdom). Since the pound needs to fall and governments can always hold down the value of their currency, the United Kingdom would be expected to intervene to lower the value of its currency by 20 percent. If inflation and productivity trends were other than expected, the interventions would be modified during the course of the year to accommodate this new information.

Exchange rates would not be adjusted to reflect capital inflows unless there was some reason to believe that those inflows were permanent. Temporary capital flows due to interest-rate differentials or political instability would be offset by government intervention. If individuals and corporations were moving money from Germany to the United Kingdom, governments would reverse this flow and move money from the United Kingdom to Germany. Basically exchange rates would be adjusted to facilitate productive investment and the flow of real trade. Financial speculations would be offset by government action.

Currency fluctuations must be dampened and adjusted to promote the long-term trade patterns that depend upon comparative rates of productivity growth and inflation. A system of crawling pegs is necessary if the world is to return to full employment and take advantage of real long-term comparative advantage. In this effort it is well to remember, however, that the more coordinated the world's macro-economic policies, the smaller interest rate differentials, the less coordination it will need in its foreign exchange policies.

THE RULES OF THE GAME

The rules of the international trading system were essentially set thirty years ago in the General Agreement on Tariff and Trade (GATT). While an adequate set of rules when they were negotiated, the world has outgrown them. If world trade is to prosper, a new set of rules for the international economic game must be developed. At the same time it is well to remember that it was not the rules of GATT that made the trading system successful in the 1950s and 1960s. It was the fact that countries were willing and able to run their economies at full employment.

With full employment, rising imports were not as threatening as they now are. In the 1960s a German steelworker did not like to lose his job to Brazilian steel imports, but he knew that another good job could be found. In the 1980s the loss of a good job in the steel industry is apt to lead to a substantial period of unemployment and even ultimately to a job paying much less. The German steelworker as a consequence demands and gets limits on Brazilian steel imports. While new trading rules are needed, they are not the heart of the problem. The heart of the problem is being able and willing to run the major industrial economies at full employment without inflation. If that cannot be done, no new set of rules is going to rescue the current system.

As President Mitterrand of France has suggested, new rules need to be developed at a new Bretton Woods conference. The conference could start by setting up a mechanism for coordinating interest rates, fiscal stimulus, and exchange rates but it would have to go far beyond these issues. When today's trading rules were set up, no one thought about nationalized industries, industrial policies, multinational companies, world capital markets, or an America that can no longer singlehandedly play the role of manager of the international trading system.

What about nationalized industries?[27] If British Steel, a government-owned firm, runs at a loss, is it automatically being subsidized and because of these subsidies "unfairly" competing against private companies? Clearly private firms cannot be expected to compete against government subsidies. Should British Steel be forced with a tariff if necessary to raise foreign prices?

If private American steel companies run at a loss, as many have, are they "unfairly" competing? If the answer is no, what is the difference? Presumably a private firm cannot sell products below cost for a long period of time while a government firm can. But how long is long? Clearly some rules need to be established as to how long a public firm can run at a loss before foreign countries are justified in levying a countervailing tariff to offset the effect of the subsidy. I would suggest that tariffs could be levied equal to the percentage deficit incurred in the previous five years. In the long run nationalized firms would be expected to run as break-even operations when they export.

What about industrial policies? Countries legimately want to promote some industries because they think that they are important to their future. Within limits there is merit to the infant industry and linkages arguments. But how long can a country protect key industries before foreign countries have a right to reciprocity? Some agreement has to be reached on the rules or everyone is going to attempt to competitively protect the same industries. Here the problem is not deciding upon the right rules—there are no right rules—but deciding upon some common rules that all agree to obey.

What about subsidized interest rates? Every country does it to some extent. That is what America's Export-Import Bank is all about. Here again the world needs an international agreement as to what is permissible. Back in 1982 when American interest rates were over 20 percent and Japanese interest rates were 7 percent, American exporters such as Boeing were not going to sell their products unless there was an interest rate subsidy. If a country wants to run high-interest-rate policy for internal reasons can it essentially rebate those high interest rates on exports, much as a value-added tax is rebated, with an interest rate subsidy through the Export-Import Bank? Here again some agreed-upon rules need to be established. One might, for example, give any country the right to rebate interest rates down to the level of the industrial country with the lowest commercial interest rates, but prevent anyone from offering rebates below this level. But whatever the rule, its precise nature is less important than having "a rule."

Multinational companies make an enormous difference in how international trade and comparative advantage actually work. In the traditional theory of comparative advantage, goods and capital travel between countries but people and ideas do not. Yet people and ideas now flow as freely as, if not more freely than, either goods or capital.

If particular skills present a bottleneck to the exploitation of some idea in a country where general labor costs are less, the multinational company can send those specialized skills to wherever they are needed. What good does it do to increase the supply of engineers if they are simply used to produce jobs abroad? The multinational company can also move its technology around the globe to wherever it can be most profitably employed. What good does it do to subsidize research and development if the fruits of that subsidy are not used at home?

Mobility may be good for the multinational company and even for world efficiency but it is not necessarily good for any one country. National governments are supposed to watch out for the welfare of their citizens—not the welfare of the world economy, multinational companies, or the citizens of other countries.

Most of the rest of the world has tried to come to grips with this reality in some manner. There are limits on what multinational companies may do in terms of borrowing, production, or export of technologies. The United States, however, has not even thought about the problem. When the multinational companies were first developing they were mostly American firms run by Americans. Given this circumstance, it was probably normal to think that whatever they did had to be good for the average American citizen. Unfortunately it isn't necessarily so. U.S. Steel may be better off buying subsidized steel from British Steel to resell in the American market but the average steelworker is not.

One of the benefits of the technological catch-up in the rest of the world is that foreign multinationals now bring to the United States products (Michelin rubber and the radial tire) or processes (the GM-Toyota car assembly plant) that Americans do not have. Where multinationals used to represent a simple one-way outflow of technology, there is now a substantial back-flow. Yet at the same time there needs to be an international agreement on what countries can do to prohibit the outflow of technology—preserve the competitive edge that they are trying to build—or require the inflow of technology. Japan, for example, required the licensing of American technology to Japanese companies before it would allow American semiconductor firms to enter the Japanese market.

It is perfectly reasonable for a country to seek to develop and preserve a comparative advantage, but it is also reasonable to place limits on this process so that technology flows at a reasonable pace, even if not instantaneously, around the globe. Or we may agree on no prohibitions. Here again the world needs an agreed-upon set of rules. Almost any set of rules is better than no rules. With no rules protectionism will swallow the system.

The political dynamics in favor of protection are particularly strong within the United States because of our legal system. "Dumping" products is illegal and real dumping should be illegal, but the United States has legally redefined dumping so that foreign producers can always be found guilty of dumping. Real dumping occurs when products are sold for less in foreign countries than they are sold for at home. Profits on the home market are used to subsidize sales in the foreign markets. Everyone agrees that this is both unfair and illegal competition. But Congress legally redefined dumping in a very different manner in the 1970s.

Dumping now legally occurs if a firm sells its products at less than cost plus a 10 percent margin for overhead expenses plus an 8 percent margin for profits. By that definition most firms dump. Few make an 8 percent profit margin on sales. If the law were applied to domestic firms, eighteen out of the top twenty firms in the *Fortune* 500 would have been found guilty of dumping in 1982.

Once foreign firms are found guilty of dumping, the courts will then impose penalties (tariffs, quotas) unless the administration acts to impose penalties first. This leads to a situation where the American government says that it is in favor of free trade but is practicing protection to stop even worse protection from being imposed by the courts. Such laws need to be altered. The rules that define dumping should be internationally written, since it is an international and not a national problem.

While the precise dynamics of increasing protection differ from country to country, similar situations exist in every country. To do nothing is to move to protection. As a result, a new Bretton Woods and a new set of rules that confront today's problems are absolutely essential if international trade is to continue to expand and provide the benefits that it should be providing. To be fair, it must be said that most of the rest of the world wants a new set of rules. The biggest obstacle to those new rules is the United States.

While it will undoubtedly take a considerable amount of time to work out a new set of international rules, America can take a number of actions quickly. First in terms of export finance and overt subsidies (mostly used in agriculture), America should act like any good competitive firm. In Boston hi-fi firms advertise that they will match the lowest advertised price of any of their competitors. As a country we should do the same. If British Steel has been running at a loss for a long time, as it has, then we will rebate that subsidy on a per-ton basis for any American exports and will impose a countervailing duty of that amount on any imports. If France is offering 6 percent interest rates and fifteen year financing on the airbus, we will offer the same on a Boeing 767. If the Common Market has a subsidy on butter exports, we will offer the same subsidy. As American firms like to say, "We will not be knowingly undersold."

THE JAPANESE PROBLEM

America's trading deficit with Japan, $37 billion in 1984 and likely to be much higher in 1985, is economically and politically unacceptable.[28] It leads American industrialists to say things about an ally that they should not be saying about an enemy. It is a problem that must be solved if we are not to poison an important international relationship.

With little growth in home markets in the early 1980s, exports became Japan's main source of economic progress. When the multiplier effects are included, exports accounted for all of Japan's growth in 1983 and two-thirds of its growth in 1984. When these exports hit the American economy, however, they cut local sales and produce unemployment. The unemployment that would normally flow from a stagnant Japanese domestic economy is essentially being exported to the United States. This was acceptable when Japan had a small weak economy and America a strong one, but it is not permissible given a large Japanese economy and a less strong American one.

Within the United States, the trade imbalance leads to irresistible political pressures to retreat into ever-widening circles of protection. Congress votes for such laws because there are simply many more voters hurt by Japanese exports than helped by being able to sell their products in Japan. In theory, consumers provide a countervailing political pressure to such legislation because they would lose the right to buy cheap, high-quality Japanese products, but in practice many consumers feel that their own jobs are threatened, and in any case consumers have little political muscle.

Americans have to take much of the blame for the trade deficit with Japan. American firms have refused to design products explicitly for the Japanese market, have been shoddy in their quality control, have refused to learn the Japanese language and customs, have demanded instant success, and have often acted as if it is the duty of Japan to run its economy precisely as the U.S. economy is run. Our government has contributed to the problem by letting the dollar-yen exchange rate rise until it is simply impossible for any American manufacturer to compete.

If the United States were the only country having trouble exporting to Japan, one could say that Americans will simply have to learn how to sell their products in foreign markets. But it isn't only Americans who are having trouble. Countries such as West Germany, with a demonstrated track record of exporting success, have found it extremely difficult to break into the Japanese market.

Japan is still operating its economy as if it were small and weak. Agriculture benefits from overt protection and other areas benefit from covert protection, such as expensive safety inspections. Even more important are history and custom. How does an American firm break in as a new supplier of industrial components when Japanese firms place a premium on maintaining long-term intimate supply relationships in the just-in-time inventory system? Ascribing blame, however, has become irrelevant. A solution is needed now.

The history of Japanese-American bilateral economic negotiations could be characterized as the dialogue of the deaf. The nature of the interchange was well illustrated in the June 1984 announcement that Japan had agreed under American duress to "open" its capital markets to international banking. The agreement was a prototypical example of the last fifteen years of Japanese-American economic negotiations. Given an imbalance in bilateral trade, Americans start yelling about some part of the Japanese economy that is closed to American participation. After a year of two of yelling and a year or two of detailed negotiations, Japan and the United States announce that they have reached an agreement "in principle" to settle the particular issue under discussion. Japan will gradually over a period of years undertake to do some of what America wants. When all of the sound and fury have died, however, nothing will have changed. The bilateral deficit will be as big as or bigger than ever.

The most recent agreement fits all of these particulars. The Reagan Administration spent almost four years yelling and negotiating but at the end got a minuscule change in the Japanese financial system. The aim of the negotiations was to raise the demand for yen, and hence its value, by making it easier to move currencies in and out of Japan. A higher-valued yen would make Japanese goods more expensive in the United States and Americans would buy fewer of them, improving the bilateral balance of trade—or so the argument went. But the negotiated changes are so modest and so spread out over three years that it was clear even at the time that they would do little to raise the value of the yen. In fact the yen went down substantially in the nine months after the agreement and the bilateral deficit rose.

The Japanese felt that they had given the Americans what they were asking for, and the Americans felt that somehow they had been cheated because nothing positive seemed to happen.

The right answer is to abolish all of our current restrictions on specific Japanese exports and to replace them with a system of general reciprocity. The current restrictions are counterproductive—leading to ever-increasing waves of protection, creating continual frictions with one of our leading political and military allies—and are robbing the American consumer.

In a system of general reciprocity America would examine world trading patterns to determine the largest bilateral deficit America could afford to run with Japan—something on the order of $8 billion per year—and still obtain overall balance in its international accounts. America would announce that Japan had unlimited access to the American market in terms of specific products—all specific tariffs and quotas would be removed—but that Japan could export only $2 billion more to the United States in this quarter than it had on average imported from the United States in the preceding four quarters. If Japan, for example, had on average imported $10 billion worth of goods and services from the United States in the first quarter of 1985, it could export $12 billion worth of goods and services to the United States in the second quarter of 1985. If it imported $20 billion, it could export $22 billion. Each quarter import licenses would be auctioned off in the appropriate amount with both American importers and Japanese exporters eligible to bid.

Such a system would preserve the advantages of free trade and competition yet still limit the bilateral trade deficit to manageable proportions. No one would be telling the Japanese how to run their economy or to change their culture. America would essentially be offering them an open door. Come into our markets. Export whatever you like. But remember, whatever you export, you have to import a comparable, even if lesser, amount.

THIRD WORLD DEBT AND THE AMERICAN BANKING CRISIS

Bad luck, ignorance, and stupidity mixed with a sprinkling of chicanery have created a banking crisis. What was once the eighth largest bank in America with $41 billion in assets—the Continental Illinois National Bank and Trust Company—needed a multibillion-dollar rescue from near collapse not once but twice: first in May and again in July 1984.[29] In August the country's largest thrift institution with $33 billion in assets—the American Savings and Loan Association of Los Angeles, a subsidiary of the Financial Corporation of America—was faced with the same problem, a sudden outflow of billions of dollars in deposits, that brought Continental to the brink.[30]

With seventy-eight banks having collapsed in 1984, that year saw a level of bank failures not seen since the sixty failures in the last year of the Great Depression.[31] In contrast only five banks per year, all of them small, failed from 1951 to 1970. Given these events, Americans may well wonder whether their banking system is sound.

The answer depends upon the questioner. Small bank depositors have not yet lost money in the current banking crisis and will not lose money! For them the American banking system is sound.

Large bank depositors, who had been losing money in recent bank closures, are unlikely to lose money in the future now that a dramatic precedent has been set at the Continental. In an effort to restore confidence in the bank—and by inference in the entire banking system—the Federal Deposit Insurance Corporation (FDIC), which normally insures deposits up to $100,000, announced that it would cover all deposits, regardless of size. With such a guarantee in place at the Continental, everyone understands that a similar guarantee has been implicitly offered at other banks. For large depositors the banking system was not sound, but now it is.

Bank shareholders have lost money and will lose more money. For them the banking system is not sound and will not soon become sound.

From the perspective at the top, no system is sound when there is a significant probability that the boss may lose his job. Bank bosses have been losing their jobs and more will do so.

As the ultimate guarantor of the soundness of the banking system the American taxpayer has not yet directly lost money, but he may. The FDIC pays for bank rescues out of its insurance funds, but these funds are now so small relative to possible losses that the agency may well have to ask Congress for an appropriation to cover expenses in future bank failures.

The banking crisis will not abort the economic recovery now under way. This might have happened if the banking crisis had arrived unexpectedly and full-blown with a Mexican default on Friday, August 13, 1982. Such a default would have wiped out billions in bank assets and might well have created a "run" (a rapid withdrawal of deposits) not just on Continental Illinois or American Savings but simultaneously on most of America's large banks. Such a run could easily have gotten out of hand. But it did not happen.

Having had three years to think about what they would do if major debtors default and having had the experience of a medium-sized crisis at Continental Illinois, it is clear that the regulatory authorities —the FDIC, the Federal Reserve Bank, the Controller of the Currency, the Federal Home Loan Bank Board—would nationalize the banking system in any major crisis and, if anything, overstimulate the economy with easy money to prevent a repetition of the 1930s collapse of the banking system.

But bottom-line answers on soundness leave a lot of relevant questions unanswered. Was Continental unique, or do a lot of other banks face similar problems? How could the banks make so many bad loans both here and abroad? The banking regulations developed in the 1930s were supposed to prevent such crises. Why have these regulations failed? Why couldn't the regulators foresee the crises and avoid them? With the rapid development of new financial institutions such as money market mutual funds and electronic funds transfers, what is a bank anyway? Should the current crisis lead to more regulation or less regulation? How do we get out of the current mess?

The Continental Illinois

The Continental Illinois was the largest bank failure since the Great Depression. The seeds of its destruction were found in the wildly imprudent energy-related loans of the Penn Square Bank of Oklahoma City.

Although it had assets of less than $500 million, Penn Square lent more than $2 billion to small wildcatters and companies servicing the oil-drilling industry in Oklahoma. At Penn Square there was a consensus that oil prices could only go up and that rising prices would bury whatever mistakes were made in the bank's aggressive lending policies. On the same assumption Continental bought $1 billion of these loans. Neither Continental nor any other bank that bought oil loans from Penn Square appears to have realized that it was impossible for a bank of its size to properly analyze and supervise that many energy loans.

No one, of course, could foresee that oil and gas prices would decline. Or imagine that the real price of gasoline—after adjusting for general inflation—would by 1984 fall back almost to where it was in 1972 before the first OPEC shock. Or forecast two back-to-back recessions, 1980 and 1981–82, with prime lending rates skyrocketing to 20.5 percent in the summer of 1981.

The role that fraud played in some of these loans is murky, but nepotism and insider lending certainly played a role.[32] At least one very large loan ($565,000) was made from the Penn Square to an executive at the Continental and several executives at Continental were fired for not maintaining adequate supervision over Penn Square lending. Internal management reports that something was wrong at the Penn Square were simply ignored by top management at the Continental.

Penn Square went broke because of its bad oil loans in July of 1982, and the loans sold to the Continental Illinois were no better.

Banks fail in two senses. They can go broke or they can run out of funds to cover withdrawals by depositors. The Penn Square made so many bad loans that it did not have enough funds to repay its depositors even after all of the funds (equity) contributed by the bank's shareholders were given to the bank's depositors. In the jargon, the Penn Square had "negative net equity."

Continental in contrast ran out of funds to pay its depositors. Although it had not reached bankruptcy with negative net equity, its bad loans so worried its depositors that they started to withdraw their funds faster than Continental could acquire money to meet their demands.

All banks lend "long" (make loans for long periods of time) and borrow "short" (accept deposits that can be withdrawn after short periods of time). If many depositors become nervous and start to demand their money, no bank can recall its loans fast enough to acquire funds to repay all of its depositors. Continental was no exception to this general rule.

If one asks why depositors should have been so worried about a still solvent bank, one has to inquire into the activities of the Federal Deposit Insurance Corporation under its head, William M. Isaac. The FDIC was established in 1933 to insure bank depositors against the kinds of disasters that had befallen them in the Great Depression. Banks went broke, causing depositors to lose their funds and forcing many of these depositors into bankruptcy. Because normal free market incentives and pressures did not insure a sound banking system in the 1930s, it became a governmental responsibility to insure bank deposits and make sure that banks did not engage in "unsound" practices.

But that was more than fifty years ago. Things are different now. Or so it was thought by the FDIC, Mr. Isaac, and the Reagan Administration that appointed him. Contrary to previous practice, where big depositors had always been protected through merger, but not contrary to previous law (only deposits of less than $100,000 are legally insured), the FDIC decided when Penn Square went over the brink that it would not protect large depositors. The strategy was to make large sophisticated bank depositors into the banking industry's policemen. Free enterprise depositors would patrol the banking industry, preventing unsound practices by withdrawal of their funds from banks engaging in such practices. The FDIC would turn its job over to private enterprise and the market.

This belief contributed to Continental's fall and its transformation into a government bank. When private depositors decided that the Continental was engaging in unsound lending practices and withdrew their money, the FDIC was not willing to carry its beliefs to their logical conclusion and see the Continental collapse—perhaps taking other banks with it.

The run on the Continental seemed to take bank regulators by surprise despite the fact that history is full of such panics. Previous to the collapse of the entire banking system in the 1930s there had been numerous panics. In the panic of 1857, for example, more than 1,400 banks went broke in the month of October. The lessons of history were clear, but ignored.

Under pressure from other banks, the Federal Reserve Board (the nation's central bank), and an incipient run on Manufacturers Hanover, the policy of not protecting large depositors abruptly ended at the Continental. Depositor protection was in fact extended far beyond even previous boundaries to include those who owned preferred shares or held the commercial paper (short-term bonds issued by the banks to raise money) of the bank holding companies. Not to do so was to insure that other banks would find it very difficult to raise funds.

But because of Mr. Isaac's announced free market strategy for getting out of the regulatory business and given the record of previous losses when the Penn Square and a number of other smaller banks failed, large depositors did not believe him when he pledged to protect their deposits during the run on the Continental and they continued to withdraw their funds even after public guarantees had been given. One-third of those smart money managers got out, taking $9 billion with them before the run stopped.

Because the FDIC's verbal guarantees could not quickly stop the run on the Continental, a solvent bank failed in a panic. And if the run had not eventually been stopped at the Continental, it was only a matter of time until runs developed at other large banks. None may have as many bad loans as the Continental, but the next weakest bank isn't much better off.

If one asks, as Senator Alfonse M. D'Amato, conservative Republican of New York, did, why the Federal regulators did such "a miserable job in allowing the situation at the bank to deteriorate to the point where it had to be bailed out by government," there is a simple answer. Regulators did not see the crisis coming, not because they were stupid but because they only expected events that were consistent with their efficient free market view of the world. And in that world an irrational bank panic was simply impossible.

When no buyers could be found for the Continental, the government had to invest $4.5 billion to keep the bank going and ended up owning 80 percent of the shareholder equity in what is essentially a new Continental bank.[33] The depositors could have been protected and the bank liquidated (the shareholders wiped out) but this would just have moved the panic into the market for bank shares and been a confession of dereliction of duty: A large bank had been allowed to slip below the line into negative net equity without the regulators' doing anything about it.

Letting market forces police the banking system presupposes that the public can determine whether or not a bank's loan portfolio is sound. Yet the troubles at the Continental show too clearly that bank executives and officers, even the regulators and auditors who have access to an institution's books, can fail to detect danger signs. Good information on the soundness of bank loans is hard to come by. After months of detailed investigations there were still large uncertainties as to how much of Continental's lending will prove to be uncollectable. That is why the FDIC insisted on a provision in the Continental rescue that shareholder equity will be further reduced to the extent that more loans are uncollectable than were expected when the bank collapsed.

Large sophisticated money managers cannot police the American banking system because they have no legal right to examine the books of the banks or the bank's customers, and they cannot be given this right since it would make them privy to confidential information about their competitors and let them engage in insider trading. Large depositors are, and will remain, dependent upon the outside rumors, innuendos and gossip that swirl around the financial markets.

In the case of Continental, the rumors of its demise began in the Far East (no one knows why) and spread to those big sophisticated rational money market managers everywhere in the world. It was rational for those big sophisticated money market managers to act on those "irrational" rumors since they had little to gain by staying in and, given the policies of the FDIC, much to lose. While there are those who believe that the free market can perceive unsound banking practices better than the regulatory authorities, as the Continental demonstrates, free market depositors too often see ghosts.

To gain the detailed knowledge that would be necessary to police the banking system takes both time and money. Large depositors have better things to do with their time and their money. They want safe places to rest their money while it is not being used for other purposes and will rush out of any place believed to be unsafe.

There is, in addition, no way for depositors to increase pressures for changes in bank lending policies by gradually reducing their deposits. Since the last depositor out the door loses his money, everyone wants to be the first depositor out the door. In real life interest rates demanded by depositors don't slowly rise as the bank's policies become more and more "unsound" but suddenly rise to very high levels when depositors discover that the bank is "unsound." Payment of the interest rates required to stop capital flight would cause bankruptcy almost as fast as the flight itself.

Banking authorities and the Reagan Administration see Continental as a one-of-a-kind occurrence and not as an abandonment of their free market principles. As expressed by Paul A. Volcker, chairman of the Federal Reserve Board, the "Continental in its totality is a unique situation . . . I don't think that we are going to see another Continental."[34] That is, of course, true. The next large bank failure was not going to be an exact duplicate of the Continental situation.

But within fifteen days of Mr. Volker's pronouncement, a new crisis was under way in California at the American Savings and Loan Association.[35] With the ability to write checks on savings accounts and to pay interest on checking accounts, the distinction between commercial banks and savings and loan associations has all but disappeared. They are banks in everything but name. If the pattern of the crisis was not identical, it was disturbingly similar. The Financial Corporation of America was a go-go bank holding company ($10 billion in large deposits were attracted in the first six months of 1984 alone).

The crisis began when the Securities and Exchange Commission (SEC) did not approve of the Financial Corporation's accounting procedures and forced it to change what had been previously reported as a second-quarter profit of $31 million into a second-quarter loss of $108 million. The losses were expected to continue since the Financial Corporation was speculating that interest rates would go down and did not protect itself against the interest-rate increases that had occurred since the first of the year. The corporation found itself in a position where the interest rate that it had to pay to its depositors exceeded the interest rate that it collected from its borrowers. Delinquent loans rose rapidly toward the $1 billion mark.

Here again the heart of the crisis was found in the nervousness of those large money managers who were holding $21 billion in uninsured deposits. In July they withdrew $1.4 billion in deposits because they were unsure whether the Federal Home Loan Bank Board (FHLBB), the first cousin of the FDIC which insures savings and loan associations, would protect them. Given recent history and the fact that the FHLBB only had $6 billion in its insurance fund, there was ample reason to worry.

Secretary of the Treasury Donald Regan saw the de facto nationalization of Continental as "bad public policy," which it was. It was a policy that is grossly unfair. There are two sets of rules for banks: Little banks can fail but big banks cannot. Large depositors in little banks can lose their money but large depositors in big banks cannot.

Under present policies bank regulators are essentially forcing large depositors to move from small banks to large banks to protect themselves. To prevent this from happening, Federal deposit insurance is going to have to be expanded to cover all deposits regardless of size. If this is not done, small banks are simply going to cease to exist—driven out of business not by their market inefficiencies but by the unfair decisions of "free enterprise" regulatory authorities.

Perhaps the greatest stupidity revealed at the Continental was the way in which the FDIC insurance fund had been run. Part of the disbelief in the FDIC guarantees was the fact that the FDIC itself did not have enough money to stem the avalanche of deposit withdrawals. The Continental had $41 billion in deposits and the FDIC had $16 billion in its insurance fund, with the authority from Congress to borrow up to $3 billion in emergency funds from the Treasury. To control the run at the Continental the FDIC ended up having to borrow $3.6 billion from the Federal Reserve System and another $5.5 billion in a line of credit from twenty-eight private banks when it was supposed to have enough funds in its own reserves. No one, and certainly no foreigner, could be absolutely sure that other private banks and the Federal Reserve would help out with the needed loans.

If one asks why the FDIC did not have the necessary funds, one uncovers an interesting practice. By law banks are supposed to pay an insurance premium equal to one-twelfth of one percent of their deposits.[36] But in 1950 the FDIC received permission to reduce that insurance premium if it was too high relative to real risks and started to issue refunds, which grew to 50 to 60 percent of the premiums collected. While one can argue whether this was or was not warranted in the late 1960s when bank failures were minimal, refunds were clearly unwarranted after 1974 when the world's economy was thrown into disarray with the first OPEC oil price hike. Yet as late as 1980 the FDIC rebated 55 percent of what it had collected, and even in 1983 the FDIC was still refunding 13.5 percent of the premiums paid. Such refunds were so unwarranted as to constitute dereliction of duty. Those running the FDIC weren't competent to run what they were running.

To compound the problem, insurance premiums are not collected on foreign deposits. Since foreign depositors are apt to be the first to flee in panic and since they enjoy the benefits of the guarantees recently given to large depositors, that practice is simply madness. And in what appears to be an extreme case of seeing one's short-run self-interest (they don't want to pay more money to the FDIC) and losing sight of one's long-run self-interest (who has more at stake in the perceived soundness of the banking system) large banks have been lobbying against collecting insurance premiums on foreign deposits.

While Continental's third-world loans were not its undoing, such loans represent a potential avalanche overhanging the entire banking system. The nine largest American banks all have more than 100 percent of their shareholders' equity at risk in just four countries— Mexico, Brazil, Venezuela, and Argentina.[37] Manufacturers Hanover is the most exposed with 240 percent of its equity at risk.

If these four countries should default, all of our largest banks would instantly have negative net equity, shareholders at our biggest banks would be wiped out, and the Federal government, as it did at the Continental, would have to provide the necessary equity capital to keep our largest banks operating. No private capitalist wants a large bank with negative net equity.

Bad luck, ignorance, stupidity, and chicanery were all present in Latin American lending. No one could foresee the two OPEC oil shocks and the resulting economic damage. Because of rising oil prices, Brazil had to export 45 percent more to buy the old volume of imports, and as a result it was noticeably poorer after the oil shocks than it was before. Banks thought that they were lending to a richer Brazil than they were.

Brazil's exports rose 16 percent per year from 1977 to 1981, but with the maxi-recession or mini-depression of 1981–82 they fell 9 percent in 1982.[38] With falling exports, debts could not be paid. To make matters worse, interest rates went through the roof. Money borrowed at 6.5 percent in 1977 was costing 19 percent in 1980 and 1981. Debts manageable at 6.5 percent were unmanageable at 19 percent.

Ignorance was widespread in that no one—here or there—knew how much money was being lent to different countries. Mexico was thought to have borrowed $35 billion in the early summer of 1982, $50 billion was rumored to be true at the height of the August 1982 crisis, and $85 billion was found to be the right number after all of the accounting was done months later. The bank lending the first billion dollars to Mexico had a perfectly safe loan; but when someone else lent the eighty-fifth billion, all of the earlier loans became equally unsafe.

No one knew how much was being lent, since banks did not share lending information with each other. (Does Macy's tell Gimbel's?) Furthermore, since loans were actually made to many different public and private groups within each country from banks in many different countries, neither the American regulatory agencies nor the governments of Latin American countries knew the extent of the borrowing.

Stupidity was not in short supply. The banks forgot that when loans, public or private, are made in underdeveloped countries, they are essentially all made to the central bank of the country. No private group can repay its loans without getting foreign exchange from the central bank. Some of the loans were good loans in the sense that the borrower had enough local currency to repay, but were bad loans in the sense that the central bank had no foreign exchange which could be used to convert local currencies into dollars. As a result banks technically met the regulatory rule that no more than 5 percent of their capital could be lent to any one borrower, but systematically violated the spirit of the rule and ended up with too many of their eggs in four Latin American baskets.

Within the banks a system was in place to reward aggressive lending. The lending officer who put together a $10 billion syndication for Argentina got a big bonus and a promotion. No one had ever gotten a bonus or a promotion by turning down large loan requests. In the late 1970s and early 1980s there was talk of oil prices going to $100 per barrel, and every such conversation led to more lending to oil-rich Mexico.

The world's big banks became engaged in a race to see who could be the world's biggest bank, and all tried to emulate Citicorp's go-go style. As with gamblers in the heat of Las Vegas action, caution, as they say, was thrown to the winds.

The banks believed that in the worst-case scenario, the United States would bail out its allies in Latin America just as the Soviet Union would come to the aid of its client states in Eastern Europe. In the last instance, it is clear that the judgment was wrong. The Soviet Union has not and will not pay the Polish loans. In the case of Latin America, the United States has not paid off any loans yet; although it has lent countries money (Argentina in the first quarter of 1984) to meet their interest payments.

Americans who deplore fraud and corruption in foreign aid programs can now deplore fraud and corruption in privately administered bank loans. Many loans were used not for the announced purposes but to finance capital flight for wealthy citizens who wanted to move their money into safer havens in Europe or America. While such movements are illegal south of the border they are perfectly legal north of the border; and based on observations in America and Europe something like $25 billion of Mexico's borrowing—$9 billion in 1982 alone—ended up in capital flight.[39] In Argentina something over $20 billion in hot money (no one seems to know exactly how much) left the country. Substantial portions of the Argentine loans were also used to buy perks and military equipment for the now discredited generals and admirals who were then running the country.

But what is being done now to convert the unsound loans into sound ones? The International Monetary Fund (IMF), essentially the agent of the wealthy industrial countries, charged with policing the international payment system, has a solution. Simple arithmetic dictates that if a country is to make interest payments or repay loans, it must have a surplus of exports over imports to earn the needed dollars. Since the IMF has no leverage whereby it can force industrial countries to accept more third-world exports, it focuses on reducing third-world imports. The recipe for doing so is simple. To get imports down the IMF forces third-world countries to pursue fiscal and monetary policies that will make them poorer. Poor people with falling incomes buy fewer imports than richer people with rising incomes.

Mexico, for instance, was forced to lower public spending by an amount equal to 5 percent of its GNP and raise its taxes by an amount equal to 4 percent of its GNP.[40] If this had been done to the United States in 1983, the Federal government would have been forced to slash spending by $165 billion and raise taxes by $132 billion. Such an expenditure cut would have eliminated Social Security's old age pensions and raised April 1984 income tax bills 45 percent. In addition, the purchasing power of the Mexican minimum wage was cut 26 percent. In America this would have meant a cut from $3.35 to $2.48 per hour in the minimum wage.

These policies worked. The Mexican GNP fell 4.7 percent in 1983 and the average Brazilian took an 11 percent cut in his income. With lower levels of economic activity, imports as expected fell, leaving more export earnings that could be used to meet bank interest charges. But such austerity measures cannot be continued for long. Eventually Latin governments will prefer default or be forcibly replaced by their disgruntled citizens with ones that will.

That such defaults have not occurred is remarkable. One could, of course, attribute it to semantics. Just as wars are no longer "declared," no one is now declared "legally" in default. Countries such as Ecuador and Poland have essentially defaulted, but big borrowers such as Brazil and Mexico are still honestly wrestling with their debts. That they haven't defaulted is partly a matter of creative bookkeeping (they are lent the money to make interest payments), partly a matter of fear (a defaulter and especially a single defaulter would quickly find essential imports such as medicine cut off), and partly a question of honor—one should pay one's bills.

Whatever the process for avoiding a legal default, however, the banks end up holding more and more questionable loans—making those large depositors more and more nervous.

Since one country's imports are another country's exports, if every country cuts back on its imports, there can only be fewer exports for everyone. What has kept this self-defeating nature of the IMF prescription from working so far is the willingness of the United States to absorb the rest of the world's trade surplus in the form of its $123 billion trade deficit. But this solution requires a world willing to lend enormous sums to the United States and a United States willing to become an ever larger international debtor. Neither condition is apt to last for long.

To remove the overhanging avalanche of third-world debt, the debts will have to be renegotiated so that long-term debt replaces short-term debt, so that fixed interest rates replace variable interest rates, and to some extent are forgiven so that countries are left with debts which they can realistically repay. With today's short-term debt structure there is a continual problem of maintaining enough confidence among creditors to roll over old debt, and whenever interest rates go up in the United States fears of default arise again. Those fears are not groundless, since for Brazil an increase of 1 percentage point means an extra $900 million more must be found to make interest payments.

The banks are resisting such renegotiations because it will make explicit the losses that are now implicit. They don't want to formally recognize in their bookkeeping what has actually happened and tell their shareholders that management has lost some substantial fraction of shareholder's equity.

But explicit losses are now occurring and they can only get worse. When Argentina did not meet its second-quarter 1984 interest payments, Manufacturers Hanover suffered a $21.4 million cut in second quarter earnings.

In exchange for making explicit the losses that the banks will suffer, however, what remains of their third-world debt after renegotiation should be guaranteed by the IMF.

Everyone gets something from such a solution. Bankers end up knowing where they stand and that the bad news is behind them. They also know that the loans that they are left with are good loans. Depositors do not have to worry about default, and the banks don't have to worry about being nationalized in a crisis.

What the industrial nations gain in exchange is the freedom to pursue appropriate domestic monetary policies. If inflation were to break out in the United States today, American monetary authorities would be confronted by the fact that attempts to tighten monetary policies and control inflation would undoubtedly trigger a third-world default and force them to nationalize America's largest banks. They also do not have to worry that the next recession will destroy their banking systems. What the taxpayer gains is the removal of a danger that a banking crisis will erupt from a third-world default and get out of hand.

To prevent the kind of banking crisis spawned by the run on the Continental requires an overhauling of America's bank regulatory system. The present system stems from the Great Depression. Some of it, such as the system of deposit insurance, springs from the legitimate need for a safety net to prevent runs. But some of it, such as the laws limiting banks to a very narrow range of activities, springs from punitive notions, common in the 1930s, that the Great Depression was caused by excessive bank speculation. It did not happen that way. A farm depression started in the mid-1920s, the GNP quit growing before the stock market crashed, and the stock market crashed well before the banks failed. Banks were victims more than they were criminals.

In contrast with the rest of the industrial world, the American banking system is marked by many more small banks and by a sharp separation between banking and other financial activities. Prohibitions upon branch banking within many states and upon interstate banking have protected small banks from the inroads of large banks, and the Glass-Steagall Act, for instance, prevents commercial banks (banks which accept deposits from the public) from engaging in investment banking (making equity investments in industrial firms)—something done in all of the rest of the industrial world.

Given the historical context which produced America's now fifty-year-old system of bank regulation, the need for reform is not surprising. The push to change regulations, however, has been generated by banks anxious to avoid old regulations rather than a conscious effort by legislators to create a more efficient banking system for the twenty-first century.

While there has been some formal deregulation, such as effectively lifting the interest rate limits on what banks can pay to small depositors, most of the actual deregulation has been of the back-door variety. Regulators simply stop enforcing provisions that they have previously been enforcing. Out-of-state banks, for example, are allowed to buy small failing banks and once in-state are then allowed to spread across the state. Using money market mutual funds upon which checks can be written, brokerage firms such as Merrill Lynch are allowed to become banks in everything but name; and banks, using bank holding companies, are allowed to enter businesses, insurance and brokerage, which are nominally closed to them.

Antitrust laws are not as rigorously enforced as they once were. Bank of America, the number two bank in America, was allowed to buy a very large Seattle bank. Financial conglomerates such as Lehman/Shearson/American Express are created by merging what is essentially a bank for travelers (traveler's checks and credit cards) with an insurance company (Fireman's Fund), a brokerage firm (Shearson), and an investment banking firm (Lehman Brothers). Today no one thinks of challenging such mergers.

Creative lawyers find loopholes in the law and banks are allowed through these loopholes where the loopholes would in the past have been quickly closed. With the discovery that a bank, by law, is an institution which accepts deposits, banks set up offices that make loans but do not accept deposits and by so doing escape the jurisdiction of bank regulators. And once such lending offices are established, everyone understands it is only a matter of time until the law is modified to reflect existing reality and deposits can be accepted.

Rewards go not to those banks that can most efficiently work within the existing regulations but to those that are the most creative in finding new ways around the old regulations. What we have now is a financial system that is reconstituting itself relative to what it thinks it can get away with.

In the anything-goes, fiercely competitive banking environment where forced mergers have become a norm, many banks have become go-go institutions to avoid being taken over, even when they do not have the resources to carry it off. And in this climate of fear and uncertainty, money starts sloshing around the system in giant whirl-pools. Just such fear and uncertainty drowned the Continental Illinois and American Savings.

Back-door deregulation is too often poor deregulation, as was seen in the FDIC decision to effectively change the system by not insuring large depositors at Penn Square. At this point, returning to the regulations of the early 1970s is also not the solution; many of those regulations were unfair, silly, and inconsistent with a modern efficient banking system. Branch, interstate, and investment banking should all be allowed. Since the Continental debacle made it abundantly clear that market forces cannot patrol the banking industry and that bank runs will occur unless all depositors are insured in full, the FDIC is going to have to extend its coverage.

After deciding what a bank is (Are the airport American Express machines that can lend you money in the form of traveler's checks a bank?), everyone operating a bank should be subject to the same regulations. And whatever laws are passed, public officials should enforce them in spirit as well as the letter of the law.

With modern computer technology and electronic funds transfers the days of state regulation are simply over. State regulations can be written but they cannot be enforced.

Regulatory officials should begin by collecting the one-twelfth of one percent insurance fee that they are supposed to collect on all deposits. This should be done until the FDIC has built up an insurance fund equal in size to the deposits of the largest bank under its jurisdiction—in 1983, it was $135 billion at Citicorp. There should be no doubt in anyone's mind that the FDIC has enough assets to protect all depositors in even the largest bank. The head of the FDIC should also be someone who agrees with both the letter and the spirit of depositor protection.

The fact that the Continental was rescued by government is not an argument for increasing bank regulation. If being rescued were an argument for regulation, then we should now be increasing regulations in the auto industry, the steel industry, the textile industry, and the aerospace industry. Large firms in all of these industries have been directly rescued with government money or indirectly rescued with government protection from foreign competition.

In deregulating banks, the basic goal should be to protect all depositors and give them the safety that they want while leaving those operating banks, both the managers and the shareholders, subject to as much market discipline as the system can stand. In doing so it must be recognized that there will always be a double standard for large and small banks as far as direct government bailouts are concerned. If large firms go down the drain, they always carry others—depositors in the case of banks, suppliers in the case of industrial firms—with them. Governments have a legitimate interest in preventing such spreading waves of failure. Small firms don't have the spill-over effects that make their demise a legitimate national disaster.

If a modicum of fairness is to exist, however, there must be substantial punishments for the managers who led the large firms into disaster. In both the Chrysler and Continental cases top managers were fired and new managers were brought in from the outside. This practice should be regarded as standard operating procedure in any rescue. Shareholders should be forced to lose much of their equity, as has happened at the Continental.

If the public is asked to absorb some of the losses from bad loans, then the public should be given some shares so that it can make some profits if the bailout works. As Chrysler was restored to profitability the value of government shares rose and returned several hundred million dollars to the U.S. Treasury. The same, it is to be hoped, will occur at the Continental.

If the regulatory authorities insist on these provisions, large banking companies are not going to become "too risky" on the assumption that they will be bailed out by government.

If many of the 1930s prohibitions on banking activities were removed, as they should be, it would be perfectly appropriate in this new, more risky environment to impose large capital requirements. Large banks now have equity equal to about 5 percent of their assets. Normal firms have to have much more equity. Any bank wishing to engage in non-traditional bank activities should be forced to raise a lot more capital. Depending upon the portfolio of activities that a bank wishes to engage in, it should be possible to work out a schedule of minimum capital requirement that would be appropriate for that portfolio of activities.

When it comes to that famous bottom line, we Americans have been lucky. Mexico did not default and take the world's banking system by surprise in August 1982. It might have. The panic at the Continental did not spread to the rest of the banking system. It could have.

One also hopes that the lessons of the 1930s have been relearned.

Efficient government regulation has an important role to play if we are to have an efficient sound private banking industry.

NEEDED: A MANAGER

While the United States is no longer strong enough to dictate economically to the rest of the world, as it did at the first Bretton Woods conference, it is still the strongest country in the industrial world. As a result it still needs to play the role of manager of the international trading system. In the next twenty years the manager's job is going to be one of seeking consensus and making compromises —not giving orders—but only the United States is capable of filling that frustrating role. For unless there is a manager who is actively concerned about the future of the international trading system, the system will simply disappear in a sea of protectionism.

Unfortunately America has abdicated on a responsibility that only it can fulfill. The international trading system won't take care of itself as the Reagan Administration seems to think. International organizations are not ipso facto bad. If the world economy is to work, a creative manager is needed, and America had better apply for the job if it wants a healthy domestic economy and healthy international alliances.

12 / Will We Do It?

The human animal is known for its adaptability. It can adjust to a wide range of circumstances but even more importantly it can adjust to *changing* circumstances. Among human animals Americans like to think of themselves as more adaptable than most. Most Americans left a familiar old world and came to an unfamiliar new world; they left kingdoms and invented a new republican form of governing themselves; harnessing individual initiative with the community solidarity they settled a continent; within a relatively short period of time they generated an economy second to none and became the world's leaders in technical change. Americans proved they were adaptable by being adaptable.

Some changes come suddenly; others occur gradually. The industrial revolution started later in the United States than it did in Great Britain. Americans did not catch up quickly but they did catch up. In the first forty years of the twentieth century, they were among the world's economic leaders although they did not stand alone. World War II saw revolutionary changes both politically and economically. America for the first time became a political and military superpower. Its economy stood alone with a huge technological gap between it and the world's next best economy.

In the forty years since then other countries have caught up with the United States. Once again, instead of standing alone, America is just one among several economic leaders. It has peers. For Americans this represents a fundamental change. Their effortless superiority is gone and they must accelerate their rate of growth of productivity to remain competitive at home and abroad.

Productivity flows from the fundamentals of who we are and how we organize ourselves. High quality inputs must be matched with shrewd strategies and good social organization. Let no one think that altering two decades of low productivity growth is a trivial task. It is not going to be done with minor policy measures adopted in Washington. The changes that will be required can only be described as fundamental structural change. Every American and almost every American institution will have to be willing to change if Americans are to meet the economic challenges facing them as they prepare to enter the third millennium.

When people ask me whether I am an optimist or a pessimist about the future of the American economy and its ability to compete in world markets, I describe myself as an intellectual pessimist but an emotional optimist. Intellectually, if I were simply a Las Vegas gambler betting the odds, I would bet no. America won't do it. The required changes are too hard. There are too many vested interests who clearly see their short-run individual self-interests but who do not recognize their long-run collective self-interests and who will oppose what must be done.

There are few examples of nations rebuilding their economies and consciously accelerating their rate of growth of productivity without the sting of a military defeat. Countries simply need the reality of a concrete defeat to break old traditional habits. Without a defeat it is simply easier on any given day not to do all of the difficult things that have to be done. Change is painful and it is only too easy to convince yourself that things are not as bad as they seem or that they are going to get better on their own. Without a military defeat today's economic performance is never a disaster that must be corrected. Japan and Germany did it; Great Britain did not.

Emotionally, however, I would place a bet on America. There are stirrings among Americans who recognize that something different must be done. Quality-control circles, an understanding that educational standards must go up, agreement that savings must rise even if there is no agreement on how, a debate about industrial policies, a wide-spread perception that something is wrong with American management—all are positive indications. When Americans get to the point where each of us is willing to admit that he or she, and not just someone else, is at the heart of the problem, America will have reached the point where change can begin.

Many of the stirrings that are now under way arise from a four-letter word—fear—the fear flowing from those $123 billion trade deficits and the economically devastated American communities those deficits leave behind. The fear of economic failure. Perhaps that fear can be used as our "moral equivalent of defeat." It can be the spur convincing us that the old ways are not necessarily good ways—that good new ways can be found.

As in any major rebuilding effort, the central problem is to harness the energy of the entire population. Few Americans are going to succeed by bailing out of the common effort and attempting to succeed as individuals on their own. American capitalists are not going to successfully compete with a low-savings American society behind them. American firms are not going to survive with illiterates on their payrolls. American managers are not going to succeed as offshore managers of foreign workers.

As America learned in World War II, a more equitable society is not in conflict with a more productive society—quite the contrary. Unfortunately, what we know instinctively in time of war we have to relearn in peacetime. One does not create the motivation and cooperation necessary for a successful team effort by increasing inequality. When sacrifices are needed in a democratic society, equity is the key. Each individual must feel that everyone else is carrying a fair share of the burdens.

It is precisely here that Democratic leadership is necessary. For what Democratic leadership can provide is the vision that America can win, a sense of what the winning strategy is, and a feeling that everyone is on the same team enduring the same hardships. In the new competitive world economy winning certainly isn't automatic. Letting the market work won't do it, since every market has winners and losers and there is nothing in market principles that insures that Americans will always be winners. In the current world market America is a loser. That is the significance of a large trade deficit. But I believe that America can become a winner in world markets and that the Democratic party both can and should lead in that effort. In the process it will gain a political agenda that will lead it to regain its political ascendancy.

The essence of the choice can be seen in a dialogue that I had with Herbert Stein, Chairman of the Council of Economic Advisers under President Nixon, at the American Enterprise Institute (a conservative Washington think tank) in mid-1983 in a joint discussion of industrial policies. Although this part of the discussion was not printed in the final transcript published by the American Enterprise Institute, it illustrates the heart of the differences between good Democrats and good Republicans.[1]

Dr. Thurow: What makes you sure that the United States at the moment isn't Great Britain circa 1900? The rest of the world is breathing at our heels and they aren't going to slow down when they catch up. They're going to zoom right by and the United States fifty years from now will have half their per capita GNP.

Dr. Stein: I'm not sure of that at all. But I'm not willing to make a major change in the system on the bet that that is the case.

Dr. Thurow: Let me ask you a question. Suppose you knew that it were true. Would you then be willing to change the system?

Dr. Stein: No.

Dr. Thurow: You are saying that the system is more important than the result no matter how bad the result?

Dr. Stein: Well, you have to give me a little room about how bad the result is, but I mean—

Dr. Thurow: I'll give you the result. Fifty years from now the American per capita GNP will be half that of the leading industrial country. Assume that were a fact. Would that then lead you to believe that we ought to change the system now?

Dr. Stein: No.

In contrast Democrats should answer yes and bet that the general American answer is also yes. The system is not more important than the results. Americans do not want to live with an economic system that produces inferior results, are inventive enough to figure out what must be changed to succeed, and are willing to make those changes once they have been identified.

The proper goal is to rebuild the structure of the American economy so that it can be fully competitive on world markets. The solution is not to circle the economic wagons and retreat into protection—to defend what we have—but to organize ourselves to aggressively economically counterattack at home and abroad. A defensive protectionist strategy is implicitly to give up on the economic race and to accept something less than finishing first, second, or even third. It is to accept a falling relative standard of living for the average American, to accept an America that cannot run even with the leaders of the economic pack, and to accept inferiority. I know of few Americans willing to accept what must be accepted.

The strategy is also inconsistent with American culture and history. Americans aren't very good when they are in a defensive mode. On the defensive we are apt to start fighting with each other. To be successful America must mobilize to win.

Now that real competition has arrived, Americans, not surprisingly, don't like it. Wherever we look we see economic defeat—not just in our old smokestack industries such as steel but in new sunrise industries such as semiconductor chips. The initial reaction is to cry foul. The world is engaged in "unfair" competition. "If America is losing it must be an unfair fight. By definition America couldn't be losing a fair fight." Yet someone else who builds a better product by working harder or smarter is not engaging in "unfair" competition. Foreign governments may help their firms compete better, but that is not "unfair" competition. Governments are elected to make their economies more productive. America needs to work with foreign governments to agree upon a fair set of rules for international competition, but the set of rules that will emerge out of those negotiations will not be the American set of rules or a set of rules that precludes an activist role for government in the economy.

American conservatives simply cannot have it both ways—claiming that any government interference at home is inefficient and that any government interference abroad is superefficient. If governments are inherently inefficient when it comes to promoting economic growth, Americans should welcome and ignore foreign intervention —it can only lower foreign growth rates. If foreign governments can be efficient at promoting economic growth, then Americans have to design their government so that it can also become efficient in promoting economic growth.

Regaining our competitive edge will not be pleasant or quick. In the words of the weight lifters, "No pain, no gain." There will be some pain in getting back into economic shape. But what needs to be emphasized is not the transitory pain but the ultimate gain. America can get back into shape and have a world-class economy. If we do so, everyone will feel better and enjoy a rising standard of living that is once again the envy of the rest of the world. The real pain comes in failing to compete and the envy that is gradually induced by falling farther and farther behind.

America cannot go back to the "effortless superiority" of the immediate post-World War II period. We aren't smarter than everyone else. America can, however, regain parity; America can remain one of the world's economic leaders. It won't happen automatically—social organization will be required—but America can have a world-class economy.

NOTES

INTRODUCTION

1. For a more detailed discussion of the data on Social Security see Chapter 7.
2. NCS News, *NBC New Decision 1984: General Election Poll Results*, page 4.

CHAPTER 1

1. Unless otherwise specified all general economic data are to be found in: United States Department of Commerce, *Survey of Current Business*, July estimates of National Income and Product Accounts; or Council of Economic Advisers, *Economic Report of the President*, Feb. 1984.
2. Executive Office of the President, *Fiscal Year 1982 Budget Revisions*, Mar. 1981.
3. Milton Friedman, "The Federal Reserve and Monetary Instability," *Wall Street Journal*, Feb. 1, 1982, Op Ed pages.
4. *Economic Report of the President*, 1984, page 308
5. Otto Eckstein, "Disinflation," in *Inflation: Prospects and Remedies*, Center for National Policy, 1983, page 11.
6. U.S. Department of Commerce, *Survey of Current Business*, July 1981, Special Supplement, page 39.
7. Sara Johnson and David Steinberg, "The U.S. Becomes a Debtor Nation," *DRI Review of the U.S. Economy*, Nov. 1984, page 23.
8. Charles P. Kindleberger, *Manias, Panics and Crashes*, Basic Books, 1978, New York, page 34.
9. U.S. Department of Commerce, *Long Term Economic Growth 1860–1970*, June 1973, page 182.
10. "The Super Dollar," *Business Week*, Oct. 8, 1984.
11. U.S. Department of Commerce, *International Economic Indicators*, Sep. 1983, page 64; and telephone update from Labor Department.
12. *Ibid.*
13. *Survey of Current Business*, July 1984, page 54.

CHAPTER 2

1. The author would like to thank Quinn Mills and Laura Tyson for their helpful comments.
2. Roger Brinner and Nigel Gault, "U.S. Manufacturing Costs and International Competition," *Data Resources Review*, Oct. 1983, page 1.15.
3. U.S. Department of Commerce, *International Economic Indicators*, Sep. 1983, page 64.
4. Council of Economic Advisers, *Economic Report of the President*, Feb. 1984, page 267.
5. Ibid.
6. "Nirvana by Numbers," *The Economist*, Dec. 24, 1983, page 53.

7. *Economic Report of the President*, 1984, page 221.
8. International Monetary Fund, *International Financial Statistics*, Mar. 1984, page 264.
9. "VCRs: Santa's Hottest Gift: The Magic Box That Is Creating a Video Revolution" *Time*, Dec. 24, 1984.
10. "Domestic Sales of VTRs Drastically Slow Down," Nov. 13, 1984, and "VTR Exports Hit Record in October," Nov. 27, 1984, *Japanese Economic Journal*.
11. David E. Sanger, "U.S. Move in Video Cameras," *New York Times*, Jan. 5, 1984, page D1.
12. Andrew Pollack, "A Move Into Microprocessors," *New York Times*, Sep. 6, 1984.
13. "NEC: A Lightning Semiconductor," *The Economist*, Dec. 15, 1984.
14. William J. Broad, "Big Japanese Gain in Computers Seen," *New York Times*, Feb. 13, 1984, page 1.
15. Steven Greenhouse, "Tool Orders Rose 2.7% in March," *New York Times*, April 30, 1984, page D1; Seymour Melman, "How the Yankees Lost Their Know-How," *Technology Review*, Oct. 1983, page 63.
16. "Business Fixed Investment," Nov. 1984, *DRI Review of the U.S. Economy*, page 61.
17. Steven Greenhouse, "A Survival Fight in Machine Tools," *New York Times*, July 8, 1984, Section 3.
18. "The Cutting Edge: Machine Tools Become an International Business," *Wall Street Journal*, Sep. 4, 1984.
19. "Sankyo Seiki to Increase Robot Exports to IBM," *Japanese Economic Journal*, Sep. 18, 1984.
20. "Thicker than R2D2," *The Economist*, Jan. 21, 1984, page 63.
21. John Holusha, "The Robot Makers Stub Their Toes," *New York Times*, Mar. 4, 1984, page F4.
22. Clyde H. Farnsworth, "Big Telecommunication Trade Gap Seen," *New York Times*, June 26, 1984.
23. Seymour Melman, "The High-Tech Dream Won't Come True," *INC Magazine*, Aug. 1984.
24. "Japan's Nuclear Plant Know-How Leaps to Worldwide Preeminence," *Japanese Economic Journal*, July 31, 1984.
25. "Japan Is Top Drug Developer for Third Consecutive Year," *Japanese Economic Journal*, Feb. 7, 1984, page 15; Harold M. Schmeck, Jr., "Report Says Japan Could Lead in Commercial Biotechnology," *New York Times*, Jan. 27, 1984, page A9.
26. MIT, *Global Technological Change: A Strategic Assessment*, June 1983; Robert C. DiIorio, "Japanese Pose Computer Threat," *Tech Talk*, July 27, 1983, page 1; Charles H. Ferguson, "The Microelectronics Industry in Distress," *Technology Review*. Aug./Sep. 1983, page 24.
27. U.S. Department of Commerce, *Survey of Current Business*, July issues 1983 and 1968, Table 6.8B and Table 6.13.
28. Ibid.
29. Ibid.
30. Ibid.
31. "America's Economic Slip Is Showing," *The Economist*, Apr. 25, 1981, page 107.
32. "The State's Piece of the Pie," *Time*, Apr. 21, 1980, page 54.
33. Bureau of the Census, *Money Income and Poverty Status of Families and Persons in the United States*, 1983, page 18; *Current Population Reports, Consumer Income*, Series P-60, page 19, 1967, page 13.
34. Ibid., page 19.
35. Ibid., page 30.
36. Ibid., page 25.

37. Ibid., page 16; *Consumer Income*, 1976, #114, page 224.
38. Ibid.
39. Ibid., page 19; *Consumer Income*, 1977, #117, page 31.
40. Mancur Olson, *The Rise and Decline of Nations: Economic Growth, Stagflation and Social Rigidities*, Yale University Press, 1982.
42. "Japan National Railways Awash in Red Ink" *Boston Globe*, Sep. 9, 1984, p. 103.

CHAPTER 3

1. To some extent the lack of "a" cause is seen in the differences among economists as to "the" causes of the slowdown—each points to different factors and all may well be right.
   Martin Neil Baily, "The Productivity Growth Slowdown by Industry," *Brookings Papers*, # 2, 1982, page 423.
   William J. Baumol and Edward N. Wolfe, "Input and Output Composition Changes: Measuring the Effect on Productivity Slowdown," mimeo.
   Congressional Budget Office, *The Productivity Problem: Alternatives for Action*, Jan. 1981.
   Edward F. Denison, "Explanations of Declining Productivity Growth," Brookings Reprint # 354.
   David M. Gordon, "Capital-Labor Conflict and the Productivity Slowdown," mimeo.
   Michail F. Mohr, "Concepts in the Theory and Measurement of Productivity," mimeo.
   Richard R. Nelson, "Technical Advance and Productivity Growth," Yale Working Paper # 815.
   William D. Nordhau, "Policy Responses to the Productivity Slowdown," Boston Federal Reserve Bank Conference on Productivity.
   Lawrence Summers, "Observations on the Productivity Slowdown," mimeo.
2. U.S. Department of Commerce, *Survey of Current Business*. July issue various years, Tables 6.2, 6.11B, 6.13.
3. Ibid.
4. Ibid.
5. H. Kemble Stokes, Jr., "An Examination of the Productivity Decline in the Construction Industry," mimeo.
6. Hal Sider, "Safety and Productivity in Underground Coal Mining," *The Review of Economics and Statistics*, May 1983, page 225.
7. Irving B. Kravis, Alan W. Heston, Robert Sommers, "The Share of Services in Economic Growth, *Global Econometrics*, page 188.
8. Bureau of the Census, *Statistical Abstract*, 1982–83, pages 71 and 75.
9. U.S. Department of Labor, *Employment and Earnings*, Jan. 1983, page 156.
10. Isadore Barmash, "Retailers Losing Theft Battle," *New York Times*, May 27, 1981, page D1.
11. Council of Economic Advisers, *Economic Report of the President*, 1984, pages 220 and 266.
12. Calculated with a standard Cobb-Douglas production function where different rates of growth of capital and labor are inserted into the function.
13. U.S. Department of Commerce, *Survey of Current Business*, July 1983, Tables 7.1 and 1.11.
14. U.S. Department of Commerce, *International Economic Indicators*, Sep. 1984, page 15.
15. "U.S. Pupils Rank Poorly in International Testing," *The Japan Times*, Dec. 13, 1983, page 10.

16. "America Frets Over the Future of Its Technical Nous," *The Economist*, Mar. 12, 1983.
17. *Economic Report of the President*, 1984, page 248.
18. *Toronto Globe and Mail*, Dec. 2, 1983; *The Oriental Economist*, Dec., 1983, page 45.
19. National Science Foundation, *National Pattern of Science and Technological Resources*, 1982, page 33.

CHAPTER 4

1. Council of Economic Advisers, *Economic Report of the President*, 1985, page 232.
2. U.S. Department of Commerce, *International Economic Indicators*, Sep. 1984, page 33.
3. Morgan Guaranty Trust Co., "Mexico: Progress and Prospects," *World Financial Markets*, May 1984, page 1; Morgan Guaranty Trust Co, "Stabilization Policies in Brazil," *World Financial Markets*, July 1984, page 1.
4. Robert A. Lawrence, *Can America Compete?*, Brookings, Washington, 1984, page 46.
5. "Study: US Is Out of the Running in Manufacturing," *Boston Globe*, Feb.4, 1985, page 57.
6. Kevin Phillips, *Staying on Top: The Business Case for a National Industrial Strategy*, Random House, 1984.
7. Charles Schultze, "Industrial Policy: A Dissent," *The Brookings Review*, Fall 1983, page 3.
8. Lawrence, op. cit.
9. Ibid., page 7.
10. Otto Eckstein, Christopher Caton, Roger Brinner, Peter Duprey, *The DRI Report on U.S. Manufacturing Industries*, McGraw-Hill, New York, 1984.
11. Ibid., page 1.
12. Ibid., page 4.
13. Ibid., page 57.
14. Lawrence, op. cit., page 94.
15. Ibid., page 48.
16. Ibid., page 44.
17. Ibid., page 95.
18. Ibid., page 47.
19. Ibid., page 46.
20. These percentages are calculated by comparing the income and price elasticities of demand for the two periods of time.
21. Lawrence, op. cit., page 49.
22. Ibid., page 121.
23. Charles Schultze, op. cit., page 5.
24. National Science Board, *Science Indicators*, 1982, 1983, page 22.
25. Eckstein, op. cit., page 5.
26. Ibid., page 74.
27. Ibid., page 79.
28. Ibid., page 102.
29. Michael C. Munger, "America's Costly Trade Barriers," *New York Times*, Aug. 19, 1983, page A21.
30. "Ford's Mr. Turnaround: 'We have more to do,' " *Fortune*, Mar. 4, 1985, page 83.
31. Yoshi Tsurumi, "How Not to Save the U.S. Auto Industry—Hidden Costs of Import Quotas on Japanese Cars," *The Jama Forum*, Volume 3, #3, 1985.

32. "U.S. May Impose Steel Duties on Brazil," *New York Times*, Jan. 28, 1983, page 1.
33. Conference on U.S. Competitiveness, "Can the United States Remain Competitive?" U.S. Senate Finance Committee, Washington, 1980.
34. Paul Simon, *The Tongue-Tied American*, Continuum, New York, 1980.
35. "Worried U.S. Companies Watch Japan Technological Advances," *New York Times*, May 7, 1984, page D12.

CHAPTER 5

1. Bureau of the Census, *Money Income and Poverty Status of Families and Persons in the United States*, 1983, Series P-60, #145, page 20.
2 "Congress Study Finds Reagan Budget Curbs Put 557,000 People in Poverty," *New York Times*, July 26, 1984, page A19.
3. Isabel V. Sawhill, "Can We Salvage the 1980s," *Challenge*, Sep./Oct. 1984, page 16.
4. Avery, Elliehausen, Canner, Gustafson, Briskman, Rochlin, and Siefert, "Survey of Consumer Finances, 1983," *Federal Reserve Bulletin*, Sep. 1984, page 681.
5 Ibid., page 689 and "Survey of Consumer Finances, 1983: A Second Report," *Federal Reserve Bulletin*, Dec. 1984, page 863.
6. Ibid., page 685.
7. Bureau of the Census, op. cit., page 12.
8. Ibid., page 16.
9. Bureau of the Census, *Historical Statistics of the United States*, U.S. Government Printing Office, 1975, page 357.
10. Danziger, Haveman, Plotnick, "Antipoverty Policy: Effects on the Poor and the Nonpoor," *IRP Conference Paper*, 1984, University of Wisconsin-Madison, page 28.
11. Gottschalk, Danziger, "Macroeconomic Conditions, Income Transfers, and the Trend in Poverty," *IRP Reprint Series*, #494, University of Wisconsin-Madison, page 203.
12. Gary Burtless, "Public Spending for the Poor: Trends Prospects and Economic Limits," *IRP Conference Paper*, 1984, University of Wisconsin-Madison, page 37.
13. Hugh Heclo, "The Political Foundations of Antipoverty Policy," *IRP Conference Paper*, 1984, University of Wisconsin-Madison, page 36.
14. *Economic Report of the President*, 1984, pages 309 and 282.
15. Burtless, op. cit., page 50.
16. Sawhill, op. cit.
17. William Serrin, "White Men Discover It's a Shrinking Market," *New York Times*, Dec. 9, 1984.
18. Arthur Okun, *Equality and Efficiency: The Big Trade-Off*, Brookings Institution, Washington, 1975.
19. Robert Kuttner, *The Economic Illusion: False Choices Between Prosperity and Social Justice*, Houghton Mifflin Co, Boston, 1984.
20. U.S. Department of Commerce, *Long Term Economic Growth*, U.S. Government Printing Office, 1974, page 210.
21. Michael J. Piore and Charles F. Sabel, *The Second Industrial Divide: Possibilities for Prosperity*, Basic Books, New York, 1984.
22. A.D. Searle, "Productivity Changes in Selected Wartime Ship Building Programs," *Monthly Labor Review*, Vol. 61, #6, Dec. 1945; Asher Harold, *Cost-Quantity Relationships in the Airframe Industry*, R-291, Rand Corporation, 1956.
23. U.S. Department of Labor, *Handbook of Labor Statistics*, U.S. Government Printing Office, 1983, page 180.

24. *The Japan Economic Journal*, Jan. 17, 1984, page 11.
25. International Monetary Fund, *International Financial Statistics*, March 1984, pages 265 and 460.
26. Bureau of the Census, *Money Income of Households, Families, and Persons in the United States: 1981*, Current Population Reports, Series P-60, page 16.
27. Harley Shaiken, "The Automated Factory: The View from the Shop Floor," *Technology Review*, Jan. 185, page 21.
28. Ibid., page 19.

CHAPTER 6

1. David E. Sanger, "U.S. Move in Video Cameras," *New York Times*, Jan. 5, 1984, page D 1.
2. "Executive Compensation," *Fortune*, Mar. 19, 1984, page 22.
3. Ichiro Hattori, "Product Diversification," *Effective Management: A Japanese View*, TBS-Britannica, Tokyo, 1983. MIT Press, Cambridge, 1984.
4. Daniel Yankelovich and John Immerwarh, *Putting the Work Ethic to Work*, Public Agenda Foundation, New York, 1983.
5. Ibid.
6. *Orlando Sentinel*, March 22, 1982.
6. Kathleen Teltsch, "Black Teen-Agers Found Eager to Work," *New York Times*, Apr. 21, 1983, page A16.
8. U. S. Department of Commerce, *Long Term Economic Growth*, 1973, page 212.
9. "West Germany Is on Its Way to a 38-Hour Week," *The Economist*, June 2, 1984, page 71.
10. Council of Economic Advisers, *Economic Report of the President*, 1984, page 249.
11. Florence Hall and Marguerite Schroeder, "Time Spent on Household Tasks," *Journal of Home Economics*, Jan. 1970, page 23.
12. Steven Rattner, "A Tale of Two Ford Plants," *New York Times*, October 13, 1981, page D1.
13. "The Japanese Way at Quasar," *New York Times*, Oct. 16, 1982, page D1.
14. *Putting the Work Ethic to Work*, op. cit.
15. "The Japanese Advantage in Autos: Quality and Cost," *New York Times*, Apr. 1, 1983, page A12.
16. David E Sanger, "Another No. 1 Rating to Japan," *New York Times*, Aug. 25, 1983, page D1.
17. "The Japanese Way at Quasar," op. cit.
18. Paul R. Lawrence and Davis Dyer, *Renewing American Industry*, The Free Press, New York, 1983, page 55.
19. Yoshi Tsurumi, "The Challenges of the Pacific Age," *World Policy Journal*, Fall 1984, page 72.
20. John Simmons and William Mares, *Working Together*, Knopf, New York, 1983.
21. Myron Tribus, "Observations," Center for Advanced Engineering Study, June 1983, page 13.
22. John Steinbreder, "Deals of the Year" *Fortune*, Jan. 21, 1985, page 126.
23. "Will Money Managers Wreck the Economy?" *Business Week*, August 13, 1984, page 86.
24. Thomas C. Hayes, "6 Top Getty Officers Leaving," *New York Times*, July 27, 1984.
25. Andrew S. Grove, *High Output Management*, Random House, New York, 1983.
26. Ken Auletta, *The New Yorker*, June 13, 1983, page 74.
27. Wolf Weinhold, "The GE-Utah Lesson," *New York Times*, Apr. 17, 1983, page F3.

28. Robert Metz, "Mixed Outlook at Polaroid," *New York Times*, Apr. 27, 1982, page D2.
29. Michael J. Piore, "American Labor and the Industrial Crisis," *Challenge*, Mar./Apr. 1982, page 5.
30. Derek C. Jones and Jan Svejnar, *Participatory and Self-Managed Firms*, Lexington Books, 1982.
31. Yoshi Tsurumi, "Value-Added Maximizing Behavior of Japanese Firms and Roles of Corporate Investment and Finance," mimeo, Sep. 1984.
32. Daniel J. B. Mitchell, "Gain-Sharing: An Anti-Inflation Reform," *Challenge*, July/Aug. 1982, page 18.
33. Hideo Ishida, "Exportability of the Japanese Employment System," mimeo.
34. Arthur M. Louis, "Business Is Bungling Long-Term Compensation," *Fortune*, July 23, 1984, page 65.
35. Arch Patton, "When Executives Bail Out to Move Up," *Business Week*, Sep. 13, 1982, page 13.
36. Gregg Easterbrook, "Voting for Unemployment," *The Atlantic Monthly*, May 1983, page 31.
37. *Encyclopaedia Britannica*, Vol. 6, 529b.
38. Council of Economic Advisers, *Economic Report of the President*, 1984, pages 220 and 250.
39. "Semiconductor Industry Asks U.S. for Trade and Tax Help," *New York Times*, May 19, 1981, page D13.
40. George N. Hatsopoulos, *High Cost of Capital: Handicap of American Industry*, American Business Conference, Apr. 1983.
41. John Tagliabue, "West German Venture Capital," *New York Times*, June 6, 1983, page D2.
42. "The Challenges of the Pacific Age," op. cit., page 79.
43. Stephen Sheffrin and Lester C. Thurow, "Estimating the Costs and Benefits of On-the-Job Training," *Economie Appliquée*, Tome XXX-#3, 1978.
44. William Serrin, "The Way That Works at Lincoln," *New York Times*, Jan. 15, 1984, page F4.
45. Steve Lohr, "New in Japan: The Manless Factory," *New York Times*, Dec. 23, 1981, page F1.
46. Piori, op. cit.
47. Makoto Sakurabayashi, *Wages in Japan Today*, Studienverlag Dr. N. Brockmeyer, Bochum, 1982; "Wage Gap Between Young Workers and Higher Age Groups Increases," *Japan Economic Journal*, Apr. 5, 1983, page 8.
48. Stan Luxenberg, "Lifetime Employment, U.S. Style," *New York Times*, Apr. 17, 1983, page F12.
49. *Participatory and Self-Managed Firms*, op. cit.
50. John Simmons and William Mares, *Working Together*, op. cit., page 194.
51. Andrew Pollack, "The Daunting Power of IBM," *New York Times*, page F1.
52. Ibid. page F9.

CHAPTER 7

1. Ken Auletta, *The New Yorker*, Nov. 23, 1981, page 157.
2. Gene Maeroff, "Task Force Reports 8% of City Youths Are Illiterate," *New York Times*, Apr. 7, 1982.
3. Gene Maeroff, "Pupils Show Gains in Easy Arithmetic," *New York Times*, Apr. 14, 1983, page 21.
4. Edward B. Fiske, "American Students Score Average or Below in International Math Exams," *New York Times*, Sept. 23, 1984, page 30.

5. Edward B. Fiske, "U.S. Pupils Lag from Grade 1," *New York Times*, June 17, 1984, page 30.
6. "U.S. Schools: Gains in Basics, Slippage Higher Up," *New York Times*, Apr. 10, 1983, page 44.
7. Barbara Lerner, "American Education: How Are We Doing?" *Public Interest*, #69, Fall 1982, page 64.
8. Ibid., page 66.
9. Edward B. Fiske, "School Seniors' Scores Rise," *New York Times*, Sep. 20 1984, pages 1 and 15.
10. "U.S. Schools: Gains in Basics, Slippage Higher Up," op. cit.
11. Linda Darling-Hammond, *Beyond the Commission Reports: The Coming Crisis in Teaching*, Rand Corporation, July 1984, page 6.
12. Ibid., page 5.
13. Leon Botstein, "Nine Proposals to Improve Our Schools," *New York Times Magazine*, June 5, 1983, page 61.
14. "Study, Pupils Taking Easier Class," *Boston Globe*. Apr. 13, 1983, page 1; "Most College Freshmen in Jersey Fail Math Test," *New York Times*, Dec. 19, 1982, page 47.
15. Edward B. Fiske, "Engineering-School Shortcomings Lead to U.S. Lag," *New York Times*, March 27, 1983, Section 12.
16. Phyllis Coons, "Reagan Defends Aid Cuts," *Boston Globe*, Mar. 1, 1984, page 1.
17. U.S. Department of Commerce, *Statistical Abstract*, 1982–83, page 25.
18. *Beyond the Commission Reports*, op. cit., page 2.
19. Merry I. White, "Japanese Education: How Do They Do It?" *The Public Interest*, Summer 1984, page 99.
20. Fred Rothenberg, "Glued to the Tube," *Boston Globe*, Jan. 25, 1984, page 1.
21. "In Public High Schools Academics Lose Ground," *New York Times*, Apr. 26, 1983, page 17.
22. Robert C. Christopher, "Who's Winning the Education Race?," *United Magazine*, Dec. 1983.
23. "Japanese Education: How Do They Do It?" op. cit., page 92.
24. "Low Teacher Pay and Status Faulted," *New York Times*, July 7, 1984, page A12.
25. "Japanese Education: How Do They Do It?" op. cit., page 91.
26. Coons, op. cit.
27. Edward B. Fiske, "Commission on Education Warns 'Tide of Mediocrity' Imperils U.S.," *New York Times*, Apr. 17, 1983, page 1; Nina McCain, "U.S. Panel Calls for Reform in Education," *Boston Globe*, Apr. 27, 1983, page 1.
28. Coons, op. cit.
29. "Materialism of College Freshmen Is Found Rising," *New York Times*, Jan. 14, 1985, page A9.
30. "School Basics Seen Creating Discipline," *Boston Globe*, Apr. 21, 1983.
31. Bureau of the Census, *Money Income of Households, Families, and Persons in the United States: 1981*, Current Population Reports, Series P-60, #137, page 178.
32. Council of Economic Advisers, *Economic Report of the President*, 1984, page 271.
33. U.S. Department of Labor, *Employment and Earnings*, Jan 1983, page 151.

CHAPTER 8

1. U.S. Department of Commerce, *International Economic Indicators*, Sep. 1984, page 15.
2. International Monetary Fund, *International Financial Statistics*, Mar. 1984, pages 460, 254, 196, 264, 188, 130, 454.

3. Council of Economic Advisers, *Economic Report of the President*, 1984, pages 220 and 250.
4 Ibid.
5. Bob Kuttner, "Growth with Equity," *Working Papers*, Sep./Oct. 1981, page 36.
6. *Economic Report of the President*, op. cit., page 251.
7. Tusuneo Ishikawa and Kazuo Ueda, "The Bonus System and Japanese Personal Savings," *The Economic Analysis of the Japanese Firm*, Ed. M. Aoki, Elsevier Science Publishers, 1984, page 133.
8. *The Oriental Economist*, Dec. 1983, page 43.
9. Ibid., page 248.
10. Ibid., Pages 250 and 220.
11. Ibid., Page 249.
12. Bureau of the Census, *Money Income of Households, Families, and Persons in the United States: 1981*, Current Population Reports, Series P-60, page 16.
13. *International Financial Statistics*, op. cit.; "America's Economic Slip Is Showing," *The Economist*, Apr. 25, 1981, page 107.
14. Malcome Sawyer and Frank Wasserman, "Income Distribution in OECD Countries," *OECD Economic Outlook*, July 1976, page 14.
15. The Conference Board, *The 1984 Budget: Compromises and Stalemates*, 1983, #4.
16. Steven Kelman, "The Grace Commission: How Much Waste in Government?" *The Public Interest*, Winter 1985, page 62.
17. *Economic Report of the President*, 1984, op. cit., page 308.
18. *New York Times*, Dec. 1, 1984, page 33; Citizens for Tax Justice, *Corporate Income Taxes in the Reagan Years*, Oct. 1984.
19. Allen Sinai and Otto Eckstein, "Tax Policy and Business Fixed Investment Revisited," Office of Tax Analysis Working Paper, Apr. 1981.
20. *Economic Report of the President*, 1984, op. cit.
21. Internal Revenue Service, *Income Tax Compliance Research: Estimates for 1973– 1981*, July 1983, page 3.
22. Based on Data Resources GNP projection for 1984, *The Data Resources Review*.
23. Department of the Treasury, *Tax Reform for Fairness, Simplicity, and Economic Growth*, Nov. 1984, page 124.
24. Joseph A. Pechman and Benjamin A. Okner, *Who Bears the Tax Burden?* Brookings Institution, Washington, 1974.
25. Senate Committee on the Budget, *Tax Expenditures*, Sep. 1978.
26. *Income Tax Compliance Research*, op. cit.
27. Internal Revenue Service, *Estimates of Income Unreported on Individual Income Tax Returns*, Publication 1104 (9-79).
28. Bill Bradley and Richard Gephart, "Fixing the Income Tax with the Fair Tax," *Tax Policy: New Directions and Possibilities*, Center for National Policy, page 19.
29. "Pumping Up Taxes," *The Economist* Dec. 15, 1984, page 10.
30. U.S. Department of Commerce, *Survey of Current Business*, July 1983, page S-28.
31. "Still as Certain as Death," *The Economist*, Aug. 18, 1984, page 55.
32. Ibid., page 23.
33. Melissa Brown, *Tax Choices*, Roosevelt Center for American Policy Studies, Washington, 1983; Joseph A. Pechman, *Tax Policies for the 1980s*, Brookings, Washington, 1982; Charles R. Hulten and June O'Neill, "Tax Policy," *Changing Domestic Priorities*, The Urban Institute, Washington, 1982.
34. "Poorer, Hungrier," *New York Times*, Apr. 10, 1983.
35. *Survey of Current Business*, op. cit., page 53.

36. Ibid.
37. Ibid.
38. Center for National Policy, *Rethinking Defense and Conventional Forces, Alternatives for the 1980s*, #8, Washington, 1983; Staff of Joint Economic Committee, "The Defense Buildup and the Economy," 1982.
39. *The Final Epidemic*, ed. Ruth Adams and Susan Cullen, Educational Foundation for Nuclear Science, Chicago, 1981.
40. Fred Kaplan, "CIA study shows 2% rise in Soviet military budget," *Boston Globe*, Feb. 22, 1984, page 3.
41. Charles L. Schultze, "Economic Effects of the Defense Budget," Brookings Bulletin, Fall 1981.
42. *Survey of Current Business*, op. cit., page 53.
43. *Money Income and Poverty Status of Families and Persons in the United States: 1982*, op. cit. page 21.
44. Ibid.
45. Ibid., page 19.
46. U.S. Department of Commerce, *Statistical Abstract of the United States, 1982–83*, page 71.
47. Peter A. Morrison, "Demographic Links to Social Security," *Challenge*, May/June 1982. page 44.
48. Bradley R. Schiller, "A Smart Retreat from Social Security Reform," *Challenge*, May/June 1982.
49. Robert J. Myers, "Bismarck Backed 70," *Wall Street Journal*, Nov. 7, 1977, page 19.
50. "Wage Questions," *New York Times*, May 13, 1983, page D3; "Chrysler Hurt by Costs," *New York Times*, March 5, 1984, page B8.
51. Bureau of the Census, *Current Population Reports: Consumer Income*, 1983, Series P60, #142, page 16.
52. Robert Pear, "Washington Drives a Hard Bargain on Medical Costs," *New York Times*, Jan. 20, 1985, page E3; U.S. Department of Health and Human Services, *Health Care Financing*, #1, Nov. 1983, page 1.
53. Richard A. Knox, "Some Local Hospitals 'Dump' the Uninsured," *Boston Globe*, Feb. 6, 1984, page 31.
54. Pear, op. cit.
55. Henry J. Aaron and William B. Schwartz, *The Painful Prescription*, Brookings, Washington, 1984; *Health Vote 1982*, Public Agenda Foundation, 1983.
56. "Urban Infrastructure," *Critical Issues for National Urban Policy*, National Academy Press, Washington, 1982; D. Kelly O'Day and Lance A. Neumann, "Assessing Infrastructure Need: The State of the Art," National Academy of Sciences, Feb. 1983; George E. Peterson, "Financing the Nation's Infrastructure Requirements," The Urban Institute, Feb. 1983.
57. John Hebers, "Alarm Rises over Decay in U.S. Public Works," *New York Times*, May 6, 1983, page 1; "Studies Focus on Decay in U.S. Physical Facilities," *New York Times*, May 9, 1983, page A13.
58. Robert Pear, "Study Says $53 Billion a Year Is Needed for Public Works," *New York Times*, Apr. 27, 1983, page A19.

CHAPTER 9

1. Daniel J. Boorstin, *The Americans: The National Experience*, Random House, 1965, page 20. I would like to thank Bruce Thomas for pointing this out to me.
2. Keiichi Konaga, "Industrial Policy: The Japanese Version of a Universal Trend," *Journal of Japanese Trade and Industry*, #4, 1983, page 21.

3. John Zysman, *Governments, Markets, and Growth*, Cornell University Press, Ithaca, 1983.
4. Philip M. Boffey, "Japan Found at Top in High-Tech Ceramics," *New York Times*, Nov. 7, 1984.
5. "Doubts raised over Law for Industry Structural Improvement," *Japan Economic Journal*, Sep. 11, 1984, page 5; Robert B. Reich, "Bailout: An Essay in Comparative Law and Industrial Policy," Working Papers on Industrial Policy, Harvard University.
6. "In Search of an Industrial Policy," *National Journal*, Feb. 26, 1983, page 416.
7. "Technology Employment and Growth," Report by François Mitterrand, President of the French Republic at the Summit of Industrialized Countries.
8. "Restoring American Competitiveness: Proposals for an Industrial Policy," *Alternatives for the 1980s*, Center for National Policy, 1983.
9. Yoshi Tsurumi, "U.S.–Japan Competition in High Tech Fields," Mar. 1983; "Japan's Challenge to the U.S.: Industrial Policies and Corporate Strategies," mimeo; Otto Eckstein, *The DRI Report on U.S. Manufacturing Industries*, Data Resources, 1984.
10. Clifford Hardin and Arthur Denzau, "Closing the Back Door on Federal Spending: Better Management of Federal Credit," Center for Study of American Business, 1984, page 6.
11. *Newsweek*, Apr. 25, 1983, page 63.
12. Office of Technology Assessment, *U.S. Industrial Competitiveness: A Comparison of Steel, Electronics and Automobiles*, 97th Congress.
13. David Treadwell, "7 Nations Agree to Curb U.S. Steel Imports," *Boston Globe*, Dec. 20, 1984, page 79.
14. James T. Bonnen, "Technology, Human Capital, and Institutions: Three Factors in Search of an Agricultural Research Strategy," in *The United States and Mexico: Agricultural and Rural Development*, Stanford University Press, 1983.
15. U.S. Department of Commerce, *Long Term Economic Growth*, 1973, page 210.
16. Council of Economic Advisers, *Economic Report of the President*, 1983, page 270.
17. Bruce Steinberg, "The Military Boost to Industry," *Fortune*, Apr. 30, 1984, page 42.
18. Ibid., page 45.
19. National Science Foundation, *National Pattern of Science and Technology Resources*, 1982, page 33.
20. "R&D Outlays to Be Upped to 3.5 Percent of National Income," *Japan Economic Journal*, Dec. 4, 1984, page 1.
21. "MITI Proposes Tax Breaks for High Tech Investment," *Japan Economic Journal*, Aug. 14, 1984, page 1.
22. National Science Board, *Science Indicators 1982*, 1983.
23. Robert D. Hershey, Jr., "Antitrust Chief Offers Guidelines on Research," *New York Times*, May 11, 1983, page 1.
24. "R&D Outlays to Be Upped to 3.5 Percent of National Income," op. cit.
25. Glenn R. Fong, "Industrial Policy Innovation in the United States: Lessons from the Very High Speed Integrated Circuit Program," 1983 Annual Meetings of the American Political Science Association.
26. Peter Behr, "Alterations Ahead in Apparel," *Washington Post*, May 13, 1984.
27. Regis McKenna, Michael Borrus, and Stephen Cohen, "Industrial Policy and International Competition in High Technology—Part I: Blocking Capital Formation," *California Management Review*, Winter 1984, page 15.
28. Celestea Gentry, "Federal Credit Programs: An Overview of Current Programs and Their Beginnings in the Reconstruction Finance Corporation," Office of Corporate Finance, U.S. Treasury, Aug. 1980.

29. The Labor-Industry Coalition for International Trade, *International Trade, Industrial Policies, and the Future of American Industry*, 1983, page 40.
30. "Time Runs Out for Steel," *Business Week*, June 13, 1983, page 84.
31. David Hecker and Mil Lieberthal, "Wage Costs and Prices in Basic Steel Products," *Labor Studies Journal*, Winter 1983, page 259.
32. William K. Krist, "The U.S. Response to Foreign Industrial Policies," *High Technology Public Policies for the 1980s*, A National Journal Issues Book, page 92; Paul Krugman, "The U.S. Response to Foreign Industrial Targeting," *Brookings Papers on Economic Activity*, #1, 1984, page 77.
33. Robert B. Reich, "Why the U.S. Needs an Industrial Policy," *Harvard Business Review*, Jan. 1982, page 74.
34. Borrus/Millstein/Zysman, "US–Japanese Competition in the Semiconductor Industry," *Policy Papers in International Affairs*, #17, University of California.
35. Philip H. Tresize, "Industrial Policy Is Not the Major Reason for Japan's Success," *Brookings Review*, Spring 1983, page 13.
36. Saburo Okita, "Economic Planning in Japan," *Effective Management: Lessons from Japan*, 1983, TBS Britannica, Tokyo, 1984, MIT Press.
37. Charles Schultze, "Industrial Policy: A Dissent," *Brookings Review*, Fall 1983, page 7.
38. View of manager from Mitsubishi Corporation at MIT seminar on industrial policy, 1982.
39. W. Paul Tippett, Jr., "Put Heat on Japan," *New York Times*, Mar. 10, 1983, Op Ed page.
40. Motorola magazine advertisment, *Time*, 1983.
41. Congressional Budget Office, *Federal Support of U.S. Business*, Jan. 1984.
42. Toshimasa Tsuruta, "The Myth of Japan Inc.," *Technology Review*, July 1983, page 42.
43. Schultze, op. cit., page 5.
44. Richard B. McKenzie, "NIP in the AIR," *Policy Review*, page 75.
45. Paul R. Krugman, "Targeted Industrial Policies: Theory and Evidence," mimeo, summer 1983.
46. Ibid.
47. Robert Lawrence, *Can America Compete?* Brookings, 1984, page 136.
48. Eckstein, op. cit., page 40.
49. Kevin Phillips, *Staying on Top: The Business Case for a National Industrial Policy*, Random House, New York, 1984, page 81.
50. Ira Magaziner, "New Policies for Wealth Creation in the United States," *Growth with Fairness*, Institute on Taxation and Economic Policy, 1983, page 29.

CHAPTER 10

1. David McClain, "The Inflation Deceleration: A Meltdown of the Core, or Just Lucky," mimeo, Nov. 1984.
2. Milton Friedman, "The Federal Reserve and Monetary Instability," *Wall Street Journal*, Feb. 1, 1982, Op Ed page.
3. Walter Guzzard, "The Dire Warnings of Milton Friedman," *Fortune*, Mar. 19, 1984.
4. U.S. Department of Commerce, *Survey of Current Business*, July 1981, Special Supplement, page 39.
5. *Economic Report of the President, 1984*, op. cit., page 305.
6. Ibid., page 291.
7. William A. McGeveran, Jr., "Recessions May Be Hazardous to Your Health,"

Wharton Magazine, Summer 1980, page 36; Maya Pines, "Recession Is Linked to Far-Reaching Psychological Harm," *New York Times*, Apr. 6, 1982, page C1.

8. U.S. Department of Labor, *Employment and Earnings*, Jan. 1983, page 150.

9. Ibid.

10. Ibid., page 154.

11. Council of Economic Advisers, *Economic Indicators*, Feb. 1984, page 13.

12. Martin Weitzman, *The Share Economy: Conquering Stagflation*, Harvard University Press, 1984.

13. The Industrial Bank of Japan, "The Japanese Economy in the World," Mar. 1983.

14. Douglas Murray McGregor, *The Human Side of Enterprise*, McGraw-Hill, New York, 1960.

15. The Industrial Bank of Japan, op. cit.

16. Arthur Ross, "Storing Oil," *New York Times*, Mar. 26, 1983, page 23.

17. Leonard Silk, "An Economic Cure: Controlling Money and Cutting Taxes," *New York Times*, Feb. 11, 1982, page D19.

18. *Economic Report of the President*, 1983, page 24.

19. Ibid. pages 166 and 240.

20. Center for National Policy, *Economic Choices: Studies in Tax/Fiscal Policy*, 1982.

CHAPTER 11

1. *Economic Report of the President*, 1985, page 347.

2. *Japan Economic Institute Reporter*, May 18, 1984, page 4; *Japan Economic Journal*, Dec. 25, 1984, page 28.

3. "Europe Central Banks Join to Drive Dollar Down," *New York Times*, Feb. 28, 1985, page D17.

4. Roger E. Brinner, "Modest Movement Toward Better Balance," *Data Resources*. U.S. Forecast Summary, Jan. 1984, page 5.

5. Morgan Guaranty Trust, *World Financial Markets*, Sep. 1984, page 4.

6. Nicholas D. Kristof, "How Import Rise Affects U.S.," *New York Times*, Feb. 1, 1985, page 27.

7. Stephen Marris, "The Dollar Problem," mimeo, Institute for International Economics, Sep. 1984, page 8.

8. Ibid., page 5.

9. "Europe's Economic Woes," *World Financial Markets*, Morgan Guaranty Trust, Dec. 1983, page 5.

10. "Europe's Technological Gap," *The Economist*, Nov. 24, 1984, page 93.

11. Calculated from data in the *Economic Report of the President*, 1984, pages 236 and 256.

12. Morgan Guaranty Trust, "Help Wanted in Europe," *World Financial Markets*, Dec. 1984, page 4.

13. Ibid.

14. Saul R. Srole, "Exchange Rate Consistent with Open Trade: The Consistent Rate as Appropriate Rate," mimeo; Rudiger Dornbusch, "The Overvalued Dollar, Nov. 1983, mimeo.

15. Fred Bergsten, "What Kind of Industrial Policy for the United States?" U.S. Banking Committee, June 8, 1983, page 4.

16. Morgan Guaranty Trust, *World Financial Markets*, Apr. 1985, page 12.

17. "A Shaken Caterpillar Retools to Take on a More Competitive World," *Fortune*, Nov. 5, 1984, page 91.

18. G. Edward Schuh, "Policy Options for Improving the Trade Performance of U.S. Agriculture," *National Agricultural Forum*, Jan. 1984, page 31.

19. Ibid., page 27.
20. "In Praise of Peasants," *The Economist*, Feb. 1985, page 86.
21. Schuh, op. cit., page 51.
22. *Economic Report of the President*, 1985, page 343.
23. U.S. House Energy and Commerce Committee "The United States in a Changing World Economy: The case for an integrated Domestic and International Commercial Policy," Staff Report, Washington, 1983.
24. "The Firm Dollar" *World Financial Markets*, Morgan Guaranty Trust, July 1983, page 3.
25. The Program on U.S.–Japan Relations at Harvard, *U.S.–Japan Relations: Toward a New Equilibrium*, Annual Review, 1982–83.
26. Nobutane Kuchi, "An Appeal to My American Friends: Resolving Trade Frictions," Aug. 10, 1983.
27. R. Joseph Monsen and Kenneth D. Walters, *Nationalized Companies: A Threat to American Business*, McGraw-Hill, 1983.
28. Consulate General of Japan in Boston, "Japan's Trade with the World and the United States in 1983," Feb. 1, 1984.
29. Gary Hector, "The Nationalization of Continental Illinois," *Fortune*, Aug. 20, 1984, page 135.
30. Thomas C. Hayes, "Thrift Unit Reports Big Loss," *New York Times*, Aug. 16, 1984, page D1.
31. "Bank Failure Rate Highest Since 1939," *Denver Post*, Aug. 30, 1984.
32. "Trial Due on Penn Square," *New York Times*, Sep. 9, 1984.
33. "$4.5 Billion Investment in Continental Bank Set," *New York Times*, July 27, 1984, page D17.
34. Kenneth B. Noble, "FDIC May Consider Rise in Bank Premiums," *New York Times*, July 31, 1984, page D1.
35. Thomas C. Hayes, "The Cash Squeeze at Financial Corp," *New York Times*, Aug. 17, 1984, page D1.
36. Noble, op. cit.
37. Morgan Guaranty Trust, "The LDC Debt Problem at the Midpoint?" *World Financial Markets*, Oct./Nov. 1984, page 5; "Burros' Debt," *The Economist*, Aug. 21, 1982, page 11; "The Third World Shadow," *Fortune*, Dec. 26, 1983, page 172; "Poor Nations' Debts Posing a Threat to Richer Countries," *New York Times*, July 5, 1983, page 1; "The Breaking of a Continent," *The Economist*, Apr. 30, 1983, page 17.
38. Morgan Guaranty Trust, "Stabilization Policies in Brazil," *World Financial Markets*, July 1984, page 3.
39. Morgan Guaranty Trust, "Mexico: Progress and Prospects," *World Financial Markets*, May 1984, page 2.
40. Ibid., page 3.

CHAPTER 12

1. "Do Modern Times Call for an Industrial Policy?" *Public Opinion*, Aug./Sep. 1983, page 2 for the printed part of the dialogue. Quotation comes from initial transcript of conversation.

INDEX